D0866962

Ezra Pound and the
Monument of Culture

Ezra Pound and the Monument of Culture

TEXT, HISTORY, AND THE MALATESTA CANTOS

LAWRENCE S. RAINEY

The University of Chicago Press
Chicago and London

Lawrence S. Rainey is assistant professor of English at Yale University.

This book was published with the assistance of the Frederick W. Hilles Publication Fund of Yale University

PS3531
082
C2876
1990

The University of Chicago Press, Chicago 60637
The University of Chicago Press, Ltd., London
© 1991 by The University of Chicago
All rights reserved. Published 1991
Printed in the United States of America

00 99 98 97 96 95 94 93 92 91   54321

Library of Congress Cataloging in Publication Data

Rainey, Lawrence S.
   Ezra Pound and the monument of culture : text, history, and the Malatesta cantos / Lawrence S. Rainey.
      p.   cm.
   Includes index.
   ISBN 0-226-70316-9
   1. Pound, Ezra, 1885–1972. Cantos.   2. Pound, Ezra, 1885–1972—Knowledge—Italy.   3. Malatesta, Sigismondo Pandolfo, signore di Rimini, 1417–1468, in fiction, drama, poetry, etc.   4. Historical poetry, American—History and criticism.   5. Tempio Malatestiano (Rimini, Italy) in literature.   6. Fascism and culture in literature.   7. Rimini (Italy) in literature.   8. Monuments in literature.   I. Title.
PS3531.082C2876   1991
811'.52—dc20   90-44410
                                                      CIP

⊗ The paper used in this publication meets the minimum requirements of the American National Standard for Information Sciences—Permanence of Paper for Printed Library Materials, ANSI Z39.48-1984.

To
Emma J. Rainey
with gratitude

Pur 6-23-92

JUL 24 1992

Contents

List of Illustrations   ix

Preface and Acknowledgments   xi

Introduction   1

1 PRODUCTION
   Ezra Pound in the Temple of History:
   Earliest Drafts and the Rites of Quotation   **25**
   A Discrepancy   29
   The Past   37
   The Future   42
   Conjunctions   50
   Roots and Routes   57
   The Politics of Quotation   64

2 TRANSMISSION
   Savage Crimes:
   (F)Acts of Transmission   **77**
   A Life and a Death   82
   Murderous Meanings   91
   Strange Shadows on You Tend   117
   The Whited Sepulchre   132

3 RECEPTION
   Desperate Love:
   Isotta and the Monument of Civilization   **155**
   The Honor of Italy   159
   Worthy of This Love   166

A Little Chronicle   173
Lyrical Center   177
The Missing Letter: Why?   186
The Last Judgment   209
Coda   226

Appendixes   229

1. The Chronology of the Manuscripts   229
2. Pound's Travels in Italy, 1922   234
3. The Principal Source for Canto 73   243

Notes   249

Index   341

Illustrations

Plates *following page 178*

1. Henry Strater, artist, and William Bird, publisher: first page for Canto 8 of *A Draft of XVI. Cantos* (1925).
2. Henry Strater, decorative capital and headpiece for Canto 8 of *A Draft of XVI. Cantos* (1925)
3. Henry Strater and William Bird: first page for Canto 11 of *A Draft of XVI. Cantos* (1925).
4. Henry Strater, detail from decorative capital and headpiece for Canto 11 of *A Draft of XVI. Cantos* (1925).
5. Henry Strater, detail from headpiece for Canto 10 of *A Draft of XVI. Cantos* (1925).
6. Henry Strater, detail from the headpiece to Canto 10 of *A Draft of XVI. Cantos* (1925).
7. Henry Strater, detail from the headpiece to Canto 10 of *A Draft of XVI. Cantos* (1925).
8. Henry Strater and William Bird: second page for Canto 10 of *A Draft of XVI. Cantos* (1925).
9. Henry Strater, inset illustration for Canto 10 of *A Draft of XVI. Cantos* (1925).

Figures

1. Reconstruction of the original facade of the Church of San Francesco, Rimini. 9
2. The Church of San Francesco, Rimini, designed by Leon Battista Alberti. 10
3. Right side of the Church of San Francesco, Rimini, viewed from the apse. 11
4. Right side of the Church of San Francesco, Rimini, direct view. 12

5. Axonometric view of a reconstruction of the Church of San
   Francesco as it would have been if completed according
   to Alberti's plans.   13

6. Agostino di Duccio, bas-relief of Sigismondo Malatesta
   at the entrance to the Chapel of the Ancestors.   15

7. Agostino de Duccio, statue of the Delphic Sybil, in the
   chapel of the Madonna dell'Acqua.   16

8. Agostino di Duccio, bas-relief depicting Cancer descending
   over the city of Rimini.   17

9. Tomb of Isotta degli Atti in chapel known as the Chapel of
   Isotta, the Chapel of the Angels, or the Chapel of St. Michael. 18

10. Detail of figure 9, the original inscription on the tomb
    of Isotta.   19

11. Lodovico Pogliaghi, *Sigismondo Malatesta Dedicates the
    Tempio Malatestiano to Isotta* (1897).   21

12. Antonio Beltramelli (1879–1930).   73

13. Charles Yriarte (1832–98).   108

14. Corrado Ricci (1858–1934).   192

15. Corrado Ricci, transcription of the original inscription on
    the tomb of Isotta degli Atti, given by him to Ezra Pound
    when the two men met in February 1923.   196

16. Henry Strater, *Margaret Strater in Red* (1922).   199

17. Henry Strater, *Little Nude by a Table* (1925).   200

18. Probably by Paul Laurent, an engraving published in
    Charles Yriarte, *Un Condottiere au XVᵉ siècle* (1882).   203

19. Process reproduction of an eighteenth-century engraving,
    printed in Charles Yriarte, *Un Condottiere au XVᵉ siècle*
    (1882).   205

20. Antonio Pisano, il Pisanello, reverse of commemorative
    medal of Sigismondo Malatesta, commissioned ca. 1455.   207

21. Probably by Paul Laurent, an engraving reproduced in
    Charles Yriarte, *Un Condottiere au XVᵉ siècle* (1882).   208

22. Church of San Francesco, Rimini, 1944.   211

23. Church of San Francesco, Rimini, 1944; the right side of
    the building, second arch.   212

24. Church of San Francesco, Rimini, 1944; the apse.   213

25. Luigi Severi, photograph of Luigi Nicoló, Adelio Pagliarini,
    and Mario Cappelli, hanged on 16 August 1944 in the central
    piazza of Rimini.   214

Preface and Acknowledgments

Most literary criticism in our time has emphasized the freedom of the reader or the arbitrary play of the text; this work, instead, focuses on constraints and conditions, on the social and material sites that not only nurture, but also pose resistances to interpretive or creative activity. Further, it adopts several strategies to incorporate this emphasis into its texture: at crucial points it abandons the impersonal voice of expository prose, turning instead to interviews, inset narrations, parodies, and free translations adapted from memoirs and other first-hand accounts, and everywhere it uses photographs that invite the reader to "de-textualize" his view of cultural works, to question and engage the sociomaterial instance that informs their genesis and transmission. Representations range from hasty snapshots to sculpted bas-reliefs, from carved inscriptions to scribbled notes, from frayed newspapers to deluxe books, and from crude sketches to monumental architecture. Such devices call attention to the essentially social and collective character of cultural production. That claim, of course, holds no less true for my own work, and I am happy to have the occasion to acknowledge the many colleagues, friends, and institutions that contributed to its formation, even as I am aware that doing so will result in a long and, for most readers, ultimately impersonal list.

I am grateful to Robert von Hallberg and Michael Murrin, who prompted my initial researches. To Professor von Hallberg I am especially indebted for more extensive criticism over a long period of time. I am also grateful to my former colleagues at the California Institute of Technology, Ronald Bush, George Pigman III, and John Sutherland, for their counsels and encouragement. Professor Bush was extraordinarily kind in reading early drafts for this book. Likewise, I am thankful to Susan Davis and David Grether for alleviating countless practical difficulties. And I especially wish to thank Jerome J. McGann, a model of scholarly generosity, for repeated provocation, criticism, and guidance.

I especially want to express my gratitude to numerous citizens, scholars, and institutions of Rimini, a city that continues to nurture a unique heritage of local erudition. I am grateful to Piero Meldini, director of the Biblioteca Civica Gambalunga, and to his assistant Paola del Bianco, for generous assistance in locating documents and photographs and in expediting their reproduction; to Angelo Turchini, professor of modern history at the Università Cattolica of Milan, for helping me with crucial materials concerning the development of fascism in Rimini; to Liliano Faenza, of the Istituto storico della Resistenza di Rimini, for help on the fate of Rimini during World War II; and to Pier Giorgio Pasini, for help with the history of art in Rimini. Above all, I am grateful to Bruno Ghigi, whose publishing house contributes indispensable resources for the study of Rimini and its past. He is the only bookseller I ever met who truly understood his craft, and no one, perhaps, has ever possessed a finer sense of the relationship between historical study and civic culture.

I am also indebted to others in Italy who kindly answered my inquiries or directed me to relevant materials: to Francesca Arduini, formerly with the Biblioteca Nazionale of Florence and now director of the library of Parma; to Matteo Guerrini, assessor of Pennabilli; to Carlo Pagannini, director of the Archivio di Stato in Milan; to the director of the Achivio di Stato in Florence, for making available the archive's administrative records; to the director of the Archivio segreto in the Vatican, for a similar courtesy; to Dr. Vittorio Mezzomonaco, director of the Biblioteca "Aurelio Saffi" of Forlì, to Vitale Beltramelli Guido, and to Francesco Rognoni, for help with records pertaining to Antonio Beltramelli; to Prof. Fausto Zevi, the Commissario governativo of the Istituto nazionale d'archeologia e storia dell'arte, and to Kenneth Haynes, for help with documents relating to Corrado Ricci; to Dr. Dante Bolognesi, of the Biblioteca Classense in Ravenna, for help with the correspondence of Corrado Ricci; to Dr. Tino Foffano, director of the library of the Università Cattolica del Sacro Cuore of Milan, for help in locating materials concerning Giovanni Soranzo; and to Dr. Domenico Berardi, director of the Archivio storico del Comune di Ravenna, for information concerning Silvio Bernicoli.

Anyone who writes on Ezra Pound must eventually confront the Ezra Pound Archive at the Beinecke Rare Book and Manuscript Library of Yale University. I was especially fortunate in receiving generous assistance from all of its guardians over the course of time. I am grateful to the library's director, Ralph Franklin, to Patricia Willis, curator of American

Literature, and to Steve Jones and the other members of the staff. Likewise, I am grateful to Donald Gallup, who kindly answered numerous inquiries and generously permitted me access to materials in his own collection.

Other libraries and librarians were also helpful. I especially wish to thank Saundra Taylor of the Lily Rare Book and Manuscript Library of Indiana University. I am also grateful to Mr. Robert Bertholf of the Lockwood Memorial Library of the University of New York at Buffalo; to Jo August Hill, curator of the Hemingway Collection at the John F. Kennedy Library in Boston; and to the curators of the Manuscripts Division and the Berg Collection in the New York Public Library.

I am indebted to private individuals as well. I still recall with gratitude the kind response of Dr. Carlos Baker, professor emeritus of Princeton University, to my rather trying questions about the dating of a certain letter. I am grateful to Mrs. Nancy Dean Watson, for having allowed me to examine the papers of her late husband, James Sibley Watson, Jr., prior to their being entrusted to the New York Public Library. And I owe a special debt of gratitude to Mrs. Valerie Eliot, who kindly permitted me to examine letters from Ezra Pound to her late husband, which proved to be crucial for resolving several questions of chronology. I am deeply grateful to Mary de Rachewiltz, who encouraged my work from the beginning and generously granted access to several important documents that were, at that time, among her private papers. I am equally grateful to Omar Pound, who was unstintingly generous in answering queries and helping locate materials. I also wish to thank James Laughlin III, publisher of New Directions, for answering so many testy questions; it was, after all, his suggestion that eventually prompted one chapter of this book. I must also express gratitude to Tim Redman, of the University of Texas at Dallas, and James Nelson, of the University of Wisconsin, for various suggestions. Still others were kind enough to read portions of this book in draft versions; I am grateful to John Klancher and Maria Rosa Menocal for their indulgence. To Michael Keller I am indebted for more kindnesses than I can enumerate. To Kathy Gaca I am grateful for having sent me otherwise unobtainable photocopies. And without the very practical assistance of Michael Urban, one chapter might not have been written at all. I am also grateful to Lys Ann Shore for her keen editing, as well as her own contributions.

I would like to thank various institutions which gave financial support for this research: la Commissione per gli Scambi Culturali fra l'Italia e gli Stati Uniti, the Mrs. Giles Whiting Foundation, and the Frederick W.

Hilles Publications Fund of Yale University, which made possible the use of illustrations in the book. I am also grateful to New Directions Publishing Corporation, agents for the Trustees of the Ezra Pound Literary Property Trust, for permission to quote from published and unpublished materials by Ezra Pound, and to A. Walton Litz for many kindnesses extended to me throughout the course of this work. Special thanks to my wife, Sonia Marathou, for more than I can name. My deepest debt of gratitude is registered in the dedication.

Grateful acknowledgment is given to New Directions Publishing Corp. for permission to quote from the following copyrighted works of Ezra Pound: *The Cantos* (copyright © 1934, 1937, 1940, 1948, 1956, 1959, 1962, 1963, 1966, and 1968 by Ezra Pound); *Guide to Kulchur* (copyright © 1970 by Ezra Pound); *Literary Essays* (copyright 1918, 1920, 1935 by Ezra Pound); *Selected Letters 1907–1941* (copyright 1950 by Ezra Pound); *Selected Prose 1909–1965* (copyright © 1960, 1962 by Ezra Pound, copyright © 1973 by The Estate of Ezra Pound); *The Spirit of Romance* (copyright © 1968 by Ezra Pound). Previously unpublished material by Ezra Pound, copyright © 1991 by The Trustees of the Ezra Pound Literary Trust; used by permission of New Directions Publishing Corp., agents.

Introduction

Monument *sb*. [from Latin *monu, moniment-um*, something that reminds, a memorial, monument, from *monēre*, to remind, to warn. Compare French *monument*, Spanish, Portuguese, Italian *monumento*.]
1. A sepulchre, place of sepulture. *Obsolete.*
2. A written document, record. (Apparently sometimes confused with *muniment*.) b. A piece of information given in writing.
3. An indication, evidence, or token (of some fact). Now *rare*. b. Something serving to identify; a mark, indication, something that gives warning, a portent.
4. Anything that by its survival commemorates a person, action, period, or event. b. An enduring evidence or example.
5. A structure, edifice, or erection intended to commemorate a noble person, action, or event. b. A structure of stone or other lasting material erected in memory of the dead, either over the grave or in some part of a sacred edifice.

O.E.D.

The monument of culture is a tomb. It commemorates death, ruin, the remains of human life. And like a sepulchre, it is ambiguous: it registers loss, irremediable erosion, the tenuous grasp of whatever time has forced us to consign to the past; and it records a promise of growth or gain, an invitation to decipher its message for the life of the future.

This study is a sustained meditation on sepulchres. While the term *sepulchre* acquires many meanings in the course of this work, a few are especially important at the outset. In the narrowest sense, it refers to a specific tomb that fascinated nineteenth-century historians and first attracted the attention of Ezra Pound in 1922. This sepulchre, originally constructed around 1450, is located in the church of San Francesco (Saint Francis) in Rimini, a town on the Adriatic coast of Italy. It contains the remains of Isotta degli Atti (ca. 1433–74), mistress and later third

1

wife of Sigismondo Malatesta (1417–68), the ruler of the city who spon-
sored construction of both the tomb and the church that contains it. The
church, too, was conceived as a vast sepulchral monument, a mausoleum
destined to house the remains of Sigismondo, his family, his ancestors,
and the humanist courtiers and bureaucrats who served him.

In the late nineteenth and early twentieth centuries, both the church
and the tomb elicited a vigorous debate about their meaning, a debate
that eventually encompassed central questions about the history and
prospects of Western culture. This debate, in turn, informs a sequence of
four poems or "cantos" written by Ezra Pound in 1922 and 1923, com-
monly known as the Malatesta Cantos. The sequence is part of the larger
work in which Pound invested virtually all of his poetic energies after
roughly 1920, *The Cantos,* and it is clearly essential to any effort to
understand his magnum opus. For while writing the sequence, Pound
came to view the church of San Francesco—a sepulchral monument—as
a symbol of his own poetic and cultural enterprise. And insofar as *The
Cantos* is the major experiment of Anglo-American modernism, a text
that embodies all its aspirations and contradictions, the sepulchre can
also epitomize the cultural monument of literary modernism—not just its
"texts" or works, but the whole field of agents, practices, institutions,
and ideological structures that have shaped its critical reception. Finally,
since the understanding of modernism has proceeded in tandem with the
changing critical methods used to assess every literary and cultural work
in our time, the term *sepulchre* can comprise the wider field of cultural
production and its interpretation: monuments from the past that are ad-
dressed to the future, monuments forever entangled within the ambiguous
dynamics that characterize all cultural transmission, at once soliciting
the interpretive freedom of readers and posing resistances to their shap-
ing imagination. Modern criticism is also a tomb.

So as we begin several semantic fields lie open before us. Yet it is
difficult to summarize the intricate pattern of tracks and circuits that con-
nect them to one another. For they are linked by strange and forgotten
trails through a dense forest of premises, arguments, and practices that
remains unmapped, and which we must explore, experience, and recon-
stitute. We must lose ourselves in a forest of details, cultivate the ac-
quaintance of forgotten spirits, listen to the remote, almost inaudible
echoes of their stories, and from these transient encounters we must fash-
ion a map of this bewildering terrain, transmitting a useful record of our
experience. For others will explore these regions after our departure, and
we shall serve them to the extent that our account offers what the anthro-

pologist Clifford Geertz has called a thick description, "sorting out the structures of signification . . . and determining their social ground and import."[1]

This study is also an allegory of the central tragedy of the twentieth century. The tragedy is double: it is a unique event—the experience of fascism that convulsed the historical consciousness of Euro-American culture; and it is an event that recurs daily—the way in which, through our present practices of critical writing and pedagogy, we transmit the cultural monuments deemed central to our collective self-understanding, our shared history—a tragedy, in which history appears only in the spectral reflections of theory and the past is annihilated in a complacent state of cultural amnesia.

While the conjunction of fascism and intellectual history, both in the past and today, is a central motif of this work, only limited attention is granted here to the titanic events and figures associated with these subjects. Today, I suspect, they can tell us little. The grandiose postures, the massive violence, the hysterical rhetoric now leave us cold. We are indifferent to them, immunized by time or benumbed by the spectral flickers from old newsreels that shudder amid television documentaries. And while they were indispensable to fascism's remarkable success, they fail to account for its prestige among intellectuals who differed widely in temperament, background, and interests. Viewed only in its moments of frenzy, fascism becomes an anomaly in the rhythm of history, devoid of authentic connection with the culture that nurtured it. Yet fascism was not an aberration, but a diverse and dynamic movement that succeeded because it could speak to intelligent contemporaries, because its ideological premises coincided with concepts essential to ordinary scholars at work on quotidian problems of their field. Fascism, in other words, thrived because it could take a "homely form in homely contexts," and only through the protracted description of those sites can we hope to understand its operations. Desire, Language, Intertextuality, Representation, Mimetic Violence—the bloated abstractions that dominate contemporary literary studies—may all be found here. Yet with few exceptions they appear in their everyday garb: wearing bathrobes, jotting notes, glancing at train schedules, reading newspapers, going to libraries, indulging in tourism, strolling amid the ruins of antiquity.

The locus of this study—not its object—is threefold. First, the sequence of Malatesta Cantos written by Ezra Pound in 1922–23. Second, an array of events invoked by those cantos, all related to the figure of Sigismondo Malatesta, the mid-fifteenth-century ruler of Rimini. Third, a body of intellectual/scholarly traditions that transmitted these events to Pound, and have transmitted his work to the present. This complex subject, in turn, becomes a field for the object of this study: to consider theoretical problems in the production, transmission, and reception of cultural works. Let us consider each of these briefly in turn.

*

The Cantos of Ezra Pound has long been considered the most important work of Anglo-American literary modernism. It is also the most intractable: its difficulties are notorious, its obscurity legendary. Though we are ignorant about many matters in Pound's work, at least one point has gradually attracted a substantial consensus: the decisive event in the formation of *The Cantos* occurred when Pound composed the Malatesta Cantos in 1922 and 1923. This event marked a catalytic moment. It enabled Pound to discover poetic techniques essential to the formal repertory of *The Cantos*, such as the direct quotation of prose documents, a device that effectively dissolved the distinction between verse and prose—a crucial development in the history of modern poetry. Equally important, the Malatesta Cantos precipitated a radical revision of all the earlier cantos, crystallizing the design of the larger poem, which had until then remained obscure for Pound himself.[2] These events, the outcome of an intense struggle with an enormous body of historical materials, consumed eleven months of his life. Yet their reverberations extended far beyond 1923. In later cantos Pound returned to historical topics connected with Malatestan material some one hundred times. In prose he treated the subject in reviews and essays of the 1930s, at times comparing himself with Sigismondo Malatesta and his work with the church Sigismondo had constructed. In his private life he talked about Sigismondo to anyone who would listen; he purchased slides and photographs of historical documents important for Sigismondo's life or times; he kept above his writing desk a bas-relief that depicted Isotta degli Atti, the woman who had allegedly inspired Sigismondo's greatest achievement; and in the closing years of his life he journeyed to Rimini again to visit the church of San Francesco one last, haunting time.[3] For Pound, it is clear, the issues he had encountered in the dramatic moments of 1922–23 became a reference point for all his subsequent thinking about civilization and cultural politics. The Malatesta Cantos are a locus for exploring the entire project of *The Cantos*, the central aspirations of literary modernism, and the intricate history of their critical reception by modern scholarship.

The Malatesta Cantos, it should be clear, are more than just a finished "text." Also linked with them is a collection of drafts and documentary materials that register their production in extraordinary detail. The earliest date from June 1922, written when Pound was traveling in Italy, and respond to his recent experiences with works by two of his contemporaries: the first publication of *Ulysses* (February 1922), and the composition and publication of *The Waste Land* (published October 1922). The latest date from late April 1923 and incorporate the fruits of his search for historical documents in libraries and archives throughout Italy, during a research tour that lasted ten weeks. Thus the materials cover an eleven-month period that was intersected by a major historical event: the march on Rome by fascist party members in Italy in late October 1922. One aim of this study is to explore the network of ideological and intellectual concerns linking these apparently disparate activities. To do so requires that we reconnoiter a still wider terrain, one that extends beyond the moment of composition, both before and after: intellectual traditions informing Pound's work, editions transmitting the Malatesta Cantos, rereadings of them in the light of later events, and the heritage of scholarly exegesis that has gathered around them.

Just as important, no vantage point in the present can pretend to be neutral or value-free. We must also address a series of issues increasingly debated in literary studies since roughly 1940, and most intensely in the last two decades. Such issues—the nature of "text," for example—are now routinely grouped under the rubric of literary theory and generally discussed in terms divorced from their relations to specific works or historical problems. Yet the wisdom of this procedure may be doubted. In cultural studies, as Geertz again has noted, theory bereft of its applications produces formulations either commonplace or vacant. To theorize concepts of "text" purified of the material complexity in which cultural works are located is to imagine the nonexistent or the unimportant. Theory advances not when it codifies empty abstractions, but when it facilitates fuller accounts. Such considerations affect the form of theoretical discussion here: the textual-historical materials are not adduced as a case to test or validate theory, but as the field in which theoretical problems are enacted. The three chapters take up issues of the production, transmission, and reception of texts, in that order. Each, in other words, considers both a historical moment and a theoretical problem. The chapter on transmission, for example, is not primarily about the reproduction of the Malatesta Cantos, though this is touched on; most of it treats a single event that has been reported in a disconnected yet coherent sequence of acts of transmission, creating a "fact" later reported by

Pound and "explicated" by scholars. This becomes the occasion for re-flections on the interplay between transmission and fact, two concepts unduly neglected in modern literary studies.

To place theoretical beside historical, or textual beside interpretive, questions violates their typical segmentation into alien (and alienated) specializations within modern literary studies. To some this may prove disconcerting, understandably. Conflict between the demands of empiri-cal and theoretical approaches is a recurrent motif in the human sci-ences. In sociology it is axiomatic, writes Adorno, that "empiricism and theory cannot be accommodated in a single continuum." In anthropology, states Geertz, the tension between them is "both necessarily great and essentially irreducible." Yet neither Adorno nor Geertz urges us to relin-quish this conflict. For Adorno such tensions were not to be concealed behind the imposing façade of an illusory synthesis, but to be "developed and made fruitful," sustained and articulated in a dialectic of growth. For Geertz, on the other hand, their relations could be best explored not through antagonism, but through acknowledging their interdependence: "The major theoretical contributions not only lie in specific studies—that is true in almost any field—but they are very difficult to abstract from such studies."[4] While neither offers a facile solution, each suggests that we can, and indeed must, endure the strains inherent in shuttling back and forth between works and frameworks, texts and contexts, his-tory and theory, interpretations and formulations of the grounds on which they are made. It is a risk worth taking.

In literary studies of recent years such risks have become increasingly uncommon. Structuralism, post-structuralism, and modern hermeneutics have shared the assumption that literary works exhaust their being in their linguistic structures. In the extreme form developed by Hans-Georg Gadamer in hermeneutics, this premise is extended further to comprise human reality in its totality; linguisticality (or *Sprachlichkeit*) is the pre-given context of all reflection, and no vantage point outside it exists.[5] It may offer the promise of meaning through a "fusion of horizons"(Gada-mer), or guarantee that meaning can never achieve plenitude (Derrida), but it remains a terrible and timeless mystery that determines all. These premises, it is clear, collapse or displace all empirical and social consid-erations into language. Their appeal to literary scholars is both obvious and patently conservative: they confirm the intrinsic and text-centered biases inherent in the disciplinary foundations of academic literary stud-ies, and especially in their constricted purview of canonical literature. In terms of practical studies, the outcome has been a chain of books showing that all works contain either self-reflective acknowledgments or disingenuous evasions of their linguistic status.

There are at least two ways in which we can begin to restore a more fruitful dialectic between work and frame, text and context, history and theory. First, we must become increasingly aware that literature is generated not in the bloodless abstraction of language, but in the material practice of writing. Literary studies can advance only through a comprehensive engagement with the entire range of graphic culture, from graffiti to train schedules, inscriptions to advertising. At present literary studies have much to learn from exactly those disciplines that have been considered "ancillary" forms of "lower criticism": disciplines such as paleography, codicology, diplomatics, bibliography, and epigraphy; disciplines engaged with writing as a social practice, not a private encounter with linguistic divinity; disciplines that scrutinize the "extrinsic" features of graphic culture because they assume that written meaning is public meaning, shared meaning, cultural meaning.

Second, we need to reconsider literary criticism's tendency to consider only moments of production or reception, to analyze either how works have been written by individual authors or how they have been read by individual readers. Inevitably this bias encourages psychologistic or privatistic theories of meaning. A central argument of this study is that we can better negotiate these two moments by reconsidering the place of transmission. Transmission is the sum of processes and forces that issue in the sociomaterial instance of every work. It is perhaps best conceived in line with Adorno's notion of a force-field: a relational interplay of aversions and attractions that constitutes a dynamic and transmutational structure.[6] Transmission is constituted at the intersection of material, institutional, and ideological mediation; it is made up of elements that are juxtaposed rather than integrated, and it is driven by conflicting imperatives. It entails semantic losses and gains, constraints and opportunities. Its status is mixed, and for this reason it offers a way to traverse—to sustain and articulate, rather than reconcile—the contradictions between empiricism and theory, or between the contexts of the writer and the freedoms of the reader. For transmission precedes every act of production or reception: writers do not engage with "intertextuality," and readers encounter only works that are presented to them in specific material forms, each presaturated with its own history of transmission. Reconstructing that history demands extended acquaintance with the sociomaterial instance of every work, with each "inscripture" of it. For every inscripture not only issues an invitation to interpretive freedom, but also offers resistance, exercises constraints on possible forms of imaginative and material reproduction.[7] How these resistances interact with specific occasions of reading and writing is the subject repeatedly explored here.

While each chapter pursues a theoretical issue, none is intended as a systematic or foundational treatment of a problem in "literary theory." Instead, I have tried to keep theoretical reflections tied as closely as possible to concrete events and occasions, and I have drawn heavily on philology's traditional strengths in exploring historical origins to forge links between interpretations and theoretical formulations. Each chapter, therefore, begins with a modest textual discrepancy, a moment of opacity. Why does Pound seem to misquote a famous Renaissance writer? Or why does he take pains to report a historical event of no apparent consequence, or even a single letter in the spelling of someone's name? Such questions, in turn, become the occasion for pursuing wider issues. Thus, the problems of production, transmission, and reception are examined through three specific themes: quotation, the nature of fact, and the construction of cultural monuments.

The materials documenting Pound's composition of the Malatesta Cantos are especially appropriate for exploring such issues. They are unique for their extent, integrity, and complexity. Nowhere else is documented so completely every conceivable moment within the process of composition, from initial conception to publication, and far beyond. The materials are massive—more than 700 pages comprising 180 documents, including over 60 drafts and draft fragments. They are also heterogeneous—roughly two-thirds of the material consists of "nonliterary" documentation: train schedules, journals, lists of books, bills and account statements from booksellers throughout Europe, call-slips from libraries in Paris, Rome, and Bologna, transcriptions taken in archives in eleven different cities, reading and bibliographical notes from an array of secondary sources, marginalia and submarginalia entered in Pound's own copies of books, letters of inquiry and administrative records, drawings and epigraphical transcriptions, photographs of epistolary seals . . . and the list goes on. It testifies to the radical interpenetration of the authorial and social worlds, and to the impossibility of distinguishing rigorously between literary and historical documents.

*

Sigismondo Malatesta, who ruled over Rimini from 1429 until 1468, is remembered by posterity for his reconstruction of the church of San Francesco in Rimini.[8] Initially, in 1447, he planned to refurbish a single chapel within the church; gradually, however, his plans encompassed a radical alteration of the entire edifice. Sigismondo entrusted the task to Leon Battista Alberti, one of Alberti's earliest and most important commissions.

Figure 1. Reconstruction of the original façade of the Church of San Francesco, Rimini. Built in the thirteenth century, the original church followed local Franciscan tradition in its emphasis on simplicity and austerity. From Franco Borsi, *L. B. Alberti: l'opera completa* (Milan: Electa, 1980), p. 134, fig. 136. Reprinted by permission.

Figure 2. The Church of San Francesco, Rimini, designed by Leon Battista Alberti. Alberti's design was the first to invoke the Roman triumphal arch as a motif for ecclesiastical architecture. The archivolt in the second order (above the main doorway) is unfinished, one of many signs that the building was never fully completed. From Borsi, *L. B. Alberti*, p. 145, fig. 149. Reprinted by permission. Photo Sergio Anelli/Electa

Originally the church of San Francesco had been a typical thirteenth-century building constructed in accordance with local Franciscan tradition (see figure 1). Its structure was simple, its style spare, and its ornamentation minimal, reflecting the basic tenets of the order's founder. But at the hands of Alberti it underwent a remarkable transformation. His handling of the façade was a dramatic innovation, the first to adapt the composition of the Roman triumphal arch to ecclesiastical architecture, making it a landmark in architectural history (see figure 2). Equally dramatic was his treatment of the church's side (see figure 3), where he fashioned a sequence of seven deep, arched niches that were divided by heavy piers; he created an austere yet harmonious rhythm that, in the words of one critic, evokes "the gravity of Flavian Rome."[9] Alberti was also ingenious in his handling of technical problems. Since the first chapel had been reconstructed before his intervention, he was obliged to

Figure 3. Right side of the church of San Francesco, Rimini, viewed from the apse. The severe rhythm of its deep, niched arches has been said to recall "the gravity of Flavian Rome." The jagged line where the marble blocks cease marks the point where construction was halted during Sigismondo's lifetime; the other portions of the church were constructed later. From Borsi, *L. B. Alberti*, p. 161, fig. 165. Reprinted by permission. Photo Sergio Anelli/Electa

Figure 4. Right side of the church of San Francesco, Rimini, direct view. This perspective of the church's side discloses the Gothic windows of the original wall. Sigismondo had already completed construction within the church's interior, which required that the original walls be retained intact; to meet this demand, Alberti designed the façade to be wrapped like a shell around the older building's core. From Borsi, *L. B. Alberti*, p. 161, fig. 158. Reprinted by permission. Photo Sergio Anelli/Electa

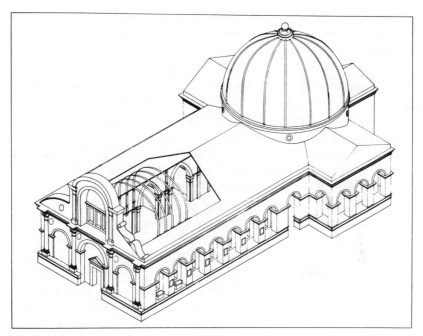

Figure 5. Axonometric view of a reconstruction of the Church of San Francesco as it would have been if completed according to Alberti's plans. From Borsi, *L. B. Alberti*, p. 137, fig. 139. Reprinted by permission.

retain the body of the earlier church; he responded by constructing the new façade as a "shell" that was literally wrapped around the exterior of the older church. One result of this was curious: a direct view of the building's side discloses, behind the Roman arches, the Gothic windows of the earlier church (see figure 4). Despite this oddity, the effect of the entire church was stunning.

By any standard the church of San Francesco is an imposing monument, perhaps more so when we know that it was never completed, indeed that only half the original project was ever constructed. Signs of its incompletion are detectable in the principal façade, for example (see figure 1), where the archivolt of the niche in the second order is left unfinished, as if caught in the empty air. However, contemporary testimonies and modern archaeological studies have permitted scholars to reconstruct the projected whole (see figure 5). The cupola would have rivaled Santa Maria del Fiore in Florence, and the building was obviously meant to be an awe-inspiring monument. Alas, history is cruel: by 1460 war and political vicissitudes had left Sigismondo Malatesta unable to support the immense costs of the church's construction, and all work had ceased. What remained was a compelling monument to thwarted aspirations.

For our purposes, three points about the church are important. First, its inscriptions and decorative sculptures aggressively celebrated the building's sponsor and patron, Sigismondo Malatesta. At the entrance to the "chapel of the ancestors," for example, appeared a portrait of Sigismondo himself (see figure 6). Above the main doorway appeared a frieze with an inscription that boasted: "Sigismondo Pandolfo Malatesta, the son of Pandolfo, made this in fulfillment of his vow in 1450." Yet in the course of time, the meaning of many inscriptions and other testimonies grew increasingly unclear, especially in the wake of shifts in the wider graphic culture, such as changes in epigraphical and writing customs.

Second, the interior of the church teemed with sculptural decorations executing an intricate program of neoplatonic and pythagorean allusions. Some involved figures associated with hermeticism, such as the sybils (see figure 7). Others contained zodiacal references, such as a famous bas-relief depicting the sign of Cancer (see figure 8). Still others represented mythological and allegorical figures, such as one bas-relief rehearsing the triumph of Diana, or another the rape of Ganymede. While scholars since World War II have increasingly agreed that the decorations derive from Macrobius's *Commentaries* on Cicero's *Dream of Scipio*, this is a relatively recent discovery, and for many centuries the sculptural decorations posed a vexing mystery.[10]

Third, the church also contained the tomb of Isotta degli Atti (see figure 9), at first a mistress and later the third wife of Sigismondo Malatesta. The tomb was prominent and striking, so much so that its relation to the other elements of the church became a matter of eager speculation. Taken together, these features—the celebratory inscriptions, the sculptural decorations, the tomb of Isotta and its inscriptions—offered a fertile field for conjecture and surmise.

As early as the sixteenth century the church of San Francesco attracted scholarly attention, such as Vasari's remarks on its architecture and sculptural decorations.[11] But in the course of time, the discussion began to take new and unforeseen directions. What emerged was something we might call "the Romantic interpretation" of the church of San Francesco.[12] The complicated development of this view is dealt with in the following chapters. For now, suffice it to say that its foundations were laid roughly between 1750 and 1800, with the dawn of Romantic culture, and that its consolidation was achieved between 1850 and 1900.

Figure 6. Agostino di Duccio, bas-relief of Sigismondo Malatesta at the entrance to the Chapel of the Ancestors *(Capella degli antenati)*. This bas-relief, with its tone of official portraiture, marks the approach to a chapel celebrating the entire Malatestan family and announces a program of dynastic aggrandizement evident throughout the building. From Borsi, *L. B. Alberti,* p. 173, fig. 175. Reprinted by permission. Photo: Sergio Anelli/ Electa

Figure 7. Agostino di Duccio, statue of the Delphic Sybil, in the Chapel of the Madonna dell'Acqua. The sculpture is one of many figures in an iconographic schema that executes an intricate program of neoplatonic-pythagorean allusions. From Borsi, *L. B. Alberti*, p. 177. Reprinted by permission. Photo: Sergio Anelli/Electa

Figure 8. Agostino di Duccio, bas-relief depicting Cancer descending over the city of Rimini. Cancer was the zodiacal sign of Sigismondo, and here it is depicted as linking the destiny of the state with that of its ruler, another part of the intricate sculptural program that fills the interior of the church. In the nineteenth century zodiacal allusions such as this would be linked with a love poem attributed to Sigismondo Malatesta. The scar in the stone, just below the claws of Cancer, resulted from the Allied bombing of Rimini during World War II. Corrado Fanti, Bologna, Italia

Figure 9. Tomb of Isotta degli Atti in chapel known as the Chapel of Isotta, the Chapel of the Angels, or the Chapel of St. Michael. In its modern form the sepulchral monument supports a bronze plaque with the inscription: D. ISOTE ARIMINENSI B. M. SACRUM. MCCCCL. This plaque was removed by the art historian Corrado Ricci in 1912, revealing an earlier inscription that had been carved directly into the stone; a photograph of the original inscription was published by Ricci for the first time in 1924. Reprinted from Corrado Ricci, *Il tempio malatestiano* (Milan-Rome: Bestetti & Tuminelli [n.d., but 1924], p. 446, fig. 534.

Figure 10. Detail of figure 9, the original inscription on the tomb of Isotta, from the photograph published by Corrado Ricci in 1924. The earlier inscription reads: ISOTE · ARIMINENSI · FORMA · ET · VIRTUTE · ITALIE · DECORI ·· M · CCCC · XLVI· Reprinted from Ricci, *Il tempio malatestiano*, p. 446, fig. 534.

In the simplest terms, this Romantic interpretation consisted of two claims: the church was a monument to Isotta, and it was a monument to paganism. The first was neatly expressed in 1860 by Jacob Burckhardt, the father of modern Renaissance studies. In his words, it was "in [Isotta's] honour and as [her] monument" that "the famous rebuilding of San Francesco at Rimini took place—*Divae Isottae sacrum*." Burckhardt was citing the "text" of the inscription from the tomb of Isotta, "sacred to the divine Isotta." However, he was not citing the inscription itself, where the word *Divae* cannot be found written in full (see figure 10)—Burckhardt, in fact, had neither traveled to Rimini nor seen the tomb—instead he was citing a transcription of it reported by various intermediaries, and his quotation of it entailed two interpretive moves. First, the abbreviation *D.* was construed to mean *diva* (divine), rather than, say, *domina* (lady). Second, the referent of the dedication was greatly extended; it was no longer the tomb that was dedicated to Isotta, but the entire church. While this was Burckhardt's only evidence for his claim, his colorful evocation of the Renaissance was so persuasive that its weakness went entirely unnoticed. Through his work the sepulchral inscription became a keystone for claims that the church was a monument to Isotta.

The other view in the Romantic interpretation was expressed by John Addington Symonds in 1874, when he called the church "a monument of

. . . the revived Paganism of the fifteenth century." Evidence for this was found in the sculptural decorations: "Their style," he charged, showed that "Christian sentiment [was giving way] to Pagan," and their ubiquity made a church where there was "no room left for God." In 1882 such views acquired new cogency and concreteness through the agency of Charles Yriarte, a French journalist and art historian. Yriarte announced that he had discovered a poem by Sigismondo Malatesta. It was a love poem, he said, and it was addressed to Isotta. And most important, it was filled with mythological and zodiacal allusions. Herein lay "the key to the enigma" of the church's sculptural decorations: "Each of its stanzas explains to us the subject of one of the bas-reliefs sculpted . . . in one of the chapels of San Francesco." Yriarte's claims were immediately accepted and widely diffused, becoming a standard feature of encyclopedias and authoritative guidebooks for the next thirty years.

Aside from the sepulchral inscription and the poem, a third testimony was adduced to support the Romantic interpretation. It was an entwined cipher, made up of the letters S and I, which is carved on heraldic devices inside and outside the church: it was assumed that the sign referred *not* to Sigismondo, but to *Sigismondo* and *Isotta*. The history of this view is also complicated. First advanced in 1718, it began to be repeated without discussion after 1813. In the wake of Yriarte's study in 1882 it became a commonplace repeated in guidebooks, travel books, encyclopedias, plays, novels, scholarly studies—a varied and yet specific repertory in the array of graphic culture. The diffusion of this belief is registered in an 1897 engraving by Lodovico Pogliaghi, which accompanied a work of popular history (see figure 11). It depicts the dedication of the church of San Francesco in 1452 and testifies to the iconography of an entire generation. In it, Sigismondo kneels before the fair Isotta, offering her the monument to their love. It is a visual recapitulation of Yriarte's memorable words: "It is not God who is adored here, but Isotta." Yet was it true? Was the church of San Francesco really not a church, but a temple, the exquisite product of an aristocratic neopaganism and the consummate testimony to the desperate love of Sigismondo for Isotta degli Atti?

A synthetic narration of this sort gives an impression of sequence and continuity. On the contrary, the formation of this tradition required a massive transmission of numerous testimonies—a multiplicity of reproductions superimposed upon one another in a complex process that was discontinuous yet coherent. For each testimony was embedded in a sociomaterial instance, an inscripture that conditioned potential forms of its reproduction. To abstract these from their settings, to collate them,

Figure 11. Lodovico Pogliaghi, *Sigismondo Malatesta Dedicates the Tempio Malatestiano to Isotta* (1897). Pogliaghi depicts Sigismondo kneeling as he offers Isotta the edifice constructed in her honor, while his retainers and attendants hold aloft banners bearing the entwined letters *S* and *I*. In 1924 Pogliaghi also furnished illustrations for Corrado Ricci's study, *Il tempio malatestiano*, and in 1927 his depiction of the dedication ceremony was reproduced in yet another work by a lesser known author. Reprinted from Francesco Bertolini, *Il Rinascimento e le signorie italiane* (Milan: Reves, 1897), p. 401.

and to establish a persuasive synthesis involved countless local deci-
sions. There were mistakes, conflicts, discrepancies, intuitions, distor-
tions, and struggles. In particular, some of the most important testimon-
ies invoked for the Romantic interpretation became the subject of sharp
debate between 1909 and 1925. Pound's reception of this uneven and
heterogeneous field is the event—composed of hundreds of particular
engagements—that is registered in the massive documentation he accu-
mulated in the course of his labors.

I have not, however, attempted to offer a global survey of Pound's stud-
ies. Such a survey is desirable, and should be issued as a narrative com-
panion to a critical edition of all the materials associated with the com-
position of the Malatesta Cantos. It would make the materials available
to a wider group of scholars and would contribute to preparations toward
a critical edition of *The Cantos*. But this study is not intended to meet
those needs. Instead it treats only a few moments within the larger event,
and its scope is rather modest. Two chapters regard only a single line in
the final version of the Malatesta Cantos. The third is more expansive,
though much of it concerns a single letter that never appears—indeed
must not appear—in the final version of the text. Still, perhaps the fate
of a single letter can tell us much about Pound, modern literary studies,
and the fate of our common culture.

The lack of a critical edition of these materials affects the organization
and form of this study in several ways. Because many drafts, notes, and
other unpublished materials are published here for the first time, and
since this study is directed to an audience whose primary interest is not
necessarily the development of Pound's work, I have adopted for these
materials a policy directed toward a high degree of legibility, employing
only a few basic conventions of critical editing. These are as follows: (1)
authorial additions or revisions to documents are placed in angled brack-
ets ⟨such as these⟩; (2) editorial interventions are indicated by square
brackets [like these]; (3) autograph materials are registered in *italics;* and
(4) typescript materials are in roman. For most readers this will prove
sufficient,[13] but a few may still find themselves puzzled by an otherwise
uncommon mark that appears in transcriptions of Pound's autograph
drafts and notes. In autograph drafts of verse, as in autograph letters,
Pound often used of a kind of double dash united by a diagonal line $=$.
At first sight this mark appears to be the functional equivalent of a dash,
but further study suggests something a bit different. First, Pound also
used a dash in many autograph manuscripts, suggesting that he assumed
a certain difference between the two marks. Second, he characteristically

used not one, but two forms of this autograph mark. The smaller, about 2–3 mm in length, usually appeared at the end of a phrase or line, placed in roughly the same position as would be a comma or period, and in some manuscripts it occurred frequently, up to twelve times per manuscript page. Obviously it did not indicate punctuation—part of a system of markings designed to increase legibility for other readers—for Pound was the only person who ever read these materials, which were intended solely as instruments for himself; instead, as its placement suggests, this mark served to record the ending of a small unit of composition, one line or less. (In a few instances it is also used to mark the beginning of such a unit.) The larger or longer version of the same mark (5–6 mm) was quite different. It always appeared between two lines, a bit like a stage direction; it was usually accompanied by more interlinear blank space between the lines immediately preceding and following; and generally it stood near the left margin. It occurred roughly two to three times in a manuscript page, and evidently registered the completion or the new beginning of a larger unit of composition, most typically some five to six lines, or something resembling a stanza. Predictably both versions of this sign fared poorly when Pound later made typed transcriptions of his own manuscripts, in part because the typewriter offered no ready equivalent for registering them. The larger mark Pound eliminated entirely, and the smaller some 80 percent of the time (resolving the rest into commas). In the following transcriptions the smaller mark is recorded thus, $=$, while the larger is registered as an elongated equal sign, thus $=$.

Since some historical information may be unfamiliar to readers, I have offered many brief narratives and cursory surveys. They should not be mistaken for systematic presentations. Frequently they synthesize extensive arguments about sources, chronology, or interpretation, which are presented in the notes; while the notes, therefore, may be lengthier than some readers might wish, they are nonetheless essential.

Finally, narratives encourage a stylistic economy that fosters a tone of great certainty. In contrast, I should like to note the provisional nature of this work. My remarks are not intended (even if occasionally delivered) as critical *pronunciamenti*, but as exploratory hypotheses. On the other hand, I insist on the dialectical relationship between the documentary and theoretical fields enacted at every level of this study. "History," as Martin Jay has remarked, "is neither a Rankean recovery of the past 'as it was' nor a Crocean reduction of the past to contemporary consciousness."[14] It is a critical, and so purposive, act of transmission—directed toward the future.

Ezra Pound in the Temple of History:
Earliest Drafts and the Rites of Quotation

That the sign detaches itself, that signifies of course that one cuts it out of its place of emission or from its natural relations; but the separation is never perfect, the difference never consummated. The bleeding detachment is also—repetition—delegation, commission, delay, relay. Adherence. The detached piece remains stuck by the glue of difference.

Jacques Derrida, *Glas*

Solea creder lo mondo in suo periclo
    che la bella Ciprigna il folle amore
    raggiasse, volta nel terzo epiciclo.

The world once believed, to its peril,
    that the fair Cyprian, wheeling
    in the third epicycle, rayed forth mad love.

Dante Alighieri, *Paradiso*, 8
Translation adapted from John Sinclair

Spande una mortale
pace, disamorata come i nostri destini,
tra le vecchie muraglie l'autunnale
maggio. In esso c'è il grigiore del mondo,
la fine del decennio in cui ci appare

tra le macerie finito il profondo
e ingenuo sforzo di rifare la vita;
il silenzio, fradicio e infecondo . . .

The autumnal May sheds a fatal
peace, as loveless as our destinies,
among the ancient walls. In it

is the greying of the world,
the end of a decade in which, for us

amid the ruins, the deep and ingenuous effort
to remake life seems finished;
silence, musty and sterile . . .

Pier Paolo Pasolini, *Le ceneri di Gramsci*

On a cool afternoon in the autumn of 1958, only a few months after his release from St. Elizabeths hospital, Ezra Pound informed his daughter that he wished to build a temple. He wished to built it, he said, on the nearby summit of Mount Mut, its white peak surging over the tree-covered slope—so close, it seemed from the terrace where they stood speaking, that you could almost touch it. A few days later they went to a nearby quarry to examine stone for the building. After that the plan was forgotten or abandoned, and the proposal never mentioned again. Nor did Pound ever discuss the origins of this seemingly quixotic impulse.[1]

Whatever its immediate source, Pound's 1958 desire was rooted in his abiding fascination with the Tempio Malatestiano in Rimini, fascination that had only deepened during the thirty-six years since he had first seen the building around 15 May 1922.[2] It had impressed him profoundly, and its hold on his imagination never relaxed. Ultimately it changed both his life and his work, perhaps one and the same for Pound. A month after seeing it, on 20 June 1922, he announced to John Quinn that he had "blocked in four cantos" for his magnum opus, *The Cantos*. One of them treated the Tempio in Rimini (officially the church of San Francesco), and the man who had sponsored its construction, Sigismondo Malatesta. Engaging in further research on the subject and revising his drafts would consume his attention for the next ten months of his life. Gradually the single "Malatesta Canto" grew from one into two, three, four cantos. One year later the fruits of these labors appeared in the July 1923 number of *The Criterion* (then under the editorship of T. S. Eliot). It comprised more than seven hundred lines of verse, Pound's most ambitious treatment of history and the largest installment of *The Cantos* to date.

The composition of the Malatesta Cantos constituted the decisive event of the Paris years (1921–25) for Pound's career as a writer. As the letter to Quinn first implied, his initial conception of a "Malatesta Canto" had also entailed a series of other cantos, and after completing the Malatestas he swiftly elaborated his original sketches: he finished the five cantos that followed the Malatestas, then revised all the previously published cantos, and at last assembled the whole into *A Draft of XVI. Cantos* (published in early 1925). As Myles Slatin recognized long ago, the writing of the Malatestas "signalled the beginning" of what he called "the climactic period of the poem's composition"; it was now that "the design of [*The Cantos*] suddenly crystallized . . . as a result of the long and intensive labor which went into the Malatesta group."[3]

Some of Slatin's remarks are borne out by a glance at the corpus of surviving manuscript materials. It comprises more than seven hundred pages of notes, drafts, and documents, including some sixty-five drafts and draft fragments. Together they tell a story of intense, unremitting labor. In the course of his research Pound examined material from libraries or archives in Paris, Rome, Bologna, Florence, Modena, Cesena, Pesaro, Rimini, Pennabilli, Fano, Venice, Milan, and Ravenna. But more important, his efforts enabled him not only to clarify his conception of the entire poem, as Slatin demonstrated, but to establish a reference point for all his subsequent thinking about "civilization" and cultural politics. Some fifteen years later, in 1938, Pound would characterize the Tempio Malatestiano in Rimini as "an apex . . . in the last 1000 years of the occident."[4] And he inscribed this view in *The Cantos* itself, for cantos following the Malatestas contain over 100 references to events or personalities related to the Malatesta story, including the recently published Cantos 72 and 73 (written in 1944 and registering Pound's anguish at the disaster engulfing fascist Italy). The Malatesta Cantos, in short, are essential not only for understanding Pound's experience in Paris, but for assessing the arc of his entire career.

That assessment, moreover, intersects with a series of issues central to the study of literary modernism. For critics such as Marjorie Perloff and Richard Sieburth, the Malatesta Cantos register a radical change in Pound's poetics, a "turn from a Symbolist mode to the art of montage, of 'documentary' surface upon which dislocated fragments are juxtaposed." The new poetics breaks with the premises of modernism: "Pound turn[s] to new models," and Dadaism now offers "a more important analogue" for his work, which increasingly resembles "a flat surface, as in a Cubist or early Dada collage, upon which verbal elements, fragmented images, and truncated bits of narrative, drawn from the most disparate contexts, are brought into collision."[5] And as such phrases suggest—note the reference to a "'documentary' surface"—this view of the Malatesta Cantos pivots on how we evaluate what is patently their most distinctive feature: the conspicuous use of quotation from "documentary" or historical sources. Yet the question of quotation, in turn, swiftly leads into wider fields of debate, such as the problem of intertextuality, its relation to the history of modernism, and the types of critical theory that we bring to bear on such literary-historical problems. The Malatesta Cantos furnish a field in which critical issues of textual and historical study are played out again and again, and therefore promise to repay our closest attention.

A Discrepancy

The manuscripts of the Malatesta Cantos are an obvious starting point for any effort to appreciate their significance, and especially the earliest drafts and notes, since they register the initial motifs and ideological concerns that animated Pound's interest. Yet discussion of the manuscripts has been impeded by difficulties in establishing their sequence of composition. One study, for example, has claimed that "the anarchic state of the manuscripts themselves" renders it "impossible to determine questions of grouping, ordering, and successive layers of composition."[6] But this is not really the case. The failure to establish their order has been due to methodological error. Previous scholars have tried to order the manuscripts almost solely by intrinsic characteristics, such as stylistic or formal criteria (a draft comprising two cantos, say, versus a draft comprising three), and have neglected to make use of their extrinsic characteristics (elements of material production, such as paper, ink, typewriter ribbon, and so on). Extrinsic characteristics, however, are essential to dating the Malatesta materials, for they can be collated with identical features in Pound's correspondence during the same period, creating a control for the establishment of a chronology. As we shall see frequently in this study, extrinsic features register a work's historical and social setting; they are, in fact, far less "extrinsic" than is commonly assumed. By analyzing the relevant features of the Malatesta manuscripts, we find that the first two drafts of the Malatesta Cantos (which I have called Draft A and Draft B) were composed between 9 and 20 June 1922 while Pound was at Sirmione, on the Lago di Garda in Italy.[7] (See appendix 1 for details.)

Draft A is the longer and probably the earlier of the two; it comprises 99 lines, compared with only 15 for Draft B (after cancellations). The two are different and yet related. Their relationship is complementary, and this is reflected in subsequent revision when Pound attempts to merge the material from both drafts into a single, unified canto (Draft C1). Draft A, one might say, provides "the raw data" of historical "fact," while Draft *B* assimilates the material to a schema of cultural history, an ideological framework. But obviously the interrelations between them are richer and more complicated, if only because the ideological intentions already exert pressure on the selection and presentation of the historical "facts."

A key example is a passage of Draft *A* that is crucial for understanding Pound's conception of the Tempio Malatestiano, which shaped his thinking at the outset of his work in 1922 and, indeed, for the rest of his life. The passage comprises lines 39–51 of Draft *A*:

> *and in the language of Pius* ⪫
> > > *built a church*   40
> > *noble but impious*
> > > > *with so many gentile*
> > > *works   that it seemed*
> > > > > *no temple of Christians*
> > *but of infidels, adorers of demons,*   45
> > *and therein raised to his concubine*
> > *a magnificent ~~pap~~ pagan*
> > *sepulchre and inscription,*
> > *To the goddess Isotta.,*
> > > > *sacro,*   50
> > > *alla Diva Isotta.*

As suggested by the phrase "in the language of Pius," it is apparently a quotation (in translation) of a well-known passage by Pius II on the Tempio Malatestiano. The original appears in his famous *Commentarii*, a loose narrative of his reign as pope from 1458 to 1464:

> Aedificavit tamen nobile templum Arimini in honorem divi Francisci; verum ita gentilibus operibus implevit ut non tam Christianorum quam Infidelium daemones adorantium templum esse videretur. Atque in eo concubinae suae tumulum erexit et artificio et lapide pulcherrimum adiecto titulo gentili more in hunc modum: Divae Isottae sacrum.[8]

It might be translated as follows:

> Nevertheless, he constructed a noble church in Rimini to the honor of Saint Francis, although he so filled it with "gentile" works that it seemed not so much a church of Christians, as of infidels worshiping demons. And within this church he erected for his concubine a sepulchral monument, very beautiful both in materials and workmanship, and bearing an epigraph in the ancient [or "gentile"] style, to this effect: Sacred to the venerable Isotta.

Yet when we examine the original by Pius II, we notice some problems with Pound's "quotation." Even a hasty comparison indicates discrepancies too serious to be explained solely by the abbreviated character of Pound's rendering. For one thing, Pound's version omits to say that the church was built "in Rimini to the honor of Saint Francis." For another, it contains the curious term "impious," which seems to have no analogue in the original Latin. And odder still, the last lines are given in Italian rather than Latin.

Clearly one must postulate an intermediary source—probably a work written in Italian, probably in the genre of popular history that flourished in the late nineteenth and early twentieth centuries. One candidate is a book by Antonio Beltramelli, published in 1912 (Palermo: Remo Sandron) and entitled *Un tempio d'amore*. It also contains the passage by Pius II, but in an Italian rendering; and if we compare it with Pound's version, we find that their translations coincide in eight points against the original Latin (line numbers refer to the lineation of Draft *A*):

(40–41) Both Pound and Beltramelli omit translation of the phrase *Arimini in honorem divi Francisci* (or "in Rimini to the honor of Saint Francis").

(41) Pound adds the description *impious* because he mistakes Beltramelli's *empì* (filled) for *empio* (impious), whereas nothing in the Latin suggests a similar rendering.

(46) Pound's *therein* is closer to Beltramelli's *vi* than to Pius's *eo*.

(46) Pound's *raised* is a literalistic rendering of *innalzò* rather than the Latin *erexit*, which would yield "erected."

(47) Pound's *magnificent* follows the Italian *magnifico*, both in contrast to Pius's *pulcherrimum*.

(47) Pound's *pagan* follows Beltramelli's *pagana*, both in contrast to Pius's *gentili*.

(48) Both omit translation of Pius's *et artificio et lapide*.

(50–51) Pound duplicates Beltramelli's Italian, rather than the original Latin.

The three passages are presented in full in table 1.

These testimonies are also supported by other evidence in Draft *A*. Lines 18–23, for example, show Pound almost in the act of leafing through his copy of the book, for the order in which he rehearses events corresponds exactly with the order in which they are discussed by Beltramelli.[9] Pound, it is clear, consulted Beltramelli's book at the outset of his work on the Malatestas, so it furnishes us with a key for tracing essential elements in his earliest conception of the Tempio Malatestiano and of Sigismondo Malatesta.

Table 1

Transmission of Pius II's remarks on the church of San Francesco in Rimini

Pius II, *Commentarii*	Beltramelli, *Un Tempio d'amore*	Pound, Draft A, lines 39–51
Aedificavit tamen nobile templum Arimini in honorem divi Francisci;	Edificò una nobile Chiesa	built a church noble
verum ita gentilibus operibus implevit	ma l'empì di tante opere gentilesche	but impious with so many gentile works
ut non tam Christianorum quam Infidelium daemones adorantium templum esse videretur.	che non sembrò tempio di cristiani, bensì di infedeli adoratori di demoni,	that it seemed no temple of Christians but of infidels, adorers of demons,
Atque in eo concubinae suae tumulum erexit et artificio et lapide pulcherrimum, adiecto titulo gentili more in hunc modum	e vi innalzò alla sua concubina un sepolcro magnifico con l'iscrizione pagana:	and therein raised to his concubine a magnificent ~~pap~~ pagan sepulchre and inscription,
Divae Isottae sacrum.	—Sacro alla Diva Isotta—.	To the goddess Isotta., sacro, alla Diva Isotta.

The title of Beltramelli's work was *Un tempio d'amore* (or in English, *A Temple of Love*), a title that effectively summarized its principal claims: first, that the church of San Francesco in Rimini was constructed by Sigismondo Malatesta as a *temple of love* dedicated to his mistress and later third wife, Isotta degli Atti;[10] and second, that the church was not really a church but a "temple," which is to say, that in its inspiration the building was an expression of neopaganism. The claims were hardly original. Beltramelli was recapitulating, albeit somewhat baldly, a corpus of ideas that had been slowly developing since the latter half of the eighteenth century, and that had gathered momentum especially in the later nineteenth century. We might call this the Romantic, or the late Romantic, interpretation.

The Romantic interpretation of the church of San Francesco focused on the reading of three testimonies: the iconography of the sculptures and bas-reliefs decorating the church's interior; the entwined letters *S* and *I* carved at various points on the building's exterior and interior; and the tomb of Isotta degli Atti within the church, especially the inscription that adorned it. (The first two are treated in detail in chapter 3.) It was the inscription, of course, that had attracted Pius II's attention in the passage we have already examined; both the inscription and his remarks on it came to constitute a key document in the Romantic interpretation of the church.

The inscription itself was brief and simple: D. ISOTTAE ARIMINENSI B. M. SACRUM. (This can be translated: "Consecrated to [or sacred to] the *diva* Riminese, Isotta, of blessed memory.") The remarks on it by Pius were delivered in the course of an introductory character sketch of Sigismondo Malatesta, portrayed as a personality with fatal flaws. To be sure, Sigismondo had constructed a notable church within his domains, nor did Pius doubt its devotional purpose: it was, he stated, built to honor Saint Francis, and thereby God (*"in honorem divi Francisci"*). (His observation is seconded by the twin dedicatory inscriptions in Greek at the sides of the church, which state that the building is dedicated to "immortal God," "Θεῶι ἀϑανάτωι"). Yet even this noble work had been marred by Sigismondo's incorrigible character, for within the monument to God he had also placed a sepulchre for his mistress (*"concubinae suae tumulum erexit"*). Thus, Pius himself noted clearly that the church was consecrated to Saint Francis, and that *only* the funerary monument was dedicated to Isotta. Yet later writers concentrated solely on the tomb—and especially on his observation that its inscription was *"gentili more,"* "in the ancient [or 'gentile'] style."

Pius's comment referred to the use of the adjective *diva* before the name of Isotta. In classical Latin *divus* had been used frequently as an epithet of extraordinary distinction or excellence (Rome, for example, was called *urbs diva* by Livy), and in the post-Augustan period it had been a common epithet for deceased emperors. But in later and medieval Latin its use had greatly declined, especially in contrast to terms such as *sanctus* or *beatus*, terms related to ecclesiastical usage and so deployed much more frequently. While it seems simple when presented in this way, the history of these terms epitomizes the historical, semantic density of the Latin language that confronted early humanists resolved to reappropriate classical Latin for use in their chancery documents and cultural works. We can appreciate the difficulty of their task if we consider that the ordinary schoolboy distinction between *eius* and *suus* was not clarified until the 1440s by Lorenzo Valla, then at the forefront of humanist scholarship. And Valla (1407–57) was an exact contemporary of Pius II (1405–64). As a highly self-conscious neo-Latin stylist, Pius knew what was involved in the programmatic effort to revivify ancient usage and diction. The use of *divus* was one such exercise, as was the use of classical *templum* in place of the medieval, ecclesiastical term *ecclesia*, both facile signs for distinguishing humanist Latin. Not surprisingly, Pius himself wrote that Sigismondo had constructed a *templum* that was in honor of *divus Franciscus*. Thus his objection to *diva* in the sepulchral inscription was not to its *mos gentilis* as linguistic usage, a mannerism he used routinely himself, but to the way that this style had been misappropriated for an object so unworthy as the *"tumulus suae concubinae."* Of course the term *gentilis* still retained some of its characteristically medieval meaning of "pagan" or "heathen"; and no doubt Pius intended it to suggest an effect of guilt by association. But in no way did he imagine, even remotely, that the inscription was the banner of a programmatic neopaganism, or that the church of San Francesco was dedicated to someone other than Saint Francis—for example, to Isotta.

What was unimaginable to Pius II became what Romantic authors were most eager to assert. This they accomplished by a strategy of quotation, a synecdoche whereby the referent of the sepulchral inscription was transferred to the entire church. The characteristic formulation of this notion was given in passing by Burckhardt in 1860, who described "[Sigismondo's] *amour* with the fair Isotta, in whose honour and as whose monument the famous rebuilding of S. Francesco at Rimini took place— *Divae Isottae Sacrum."* [11] Yet Burckhardt did not elaborate a companion notion implicit in his work—that the term *diva* was not a stylistic mannerism but the authentic sign of neopaganism, or that the church itself expressed this neopaganism. John Addington Symonds (1874) likewise did not explicitly discuss the term *diva*, but he made his understanding of it clear enough. He quoted the abbreviated form of the inscription transmitted by Pius II and Burckhardt, then concluded that the church was "a monument of first-rate importance for all students who seek to penetrate the revived Paganism of the fifteenth century";[12] it was "one of the earliest extant buildings in which the Neopaganism of the Renaissance showed itself in full force."[13] Together Burckhardt and Symonds had formulated the poles of interpretation for the building: a monument to Isotta, a monument to paganism. Yet these were but two sides of the same coin, and inevitably they were fused into a singular fantasy.

The Romantic interpretation of the church received its definitive synthesis in the work of Charles Yriarte (1832–98), an obscure journalist who published a biographical and art historical study of Sigismondo Malatesta in 1882, *Un Condottiere au XVe siècle* (Paris: J. Rothschild). Yriarte had discovered a poem that he attributed to Sigismondo, and he claimed that it unlocked the mystery of the building's sculptural iconography. It was a love poem, he said, from Sigismondo to Isotta (pp. 218–19). He also borrowed bits from earlier authors to claim that the carvings on the robes depicted in certain bas-reliefs contained hidden inscriptions to pagan gods, a "légende païenne" (pp. 236–38). And in short, the church of San Francesco was a pagan monument to Isotta: "It is not God who is worshiped here; instead it is for her that the incense and the myrrh are burned." ("Ce n'est pas Dieu qu'on adore ici, c'est pour elle que brûlent l'encens et la myrrhe," p. 198).

Yriarte's views were diffused through books and studies of every sort: novels, plays, travel guides, encyclopedias, and scholarly monographs. To a later age some seem improbable vehicles indeed. There was Pasquale Villari, for example, who had spearheaded the school of positivist historiography in Italy. Yet in his article for the 1886 edition of the *Encyclopaedia Britannica*, Villari repeated all of Yriarte's principal claims: the Tempio was meant "to celebrate the tyrant's [i.e., Sigismondo's] love for Isotta"; it was "dedicated . . . to the glorification of an unhallowed attachment," and Isotta was its "ruling deity"; and the sculptural decorations were "derived, it appears, from a poem in which Sigismondo had invoked the gods and the signs of the zodiac to soften Isotta's heart and win her to his arms."[14] The 1900 and 1908 Baedeker travel guides for central Italy also reported that the sculptures in the Tempio were "from a poem by Sigismondo in honour of his mistress";[15] and the same view was rehearsed in the French travel guides of André Maurel (thirteen editions, 1906–20).[16] In a 1906 novel, Edward Hutton asserted that the Tempio was built "to Madonna Isotta, *Divae Isottae Sacrum*," that it was "a monument to Sigismondo and Isotta."[17] In 1907 Luigi Arduini affirmed the "exclusively pagan spirit" of the Tempio ("spirito esclusivamente pagano"), which was "an apotheosis of their love, or even a temple transformed into a sanctuary of their passion" where Isotta was "the true and only ruling divinity" ("un'apoteosi del loro amore, perfino un tempio mutato in santuario della loro passione" where Isotta was "la vera e sola divinità dominatrice").[18] In 1908 Giuseppe Albini published a poetic drama depicting Sigismondo in the act of ordering the architect to erect the "monumento de la divina Isotta."[19] In 1911 the *Encyclopaedia Britannica*, in its famous eleventh edition, reprinted exactly the same article that had appeared in the 1886 edition.[20] And as if to epitomize the cumulative fantasy of three decades, in 1912 Antonio Beltramelli published *Un tempio d'amore*, the work consulted by Pound. For him the church of San Francesco was "the supreme tribute of adoring reverence paid to Isotta" (p. 55). It offered homage to her beauty, her simplicity, her figure ("diritta come il pino"), even her brow and her eyes ("grandi e dolcissimi"): "Behold, then, the 'divine Isotta', the beloved whom Sigismondo adored and for whom he wanted to erect one of the most beautiful monuments of the Renaissance: the Temple of Love" ["Ecco adunque la 'divina Isotta' la creatura che Sigismondo adorò e per la quale volle elevato uno fra i più bei monumenti del Rinascimento: il Tempio d'Amore"] (pp. 51–52). His nod to the inscription—"*la 'divina Isotta'*"—made explicit the interpretative procedure of two generations. And the heir to this problematic heritage was Ezra Pound. Over and over Draft *A* rehearses the basic poles of the Romantic interpretation of the Tempio. In line 20—"Diva Isotta, erected a temple"—Pound again cites the sepulchral inscription to signal his belief that the church was constructed in honor of Isotta degli Atti. In line 37 he notes tersely that Sigismondo "adored graven images," referring to the church's sculptures with a biblical allusion to suggest that they signaled a new ethical and cultural order, a neopagan culture. Yet in adopting the late Romantic tradition from Beltramelli, Pound was receiving more than merely a corpus of historical claims about a determinate event in the past. For Beltramelli's work differed from its predecessors not in its claims but in its style—the tone of lyricism and violence, the note of aggression that gave the "traditional" interpretation a strange, compelling insistence. It was distinguished by the urgency with which it granted the late Romantic view of Sigismondo an exemplary status and offered it as a resource at the disposition of contemporaries, a spur to imagining new forms of cultural life in the present and the immediate future. Quotation, one might say, is always Janus-faced—looking backward and forward.

The Past

Pound, insofar as he adopted Beltramelli's historical claims, was doing little more than rehearsing assertions common to a broad—though not unchallenged—consensus of recent historiography and popularizing literature. Yet his reception of the late Romantic tradition transmitted by Beltramelli was by no means passive. Indeed he transformed it decisively by integrating it within a wider understanding of the past and a wholly new assessment of its implications for the future. Both maneuvers unfold with dramatic force in Draft *B*:

> *I have sat here for 44,000 years*
>   *yes precisely,*
>   *and Tontolini has finished*
>   *his turn in the arena.*
> *(44,000—gradins—etc.)*   5
> *And the world began again last October—*
>   *and the Tempio -   in October* ⳤ
>
>   =
> *And he commanded and commended*
>   *it Sigismundo* ⳤ
>   *the feast to be upon May day* ⳤ   10
> *Kalenda maya -*
>   *Kalenda maya,*
> ~~*and the priests of Faunus*~~   12.1
> ⳤ ~~*as Valturio says*~~ ⳤ   12.2
> ~~*were ordered*~~   12.3
> ~~*to serve fau*~~[*nus*]   12.4
> *"Els fueills de glaya."*
> *The turn of the Adige* ⳤ
>   *and the grey turn of the circus* ⳤ   15
> ~~*The f the regard stoic*~~   15.1

With respect to the past, Pound sought to assimilate the late Romantic view of the Tempio to his own understanding of medieval Provençal culture, an effort that emerges in Draft *B*, lines 11–12 and 13, where he cites bits of several verses in Provençal from the poet Raimbaut de Vaqueiras:

> Kalenda maya–
> > Kalenda maya,
> "Els fueills de glaya."

The lines from which Pound is quoting read (italics mine):

> Kalenda maya
> Ni fuelhs de faya
> Ni chanz d'auzelh ni flors de glaya
> Non es que·m playa.

Raimbaut's song is a love lament, and as a contrast to his unhappy condition he begins by reporting the arrival of spring and May Day. The lines can be translated: "May Day: no leaves of beech-tree, no song of bird, no flowers of iris [or gladiolus] are there which please me." However, Pound's selection emphasizes only the elements of spring, eliminating the negative particles that signal Raimbaut's infelicity. The phrases he quotes can be translated: "May Day, May Day" (lines 11 and 12) and "the leaves of iris [or gladiolus]" (line 13). On the simplest level Pound seeks to suggest that the Tempio's construction heralds a new cultural era, the dawn of the Renaissance and the spring of a neopagan revival. Yet Pound also has precise motives for doing so by means of this poem, which he uses to evoke a rich complex of ideas. Some of these derive from the biography of Raimbaut, a Provençal poet (ca. 1160–1207) who was among the earliest of the troubadours to practice his craft outside France. Between 1175 and 1178 he made his first visit to Montferrat in northern Italy, where he met and grew close to Boniface, prince of the ruling house. When Boniface succeeded to the marquisate in 1192, Raimbaut hastened to renew their friendship. He assisted Boniface I in his battles against Asti and neighboring communes of the Piedmont in 1192–93, and in the conquest of Sicily in 1194. And though he apparently went back to Provence briefly in 1195–96, he returned to the court of Montferrat again from 1197 to 1202. By now the cultural life of the court was flourishing and eager to host Provençal poets, such as Peire Vidal and Gaucelm Faidit, and it was in this period that Raimbaut also wrote most of his best work. In 1203 he joined Boniface in the Fourth Crusade, which eventually conquered Constantinople and established the Latin kingdom, resulting in Boniface being declared the feudal lord of Thessalonica (Salonika). It is most likely that Raimbaut died with Boniface in 1207 when he was mortally wounded by a troop of the Bulgarian forces then invading Greece.

Raimbaut is important because he was among the earliest troubadours to arrive in northern Italy when the prestige of Provençal lyric was spreading over the Alps and becoming fashionable among the lords of Montferrat, Malaspina, Este, and Ravenna. His poetic activity furnished "the first real impetus towards the diffusion of the Provençal lyric in the peninsula" and contributed "greatly to the development of the art of the troubadour in Italy, at first in the Provençal language and later in the native idioms."[21] (Among his works is a multilingual *descort* imitated by Dante.) Raimbaut, in other words, was a figure whose activity marked a cultural transition, a bridge between Provençal and Tuscan lyric of the duecento, and in this respect not unlike Sigismondo, whose construction of the church of San Francesco signals a landmark in the change from Gothic to early Renaissance architecture.

Yet the significance of invoking Raimbaut went beyond the general thematic connection suggested by his biography. Pound was invoking not only Raimbaut, but specifically his lines about May Day—a device allowing him to suggest his own view that the link between the poetry of Provence and the Italian duecento was charged with values that were extraliterary. It marked not just the spread of specific literary forms and practices, but the transmission of an ethico-religious culture whose most salient expression had been the poetry of the troubadours. That is to say, it was a literary culture whose vitality, he believed, stemmed from its unique relation to the spring rituals of May Day. This belief underlies his selection of Raimbaut's lines regarding "*Kalenda Maya*." As Pound wrote in 1912:

> . . . remember how Provençal song is never disjunct from pagan rites of May Day. Provence was less disturbed than the rest of Europe by invasion from the North in the darker ages; if paganism survived anywhere it would have been, unofficially, in the Langue d'Oc. That the spirit was, in Provence, Hellenic is seen readily enough by anyone who will compare the *Greek Anthology* with the work of the troubadours.[22]

In miniature the passage outlines a historiographical matrix to which Pound repeatedly assimilated events from other periods, pre- and post-medieval.[23] Yet as so often, his view had an intricate relationship to contemporary scholarship. His immediate source for this belief was Justin H. Smith, *The Troubadours at Home: Their Lives and Personalities, Their Songs and Their World* (New York: G. P. Putnam's Sons, 1899), a work that Pound had read by at least 1912.[24] In his chapter on "The Origins of Troubadour Poetry" (vol. 2, pp. 324–39), Smith had voiced the theory on which Pound drew repeatedly when offering his own account of the same question. Synthesizing earlier views, Smith conceded that the emergence of Provençal culture owed much to the *sermo plebius* of late antiquity, and also to contributions offered by "several foreign elements" from ancient Greek, Visigothic, Arabic, and Celtic cultures (pp. 324–33). Together these had formed a kind of dormant basis for the cultural flowering that followed. But the catalyst, claimed Smith, was to be found in "a little meadow among the hills of Aquitaine,—of southern Poitou, let me say" (pp. 333–34), for it was here that the dances of May Day had taken place, dances that offered a key to the nature of Provençal culture: "These May festivals had their origin in pagan celebrations in honor of Venus. The character of the dances is inferred from dances still found in remote districts of France" (p. 464, n. 5). This view Pound had echoed as early as 1910 in *The Spirit of Romance*, when he discussed the late antique poem known as the *Pervigilium Veneris*. "It celebrates a Greek feast, which had been transplanted into Italy, and recently revived by Hadrian: the feast of Venus Genetrix, which survived as May Day" (*SR*, p. 18).

Smith gave no evidence for his claim that the May Day festivals derived from the cult of Venus, but he was unequivocal in citing his source for the idea that May Day, in turn, had constituted "the definite starting-point of troubadour poetry" (p. 338). This was "the theory of Gaston Paris" (p. 338), especially as elucidated in his *Origine de la Poésie lyrique en France au Moyen Age* (Paris, 1892). It was a name Pound knew well, that of a highly respected medievalist whose views he cited repeatedly in the 1910 *Spirit of Romance* (pp. 73, 74, 75), and whom he still remembered with approval over two decades later.[25] Yet while Pound's belief had roots in a solid, if controversial, scholarly tradition, his argument altered the shape and texture of earlier claims in crucial ways. For example, it placed less stress on May Day as the point of departure for a new culture, and instead emphasized the elements of continuity with earlier or ancient culture—especially ancient Greece. Further, it eliminated the main category of evidence used by Smith and Paris, contemporary folk custom, and in its place adduced only literary and poetic texts.

In some respects Pound's argument was transparently self-serving. By asserting that "paganism" had survived "unofficially" he avoided the inconvenience of having to buttress his argument with actual documentation. By claiming that the "Hellenic spirit" of Provençal culture was "seen readily enough" by comparing the *Greek Anthology* with unspecified poems, he evaded the labor of citing the specific texts that would substantiate his claim. Further, the argument was exquisitely "cultural," depending solely on poetic texts disconnected from any other type of documentation. And its terminology was vague, at best; it encompassed under "paganism" phenomena as diverse as the pre-Roman customs of May Day and the far different culture of ancient, especially Hellenistic, Greece.

Yet Pound was deeply committed to this historiographical matrix. As early as 1910 he also sought to extend its chronological perimeters to encompass the Italian culture of *stilnovismo*. He stressed elements of "the pagan lineage" in the "rise of Mariolatry"; he claimed that "the consummation of it all" was discernible in "Dante's glorification of Beatrice" and in "the final evolution of Amor by Guido and Dante," developments that had created "a new and paganish god."[26] Moreover, he apparently held to these beliefs consistently throughout the period 1910–30, for in a 1931 article he wrote that "it is equally discernible upon study that some non-Christian and inextinguishable source of beauty persisted throughout the Middle Ages maintaining song in Provence, maintaining the grace of Kalenda Maya."[27]

Such continuity suggests how eagerly Pound must have read a passage in Beltramelli's book claiming that the cultural tradition of Rimini (expressed fully only in the Tempio) was distinguished by its capacity for passion, passion that had enabled it to soar to new heights, had "lift[ed] it into the serene dominion of thought, into the Hellenic religion of love as the sole wellspring of eternal beauty, whence art landed upon her shores and shone upon her with its magic spell that never decays" (pp. 10–11). Or again, another passage by Beltramelli that described the Tempio as it struck a visitor in 1912, a view surely not dissimilar to Pound's own a decade later in 1922: "It rises in the heart of Rimini, alone, in a silent piazza; it appears unexpectedly, since everything around it is impoverished and nothing announces its presence; it emerges into view like an extraordinary flower arising from the mud of May" (p. 56). Pound was eager indeed to view the culture of Renaissance Rimini as the heir and renovator of a "secret" spiritual tradition stretching from ancient Greece to medieval Provence. Consider only the marginalia that he entered in his copy of Charles Yriarte's work, *Un Condottiere au XVe siècle*, shortly after he obtained it on 3 August 1922 (seven weeks after writing Drafts *A* and *B*).[28] Of the 150 markings Pound entered in this copy, the two longest are notes implying that Sigismondo and Isotta had enacted an ethos of amour that constituted a revival of practices and attitudes found earlier in Provençal and ancient Greek cultures. When

Yriarte comments with surprise on how unabashed was the public display of Sigismondo's passion for his mistress,[29] Pound hastens to remark: "*Prov*[encal]. *customs. Y*[riarte] *ignorant of middle ages*." And again, when Yriarte quotes a line from a poem written in Isotta's honor by a poet of the Malatestan court—a line that compares her to a goddess, "*Nulla tibi par est foemina, nulla dea*"—Pound hastens to adduce in the margin a passage from Homer, the famous lines in which the Trojan elders compare Helen to a goddess. Together these marginalia delineate the boundaries of a hidden cultic tradition that Pound wished to discern, a tradition leading from ancient Greece to Provence, and revived in Malatestan Rimini.[30]

Thus Pound's citation of these few lines from Raimbaut de Vaqueiras asserts a core of ideas and a rich complex of analogies behind his thinking about the church of San Francesco in Rimini. First, the evocation of May Day establishes a simple analogy: as May Day announces the arrival of spring, so the Tempio Malatestiano announces the cultural rebirth of the Renaissance, viewed by Pound as a neopagan revival in accordance with Burckhardtian historiographical tradition. Second, the poem's author embodies the transferral of the "Hellenic" spirit and "paganism" from Provence to the soil of Italy, prefiguring its later revival by Sigismondo Malatesta and its actualization in the Tempio Malatestiano. Third, the reference to "Kalenda Maya" in Provençal recalls the specific claim that "Provençal song is never disjunct from pagan rites of May Day." And there is yet a fourth point—but to understand it we must explore one last transformation of the late Romantic tradition regarding the Tempio, a transformation linked not with the past, but with the future.

The Future

While Pound adopted without change many elements from the late-Romantic tradition regarding the Tempio, he also assimilated the entire tradition to the crisis of contemporary Europe. The process unfolds in two critical passages, one of which is Draft *B*, lines 6–7:

> And the world began again last October—
> and the Tempio–   in October

Here the construction of the Tempio Malatestiano is presented as an analogue for the birth of a new era in the modern world, an era purportedly begun "last October" of 1921 (line 6)—at first sight an obscure, indeed hermetic, claim. Yet its sense is clarified by reference to a "mystical" calendar that Pound had published some four months earlier in the spring

1922 issue of *The Little Review.*[31] Accompanying the calendar was a brief
note by Pound that "explained," "The Christian era came definitely to an
END at midnight of the 29–30 of October (1921)." Pound no doubt had
initially selected this date to end the Christian era because it solemnized
the evening when he had received a handwritten note from James Joyce,
informing him that "the writing of *Ulysses* is ended."[32] Yet the signifi-
cance of the calendar rested less in the ending of one era than in the
beginning of another.

The Christian era's end, his note observed, had been followed by two
sacred days that would be extracalendrical in the new calendar, days that
were designated the feast of Zagreus (30 October or "Demeter") and the
feast of Pan (31 October or "Demeter"). It was the latter that interested
Pound in relation to the Tempio. For on 31 October 1447 the bishop of
Rimini had blessed the first stone laid for reconstruction of the chapel of
San Sigismondo in the church of San Francesco. The chapel was the first
portion of the church to be rebuilt, and not long afterwards this initial
project was incorporated into Alberti's more ambitious redesign of the
church's exterior; yet because it had led into the subsequent reconception
of the entire project, the date when work began on the chapel was tradi-
tionally viewed as the inauguration of the Tempio Malatestiano.[33] In other
words, 31 October marked both the birth of the Tempio and the eve of the
new era initiated in 1921. It also followed by one day the birth of Pound
himself, born on 30 October 1885, and no doubt this had been an impor-
tant motive for beginning the new era with exactly this date. For it was
not by chance that Pound's appointed biographer described the new ep-
och (post-1921) as "a new pagan age called the Pound Era."[34] In the
coincidence of dates Pound detected—well, slightly more than coinci-
dence. For behind the superficial toying with calendrical motifs (and
Pound himself probably regarded it as such) were hidden more serious
claims that Pound wished to assert, claims central for his understanding
of the church in Rimini, his own work, and its place in the new era that
he longed for. From the outset he wished to discern a parallel between
himself and Sigismondo Malatesta, between his vague hope for a new
cultural era and the construction of the Tempio Malatestiano, between
the magnum opus he wished to write and the unfinished monument of
Rimini.

The analogy, however, was more resonant than even Pound imagined,
as becomes clearer if we examine the second passage crucial for his
transformation of the late Romantic tradition, a passage in Draft *B*, lines
8–13:

And he commanded and commended
it   Sigismundo ⪰
the feast to be upon May day ⪰   10
Kalenda maya -
Kalenda maya,
~~and the priests of Faunus~~   12.1
~~⪰ as Valturio says ⪰~~
~~were ordered~~   12.3
~~to serve fau~~[*nus*]

Here Pound sketches a sort of historical fantasia. The lines of Raimbaut de Vaqueiras concerning May Day have been inserted into a narrative that recounts an obscure ceremony conducted by Sigismondo Malatesta. As before, the point of departure is the chapel of San Sigismondo—this time not the start of reconstruction, but its completion, celebrated in a consecration ceremony that took place on 1 May 1452. Yet the account that Pound presents is so striking and singular that we must consider the primary sources that register this event.

The only contemporary source that reports the consecration is the anonymous *Cronaca malatestiana*. The ceremony, it recounts, was attended by six bishops and two abbots, and the service was "very solemn" (*solenissimo*). Afterwards the dignitaries enjoyed a large meal hosted by Sigismondo in the Franciscan convent attached to the church, and there was also a public race or contest in honor of the festival. The chronicle says nothing more.[35] Another source adds no details about the ceremony, but briefly mentions a topic that later authors often incorporated into their own accounts—relics that were placed in the sacristy attached to the chapel. They were valuable and magnificent, according to Roberto Valturio, a contemporary of Sigismondo who served as his secretary and councilor.[36] For subsequent authors the relics offered the principal, indeed only, occasion for embellishing the narrative transmitted by the *Cronaca*. In 1582 Francesco Sansovino's account (written over a century after the event) added that the relics from the chapel's sacristy had been displayed from the church's pulpit during the ceremony.[37] And some thirty years later a fourth account repeated Sansovino's claim, noting that the practice of enumerating the relics was still being followed on each 1 May (as of 1617).[38]

None of these accounts served as Pound's source, it is clear, for at this point he was just beginning his research and was scarcely aware of their existence. Yet they help us to demarcate the field from which some later, secondary source may have reported its own version of the 1452 consecration, a version that at least (*a*) mentioned the date of 1 May and (*b*) reported the name of Valturio; and which (*c*) perhaps stressed claims about the "pagan" character of the Tempio and (*d*) may have contrasted this with the ecclesiastical character of the consecration. Such features suggest a work from the latter half of the nineteenth century, but I have found none that narrates anything resembling the remarkable account given by Pound. Most likely there was no single source, and Pound was using sketchy notes as the basis for a fantasy of the 1 May consecration; or perhaps he misunderstood his own notes and turned his misunderstanding into a point of departure.[39] In either case, the attribution of the story to Valturio ("as Valturio says," 12.2) is patently false, and the account itself is equally so.

Yet inasmuch as the story is largely Pound's invention, it is all the more significant for how much it reveals about the emerging form of his aspirations. For his account of the 1 May ceremony is both startling and disturbing. At its core are two elements. First, Sigismondo has "commanded" that "the feast"—and the word is crucial—be held "upon May Day" (8–10). Here again the term "feast," refers to *The Little Review* calendar and the explanatory note that listed "feasts" to be instituted in the new, post-Christian era. Among them was one for May Day, this one called "the feast of Priapus." It is to this "feast" that the 1452 ceremony consecrating the chapel of San Sigismondo has been assimilated, a feast plainly celebrating the powers of human sexuality and generation as the keystones of a new ethical and cultural order, and a feast to be observed on the very day that had served as the catalyst for the culture of Provence—whence the embedded quotation of "*Kalenda maya, Kalenda maya.*" It suggests an intricate alignment of history, ideology, and mythological lore. For as Priapus represents the power of generation, so Faunus is the Roman deity charged with assuring the fertility of the flocks and often assimilated to the Greek Pan, both *numina* who haunt the forests or mountains and live at the borderlines of civilization. These borderline figures are now recuperated, turned into protagonists of a cultic vision stretching from ancient Greece to Provence to Malatestan Rimini, and invoked to prefigure a new ethical-cultural order in the modern world.

Equally important is another element in this presentation, its report that the ecclesiastical dignitaries have become "priests of Faunus" at Sigismondo's behest, or more exactly, have been "ordered" by Sigismondo "to serve fau[nus]" (12.1, 12.3–4). Entirely Pound's invention, the account is especially revealing. For here the neopaganism of the new culture is inaugurated in a fantasy with disturbing connotations, a fantasy that portrays the new order achieved not by transition, persuasion, or consensus, but by forceful imposition on the unwilling figures of ortho-doxy, the ecclesiastics who are (in Pound's words) "ordered to serve" the neopaganism that seals the new age.

It is here, in the hint of violence and the tone of aggression, that Pound's presentation shares a common ground with Beltramelli, whose book we have seen that he consulted. For in contrast to earlier writers in the tradition of Malatestan historiography, Beltramelli was distinctive for employing a tone of violent lyricism to make his portrait of Sigismondo emphasize the concepts, obviously derived from Nietzsche, of will and struggle. In his words, "the mere presence of Sigismondo was enough to impose subjection, and in this trait lay the secret of his fascination over the masses" (p. 40). Or as he put it again, "if Sigismondo failed in his effort to kill pope Paul II, it was hardly for lack of will" (pp. 43–44). In Beltramelli's portrait, as in Pound's, will and its forceful imposition char-acterized Sigismondo and his activities in the construction of a new moral-cultural order, and marked his exemplary status for the imagining of a new man in the present, and the coming era.

The new order envisioned by Pound and Beltramelli pertained not to the past but to the present and the imminent future (as the calendrical motifs of Draft *B* make quite explicit). And it was approaching with fear-ful speed, indeed was already at hand. For in June 1922—that is to say, exactly when Pound was at work on Draft *B*—Beltramelli was laboring on another book, this one entitled *L'uomo nuovo* (or in English, *The New Man*), released a year later.[40] It was the first biography of Mussolini. And it was Beltramelli's finest book—tense with rugged lyricism, charged with violent evocations of the land he loved, his native province of Rom-agna, and the man who had risen from it to seize the leadership of modern Italy. His regionalist sympathies led him to create a kind of myth about the *romagnolità* of Mussolini, setting an impressive pattern followed by all the apologetic biographies published in the next twenty years.[41] Not surprisingly, when Beltramelli sought to establish forerunners for "the new man," he dwelled on figures from the house of Malatesta, since they too were from the province that gave birth to Mussolini. There was Mala-testa da Verucchio, for instance, the man who had founded the house of Malatesta by virtue of his will: "He knows what he wants and he places his life as a pledge for his will" (p. 55). His descent from the mountains (the abode of Pan) and Verucchio was an exemplary journey, the arrival of a figure from the borderline who wrested Rimini from the factious forces of the democratic commune. (One should compare this scene with Pound's treatment of the same figure in the final version of the Malatesta Cantos.) And of course there was Sigismondo Malatesta, "warrior and artist" with "the heart of a poet," whose "desperate energy" and "passionateness" impressed itself in every deed, a true forerunner of Mussolini (pp. 56–57). The regime, it must be noted, was duly pleased. A letter from Mussolini to Beltramelli appeared in facsimile at the close of the volume, lending its portrait still greater "authority."

Beltramelli's treatment of Sigismondo Malatesta helps us gain insight into Pound's motives in Draft *B*. Pound shared with Beltramelli the desire to evoke a new ethico-cultural order, and an aspiration to see this order embodied in (and through) a new type of man. As he wrote in January 1922, five months before Draft *B*, "in trying to synthesize the change of the last years of calamity we may find that the type 'gentleman' is played out, that the term should take its place with *corteggiano, muscadine, courtier.*" It was a new era, he suggested, with its own particular needs. It was time to "demand some caste debarring that inaction, that mental timidity, that defensiveness, that general nullity so wholly compatible with, and even invited by the gentleman." It was time "to turn to and build rather than scratch round for remnants and bric-à-brac," and this task would require "acute and violent effort." The model for this "violent effort" was the early Renaissance: "our envy must be for a period when the individual city (Italian mostly) tried to outdo its neighbour in the degree and intensity of its civilization, to be the vortex for the most living individuals."[42]

The vehemence of Pound's desire to invoke a new age derived from a complex of motives, some social and some personal. In his own life, Pound had suffered a series of intense, humiliating setbacks in his economic fortunes and literary career during 1920 and 1921. Some had issued directly from the "panic" that struck the stock market in late 1920 and carried into the depression of 1921. In late December 1920 he learned that the "panic" had made it "out of the question" to pursue John Quinn's proposal for a syndicate to grant him a lifetime endowment.[43] In January 1921 he was informed that *The New Age*, his principal means of income, would no longer be able to pay contributors—another result of the troubled economic conditions.[44] In April he learned that his contractual arrangements with *The Dial* would not be renewed, and a day later he confessed to one correspondent his fear that he would soon "perish in the unwatered deserts."[45] By June he was reduced to translating what he dismissed as "pornography for pastors of [the] U.S." in order to "pay the

rent."[46] And although he managed to persuade *The Dial* to renew a por-
tion of the earlier agreement in July, his duties and salary were halved.[47]
The situation continued to worsen. By October he was constrained to ask
John Quinn for a loan.[48] In December 1921, when informed that Elkin
Mathews (his principal publisher from 1908 to 1920) had died, he could
think of nothing to say except to inquire about what might "become of his
business; and if there is any chance of its continuing, or the estate paying
the royalties due."[49] Little wonder that his "Paris Letter" of the next
month should call the recent period "the last years of calamity."

It was not until January 1922 that Pound could rectify the distressing
state of his personal finances, when he signed a long-term contract with
Horace Liveright promising a guaranteed income for the next two years
($500 annually, plus translator's fees for any work from French agreed on
by both parties).[50] How soon he began receiving money from the new
contract is unclear, but already by 3 February he was planning a journey
to Italy, the trip that would take him to Rimini and his first view of the
church of San Francesco, and to Sirmione where he would write Drafts *A*
and *B*.[51] Yet as Pound began to restore a precarious equilibrium to his
finances in the wake of the economic downturn of 1920–21, he emerged
with a sensibility reshaped by trauma. On the one hand his comments on
any question touching his personal finances revealed a novel mordancy.
In March 1922 T. S. Eliot proposed that he write a regular report from
Paris for his forthcoming journal (soon to be named *The Criterion*), and
that he serve without pay as a scout for new talent. His reply was acidic:
"I don't, damme, see why I should write a letter to London for £3." Cer-
tainly he had no intention of furnishing "free services as unpaid foreign
editor." His tone was bitter and virulent: "I have beggared myself, and
kept down my rates for years by contributing to every free and idealistic
magazine that has appeared."[52] And he scarcely troubled to conceal the
fact that he was reacting to the recent trauma; two weeks after writing the
Sirmione drafts he reminded John Quinn, "You know how damn near a
squeak I have had more than once, and even so recently as last winter."[53]
On the other hand, he was resolved to assume a new, more assertive
posture toward the future. By now he felt keenly his need of personal and
creative renewal. Sirmione, he explained to one correspondent, was
"where I always go to refit"; it was a place where even three weeks might
"make a new man of you"—a phrase suggesting the affinity between his
own state of mind and the cultural psychology animating Beltramelli's
biography of Mussolini.[54] When he was in Sirmione, then, Pound epito-
mized his resolve for personal and cultural renovation by rehearsing an

enactment of these motifs in the past through the figure of Sigismondo. Years before, when he had first begun *The Cantos,* he had depicted the ritual of Odysseus and his *nekuia* as a figure for his efforts to find the knowledge of the past. Now to renew his work he elaborated another ritual, the ceremony of "Sigismundo" that heralds the knowledge of the future, the announcement of a new age.

The ceremony enacted by "Sigismundo," however, differs sharply from the earlier ritual of Odysseus, and the differences between them suggest social rather than biographical motives. The figure of Odysseus had occupied a smaller stage, had operated in a more private sphere: he communicated with the past alone, and he was content to rehearse ceremonies already sanctioned by his community. The "Sigismundo" of 1922 is conspicuously different: he is a figure of authority, a "new man" of the future, a leader who introduces a cultic vision into a community that is passively silent, and who does so by forcefully imposing his beliefs on the timid figures of orthodoxy obeying his "commands" and "orders." His position in the social order is ambivalent: inside it by virtue of his power, outside it by virtue of a cultic vision heralding the new age. Above all, he possesses the power to humiliate the figures of orthodoxy. For now the introduction of a new order entails the settling of old scores.

Here, too, comparison with Beltramelli is suggestive. In his 1912 work on Sigismondo, Beltramelli had given only passing attention to an incident in 1467, when Sigismondo allegedly attempted to murder Pope Paul II; but in his 1922 biography of Mussolini he presented it as the central episode in his portrait of the Renaissance ruler. His shift in emphasis parallels a hardening in Pound's own deliberations, for in subsequent drafts Pound also gives the same incident increasing prominence, and by the final version of the Malatesta Cantos his narrator calls it a "damn pity he didn't . . . get the knife into him." Again, growing intransigence also characterizes Pound's later treatment of Raimbaut de Vaqueiras, the Provençal poet invoked in the lines "Kalenda maya, Kalenda maya." For in subsequent drafts Raimbaut is eliminated entirely, and is replaced with the keener, more aggressive figure of Guillaume IX, the warrior duke who was the first of the troubadour poets. The difference between them was clear. Raimbaut had epitomized a process of transition, while Guillaume signaled a sharp break, the abrupt entry of a new cultural era— and violent transformation was now at stake.

Growing impatience and intransigence were not restricted to Pound, but were part of the increasing alienation felt by broad sectors of European society in the wake of the war and the economic dislocations that had ensued—dislocations that had directly affected Pound himself. These sectors regarded with equal hostility the mainstream parties of the center and the socialist reformists of the left. Both were viewed as integral, compromised elements in the same unholy alliance of capitalist production, materialism, and philosophical positivism that had created the war. They shared Pound's belief that the time had come "to synthesize the change of the last years of calamity," and increasingly they demanded a new spirituality, a new age ushering in the revendication of spirit without invoking the decayed authority of Christian orthodoxy. At its core, this was the new cultic vision prefigured by "Sigismundo."

Conjunctions

While the private trauma of Pound converged with the public sense of dislocation in the aftermath of the war, it did so through numerous levels of mediation, both institutional and discursive. The new spirituality that he sought to articulate intersected with other voices in an intricate network of discursive genealogies—some deeply private, some widely shared. A case in point is his effort to assimilate the construction of the Tempio with the "feast of Pan" in the "post-Christian" era, an effort that might seem abstruse antiquarianism were it not grounded in the intense colloquy of contemporaries. For Pan elicited remarkable interest in the culture of Edwardian England, interest that centered on a set of structural and historical ambiguities that had come to inhere in the figure. Pan was the half-beast and half-man who was divine, and so could epitomize an affirmation of the divided nature of the human: the precarious equilibrium between impulses toward the forces of libidinal, irrational energy and the contrary claims of restraint through the control of reason. A similar dichotomy structured the topography associated with Pan: linked with mountains, woods, or rural life in general, he could represent a gamut of values ranging from Arcadian escapism to the experience of natural beauty, from the intoxicated revel of life and procreation to the more aggressive, fearsome sexuality rooted in primitive instinct. In both cases he remained a native of that "other" zone outside the boundaries of urban and particularly industrial civilization. Yet this topography became more complicated when viewed as a landscape of the mind. Here Pan became not the half-beast and half-god who lived "outside" the pale of civilization, but one who resided "inside" the private and collective psyche, a joyful or barbaric force perennially seeking escape, fulfillment, or the usurpation of power. These dichotomies, in turn, could overlap with axes of class and social structuration, so that Pan could figure the vital energies of popular or lower class cultures, or be an oppositional gesture against the exhausted "high culture" of the educated bourgeoisie. And still another dichotomy appeared in a historical assessment of Pan, this one derived from the late antique story recounting that Pan had mysteriously died in the reign of Tiberius—"Great Pan is dead," a ghostly voice had shouted to a passing ship, or so reported Plutarch—for inasmuch as subsequent interpretation had linked this event with the moment of Christ's crucifixion, Pan could also evoke the demise of antiquity and the birth of the Christian era.[55]

Pan, then, was a cipher in which late Victorian and Edwardian society registered the anxiety of its transition to an increasingly secular culture. Edmund Gosse, writing in 1907, saw Pan as a figure for the psychic and intellectual dilemma of his age. "I was at one moment devoutly pious, at the next haunted by visions of material beauty and longing for sensuous impressions. In my hot and silly brain, Jesus and Pan held sway together." But Gosse was already well past middle age when he wrote this; for younger intellectuals the figure of Jesus had long since vanished altogether. Rupert Brooke spoke for a new generation in 1906 when he reported, "I myself have heard Pan piping among the reeds, down in Surrey." And Gosse and Brooke were hardly alone in their attention to Pan. Cultural works invoking Pan appeared in every genre—poetry, fiction, and intellectual prose. Consider only a sampling of short stories and novels that appeared between 1901 and 1916: H. W. Nevinson, *The Plea of Pan* (1901); Richard Garnett, "Pan's Wand" (1903); E. M. Forster, "The Story of a Panic" (1904); James Huneker, "Pan" (1905); E. F. Benson, "The Man Who Went Too Far" (1906); Forrest Reid, *The Garden God* (1906); Kenneth Grahame, "The Piper at the Gates of Dawn," which is chapter seven in *The Wind in the Willows* (1908); Victor Neuburg, *Triumph of Pan* (1910); Saki, "The Music on the Hill" (1911); Algernon Blackwood, *Pan's Garden* (1912); Lord Dunsany, "The Death of Pan" and "The Tomb of Pan" (1915); and Eden Philpotts, *The Girl and the Faun* (1916). Poetry was no less abundant: between 1880 and 1914 (a period of thirty-five years) there were at least one hundred forty poems that made use of Pan. In Cambridge there was even a Pan Society. A curious world of desires—both private and social—was epitomized in the affecting cry of Amelia J. Burr, writing in 1915: "Blow, Pan, blow! I am thy pipe, | Let me thy music be."[56]

During his London residence, when Pound was eager to catch the ear of his contemporaries and responsive to topics of current discussion, Pan appears five times in his poetry and prose. His treatment shows him adopting contemporary motifs while attempting to invest them with a particular significance for his own life and work. In *Ripostes* (September 1912) Pan appears in two poems, once in "N.Y." where the city is depicted as a reed and the poet as Pan; and again in "Pan is Dead," where the speaker and a group of women probe the cause behind Pan's disappearance from the world. In these works Pan is a register of Pound's cultural aspirations and a mark of his ambivalence toward the discrepancy between them and the contemporary milieu. "Pan is Dead," in particular, indicates Pound's familiarity with an anthropological interpretation linking Pan with the dying god of spring, and his understanding of its relevance for contemporary cultural discussion. In March 1914 the figure is invoked in two more poems, "The Faun" and "Tempora." Both are written in an ironic vein, and their wry detachment comments on the anachronistic incongruity of Pan appearing in a cultural setting wholly urbanized. Yet the irony hardly means that Pound had lost interest in the figure or abandoned its utopian implications, for in January 1915 he published a prose article in which he reported, with the utmost seriousness, that he had seen the god in a vision.[57] In short, within his own work the figure of Pan was also a complex and contradictory one: a token of his aspirations, the vision he hoped to register in his work, or a sign of its impossibility in a culture deemed hopelessly trivial.

Yet discussion turning on the figure of Pan reached far beyond either Pound or England. It extended throughout Europe.[58] In part this was due to the influence of Nietzsche and the explosive complex of values that accrued to the figure of Dionysius as a result of his work. Since one mythological tradition made Pan an offspring of Dionysius, and others portrayed them as frequent companions, the invocation of Pan could signal (yet also obscure) an intellectual genealogy within the Nietzschean heritage, linking one to a common project and yet enabling one to retain a certain independence. But in part the figure of Pan offered structural analogies with issues of contemporary thought so compelling that intellectuals often came upon it by quite independent routes. Here again a few examples suggest the extent of the phenomenon. In 1894 the Norwegian writer Knut Hamsun published *Pan*, a novel of unabashed primitivism; its apparent relevance to the postwar crisis was self-evident when the work was translated into English in 1921. In 1895 Julius Meier-Grafe and Otto Julius Bierbaum founded a magazine named *Pan* in Berlin, its cover depicting the goat-god as the seal of a new stylistic movement, often called Jugendstil. Oddly, Jugendstil took its name from the more popular

Munich periodical named *Jugend,* and that periodical itself portrayed Pan repeatedly on its cover (twice in 1908, for example). Indeed, it contained advertisements representing Pan as well. (Another magazine named *Pan* was founded in 1911.) In 1908 Gerhart Hauptmann wrote *Griechische Frühling,* a travel account that mingled aggressive primitivism and neopagan sentimentality centered on the death of Pan. In France, meanwhile, André Gide expressed his own interest in the myth, which he began to see as the embodiment of all his work. And in Italy Pan was typically represented by his more "native" counterpart, Faunus. It will come as no surprise that in 1904 Antonio Beltramelli wrote a short story entitled "Il Fauno," or that in 1908 he published a book entitled *I Canti di Faunus* (or *The Chants of Faunus*), a collection of poems and aphorisms echoing the assertive individualism of Stirner and Nietzsche. A copy of it is preserved containing marginalia by Mussolini, who also reviewed it with perceptive remarks on the author's enthusiasm for Max Stirner—the same Stirner whose philosophy of "egoism" gave its name to the London journal *The Egoist,* with which Pound was closely associated.

Such works constitute the matrix informing Pound's effort in Draft *B* to link the Tempio with the "feast of Pan" in the new post-Christian era, and to his fantasy of the ecclesiastical dignitaries commanded to become "priests of Faunus." Pan was an ambivalent figure who had become invested by contemporary culture with an enormous power to absorb heterogeneous contents and to address extremely diverse audiences; its "meaning" was not a given of mythological bedrock, but an outcome of congruity and tension between fault lines already inscribed in the figure through history and fault lines inscribed in a determinate use-context. Which is to say, its "meaning" resided neither in the past nor in the present, but in the structure of relations that appertained between these and the future. It was an ambiguous cipher that "claimed the energy of youth and the prerogatives of ancient wisdom," promised unity of experience (god, man, and beast) against alienation and fragmentation, offered the immediacy of music and sensuous impression in unison with the resonance of spiritual depth, and suggested the force of an elite (classical) knowledge at one with the roots of the people. Here was the culture of emerging fascism.[59]

To be sure, "the people" are not a conspicuous presence in the ceremony rehearsed in Draft *B.* They appear nowhere in the central tableau, but only in the curious framing device that opens and closes the draft:

I have sat here for 44,000 years
yes   precisely,
*   and Tontolini has finished*
his turn in the arena.

It is through the figure of "Tontolini" that the people appears onstage, refracted in the traveling variety show of Ferdinando Guillaume (whose stage name was Tontolini) which performed in the "arena" of Verona every evening from 1 to 6 June 1922. Pound attended one of the performances, together with his wife Dorothy, T. S. Eliot, and Bride Scratton.[60]

Ferdinando Guillaume (1887–ca. 1965) was born and raised in a family with deep roots in the circus and variety-show business. But Ferdinando soon associated himself with a newer, emerging form of entertainment, the cinema. The earliest comic films in Italy began to be made in Turin around 1905. They were short (each about fifteen minutes), simple, ingenuous, and farcical. They were also anonymous, for the new medium was shunned by the comic actors of traditional theater, who were incapable of responding to its rapid rhythms; instead the new comedians emerged from the comic art of clowns and variety performers. In 1908 André Deed (André de Chapois), formerly an acrobat and singer in concert-cafés, brought the comic shorts out of anonymity by creating the character Cretinetti, who in a rapid series of films (one per week) underwent adventures ever more extravagant and popular. His successor was Guillaume, who made his debut in 1910 with the stage name of Tontolini. In 1912 Guillaume changed studios, and legal reasons obliged him to create another character, "Polidor" (named after the horse used by his mother in the equestrian circus). He enjoyed great success during the prewar years, and in the hope of still greater gains he began his own production company shortly after the end of the war in 1918. The moment was unpropitious: the invasion of American film comedy was soon sweeping away the comic sector of the struggling film industry; and by 1921 the panic and depression of late 1920, combined with unpaid loans, forced the collapse of the principal backer of Italian films, the Banca italiana di sconto. Guillaume was forced to begin his career anew. After a visit to England he decided upon his next venture, a traveling variety show that would combine elements of the circus (his family background) with motifs drawn from English music halls. He called it Il Teatro della Risata or La Compagnia della Risata di Polidor, and the show began touring in late 1921. When it arrived in a new town it would stage a grand parade to publicize its presence, perhaps the event that first attracted Pound's attention in June 1922. A typical performance lasted some two hours and featured tumblers, jugglers, dancers on tightropes, singers, and other attractions. These heterogeneous elements were unified by the presence of Tontolini-Polidor himself, who had contrived a side box placed on the stage, from which he would comment on the show and perform various feats between numbers: skits, brief concerts with glasses and bells, antics such as dropping his gloves and recapturing them with a broom and dustbin, or throwing crackers at the other performers during their routines. In effect the scripted performance became a pretext for the antics of Tontolini/Polidor, generating simultaneous performances shaped by internal, improvisational rhythms.[61] Seen in sociological terms, the double performance responded to changing social conditions of Italy: elements drawn from circus acts and music halls appealed simultaneously to traditional and emerging social formations, to both a peasant and a lower class urban public, and especially to those of the urban public who had only recently migrated from the countryside.

Evidently the show left an impression on Pound, and in later drafts (e.g., the entire series of *C* drafts) he described it at greater length (*C1*, 83–85):

> [. . .] *the footlights* $=$
> *the clowns- dancers* $=$
> *performing dogs* $=$

On the other hand, he was apparently disturbed by the "vulgarity" of the show, uncertain how to react to the social and cultural ambiguities it represented.[62] His dilemma is exemplary for what it suggests about the interaction of popular and elite culture in modernism's formation, an interaction that affects how we view the larger problem of history and myth both in *The Cantos* and in modernism more generally.[63]

Pound's apparent interest in the show indicates that, like other modernists, he sometimes viewed popular culture as a source of antibourgeois sentiment that could be used—if only by juxtaposition—as the grounds for a critique of elite bourgeois culture. On the other hand, the show presented by Tontolini represented a "contamination," a hybridization of peasant culture by the tastes of an urban lower class public, a disintegration of traditional popular culture in favor of "popular" bourgeois culture. The dances of May Day, which had furnished a key to the culture of Provence, were disappearing, supplanted by a "popular" culture that tended toward repetitive, nonparticipatory, and nonregenerative banality. Tontolini represents a bastardization of authentic popular culture; he is the illegitimate heir to debased traditions that he himself no longer understands. Sigismondo, in contrast, is the legitimate heir of Pan who represents an authentic unity of popular energy and aristocratic classicism. The point is made explicit in subsequent drafts when Pound mistranslates the dedicatory inscription that crowns the façade of the church. The original Latin reads: "*Sigismundus Pandulfus Malatesta Pandulfi F. V. Fecit . . .*" (or "Sigismondo Pandolfo Malatesta, the son of Pandolfo, Built This in Fulfillment of his Vow . . ."). But Pound's recollection of the inscription wavers, and he assumes that the phrase *Pandulfi F.* (or "son of Pandolfo") is abbreviated as *Pan. F.*, an abbreviation that might suggest that Sigismondo was "the son of Pan." Thus, in one draft Pound renders the inscription: "Pan's son hath built this place."[64] Though swiftly canceled, it indicates the counter-genealogy that informs his treatment of Tontolini, whose hybridized culture is occupying the stage in the arena of history, whose banal performance is usurping the space that might better nurture a regeneration of classical culture. And yet, as Pound had written a few months earlier, it was no longer time to "scratch round for remnants and bric-à-brac," and therefore the culture of the urban lower class represented by Tontolini is declared a spent force in history: "and Tontolini has finished | his turn in the arena." This judgment, in turn, is reinforced by evoking a wider perspective in time, the arena that antedates and outlasts his performance, that testifies to the real perdurance of classical culture.

Moreover, what is here a synchronic feature within a single draft is recapitulated diachronically in the development of later drafts. The performance of Tontolini is gradually eliminated, while the image of the arena is retained and invoked repeatedly throughout the early cantos as a haunting symbol of permanence amid change. This compositional history, in turn, recapitulates a social desire: real, emerging forms of "popular" bourgeois culture, those linked with an urban lower class public, must be erased in order to conserve the privileged site of traditional popular culture that is linked with a rural public, the natural domain of Pan and Faunus. The terrain must be cleared of a historical encumbrance in order to secure the dream of an elite knowledge that, like a centaur, finds in traditional and popular culture its back and strong legs.[65]

The interaction of popular and elite culture in the formation of modernism (and Pound's text in particular) is related axiologically to the interplay of myth and history, to the tension between two apparently different temporal perspectives that are invoked in both *The Cantos* and modernism. Studies of Pound have been especially sensitive to this debate. Daniel Pearlman, for example, has argued that initially *The Cantos* present a contrast between the perspective of conventional or historical temporality and an "organic" or ahistorical perspective, but that the disparity between these is later overcome through "the reconciling synthesis of love." (The atemporal perspective has also been termed a mythical, cyclical, or primitive perception of the world.)[66] Michael André Bernstein, on the other hand, has charged that the poem effectively fails to reconcile these perspectives, that instead it offers "only the deep-seated contradictions upon which the poet's own hopes for a fruitful synthesis run aground."[67] Yet the contradiction between temporal perspectives is more illusory than real, at least if we attend to the interaction between the calendrical invocation of "the feast of Pan," the ceremony of "Sigismundo," and the problematic presence of Tontolini. At stake is not so much contradiction as sociohistorical reciprocity: the perspective of mythical/organic time draws its force—exists at all—only in symbiosis with the historicist tendencies of elite bourgeois culture, and the site of its production is secured only through the marginalization and repression of other cultural forces that threaten their common terrain. The dichotomy between organic and historical temporality is a sociohistorical construction, not an authentic antinomy, for in the twentieth century there *is* no mythical perspective of time, only the anxiety of history that is displaced in specific discursive strategies. "Myth" is already saturated with history—and half-perishing with longing to escape.

Roots and Routes

The heterogeneous contexts informing Drafts *A* and *B* converge and interact through quotation, an issue that is also thematized within the drafts themselves. In Draft *B* especially, the new age is inaugurated through the reconstruction of a fractured chain of transmission—"*kalenda maya*"—and the new culture is presented as a ritual recovery of quotations. New culture and new poem are consecrated in a ceremony that ratifies and is ratified *by* quotation, as if citation were the discursive counterpart to the theme of human and cultural regeneration. Nor is quotation prominent only in the earliest drafts of the Malatesta Cantos; in the final version it proliferates even more, as raw patches of what appears to be prose are rendered without the slightest deference to poetic conventions, creating a text that bristles with vivid juxtapositions. The presence of such patches has hardly gone unnoticed. For Hugh Kenner, "there is no more dramatic moment in the *Cantos*," while for Michael André Bernstein this "represents one of the most decisive turning-points in modern poetics."[68] Both are surely right. Quotation is central to any assessment of *The Can-*

tos, and we must give it careful consideration. But to do so, we need to consider how, and why, quotation itself has become a particular problem for recent criticism and theory.

Quotation is a salient feature of major modernist texts, whether *The Cantos* or *The Waste Land, Ulysses* or *To the Lighthouse.* Its appearance in the modernist novel may not be surprising: after all, quotation has typified the novel since the day when Don Quixote recited Petrarchan sonnets and the formulas of chivalric romance.[69] But quotation is also ubiquitous in modernist poetry—seven of the last eight lines of *The Waste Land,* for example, are quotations—surpassing the boundaries of generic expectations. Further, the modernist practice of quotation is not only pervasive, but qualitatively different: in addition to earlier poems or traditional literary materials, it cites tags from popular songs (O O O O that Shakespeherian Rag—), or the nightly injunction of pub-tenders (HURRY UP PLEASE IT'S TIME), materials wrested from outside the conventional literary domain. And the citation of historical documents, a procedure first adopted in the Malatesta Cantos, seems an especially intransigent form of this practice. The source texts are aggressively quotidian and antiliterary, invoking materials so alien to conventional notions of the "poetic" as to reconstitute the boundaries of subject matter acceptable in poetic discourse. Morever, they are presented without ragged right margins, miming the graphic characteristics of prose as if to emphasize their departure from poetic norms. In part, then, they have elicited critical interest because evaluating them is essential to our understanding not only of *The Cantos,* but of literary modernism. Another reason for interest is that criticism of the last two decades has virtually defined itself by the problem of quotation.

Quotation is the simplest yet most pervasive form of intertextuality— "la relation interdiscursive primitive," it has been called.[70] For Barthes it was the constitutive feature of text itself ("The text is a tissue of quotations drawn from the innumerable centers of culture"), a view that informs a wide array of studies considering quotation's formal, semantic, structural, and phenomenological features.[71] But quotation also consists in the exact or apparent reproduction of a previous textual sequence, and so invokes the binary oppositions between original and copy, object and representation, referent and sign, that have been the target of deconstruction. As deconstruction has disclosed and inverted the hidden privileges or hierarchies grounding logocentric dichotomies, quotation has been decisively revaluated. Derrida, in particular, has called attention to a single sentence that appears in quotation marks in Nietzsche's *Nach-*

lass, "I have forgotten my umbrella" ("Ich habe meinen Regenschirm vergessen"). The sentence stands isolated amid Nietzsche's fragmentary notes, and the presence of quotation marks does not facilitate but prevents the identification of referents or context. Thus quotation becomes an emblem of undecidability, like *l'écriture.* One inaugurates "the epochal regime of quotation marks," writes Derrida, a regime that encompasses "every concept belonging to the system of philosophical decidability, disqualifies the hermeneutic project postulating a true sense of the text, frees reading from the horizon of the meaning or truth of being, from the values of the product's production or the presence of the present." [72] Here quotation is revaluated not to assess a historical practice, but to celebrate an inversion of the hidden privileges embedded in the notions of source and referentiality. Here, then, the roots of reference are unearthed, exposed—and found to be illusory. Yet much, and perhaps too much, is omitted from such a view: in the problem of quotation, many of the central questions concern not just roots, but routes of reference—not just origins, but functions.

Theorists and linguists, disposed to investigation only through intersystemic orders, have discussed extensively the intrinsic dimensions of quotation, taking for granted that the relationship between inset (the quoted item) and frame (the quoting agency) is purely "textual" in character: a relationship between text and text. Seen thus, every quotation reproduces not only or primarily a source (or referent), but its own status as part of a linguistic order, which is to say, as part of a structure assumed to function apart from human agency (which is displaced by linguistic agency) and to possess a quasi-ontological status. Arguments of this sort are often presented as part of the generalized attack on privacy theories of meaning that has characterized much of twentieth-century thought, a strategy that is also pursued by Derrida. Quoting a sentence of his own, he notes that it "survives" not only himself, but also "the presence or assistance of any party, male or female. The statement survives them a priori, lives on after them." [73]

Such arguments undermine psychologism insofar as they attack the belief that texts are a transparent reproduction of the intentions, thoughts, or concepts held by an autonomous subject. But in some respects they also reinforce psychologism's essential premise, a notion of textual production in which agency is fundamentally desocialized. The freedom that privacy theories of meaning accord to the autonomous author is displaced into the psyche of the reader, whose appreciation of "textual" play is licensed to bypass rather than address the resistance of the "referent." While psychologistic premises are challenged at the point of production, they are reconstructed at the point of reception—reception, to be sure, in a particular and displaced sense. For when Derrida declares that his intentions as a writer are invalid as a "referent" he secures the freedom of Derrida the reader; but as Derrida the reader appears only in the written work (or "text") that registers his reading, his freedom is effectively submerged into the text's. Derrida does not write the text, it writes Derrida. Agency vanishes, or rather is blurred into text itself, conceived as a subject free from every limitation in accordance with impulses that strike some observers as deeply romantic or anarchic. Focusing on the intrinsic dimensions of quotation becomes a means of bracketing from analysis the kinds of forces that are registered by its extrinsic dimensions—quotation's functions within social groupings, its historical transformations, its transmissional dynamics, everything that might be summed up in routes of reference.

Quotation is not a purely private exercise, it is an activity conducted within the contours of specific institutional practices—a citationary institution that frames the entire practice. Consider the most typical form of extended quotation: the transmission of texts, the publication of documents, manuscripts, or other cultural works. Historically, this has repeatedly and decisively been affected by shifts in the routes of reference, by changes in the wider quotational culture. The most important event in the history of the book, the disappearance of the roll in favor of the codex, came about as the result of a new culture of quotation; the codex was more capacious and easier to consult, and facilitated the kind of cross-reference essential to the study of sacred, authoritative texts that emerged with Christianity. And needless to say, many works by pagan authors failed to survive the gradual but wholesale transference from roll to codex. They were the earliest victims of new citationary practices, *not* quoted and *not* transmitted. Quotation is always doubled-edged: it includes and protects, excludes and eliminates.

The routes of quotation are not governed by the infinite play of "textuality," but are regulated in configurations of literacy, schooling, the distribution or prohibition of texts, and in axes of class, power, and property—dimensions deemed irrelevant in structuralist and post-structuralist accounts. Classes sometimes define themselves by their citationary practices. Between 1820 and 1840, for example, Shelley's *Queen Mab* was quoted over a hundred times in working class and radical periodicals, and still more extensively in pirated editions, precisely because it was considered a seditious work. This view effectively vanished as its author was gradually assimilated into the canon.[74] And the possibility of such appropriations can threaten the interests of property: Peter Ackroyd, in his 1984 biography of T. S. Eliot, confesses that he was "forbidden by the Eliot estate to quote" from Eliot's works and correspondence.[75]

Such cases make only too clear quotation's power and menace. Implicit in the sociomaterial and institutional frame of each quotation is a certain interest in regulating the routes of reference in determinate ways, in blocking or shunting some intersections and in facilitating others. Every quotation bears an imaginary map, one might say, that charts an ideal discursive topography plotted both spatially and temporally. This map graphs other quotations organized both synchronically and diachronically, with appropriate genealogies and relations arranged to culminate in the moment of its own understanding, a future where its own discursive plenitude is fully realized—the city of God, or that happy land where people fish in the afternoon and are critical critics at night, or the new age imagined by Pound and Beltramelli. By its embeddedness in specific routes of reference, quotation is never merely re-production, but also pre-production binding inset and frame in an imagined futurity.

This future is never fully achieved. Indeed, its plotted conjunctions are always being undone. As Derrida remarks about the sentence from Nietzsche: "It knows of no proper itinerary which would lead from its beginning to its end and back again, nor does its movement admit of any center" (p. 131). The future, as often as not, reproduces precisely those other quotations from the past that were excluded or marginalized in the ideal map. The pagan texts that survived the transition to Christian culture now command far more interest than all the patristic exegesis that gave birth to the codex. Marx, in *The German Ideology*, amasses hundreds of quotations to heap scorn on Max Stirner, the philosopher of egoism; yet his *German Ideology* was not published until 1926, and then only in part, while Stirner's *Der Einzige* was rediscovered and reprinted in some forty editions in German, Italian, French, Spanish, and English between 1880 and 1930. Or in 1987 one reproduces forgotten articles written by Paul de Man in the 1940s for a Belgian newspaper named *Le Soir*, and everything that he ever wrote afterwards, his unprecedented influence on criticism between 1970 and the present, indeed the entire history of criticism in that period—all are reinscribed in a new context, reread and rewritten.[76]

Derrida has always appreciated the aleatory element of futurity, its capacity to graft an utterance onto a new context or to unleash the explosive power of iteration in different circumstances. Indeed, it stands at the basis of his thought: "This is my starting point: no meaning can be determined out of context, but no context permits of saturation."[77] For context, viewed in historical terms, is infinite: as long as history is still unfolding, it remains open. There are always events in the future that will alter irrevocably the meaning of earlier textual events. In 1985, for example, the disclosure of de Man's wartime journalism was an event that had not yet taken place; yet when it did, it reshaped the grounds for assessing all his later writings and influence.

De Man's case is important because it epitomizes essential features in the problem of quotation—the 1988 disclosures, after all, are simply instances of extended quotation, the reproduction of texts originally printed between 1939 and 1942. Their meaning, as Derrida would point out, would not achieve saturation through the reconstitution of their immediate context, assuming that context was restricted to events that occurred before they were written. For much of their meaning stems from events that occurred only later. When we read de Man's essay on "The Jews in Current Literature," published on 4 March 1941, our reading is inevitably informed by the decision (probably reached in the autumn of 1941) to proceed with the Final Solution.[78] Its "statement survives" the mind of de Man the writer because meaning does not reside solely in some inferred intention on the part of the speaker, because it is grounded in the future, in histories that invite us to perceive linkages between events that were unclear or unknown to contemporaries.

But meaning is also public, and therefore many of its essential dimensions are embedded in the sociomaterial instance of any work, which we may term an *inscripture* (as opposed to specific forms of this, such as book, papyrus, newspaper, inscription, or codex). The same article of 4 March 1941, for instance, acquires particular relief when viewed not simply as "text," but as an element within a particular page of *Le Soir*, a Brussels newspaper whose editors had been appointed by the Propaganda Abteilung of the occupation army. The page is dedicated to "The Jews and Us," and the article is surrounded by other essays entitled: "Jewish Painting and Its Repercussions," or "Freudianism: A Jewish Doctrine," or "The Two Faces of Judaism." Here, too, we see how meaning never achieves saturation only in a particular inferred intention on the part of the speaker, for much of this article's significance consists in its place within an institutional order, a campaign of anti-Semitism conducted in collaboration with occupation authorities, a programmatic effort disclosed precisely by its inscripture.

Quotation, finally, does not acquire its meaning only by reference to its original, but by its place within a citationary institution, by its function, and by its address to a specific audience. All these dimensions are registered in partial yet important ways by the appearance of de Man's "text" in *Le Soir*, itself a quotation of the manuscript that de Man presumably consigned to his editors. Yet even their inclusion in an account of quotation or meaning would not significantly alter Derrida's view of the isolated sentence by Nietzsche, or the articles by de Man, for none of them would affect his central claim that "there is no infallible way of knowing the occasion of this sample or what it could have been later grafted onto. We will never know *for sure* what Nietzsche wanted to say or do when he noted these words, nor even that he actually *wanted* anything" (p. 123). He further speculates: "Could Nietzsche have disposed of some more or less secret code, which, for him or for some unknown accomplice of his, would have made sense of this statement? We will never know" (p. 127). Derrida's point is to insist on the limits of certitude: we have "no *infallible* way of knowing," we "will never know *for sure*," and "no context permits of *saturation*" (first and last italics mine). These claims may be true, or even self-evident, but they seem based on a remarkably crude assumption that our alternatives are either complete belief or complete disbelief, either the illusion of certainty or the certainty of illusion. In practice, however, we entertain many degrees of credence, and we seek to give just that degree of credence which is warranted by the evidence at hand. The de Man case is not unusual in this regard. It is always possible, after all, that de Man disposed of some secret code, that his articles transmitted secret warnings to endangered Jews in Belgium, or were a subterfuge designed to distract authorities from his participation in an obscure resistance group. "We will never know," it might be said. Perhaps not. Yet we are not obliged to wish to know in the unshakable, absolutely unquestionable, "infallible" sense premised by Derrida; we may prefer to settle for hypotheses that are more plausible, for speculations more cogent and more comprehensive in their treatment of evidence. And if so we will lend little credence to such speculations about de Man, or Nietzsche. Our support for other hypotheses will hardly be an "infallible way of knowing," but it will be sufficient for the task at hand. That is all we ask of human belief, or meaning: that it be sufficient for our purposes, that it fulfill pragmatic ambitions or serve functions as best it can, and not that it be absolute, "infallible."

And that, of course, is probably what Nietzsche's sentence in quotation marks was meant to do as well. It was a note addressed to himself in

the autumn of 1881, a text whose audience was only its author, whose
function was probably an aide-mémoire, and whose referent therefore
needed no mention. Once its function had vanished, it became a mystery.
Deprived of its original audience of one, it was effectively dead, for texts
have no life apart from readers, or from a social world. Thus it became a
work not unlike countless epigraphs and papyrus fragments of the ancient
world, citing referents that we cannot identify, testimonies to the fragility
of transmission, monuments of culture. For Nietzsche's isolated sentence
begins its second life only when it is included in the edition of his com-
plete works cited by Derrida, a life that is nurtured with its integration
into the codes of post-structuralist theory by Derrida's discussion. What,
finally, is mystified by Derrida as the aleatory freedom of the sign is the
historical dynamics of transmission. That process will always comprise
moments when the text is freed of the logic implicit in its production; yet
we will be better able to assess disjunctions between origins and func-
tions through careful descriptions of both, rather than arbitrary and uni-
lateral speculations. Even the freedom of the text, even quotation, is
grounded in sociohistorical differentiations through which meanings are
always created and sustained. We shall need to recall this, because in
the rest of this book we shall pursue in detail the history of many quota-
tions—some cited, others ignored or forgotten by Pound—each with its
own origins and functions, its own set of transformations forming a dy-
namic complex, and its own routes of reference.

The Politics of Quotation

By the early years of the twentieth century, the quotation of historical
documents had become an activity informed by an intricate genealogy—
a particular intersection of historiography, philological tradition, and dip-
lomatics. The last of these, diplomatics, had originated in the wake of
the Reformation amid erudite disputes about the validity of legal claims
based on medieval documents. Its foundations were laid by Benedictine
monks associated with the monastery of St. Germain des Prés in Paris.
Already by 1632 they were assembling a documentary collection not only
of legal documents, but of materials related to French writers, the *Histo-
riae Francorum scriptores coetanei*. By 1681 their activity led to Jean
Mabillon's classic book, *De re diplomatica*, the first systematic study of
the extrinsic and intrinsic features of medieval documents, and it was
around this time that their activities began to interest secular historians,
especially those connected with a tradition of erudite antiquarianism.
The most famous of these was Lodovico Muratori, who in 1723 began to

publish his collection *Rerum italicarum scriptores,* whose title suggested its debt to the earlier Benedictine publication. The collection consisted mostly of medieval chronicles, none linked by any narrative outside the documents themselves (apart from a brief introduction and a few notes), and its success led to numerous imitations, such as Mencke's 1728 publication of the *Scriptores rerum Germanicarum praecipue saxonicarum.* But it was in the nineteenth century that the erudite and antiquarian collections acquired new value as instruments of national policy and history. In 1821 the École des Chartes was founded in Paris, while in 1819 arose the Societas aperiendis fontibus rerum Germanicarum, which in 1824 began its massive (and still ongoing) publication of the *Monumenta Germaniae Historica.* The *Monumenta* became the model for all subsequent collections and helped engender the English expression, "a monument of scholarship." For better or worse, the diplomatic collection of documents had become indissolubly linked with the emergence of the bourgeois hegemony.

Yet diplomatics was Janus-faced: though assimilated to the programmatic unfolding of national history and bureaucratic modes of cultural production, and still later to the development of positivist historiography and the broad respect for science in the second half of the nineteenth century, it could also appeal to a deeply romantic sensibility. For original documents offered a special *frisson,* a magical sense of vivacity or spontaneity undiluted by narrative conventions. In 1871, for example, Charles Yriarte published an account of the Prussian seizure of Paris and the Commune, which was based entirely on direct quotation from official dispatches. As he explained: "There and there alone [in the original document], are we to find the true elements of history. For there is nothing that can be added to the harsh language used in telegrams, especially when written under the force of such compelling events, nothing that could lend them greater narrative vivacity, greater tone or particularity."[79] What held for contemporary history could also be applied to remoter periods. Influenced by Armand Baschet, who had discovered the Venetian archives in 1852 and published several books based on its holdings, in 1874 Yriarte wrote his first historical biography, also drawing on archival sources from Venice.[80] Eight years later he wrote his biography of Sigismondo Malatesta, the work that synthesized the late Romantic interpretation of the church of San Francesco as a temple of love, replete with a massive appendix composed of documentary transcriptions. It would be Pound's reading of this appendix, in late 1922, that would spark his first attempts to reproduce "historical" quotations rendered with the graphic conventions of prose. Pound, in other words, would encounter a generic convention—the use of documentary transcriptions—that had become fundamentally ambiguous: a practice that could contain, in a fragile synthesis, the competing claims of science and art, reason and experience, positivism and romanticism. The precise relationship of these values depended not on their inherent properties, but on their utilization within a complex of institutional practices—as Pound had learned only too well when he had been a graduate student in Romance philology.

Pound's training in Romance philology at the University of Pennsylvania (1905–6) has been insufficiently studied, but its salient features are clear enough. It is a commonplace that graduate education in the United States, inaugurated in 1876 with Johns Hopkins University, was characterized by a double genealogy: it was based on the German model of the research institution, and it was "a vital part of the culture of professionalism" that emerged under the aegis of a new middle class.[81] Both features affected the conjunction of philology and Provençal literature that interested Pound. The study of Provençal language and literature had been created almost overnight in 1834 through the work of Friedrich Diez; its central corpus of texts had been assembled in 1885 by the German scholar Karl Otto Appel, and its major critical editions and research instruments (such as Levy's *Wörterbuch*) were all the products of German philological tradition. Yet philological method was also explicitly linked with habits and practices of capitalist culture in the United States. Consider the remarks of Richard G. Moulton, a Ph.D from the University of Pennsylvania who went on to teach at the newly founded University of Chicago; in his 1885 book subtitled "A Popular Illustration of the Principles of Scientific Criticism," he explained that the task of the "inductive" critic was to "investigate patiently" the entirety of a work, "putting together with *businesslike exactitude* all that the author has given, weighing, balancing, and *standing by the product*" (italics mine).[82] Seen thus, philology—a specific set of citationary practices—epitomized the ensemble of science, capitalism, and positivism that had driven the apparatus of high industrialism.

Throughout his career Pound was acutely interested in the complex of values associated with philology and its institutionalization. His first published essay (1906) was a book review that damned "the Germanic ideal of scholarship" and savaged "the scholar" engaged "in endless pondering over some utterly unanswerable question of textual criticism."[83] His first book of prose began with a declaration equally blunt: "This book is not a philological work." The preface attacked "the slough of philol-ogy," its tolerance for "mediocrity," its effort to be a "science," its "pas-sion for completeness" and "facts," its reliance on the mediation of "com-mentaries," its appeal to people who were "earnest" and "dull," and its tendency to atomize literature into "rags of morphology, epigraphy, *pri-vatleben.*" In opposition to this he posited his own criticism and "the river [of] art" (versus "the slough of philology"), criticism that indulged in a "primitive religion" of "hero-worship," cultivated "refinement of style" and a cult of the "masterwork," reveled in "levity" and "laughter," and emphasized "selection" and "direct study of the texts themselves."

Yet as the term "refinement" suggests, these values also intersected with specific linguistic codes and social groupings, a point that is made explicitly by Pound in a 1917 essay, "Provincialism the Enemy," an in-quiry into the causes of the Great War.[84] For Pound, the war was the outcome of a specific cultural *mentalité* of which philology was merely a salient expression. In terms of academic life, its symptoms were "the attempt to raise 'monuments' of scholarship" (p. 195), interest in "unvital detail" and "questions of morphology" (p. 192), the "apparatus criticus" (p. 197), and the entire "Germano-American 'university' ideal" (p. 191). Behind these symptoms, however, was a deeper structure far more insid-ious: a new form of tyranny, and specifically a "personal tyranny" com-posed of "personal oppressions" (p. 189) that were directed against "per-sonality" (p. 194) and "the rights of personality" (p. 195). Philology was only the academic manifestation of this structure. Its political form was socialism. For socialism did not "offer as much protection to the individ-ual as any other known system." Its "general tone" tended to "emphasize the idea of man as a unit, society as a thing of 'component parts'," and it was only a variant of the same "heresy" that had produced philology— "the denuded or mechanised life." Socialism offered "mechanical simpli-fication," while philology presented "mechanical complication" (p. 196). But it was one and the same. Both favored the mass of mediocrities, whether workers or members of an intellectual bureaucracy, people de-void of authentic personality.[85] For the gift of personality was not some-thing possessed by everyone, but by only "a few, a very few 'unpractical', or, rather, unexecutive men" who were actually working "to prevent [the] new form of tyranny" (p. 194). They were the ones who really counted, and the "new tyranny" was all the more odious precisely because it was directed against them, the spiritual elite who had always been the real foundation of civilization. "Civilisation is made by men of unusual intel-ligence. It is their product" (p. 202). Here, of course, is the same discursive configuration we have seen at work in the treatment of Pan and Tontolini: distaste for the world engendered by capitalism is structured through a radical antimaterialism that rejects both the historicist trend of elite bourgeois culture and the repetitious "uniformity" of an urban lower class public associated with socialism. Meanwhile the "middle" (read also "mediocre") socioeconomic strata are rejected in favor of an imaginary cultural aristocracy that embodies and is unified with the vitality of a traditional-rural folk, and this imaginary construct becomes the vehicle for values uncontaminated by the *mentalité* that has engendered the culture of capitalist industrialism, materialism, or its academic exponent, philology. And it was but a short step from the 1917 essay to his 1922 view of the courtly culture of Rimini, where the "men of unusual intelligence" become "men of unusual genius" as Pound approvingly cites (in the final version of the Malatesta Cantos) Bartolomeo Scacchi's report that Sigismondo typically discussed "books, arms, | And men of unusual genius." This was the background to Pound's use of historical quotation in the Malatesta Cantos—an aggressive, accusatory assault on the historicist trend of elite bourgeois culture.

Viewed in Pound's own terms, the quotations in the Malatesta Cantos are not structured by philology, but against it: the "passion for completeness" is replaced with "selection"; the consultation of "commentaries" gives way to "direct study of the texts themselves" (ten long weeks of archival research from February to April 1923); the method of "science" is superseded by "art"; the "dullness" of "the earnest" is met with "levity"; and the study of "mediocrity" is supplanted by the "primitive religion" of "hero-worship." Pound invokes the standards of philological accuracy only to savage the institutional apparatus that sustains them. His literalist translations parody the typical features of the loathed institution. Consider his citation of a single phrase from a letter of 1454: "the bay pony (ronzino baiectino) the which you have sent me." Here are the gestures of philology—meticulous report of the original wording in parentheses (ronzino baiectino), and a translation so literal as to skirt the absurd ("the which" for *il quale*). It is, of course, *too* literal, a cruel parody of the philological fetish with "unvital detail." Or again two lines cited from another letter of 1449:

> And it wd. be merely work chucked away
> > (*buttato via*)

Here the evocation of a colloquial idiom serves to foreground the departure from philological decorum. Still, in itself the gesture is insufficient, liable to be dismissed as a matter of mere taste: therefore Pound explicitly cites the original Italian as his justification (*buttato via*), a sign that his quotation *is* based on "direct study of the texts themselves" rather than "upon commentaries," a tacit claim that he has examined the original letter conserved in Florence. For here again he cites not merely a text, or even an inscripture, but also an institutional practice of citation through the meticulous report of the original wording in parentheses. And every aspect of his claim is borne out by external evidence: the Archivio di stato of Florence conserves his registration there, dated 3 March 1923,[86] and the notes he took as he examined the letter are likewise conserved, showing that he not only transcribed *buttato via* from the document, but took pains to underline it twice.[87] Pound's claim is thus a double one: that his citation follows the rules of his antiphilology, and that only an instrument of this sort enables one to perceive, rescue, and represent the lost vitality of a culture where courtly "refinement" and colloquial "levity" had been one. Here, in this nuanced manipulation of philological method and discourse, Pound establishes a combative critique of the culture that has engendered its very structures. For he understands fully what is implied in the elegant formulation of Voloshinov: "Reported speech is speech within speech, utterance within utterance, and at the same time also *speech about speech, utterance about utterance.*"[88] He understands, in other words, that citation concerns not only the roots of reference, but the routes of reference.

Pound's use of quotation was ambiguous and ambivalent. It invoked the standards of philological accuracy in order to juxtapose them against a higher accuracy of the spirit. It enacted a critique of the bourgeois *mentalité* and a radical rejection of the reformist socialism that allegedly shared its foundations; yet the result was a utopian aspiration imperiled by its own emptiness, a threat that could only be met by authorization from the past, by the invocation of historical precedent—which meant a return to the terrain of philology and history. The cycle became vertiginous and inescapable, its gestures both rebellious and conservative, its implications poised on an abyss of ambiguity.

This highly determinate form of ambiguity, however, has received little attention in recent criticism regarding the Malatesta Cantos. The case of Marjorie Perloff is instructive, for hers has been an influential voice in recent criticism of Pound, while her critical practices are representative of the professional mainstream in the last decade.[89] Her argument proceeds in three steps. First, she advances a reductive notion of content: that the Malatesta Cantos depict "Pound's hero—the Renaissance ruler

as beneficent patron of art." She then claims that the work *must* exceed
the grasp of criteria so patently trivial. Yet Pound, it should be noted,
was a poet deeply interested in subject matter and content, and one es-
pecially concerned with the problem of patronage, a form of cultural pro-
duction that was, indeed, the central economic resource of literary mod-
ernism. From March 1922 to mid-1923, while composing the Malatesta
Cantos, Pound was actively engaged in organizing the Bel Esprit project,
a plan to create a lifetime endowment for T. S. Eliot. Two years later, in
March 1925, when Pound was approached by Henry Allen Moe of the
John Simon Guggenheim Foundation about candidates for its newly cre-
ated awards, Pound launched into a thirty-page letter extolling patronage
and urging the merits of Wyndham Lewis, T. S. Eliot, and George An-
theil as potentially worthy recipients. After ten pages of pleading for
Eliot, he paused to define his ideal of patronage:

> Incidentally I mean⟨t⟩ to cite chiefly /re Eliot, a letter of Sigismund[o]
> Malatesta's which I have quoted at length in my VIIth [*sic*] Canto (Canto
> VIII, in the Malatesta Cantos, Criterion, I think Aug. 1923) Canto VII in
> the Three Mountains Press Edtn.
>
> I take Malatesta as a prime example of a man who wanted civilization
> in a small town, and GOT the goods delivered. He had Pisanello, Pier
> della Francesca, Battista Alberti, the architect, Mino da Fiesole, four
> certainly of the best men of the time down in Rimini. This letter is to
> Giovanni dei Medici, persumably re/ Pier Francesca; and says he wants
> the master painter for life, with a set provision, security to be given, and
> ends up[:]
>
>> affitigandose per suo piacer o no,
>> So that he can work as he likes or not.
>
> Ma⟨l⟩atesta got the goods. And he was enough of an artist himself to know
> that you can't always tell when an artist is loafing. Real work may be done
> on tennis court or in trolley car, and sham work at desk.

Pound, it is clear, was far more eager to address the issue of subject
matter and contents than his critics have been.[90]

Perloff's remarks, however, proceed not from an engagement with
either the poem or its relevant context, but from systematic assumptions,
which she shares with modern criticism, about the very nature of the
literary object. Her tart dismissal of contents and authorial intentions is
only a preliminary step toward "beating the material into shape," forcing
it to conform to the reigning paradigm of critical practice. By extension,
the work's "real contents" must reside elsewhere: "you would hang your-
self" if you attempted "to read the Malatesta Cantos for their thematic

interest" (p. 181). Rather, it must reside in its formal or systemic features, and therefore she offers a series of local readings that focus on stylistic minutiae. One, for example, concerns a phrase from a 1454 letter which we have already seen, "the bay pony (ronzino baiectino) the which you have sent me." Perloff remarks:

> Translated thus literally, the letter has neither the status of fifteenth-century document nor twentieth-century adaptation; it remains a curiosity, removed from a specific time-space context. The introduction of the Italian phrase "ronzino baiectino" is particularly skillful: "ronzino baiectino" does mean "bay pony," but in the context it sounds more like a zoological specimen or a rare disease. (p. 185)

"Context" is tacitly restructed to minutiae of style, discursive practices stripped to mere phonetics ("it sounds like"), and every link with sociohistorical reality dismissed a priori: "removed from a specific time-space context." And these maneuvers are repeated over and over, as in a discussion of the two lines cited earlier from a letter of 1449. Perloff comments (p. 186):

> Closely related to such artful mistranslation is the *purposely incorrect* [italics mine] rendering of the Italian itself. In the letter to Giovanni di Medici which opens Canto VIII, for example, Pound has Sigismundo say: "[. . .]And it wd. be merely work chucked away / (*buttato via*). . . ." In the original, the Italian phrase is *gettata via*, which means "thrown away." Pound substitutes the harsh "*buttato via*," partly to suit his own meaning—"chucked away"—and partly, no doubt, for comic sound effect.

By "the original" Perloff refers not to the actual document located in Florence and consulted by Pound, but to the published transcription of it that appears in Charles Yriarte's book of 1882 (as her note declares, p. 186 n. 1). Her failure to distinguish these is merely a logical outcome of the assumption that the relationship between inset (quoted item) and frame (quoting agency) is purely "textual" in character: a relationship between text and text, rather than a social dynamics of transmission that comprises numerous inscriptures. Perloff takes for granted that investigation proceeds through purely intersystemic or "intrinsic" orders, and when faced with recalcitrant evidence she achieves those orders by systematically destroying its "extrinsic" dimensions: its specifically material form, its thematics, its problematic textual features. For precisely those features deemed "extrinsic" in ordinary critical discourse are *intrinsic* for understanding the dynamics of transmission. Indeed, by now it must be clear that the "incorrect rendering" is purely Perloff's creation, and the "comic sound effect" mere speculation. And yet even these local misreadings are significant only insofar as they lead toward the final solution of the work's social actuality in every form. In the Malatesta Cantos, she concludes, "history becomes the impetus for the play of language" (p. 182). It is only an occasion "to create new verbal landscapes" (p. 182), a site where "fact, in other words, is repeatedly transformed into fiction" (p. 183).

To the contrary, the case of the Malatesta Cantos suggests a scenario that moves in the opposite direction: a space where fiction will be repeatedly transformed into fact—at least if we take seriously the affiliation between Beltramelli's portraits of Sigismondo Malatesta and Benito Mussolini, or the genealogy of the new age imagined by Pound in Drafts *A* and *B* and its fateful reinscription in later years. To be sure, this may be only to say that social actuality is constituted by a network of real and discursive practices that is exceptionally intricate, and that the distinction between "fact" and "fiction" is a device too crude to ground any account of its essential features. For discourse, like its paradigmatic form the quotation, is Janus-faced: it looks backwards and forwards, soliciting the past in order to imagine the future.

As he wrote Drafts *A* and *B* in the summer of 1922, it is certain that Pound knew nothing about Beltramelli, or his biography of Mussolini, or his effort to furnish Mussolini with genealogical links to Sigismondo Malatesta. And yet the routes of reference traced in his quotation from Beltramelli were both wider and deeper than anything Pound could encompass—wider in the sense that they were more intricate, more extensive, and more problematic than he could imagine; deeper in that they extended into the past and future in ways that could hardly have been predicted in the summer of 1922 and yet appear already inscribed in the quotation from Beltramelli. Historical criticism, we begin to perceive, is understood wrongly as the mere recovery of a context that has existed in the past; its most important contexts are those that exist only in the future.

As for Beltramelli himself, his course was increasingly fixed as a party militant (see figure 12). In March 1925 he served as a principal speaker at the Convention of Fascist Culture (also called the Congress of Fascist Institutes of Culture), the pivotal effort of the regime to organize the nation's intellectual life; in April 1925 he signed the "Manifesto of Fascist Intellectuals," the central document of its program. Under party auspices he undertook direction of *La rivolta ideale*, the organ of the "University Youth" movement, and for two years he also served as co-director of *Il*

Figure 12. Antonio Beltramelli (1879–1930). Journalist and novelist, Beltramelli wrote *Un tempio d'amore (A Temple of Love)* (Palermo: Remo Sandron, 1912), a crucial source for Pound's earliest conception of Tempio Malatestiano, and *L'uomo nuovo (The New Man)* (Milan: Treves, 1923), the first biography of Mussolini. Reprinted from *L'illustrazione italiana*, 23 March 1930, p. 483.

raduno, the weekly newspaper of the "syndicate" of fascist authors and writers.[91] He died in 1930, and in 1937 the anniversary of his death was commemorated by an article that reprinted the marginalia written in 1908 by Mussolini in his own copy of Beltramelli's *The Chants of Faunus*.[92] Yet though well known in Italy, Beltramelli's work attracted little attention abroad, and holdings of his works are often uneven in other countries. In the United States, for example, only one library reports a copy of the book consulted by Pound, *Un tempio d'amore*, and surely this is one reason why American scholars have never identified his role in the genesis of the Malatesta Cantos, even though direct quotation from his book is a prominent feature in the final version of the Malatesta Cantos (on this, see chapter 3).[93] For the routes of transmission affect every effort at understanding.

As for the passage from Pius II/Beltramelli quoted by Pound, it was only beginning its itinerary. In Draft *A*, as we have seen, Pound expressly claims to report "the language of Pius," a claim that is reiterated in the next major draft, *C1:* "(Pius the 2nd speaking)." When he wrote the third draft, however, Pound removed the explicit attribution to Pius II. By now he was reading widely in the relevant historiography, and understood that the passage from Pius II was a standard feature in discussions of the church of San Francesco. Yet as he deleted the explicit attribution, he also added for the first time quotation marks, those ambiguous prongs. In subsequent revisions the quotation marks were left intact, while more and more of the actual passage was deleted, until in the final version of the Malatesta Cantos it appears as an isolated sentence in quotation marks:

"and built a temple so full of pagan works"

Seen thus, of course, it is a sentence rather like Nietzsche's, one that "knows of no proper itinerary which would lead from its beginning to its end and back again, nor does its movement admit of any center." For commentators subscribing to a naïve historicism, it has never posed a problem: uniformly they have returned the citation to its origins, to its roots in the work of Pius II—perhaps the least significant thing about it.[94] As for Pound, his own understanding of its routes of reference altered with the passage of time: in 1922 an analogy between Sigismondo Malatesta and Benito Mussolini had been only one possibility, and at that a remote one, among many; by 1932, however, it would strike Pound as the central axis for the shape of his magnum opus and his understanding of its place in the modern world. As he would write to John Drummond in

February 1932: "Don't knock Mussolini, at least not until you have weighed up the obstacles and necessities of the time. He will end up with Sigismundo and the men of order, not with the pus-sacks and destroyers." [95]

The letter to Drummond is consoling, if only because it seems to confirm our darkest suspicions, to ratify what we know about Pound and the tragedy to come. Yet our sense of security may be unsettled if we glance again at the line as it appeared in the final version:

"and built a temple so full of pagan works"

For as it stands in isolation this way, the sentence has no subject. It specifies no agent—as if to suggest that it was spoken by the entire course of Western history stretching from ancient Greece to medieval Provence, to Renaissance Italy, to nineteenth-century France, to an American living in Paris in 1922, and to the present site and very moment of our reading—here and now, or nowhere and never. Pound, to be sure, tries to erase this momentary ambiguity; in the next line he hastens to add a subject: "i.e. Sigismund." But to a generation of readers that has been surprised by sin and nurtured by the skeptical readings of de Man and Derrida, his haste seems too transparent, his fear too apparent. Who will believe him? For perhaps it was not "Sigismund" at all who built this monument of culture, this "temple so full of pagan works." And if not, then who? Perhaps Tontolini, or Ezra Pound? Or could it be Jacques Derrida? Or perhaps it is only that familiar of our nightmares, the *hypocrite lecteur*.

It will not remain here, of course. Its passage is necessarily brief, and its meaning unsecured by any recovery of contextual origins. For there can be no recovery of a ground of origin in the moment of production, only an act of transmission that is itself another production—this one, for example, which you, *mon frère*, are reading now. Grafted onto many other quotations, juxtaposed with other voices—some, like Tontolini's, which it had once silenced—it must face the dangers that attend every ritual of recovery and every drama of citation and above all those that push their efforts as far as Pound's. Iterability and meaning, to read the same words and yet perceive them differently, transformed by the power of grafting, by their appearance in a new inscripture, by transmission: On a cool afternoon in the autumn of 1958 . . . there, he said . . . so close, it seemed from the terrace where they stood speaking, that you could almost touch it.

Savage Crimes: (F) Acts of Transmission

For ye are like unto whited sepulchres, which indeed appear beautiful outward, but are within full of dead men's bones, and of all uncleanness.

Matthew 23:27

Anche la Speme,
Ultima Dea, fugge i sepolcri; e involve
Tutte cose l'obblio nella sua notte;
E una forza operosa le affatica
Di moto in moto; e l'uomo e le sue tombe
E l'estreme sembianze e le reliquie
Della terra e del ciel traveste il tempo.

Even Hope,
The final Goddess, flees sepulchres; and oblivion
Entwists all things in its night,
And a laborious force exhausts them
In eddy upon eddy, and time
Transmutes man and his tombs,
And every last vestige, and the relics
Of earth and of heaven.

Ugo Foscolo, *I Sepolcri*

Come, perché di lor memoria sia,
   sovra i sepolti le tombe terragne
   portan segnato quel ch'elli eran pria,
onde lí molte volte si ripiagne
   per la puntura della rimembranza,
   che solo a' pii dà delle calcagne:
sí vid'io lí . . .

Just as, above the buried dead, so they might
    be remembered, the pavement tombs
    bear designs of what they were before,
whence tears are often shed there
    at the prick of memory
    which spurs only the pitiful,
so saw I . . .

Dante Alighieri, *Purgatorio*, 12
Translation adapted from John Sinclair II

What is a fact, and how is it constituted? Such queries seem absurd in the wake of recent critical theory, in which "intertextuality" has become the paradigm for analysis of the past and present. We are by now so accustomed to "the generation by models of a real without origin or reality, a hyperreal," that the notion of a fact strikes us as quaint.[1] If we read the writings of positivists from the turn of the century we marvel at their boundless confidence in the solidity, virtue, and power of fact. For us it is all different: as soon as we see the word we hasten to drape it in quotation marks, "fact," as if averting our gaze from an unseemly display of reality, an embarrassment. Fact, we sense obscurely, was somehow the desired Other of an earlier era; but for us it is a scandal, and at most it provokes not desire, but questions:

> What is your substance, whereof are you made,
> That millions of strange shadows on you tend?

In literary studies the problem of fact has been especially acute because it drives to the heart of disciplinary competence and activity, raising disagreeable questions about the relationship of fact to fiction, or history to literature. Why study literature at all if it regards only fictions? So runs an old refrain in a long-standing yet central debate. As fact has become a problematic notion, readers of *The Cantos* have felt its difficulty in three particular forms. First, at the simplest level, the work rehearses thousands and thousands of little facts. Every page, every line it seems, spews forth another proper name, such as "Bernicoli in Ravenna, and that stuffed shirt who | wrote such an elegant postcard."[2] The outcome is a referential quagmire. Who *are* these people? The disconcerted reader consults a two-volume *Companion to the Cantos*, but learns little: Bernicoli is "unidentified, not in source," while the "stuffed shirt" and his "postcard" are left unmentioned, veiled in mystery beyond mystery. As the minutiae accumulate and gather momentum, the reader begins to experience vertigo, fearing it is all gibberish.

Second, the accumulation of facts is distressing because so many of them are related to history—a dimension of our common culture that we hesitate to view as mere gibberish. Our everyday notion is that historiography reports *facts*, or what really happened (as one famous historian expressed it). Yet *The Cantos* presents a documentation of the past so massive, so overdetermined that it taunts us with its incomprehensibility. It suggests that our cultural heritage is a tale told by an idiot. Typically, there have been two responses to this. One, citing ordinary notions of fact, history, and formal coherence, has dismissed *The Cantos* as an aberration, the impetuous scrawlings of a madman—a maneuver that secures the cultural tale by declaring the teller an idiot. Another, rejecting appeals to everyday notions of history and art, argues that factual discrepancies and formal incoherence are problematic only if viewed in traditional terms, but can be reevaluated in the light of recent conceptions of intertextuality. The Malatesta Cantos, not surprisingly, have served to focus the debate. For Christine Froula, the Malatesta Cantos are a "brilliant rendering of . . . history" because they represent events in their "incompleteness and doubtful meaning," and because therefore "it is historical 'process' and not isolated facts which Pound aims to represent."[3] For Marjorie Perloff, they offer a locus where "fact . . . is repeatedly transformed into fiction," and "history becomes the impetus for the play of language."[4] And for Richard Sieburth, they force us to confront the question: "For what, more often than not, are the 'facts' to which the *Cantos* refer but texts in their turn, what is the 'history' that the poem includes but a body of written traces?"[5] On this view, the teller may be an idiot indeed; but all the better, for the tale to be told is equally idiotic.

Third, fact reenters the debate in a more virulent form, for every reader is painfully aware that the *The Cantos* intersects with the salient fact of Western history in the twentieth century: the Holocaust. Indeed, in the holocaust of fact enacted by criticism in recent decades, the fact of the Holocaust has been the only survivor. And because Pound was outspoken in his support of Mussolini and most outrageous in his anti-Semitism at exactly *that* moment in time, we are certain that his work must be seriously or irremediably flawed. Froula distrusts facts, yet declares it a "fact that as [Pound] said, 'my errors and wrecks lie about me.'"[6] The allusion is plain enough. Others applaud when "history" is dissolved into "the play of language" at the hands of Pound, yet hasten to censure Paul de Man—who popularized these very phrases—for his wartime articles in the collaborationist newspaper *Le Soir*.[7] (But why not view de Man's activity as further "impetus for the play of language"?) Clearly such views reveal serious contradictions. We banish fact and ostracize history in order to execute the business of "criticism as usual," but reinvoke it when it serves as a platform for ingenuous appeals to the postwar ethical consensus, when it enables us to point accusing fingers at *others* allegedly responsible for—but who would dare say, "the fact" of the Holocaust?

If the Holocaust and *The Cantos* expose fault lines in our usage of fact, they can do so because similar problems recur in everyday moments of literary critical activity. We can best approach them by such a quotidian moment: a modest historical fact mentioned briefly in the Malatesta Cantos, the death of a woman in 1449, which is registered in a single line: "and Polixena, his second wife, died." What does it mean? It is, clearly, a prosaic line (ND70[10] 9.57). Its first word ("and") sidesteps the temporal and logical relations of more formal writings. Its diction is modest, and its syntax plain, with only a brief apposition that reports lean information. Its tone is flat and calm, as if assuring us that the subject matter of this line is unimportant, an effect that depends on an implicit contrast with other procedures found elsewhere in *The Cantos*. Consider a moment when Pound hints, through alliteration, at a saturation of significance: "In the gloom, the gold gathers the light against it." Yes, this bristles with local obscurity—who can unveil the symbolism of "gold" or "gloom," or the referent of that enigmatic "it"?—but it resonates with notes of cryptic plenitude and cosmic significance. Or compare the line that immediately precedes the claim about Polissena: "And he began building the TEM-PIO." Here even typography is recruited to announce the subject matter's gravity—*this* is important, *this* is a monument of culture and civilization. Not so the line about Polissena. It lacks both musical knickknacks and typographical gewgaws. And we understand the difference: the Tempio may live forever, but Polissena simply "died."

The line about Polissena also deploys plain yet forceful prosody. It is made up of three successive phrases: in each the number of syllables is gradually reduced (from five to four to one), while the ictus is gradually advanced (from fourth to second to first syllable) until it coincides with the entire phrase. The last is a terse monosyllable that reports an event with finality—"died." It excludes every other prosodic possibility, as if enacting in rhythm the rejection of every other possible content: Polissena was not poisoned, or strangled, or murdered, or stabbed, or suffocated—she "died." And the veracity of this assertion is reinforced by an

orthographic device, the conspicuous spelling of Polissena as "Polixena."
If we indulge the fiction that this line simulates a quattrocento chronicle,
the orthography implies that it has been executed scrupulously; and if we
are conscious that this fiction is played out in the early twentieth century,
it implies that our author has examined relevant sources, perhaps pri-
mary documents, and is asserting his competence. Together, the diction,
syntax, prosody, and orthography evoke a complex unity: an event is reg-
istered tersely yet emphatically, its veracity is authenticated, and it is
assigned a place within the stylistic hierarchy of *The Cantos*. But why so
much trouble for a simple fact?

One wonders what the line about Polissena really means. In theory
there are many answers to that question. In practice, however, the ques-
tion is altered when framed in specific forms. What did the death of Pol-
issena Sforza say to her contemporaries? Why did it interest Pound so
much, writing some five centuries later, and why did he report it in this
oblique yet emphatic manner? And how can these questions speak to us,
readers who confront Pound's text some seventy years later? To approach
them, we need to examine the relations among four distinct historical
moments: (1) the genesis of contemporary documents regarding the death
of Polissena; (2) their transmission to the early twentieth century; (3) the
steps in which they were received and reconstituted by Pound; and (4)
the historical reception of Pound's reconstitution. A concrete subject
such as the death of Polissena gives us a vantage point from which to
survey a vast network of contradictory uses constituting a fact, and also
to acquaint ourselves with a cast of characters who will reappear later.
The story, to be sure, is complicated, but complication is itself one of the
issues at stake.

A Life and a Death

Polissena Sforza (1428–49) was the illegitimate daughter of Francesco
Sforza (who fathered thirty-five children) and Giovanna d'Acquapen-
dente. Her father is well known to students of the Renaissance: he is
often viewed as the type of the opportunist condottiere who managed to
convert his position into that of a respected prince (born 1401, duke of
Milan, 1450–66). Her mother is known only as one among the many
women who gave birth to Sforza's illegitimate children. Polissena, her
third of five, was born in Mortara (fifty kilometers south of Milan), where,
in March 1428, Francesco had been ordered to remain in readiness at
the command of his employer, Filippo Maria Visconti (duke of Milan,
1412–47). She was named after Polissena Ruffo of Calabria, Sforza's first

wife from 1418–20.[8] Like most women of her class and status, Polissena passed her life as an instrument for her father's political ambitions. In early 1441 she was offered in marriage to Malatesta Novello, Sigismondo's brother, part of an effort to enlist him on Sforza's side in his struggles with Filippo Maria Visconti (at this time Sforza's enemy).[9] When nothing came of this she was offered to Sigismondo himself. The contract of marriage was signed on 26 July 1441, and aside from her own possessions and furnishings, her dowry was established at 15,000 *ducati d'oro*.[10]

The marriage was meant to seal a political alliance significant for both Sigismondo and Sforza. Sigismondo wished to receive support and patronage from the most powerful condottiere of his time, while Sforza hoped to gain strategic access to the Riminese territory under Sigismondo, a base of action and a haven in the event of difficulties in his struggle to retain the Marches, a nearby province. (Sforza had seized the province from the church in 1433, and now was defending it against ecclesiastical efforts to reassert control.)[11] The impending union was important, and Sforza sought to endow each step toward the marriage with ceremonial dignity. He demanded, for example, the collaboration of towns that were under his control and in the path of Sigismondo's projected journey to the betrothal ceremony; on 3 September the council of Macerata decided to comply with his "request" that it furnish Sigismondo with an honorable reception when he passed through the town:

> Upon receipt of a letter from Contuzio, reporting in effect how His Excellency the Count [Francesco Sforza] has given his distinguished daughter Polissena to the magnificent and powerful lord Sigismondo Malatesta; and the aforesaid magnificent lord Sigismondo must soon go to Fermo, and both en route and on his return will stay in this city, and the will of the Count is that he be received honorably.[12]

A few weeks later, on 22 September, Sigismondo left Rimini for Fermo "a spoxare la figliola," that is, to take part in a formal ceremony of betrothal.[13] Presumably he stopped in Macerata both going and returning, according to plan. By 16 October he was back in Rimini, and signs of the new union were already in evidence; the same say he received a visit from Alessandro Sforza, Francesco's brother and later the ruler of nearby Pesaro.[14]

Polissena's wedding with Sigismondo was celebrated seven months later in April 1442. Once more preparations were made to lend the occasion solemnity. Polissena had to be escorted to Rimini, for example. On 21 April a letter from Alessandro Sforza was read to the *Consiglio* (town council) of Recanati requesting "horses to be sent to Fermo for accompanying lady Polissena to lord Sigismondo" ("equos mictendo[s] Firmum pro assotiando dominam Polissenam ad dominum Sigismundum").[15] Presumably the horses were furnished; a few days later Polissena began traveling northward, and eight days later she arrived in Rimini, on 29 April. Her reception sparked three days of festivities, meticulously described by the city's anonymous chronicler:

> Our magnificent lord, lord Sigismondo Pandolfo di Malatesti, took as his lady the magnificent lady Pullisena [*sic*], daughter of the magnificent lord Count Francesco. She was accompanied by many lords and noblemen through great triumphal processions; and the street was covered with cloth of fine wool all the way from the Arch of Augustus to the court. The second day a fine and renowned feast was held in the palace, with enormous triumphs, and in attendance were nearly all the ladies and citizens of Rimini appropriate for a *festa* of this kind; and there was a banquet that was solemn and beautiful and bountiful. At the feast our aforementioned magnificent lord made a knight of Piero Giovanni from Cesena, and gave him a fine vest with a gold brocade and a sword and spurs. The third day, which was the first of May, a beautiful joust was held in the forum [or main piazza], and the prize was a piece of blue velvet which was obtained by a retainer of our magnificent lord, named Giovanni da Riva, because to him was given the honor of the joust. On the second of May, the escort which had accompanied the said magnificent lady [Polissena] left and returned to the Marches. The wedding celebrations were beautiful indeed, renowned and sumptuous, with quality and care in all the provisions.[16]

The triumphal entry through the Arch of Augustus, the *festa* in the commune with the knighting of Pier Giovanni Brugnoli, and the jousting in the forum on May Day[17]—all indicate the ceremonial dignity the court sought to lend to the occasion. Twelve days later (13 May) Polissena's father came to Rimini, again with much ceremony, a visit that also was duly recorded by the anonymous chronicler of Rimini:

> The magnificent lord and captain, count Franceso, came to Rimini, now as both captain and standard-bearer of the holy Church, and he entered the city with seven flags: one from the Church, another from pope Eugene IV, another from the Republic of Saint Mark, another from the Florentines, and three others that were not unfurled. And also with him came his wife the magnificent lady Bianca, daughter of the duke of Milan, with eight young girls on white horses, and all were dressed in green in the same style. And she came under a white baldachino in a stately procession, and the entire street was covered with white cloth from the gate of

Saint Julian [at the bridge of Tiberius] all the way to the court; and there was a beautiful feast with dances and triumphs, and meals that were large, solemn, and much celebrated. And with the aforesaid magnificent count there were many men of arms, both foot and horse, of choice and beautiful company.

But after only two days Sforza departed, heading southward for the Marches and leaving young Polissena to settle into her new life at court.[18] She was now fourteen years old.

Some eight months after her arrival Polissena gave birth to her first child, Galeotto, in January 1443. The baby was baptized on 17 January. The ceremony was performed by Ariminuccio Martini, canon and parish priest of Sant'Agnese of Rimini. And young Galeotto was held by Fra Bartolo (or Bartolomeo) di Iacopo Mercati de Cesena, the rector of the monastery that housed the Eremites of St. Jerome, located on the hill of Scolca near Rimini—a place important for later historians discussing Polissena's mysterious death.[19]

In 1444 or 1445 Polissena gave birth to her second child, Giovanna, betrothed in 1451 (age six or seven) and married in 1454 (age nine or ten) to Giulio Cesare de' Varani of Camerino.[20] Also from 1445 are the first testimonies indicating Sigismondo Malatesta's love for Isotta degli Atti, then twelve or thirteen years old.[21] And also from 1445 is the sale of Pesaro: Galeazzo Malatesta, the town's ruler and member of a collateral branch of the Malatesta family, delivered the city to Alessandro Sforza for a price, thwarting Sigismondo's ambition to incorporate it into his own domains. It signaled the end of the alliance between Francesco Sforza and Sigismondo Malatesta. Nothing is known about how these events affected Polissena or her life in Rimini.

As befitted her growing maturity, Polissena began to assume a larger role in the social and ceremonial life of the court. Her activities in 1447, at age nineteen, are reported in glimpses by the city's chronicler: on 15 June she goes "magnificamente" to Cesena to visit Violante, the wife of Sigismondo's brother; on 9 August she visits her father, who was camping near Rimini while leading his troops northward to Milan in anticipation of the death of Filippo Maria Visconti; and on 25 November she attends the betrothal of Lucrezia, Sigismondo's illegitimate daughter (by Gentile di Giovanni of Bologna), and the ruler of a nearby town.[22] Meanwhile, other events were intersecting with her life. In May 1447 Isotta degli Atti gave birth to her first child by Sigismondo, Giovanni, who died after only a few days of life; and in 1448 she gave birth to another, Malatesta.[23]

On 1 November 1448 Polissena was finally declared legitimate by a bull from Pope Nicholas V.[24] By this time, it would seem, her son Galeotto was dead.[25] Seven months later she herself died, on 1 June 1449. Her death was recorded in the city chronicle:[26]

> The magnificent lady Polisena [sic] died, wife of our magnificent lord. At her funeral ceremony there were 120 doubled-branched candelabra. She was interred in the church San Francesco, with all the people [in attendance]. All of her servants and retainers were dressed in new clothes. The bishop of Cesena and all the clergy of Rimini were in attendance. May her soul rest in peace.

The chronicle said nothing about the cause of death.

Notwithstanding her demise, there was no end to the political commerce that had stamped Polissena's life. Two years later, on 5 September 1451, her father, who was now duke of Milan, signed a *condotta* with Sigismondo Malatesta, in which the two men stipulated that they would forget all past injuries and offences—implied were the sale of Pesaro in 1445 and Sigismondo's service for Venice to prevent Sforza's conquest of Milan in 1449–50—except the debt still remaining on the dowry of Polissena.[27] But this was only the beginning.

Polissena's death became the object of intense political maneuvering about twelve years after the event. This is reflected in five documents, all of them authored by three men: Francesco Sforza, Pope Pius II, and Giovanni Simonetta. The first is a letter from Sforza to Ottone del Carretto, his ambassador at the papal court. It is dated 10 January 1461.[28] The date is important because four months earlier Sigismondo Malatesta had struck an alliance with the Angevin party in its effort to unseat the occupant of the throne of the kingdom of Naples. Francesco Sforza was determined to block this effort, a cause in which he was united with Pius II, both resolved to prevent a French presence in the peninsula. But each also had his own aims. Pius II was eager to punish Sigismondo, to use the occasion to regain ecclesiastical control over the Malatestan domains (nominally held by the Malatesta as vicars of the Church), while Sforza was more concerned with the kingdom of Naples, a key state in the peninsular balance of power. Sforza had been placed in a delicate position when Pius II requested that their combined forces, which were now engaged in military operations in the south, be directed against Sigismondo. On the one hand he had to please Pius II in order to maintain their alliance, and thus he had to evince interest in the Malatestan affair. On the other hand, he wanted no action that would distract resources from his main objective: he had to ensure that Pius maintained his commitments to Naples, and to remind him of the principal task in order to keep him from diverting his resources into the Malatestan adventure. His letter of January 1461, therefore, ordered his ambassador to agree with Pius II in wishing to punish the Malatesta, and to declare that Sforza himself had reason to favor the undertaking, for no man in the world had been more offended or injured by Sigismondo "in le carne et sangue," in flesh and blood. However vague or equivocal the allusion, its meaning was evident. Probably it was supplemented by the verbal testimony of Benedetto Reguardati of Norcia, a special ambassador sent by Sforza to Rome at the same time.[29] Reguardati's testimony, in fact, probably furnished the basis for the charges contained in the second document.

Less than a week after Sforza's letter to del Carretto, Andrea del Benzi read aloud, in a public consistory, an invective written by Pius II. It urged that Sigismondo be formally tried for numerous crimes against ecclesiastical law and common morality. Among them: he had strangled Polissena.[30]

A third wedding ceremony (*tertiae nuptiae*) took place, and a new dowry accompanied his new wife, the daughter of Francesco Sforza, at that time Count of Cotignola, and now the renowned and most excellent Duke of Milan. Although she was very modest, and endowed with singular virtues, her fortune was no better, and her husband no kinder than he had been to the former [wife]. Sigismondo, that atrocious and bloody parricide, offered not the companionship of a faithful marriage, but strangled this wife as well, who was deeply religious and devoid of any fault, even though no cause of death could be established afterward.

In addition, the oration charged that Sigismondo had killed several Franciscan friars because they had refused to violate the sacrament of confession by revealing the secrets of Polissena (and other women as well). The invective is the second document in the affair, and the first to offer an explicit accusation.

The third is another letter from Sforza to Ottone del Carretto, this one written on 23 August 1462, some nineteen months after the previous letter. Though it was motivated by similar exigencies, circumstances had changed. In the intervening period, the plan to overthrow the throne of Naples had begun to run aground, bringing misfortune for Sigismondo Malatesta, Giacomo Piccinino (another condottiere), and other supporters of the Angevin cause. The decisive events were two battles in August 1462. The first took place on 12 August. Sigismondo, after a siege of several days, received the surrender of the fortress and town of Senigallia. It seemed an important victory, and the news was immediately dispatched to Francesco Sforza by Niccolò de Palude, a Sforzescan governor in nearby Pesaro, and again by Agostino Rossi, a Sforzescan agent also nearby.[31] Yet the victory proved ephemeral indeed. A few hours later, ecclesiastical forces led by Federigo da Montefeltro arrived outside the town and set up their own siege; seeing himself outnumbered, Sigismondo tried to escape with his troops the same evening. They were pursued by Federigo's men and overtaken; by early next morning, 13 August 1462, the fighting had ended in a decisive rout of Sigismondo. Again the news was rapidly diffused. Federigo, for example, wrote that very morning to Piero, his *cancelliere* at Rome, announcing the victory.[32] The same day Niccolò de Palude wrote again to Francesco Sforza, this time reporting Sigismondo's rout.[33] But news traveled slowly in this era. By 16 August, only the report of Senigallia's initial fall to Sigismondo had reached Pius II, then in Pienza; disheartened, he wrote to Sforza to assess the implications of the event. Despite the loss, he said, he considered it best to send Federigo's troops *northward* to attack Sigismondo; still, he would await Sforza's advice.[34] It was in reply to this that Sforza wrote his letter of 23 August 1462, the letter that interests us. However, its contents make sense only in light of a second battle, one that Sforza still knew nothing about.

On 18 August, at Troia, the Angevin forces under Piccinino were defeated by the king of Naples and Alessandro Sforza. The defeat was decisive, marking the end of the revolt and of Francesco Sforza's worries. Once more, however, communications were slow. By 23 August, when Sforza was planning his reply to Pius II, the news had not reached him. He knew that troops were massing in the area and suspected that the engagement might prove crucial. In the interim, moreover, he had also received a report of the other battle, Sigismondo's undoing outside Senigallia, for he refers to it explicitly in his own letter—more than Pius II had known on 16 August when he had written to Sforza, urging his cooperation in a plan to send troops northward against Sigismondo, instead of southward against Piccinino.

These, then, were the circumstances in which Francesco Sforza wrote his letter to Ottone del Carretto—or more precisely the minute of his letter, since the letter itself has not been found. Sforza's minute instructs del Carretto on what to say to Pius II. He must, above all, stress the urgency of sending Federigo's troops southward to support the king of Naples, rather than diverting them into an attack on the Malatestan domains. To show that this counsel is not motivated by a lack of severity toward Sigismondo, but solely by tactical considerations, del Caretto should list all the crimes of Sigismondo against Sforza, proof that Sforza must be as interested as Pius in punishing him. At this point Sforza adduces a long list of alleged injuries. Now the murder of Polissena is described in detail for the first time.

The deed, claims Sforza, was done by an agent of Sigismondo: "one of his men, named Count Antonio" ("uno suo, chiamato el conte Antonio"), who suffocated Polissena with a small cloth ("panixello"). Further, Sigismondo killed a priest who had refused to testify falsely that Polissena had confessed adultery to him, a part of his effort to create an excuse for the crime. His motives were two, hate for Sforza and the desire to make Isotta his wife: "per lo innato odio ne ha portato et porta de sua natura, per tôre per mogliera la Isotta, sua femina." In addition, says Sforza, all this information has been obtained from a person who actually witnessed the events ("da persona che se trovò a vedere tucte queste cose"), though he is not named. Finally, Sforza specifies the effect this information (and the other injuries mentioned) should have: it should convince Pius II that Sforza has no reason whatever ("nè casone alcuna") to be merciful to Sigismondo, and that his counsel is disinterested when he urges Pius to order Federigo da Montefeltro *southward* immediately in order to win the war against the Angevins.[35]

If these instructions were sent to del Caretto, they were soon superseded by others that countermanded them. For the message, we know, was never delivered. And the reason is clear: news of the Angevin defeat at Troia must have reached Sforza shortly after the minute was drafted, rendering the argument purposeless. This is confirmed by the fourth document regarding Polissena's death, Pius II's *Commentarii*, a loose narrative of his reign as pope. Though it was revised as late as June 1464, its version of the murder omits every detail offered by Sforza's letter of 23 August 1462: "Two wives, whom he had married prior to the concubinage with Isotta, he killed one after another by means of poison or a sword." Instead its account looks back to the oration delivered by Benzi, making Sigismondo himself the agent of the crime. Indeed, it alters only one detail: the earlier oration had accused Sigismondo of strangling Polissena, while the later work charged him with either stabbing or poisoning her.[36]

The last document concerning Polissena's death is a biography of Francesco Sforza written by Giovanni Simonetta, the brother of Francesco's loyal secretary, Cicco Simonetta. Its version of the story resembles that of the instructions of 23 August 1462, and since Simonetta worked in the Sforzescan chancery, he probably had access to the minute that is still preserved.

> For Sigismondo greatly feared an encounter with Francesco Sforza. After all, Polysena [sic], his wife and Francesco's daughter, had been killed at his command, in part to make her father suffer greater sorrow, and in part, due to his insatiable and exacerbated loathing for her father, to prevent her from giving birth to male children, and in part so that he could marry his concubine Isotta, whom he loved passionately. Thus, though in fact his innocent and chaste wife had suffered a horrible death, he feigned that she had been snatched from life by a plague-like disease, and ordered it spread abroad that her life had ended naturally.

Simonetta's version states that Polissena was killed at Sigismondo's orders, not by himself, and that Sigismondo ordered the story to be given out that she had died of the plague. It invokes the two motives given earlier by Sforza's letter, but adds a third for good measure: a wish to prevent a male heir by Polissena ("ne . . . virilem ex ea prolem susciperet"). Finally, it says, fear of Sforza's vengeance had motivated Sigismondo's desultory conduct of the 1449 campaign against him, when as condottiere of the Venetians he was entrusted with preventing Sforza's victory over the Ambrosian Republic of Milan.[37]

Together, then, five documents reported the murder of Polissena Sforza:

10 January 1461, letter of Francesco Sforza to Ottone del Carretto;
16 January 1461, invective, written by Pius II, recited by Andrea del Benzi;
23 August 1462, minute of letter of Francesco Sforza to Ottone del Carretto;
ca. 1461–64, passage in Pius II, *Commentarii;*
ca. 1475, passage in Giovanni Simonetta, *Rerum gestarum Francisci Sfortiae mediolanensium ducis commentarii.*

Each of them underwent a different process of transmission, its dynamics subject to questions of class and social power, geography and modes of reproduction, techniques for reproducing and assessing written materials, ideologies and aspirations. Now the routes of reference were coming into play—and with a vengeance. What would reach Ezra Pound in 1922 was not a collection of documents arranged in sequence and integrated into a synthetic narrative, but a cluster of accounts in which the original documents had been transformed by practical and symbolic uses, modifications in institutional configurations, historical occasions and constraints, and imaginative reading.

Murderous Meanings

Of the five documents, only three were published before 1910, and the order of their transmission decisively influenced discussion. The first to attract attention was the invective written by Pius II and recited by Andrea del Benzi in 1461. In 1462 it was incorporated by Pius II into a papal bull, *Discipula veritatis,* so becoming part of an official document by the head of Christendom. As such it was the first of the five documents to be published, included in gatherings of his most important letters, among them a collection he made himself. It was also the first to be printed, appearing in early editions of his letters (1473, 1481, 1487).[38]

The authority behind its account legitimized it as a resource at the disposition of others, increasing its diffusion, while its diffusion further augmented its influence. Consider a single example: the universal chronicle, or history of the world, written by Fra Jacopo Filippo Foresti da Bergamo (1434–1520). Beginning with his second edition in 1485, Foresti drew on the oration/bull for his account of Sigismondo's life and times. He paraphrased its incisive rhetoric and left a striking narrative of the charge that Sigismondo himself had strangled Polissena. His work enjoyed astounding success, serving as a standard work of reference throughout the next century. In Latin, new editions appeared in 1486, 1490, 1492, 1503, 1506, 1513, and 1535; in Italian, in 1491, 1508, 1520, 1524, 1540, 1553, 1575, and 1581 (sixteen editions in less than a century). And because it was published in Venice the work reached the international book market controlled by the maritime republic.[39]

In charging that Sigismondo had tortured several Franciscans for refusing to violate the sacrament of confession, Pius II had also created new martyrs for the faith. As one tradition of ecclesiastical erudition represented by Foresti was beginning to wane, a new one was arising, and in the wake of the Counter-Reformation, martyrdom was a serious issue indeed. Drawing on the accounts of Pius II and Foresti, earnest ecclesiastics never failed to record the murder of Polissena in chronicles, Franciscan martyrologies, and local devotional works: Fra Paolo Clerici Veronese (ca. 1570), Padre Haroldi (1612), Father Luke Wadding (1642), A. R. P. Arturo (1653), Don Silvio Grandi (1702), Padre Flaminio Bottardi da Parma (1760), unpublished works by Padre Righini (eighteenth century), Giambattista Braschi (eighteenth century), and Mgr. Giacomo Villani (date unknown), and even a last martyrology from the early twentieth century by Padre Giacinto Picconi.[40]

Aside from its martyrological fervor, the new tradition exhibited a certain confusion regarding details, an inevitable result of such widespread transmission. Some authors, for example, preferred to assign the martyred confessor not to Polissena, but to Ginevra (Sigismondo's first wife); others took the safer course and assigned him to an indeterminate "moglie."[41] But these variants were modest when compared to the inventiveness of a zealous monk from Rimini writing around 1650. His object was to endow the martyrdom with new specificity, to link it with the sacred relics housed in a nearby monastery. Drawing upon the account provided by Wadding, he fabricated a brief but "ancient" chronicle, attributed it to one "Alessandro," and recounted a story replete with ghastly detail. The nearby relics included a skull marked by dark stains: they were the signs of martyrdom, formed when Sigismondo had pushed a burning helmet over the head of the devout sacerdote.[42] This strange work was to play a major role in later discussion.

The oration/bull influenced not only ecclesiastical writings, but also humanist historiography. Its effects can be easily traced, for the oration/bull contained a small ambiguity that had curious repercussions. In its overview of Sigismondo's wicked deeds, it reported that he had broken his engagement with the daughter of Carmagnola after her father's execution in 1432, and had married and murdered his first wife, Ginevra d'Este.[43] Inadvertently it suggested that Polissena was not his second wife, but his third, as it explicitly referred to their marriage as *tertiae nuptiae*. The ambiguity prompted more explicit mistakes in others, such as Foresti, who gave three wives to Sigismondo in every edition from 1485 to 1581. When the editor of the last edition, Francesco Sansovino, wrote his own book of history in 1582, he also repeated the mistake. Others found it elsewhere. In 1570 Giovanni Battista Pigna published an aulic history of the d'Este family that duly reported Polissena's murder, citing the manuscript chronicle of Fra Paolo Clerici, which had been based on Foresti and Pius II.[44] The humanist works, in turn, enjoyed their own particular *fortuna*. Sansovino's, for example, became a nineteenth-century favorite, an antiquarian's delight that teemed with colorful matter for historians seeking a good tale, such as John Addington Symonds. Ignorant of Renaissance paleography and epigraphy, yet eager to posture as an authority, Symonds lacked the requisite skills to assess earlier inscriptural forms, so he had no choice but to surrender to the "text" of

Sansovino.[45] In 1874 he wrote that Sigismondo had "murdered three wives in succession, Bussoni de Carmagnuola [sic], Guinipera d'Este [sic], and Polissena Sforza, on various pretexts of infidelity." In a footnote he confessed to some "doubt" about a third murder or wife. But two years later he declared flatly that Sigismondo had "killed three wives in succession."[46] As the standard authority on the Renaissance in the English-speaking world, Symonds would also influence Pound.

The second of the five documents to appear was the work of Giovanni Simonetta which, like the oration/bull by Pius II, enjoyed an ample diffusion that derived from institutional affiliations. Simonetta's narrative offered a humanist apology of Sforza's career as condottiere and ruler of Milan. It was dedicated to his grandson Giangaleazzo, its aulic aspirations obvious enough that at least one contemporary assumed it had been written at the mandate of Sforza himself. It was quasi-official historiography and was duly recognized by other members of the class of humanist functionaries to which Simonetta belonged.[47] Largely finished by 1475, it was published in 1482 and again in 1486. At the suggestion of Lodovico il Moro (ruler of Milan) it was translated into Italian by Cristoforo Landino, a central figure of Florentine humanism, and so republished in 1490, 1544, and 1545. Much later, in 1732, another edition in the original Latin was edited by Lodovico Muratori, earning it renewed attention as Muratori's documentary collection became a standard resource for the writing of Italian history.

Finally, in 1584 another of the five documents appeared, the third to be printed: the *Commentarii* of Pius II, published in Rome, and later reprinted in Frankfurt (1614). Yet due to its strictures on contemporaries whose descendants continued to occupy positions of power and prestige, the work was severely edited and many passages omitted—among them the one on Polissena. It would not be printed until 1883, when one scholar attempted to publish all the expurgated passages together. Yet the work's effect on the debate concerning Polissena was no less serious, for one of its central themes was the papal struggle against Sigismondo Malatesta. Further, manuscripts with the deleted passages intact had long been widely circulated—at least fourteen are known.[48] At the very least, publication of the *Commentarii* tended to reinforce the impression already given by the oration/bull: the principal source of the accusations against Sigismondo was not the chancery of Francesco Sforza—those documents were still unpublished—but the papal court of Pius II.

By the seventeenth century, ecclesiastical and humanist consensus had combined with the impulse of post-Tridentine pietism to establish an uncontested hegemony in the debate regarding Sigismondo and his alleged crimes. Even authors who were acquainted with other documents still unpublished were loath to reconsider the charges. An example is Cesare Clementini, a diligent historian from Rimini, whose two-volume history of his native city appeared in 1617 and 1627. Clementini clearly had access to the anonymous chronicle from the fifteenth century; indeed he was the only author to cite it before its publication in 1729, and he even quoted its account of Polissena's funeral (though he modified its date of her death by one day, from 1 June to 2 June). Yet he ignored its failure to specify the cause of her death and instead followed the massive array of secondary materials that reported the murder. He cited Pigna and the manuscript chronicle of Fra Paolo Clerici Veronese to show that all of Sigismondo's wives were considered "pudiche." He cited Simonetta for the charge that Sigismondo had declined to engage Sforza in 1449 for fear of retribution. And he cited Pius II's oration/bull for the principal accusation. Rendered in the baroque style of Clementini, Pius II's charge gained greater specificity: Polissena had died "not without suspicion of a cloth having been twisted around her neck," or "by a noose" ("non senza sospetto d'un asciugatoio involto al collo," or "col laccio").[49] The result was paradoxical: though Clementini neglected the chronicle, his association with it gave his version of the charge new force. To later readers it suggested that he had been persuaded of its truth, that his persuasion derived from the examination of unpublished materials available only in Rimini, and that his own testimony offered independent confirmation of the charges by Pius II and Simonetta. Within a century of publication Clementini's work was widely recognized. His status as a local historian lent it a patina of authority, and in subsequent centuries its views would prove decisive for more than one author.[50] Pound, in fact, would take notes from it carefully.

It was not until the eighteenth century that new intellectual formations emerged that facilitated the communication and publication of new documents and reconsideration of the extant documentary corpus. Three writers (Mazzuchelli, Amiani, Battaglini) show these forces at work in different ways. Gianmaria Mazzuchelli wrote the first (and only) biography of Isotta degli Atti, published in 1756 in Milan and again in 1759 in Brescia—both territories outside papal control. His experience was typical of eighteenth-century intellectual life in Italy, increasingly organized in lay academies associated with local patriciates. The academies encouraged documentary studies that used techniques from the emerging field of diplomatics (the most famous example being Muratori's vast collection, *Rerum italicarum scriptores*). They published journals of erudite antiquarianism and annual miscellanies, and they cultivated an elaborate network of correspondence—practices that complemented one another, since the articles issued by the journals and miscellanies were typically written as familiar letters. (Mazzuchelli's biography of Isotta was first published in an annual miscellany as a letter to Bernardo Nani, and the epistolary form was retained in its publication as a book.)

In his expressed views on the death of Polissena, Mazzuchelli added little that was new: he cited Pius II and the ubiquitous Fra Foresti da Bergamo, and he was forthright in acknowledging his principal source, Clementini. His originality lay elsewhere, in a footnote adding that Clementini's assertion was "confirmed" by "manuscripts from the period" ("manoscritti di quei tempi"). The plural manuscripts turned out to be a single document—the false chronicle by "Alessandro." Mazzuchelli described it in detail, noting that some people thought it a rather recent production. Equally important, he acknowledged his source for this information, "the illustrious Doctor Giovanni Bianchi of Rimini, who with his letter offered me a sign of his kindness."[51] Bianchi was head of the local Riminese branch of the Accademia dei Lincei, which he had revived in November 1745 (assuming for himself the delightful title, *Lynceorum restitutor perpetuus*) Yet that was only the beginning: he belonged to the Accademia dei Congetturanti of Modena, the Accademia della Crusca, the Accademia Etrusca, the Accademia del Buon Gusto of Palermo—to mention only a few. He corresponded extensively with Muratori (seventy-nine letters from him are preserved) and he collaborated on the *Novelle letterarie* of Florence (an annual miscellany). In short, here was the institutional network behind the major innovation in Mazzuchelli's treatment. This was that it marked the first time that an unpublished document in Rimini had been communicated and published abroad. Geography was being superseded by sociocultural formations, and new documentary sources could take their place alongside the traditional array of published books. Aside from this innovation, Mazzuchelli also introduced two other novelties, both seminal for later discussion. By quoting extensively from parts of the chronicle of pseudo-Alessandro, he made them more widely available to others.[52] Moreover, he was the first to invoke the motif of love. Isotta, he said, was a paragon of beauty and wisdom who had merited Sigismondo's passionate devotion, passion that may have led to Polissena's death: "perhaps his love for her was the cause of the death of the aforementioned Polissena."[53] This was a new note, the pre-Romantic dawn. No one before him had linked the question of Polissena so directly with Isotta; the effect was to raise an urgent question: had Isotta prompted the murder?

Contemporary with Mazzuchelli was Pietro-Maria Amiani, a resident in the nearby town of Fano who, in 1751, published a local history buttressed by an elaborate documentary apparatus. Amiani was derivative and uncritical in ascertaining the relative value of conflicting testimonies; he relied heavily on secondary sources, especially a manuscript history of Fano from the seventeenth century by Vincenzo Nolfi. Yet his work was destined to play a pivotal role in the long debate about Polissena's death, and from it would stem, directly or indirectly, the entire dissenting tradition that rejected the charges against Sigismondo. Consequently his report of her death has an importance far beyond its merits—or its modest appearance within a tepid chronicle of the year 1449.[54]

> The plague continued to desolate the city [of Fano] . . . this year, in which the contagious evil spread throughout Italy . . . which, having finally subsided due to the intercession of our glorious patron San Paterniano, lady Violante (wife of Malatesta Novello of Cesena) came to reside in the palace of Sigismondo here in Fano, and upon her arrival was given candles and sweetmeats by the town Council (o). Her example was followed by Margherita, the widow of Galeotto Roberto Malatesta [Sigismondo's older brother], who abandoned Rimini after she saw Polissena, the wife of Sigismondo, die on 2 June or the second day of Pentecost; Polissena was the daughter of Count Francesco Sforza, and several writers assert that she was strangled at the orders of her husband, wherefore Pius II said that Sigismondo freed himself of three wives, one by repudiating his obligations, one by poison, and one by the noose, though all three were chaste and wise. To Rimini our city immediately sent Angelo di Gabriele de' Gabrielli, Malatesta d'Andrea Torelli, Taddiolo di Niccola di Andrea Galassi, and Niccola di Pier-Antonio di Giovanni Francesco Bertozzi, dressed in mourning clothes so they could attend the funeral of Polissena, from which they returned on the eighth of the month, bearing letters from Sigismondo to our city, which reported the death of the bishop Bartolommeo Malatesta and the investiture of Cervia . . .

In his notes Amiani cited a source only for his claim about Violante: "(o) *Acts of the Council for the said year, page 180*" ("*Att. de' Cons. al det. ann.* [1449] *car. 180*").

Amiani's passage combines several sources. One is Clementini, from whom he adopts the date of Polissena's death (2 June rather than 1 June) and his version of Pius II's charge that Polissena had been strangled. Another is the unpublished chronicle of Nolfi, from which comes the report that Violante (wife of Sigismondo's brother) came to Fano from

Cesena in order to avoid the plague. A third is the records from the *con-siglio* of Fano (cited in his footnote). The records have been located, and they confirmed his report about Violante: dated 28 April and 27 May 1449, one states that she left Cesena "pro evitanda epidemia," establish-ing that the city was suffering from the plague at this time (though it proves nothing about the contemporary situation in Rimini). A fourth stands behind the claim that Fano sent four representatives to attend Po-lissena's funeral. Clearly this source cannot be the chronicle of Nolfi, for it reports nothing about the funeral. By its nature it suggests an archival or notarial document: after all, the four names given by Amiani were citizens of Fano alive in 1449, and there is no apparent motive to invent a story with so many details. Yet the document has never been located. Further, other claims about the funeral embassy are transparent anach-ronisms: the bishop Bartolomeo de' Malatesti had died in 1448, a year earlier, and the papal bull for the investiture of Cervia also dated from 1448. The upshot of these comparisons is clear: the seventeenth-century history by Nolfi is generally reliable because it coincides with archival documents; but Amiani is reliable only insofar as he follows Nolfi, and alas, he stops doing so precisely when he offers his crucial claim, that Margherita d'Este came to Fano after having "seen" (Amiani's *vide*) Po-lissena die in Rimini. It is supported by no other source, and indeed is contradicted by the testimony of the Riminese chronicle (usually accu-rate in such matters).[55] Still worse, Amiani himself apparently failed to perceive its implications for the traditional charge that Polissena had been strangled, for he proceeded to report the accusation without a mur-mur of dissent. Yet his entire passage was suggestive: it reminded later authors that the plague had been crawling across central Italy during the years 1448 through 1451—and that it could be a convenient explanation for Polissena's death.

Amiani's book was a local history with no appeal to a wider audience, and its claims might have gone unnoticed had they not been appropriated by Francesco Gaetano Battaglini (1753–1810). Born in Rimini of a patri-cian family, he was nurtured in the intellectual tradition left by Giovanni Bianchi and ideally suited to undertake the biography of Sigismondo Malatesta that he published in 1794, a work that is still the most organic treatment of its subject. Every page demonstrates his intimate knowledge of the documentation in Rimini. It also shows how data that had seemed only anomalous to others could be integrated within a new conception of the subject; for now the Romantic hints of Mazzuchelli were integrated with the suggestive report from Amiani. Battaglini firmly rejected Simonetta's old charge that Sigismondo had avoided battle with Sforza in 1449 because he feared reprisal for her murder. Indeed, he dismissed the murder accusation itself as mere calumny by "someone attempting to denigrate in whatever way possible the reputation of Sigismondo." It was the first denial, based on a systematic recapitulation of details mentioned by Amiani:

> But I shall lend greater credence to the author who has written that Polissena must have succumbed to the plague, which, raging throughout our region at that time, took from this world the bishop Bartolomeo de' Malatesti; wherefore the wife of the lord of Cesena [Violante] and the widow of Roberto [Margherita] both took counsel to betake themselves to Fano.

Battaglini—uncharacteristically—offered no source for these lines. And yet what source could he furnish? No one before him had written that Polissena "must have succumbed to the plague," and in effect he was saying only that he preferred to believe himself, or his understanding of Amiani.[56] It was elsewhere, in his lyrical evocation of the figure of Isotta based on motifs adopted from Mazzuchelli, that his work established the implicit rationale for his rejection of the murder: a defense of individualistic passion would run aground if it were shown that its fruit was murder. And in the years to come, this rationale would become both more explicit and problematic, as the question of Sigismondo began to intersect with crucial issues of ethical and political identity.

In the nineteenth century, the debate on the alleged murder was thrust into new contexts that altered all its implications. Consider the article "Rimini" by Gaetano Moroni, a Catholic priest, published in 1852 as part of his *Dizionario di erudizione storico-ecclesiastica da S. Pietro ai nostri giorni*. At first sight his treatment of the incident seems brief and insignificant: "Sigismondo I [*sic*], impassioned for Isotta, wanted to remove the obstacle necessary to marry her, and in June 1449 he had Polissena—once so beautiful and so desired by him—strangled, as Amiani and other historians affirm." To Moroni, Amiani's ambiguous passage about Polissena's death suggested a conclusion exactly the opposite of Battaglini's. Moreover, Moroni no longer speculated, he *insisted* that the motive for the crime had been Sigismondo's unbridled passion for Isotta and his unscrupulous opportunism.[57] Romantic love, which Mazzuchelli had briefly considered as a possible motive, was now a reality with tragic consequences. Why?

Moroni's view of the murder was inseparable from his treatment of recent events. In 1831 Rimini had participated in an abortive attempt to overthrow papal control. In September 1845 it had witnessed a violent uprising led by Pietro Renzi, one of the first battles of the Risorgimento that led to the unification of Italy. Moroni fulminated against the revolt, which had left Rimini "groaning under the rapacious and cruel desires of the horde, intent only upon theft," while the "good and faithful subjects" of Rimini had been overjoyed when they first viewed papal troops besieging the city, indeed had greeted them with "festive demonstrations."[58] Recent events were still more distressing—and some went unmentioned. In 1846 Massimo d'Azeglio had published his harsh denunciation of papal misgovernment in Romagna.[59] On 22 March 1848 the Austrian garrison in Venice (where Moroni's own work was published) had capitulated to revolutionary forces that proclaimed the restoration of the old Venetian Republic. The next day, after five days of street fighting led by a Council of War under Carlo Cattaneo, Milan had been freed from the Austrian garrison of General Radetsky. In November a minister of the papal government had been assassinated in Rome, and a few days later Pope Pius IX had been forced to flee the holy city. To be sure, all the uprisings had been quelled by 1849: the pope was protected by a French garrison in Rome, while Venice and Milan were conceded to Austria again, and Rimini was restored to the papal state. But restoration had not stilled the threat of another revolution, a specter that haunts Moroni's portrait of Sigismondo Malatesta. For in the new world of the Risorgimento, a figure such as Sigismondo could assume dimensions otherwise unexpected, even bizarre. His resistance to the growing power of the Renaissance papacy could betoken the Risorgimento struggle itself; the artistic vitality of the Renaissance could epitomize the cultural glory of the past and foreshadow the promise of a new unified Italy. In nineteenth-century Italy, the idea of the Renaissance was always inseparable from contrasting conceptions of the new "renaissance" proposed by diverse political currents. Implicit in every judgment of it was a larger evaluation of all Italian history, past and present. (Indeed, until around 1870 the same word, *Risorgimento*, was often used for both periods.) In this light Sigismondo became a representative figure in a laicizing reinterpretation of the Italian past. Now the charges against him assumed new relevance: if corroborated, they served as an object lesson on the dangers of secularism, on the moral degeneration that followed from life led without God or his earthly representative; but if disproved, they epitomized the ecclesiastical falsification of the Italian past, historiography that had severed

the temporal continuity of the nation as surely as the papal state had
sundered its geographical unity. Here was the impetus behind Moroni's
eagerness to link the murder with Isotta, to fashion a cautionary tale that
identified the moral corruption of secularism and implicitly damned the
contemporary programs associated with it.[60] Sigismondo now appeared in
a new costume, wearing the black coat of the liberal bourgeois.

The liberal reply to Moroni appeared in an article on the Malatesta
that was published in 1869 as part of a biographical collection on re-
nowned Italian families. The collection had first begun publication in
1819, edited by Pompeo Litta, when it offered little more than a retarded
example of aristocratic antiquarianism. But by 1869 it had assumed new
dimensions in the context of the Risorgimento. Litta himself had served
as minister of war in the provisional government of Lombardy during the
abortive revolution of 1848, and had worked closely with Carlo Cattaneo,
the energetic spokesman for the bourgeoisie. When he died in 1852, his
mantle was assumed by Luigi Passerini, and by now the collection was
on its way to becoming a national history.[61] Recounting the fortunes of
illustrious families had become an occasion for asserting the continuity
of Italian secular history, for restoring the national past to the readers of
the new unitary state created after 1860. The collection's format had
proved ideal for presenting a mix of families with bourgeois and aristo-
cratic origins, recapitulating the same compromise that had molded the
guiding class of the new Italy, as exemplified in the cooperation of Litta
and Cattaneo. Even the work's publication in Milan bespoke its affilia-
tions with the economic center of the new state, where bourgeois capital
financed new publishing houses eager to serve an emerging readership.[62]
Yet in 1869, despite all the recent achievements, one problem was still
unresolved: Rome, the historic capital of Italy, remained under the con-
trol of the papacy. And the church was growing intransigent. The Sylla-
bus of 1864 and the doctrine of infallibility proclaimed in 1869 were
virtually a declaration of war on liberalism. Could any bourgeois reader
of 1869 follow the struggle between Sigismondo and Pius II without re-
calling the struggle between modern Italy and Pius IX? Passerini con-
tested every accusation leveled against Sigismondo by Pius II, even the
alleged murder:

> Polissena died on 1 June 1449, most likely of the plague, even though it
> has been written that her unfaithful consort had her strangled to punish
> her for infidelity. But regarding this claim, it should be noted that Sigis-
> mondo and Sforza remained on terms of goodwill for some time, and that
> Sforza never mentioned this tragedy in the many attacks he later launched

against his son-in-law, an event he certainly would never have forgotten if
it had really occurred. Nor would he have saved him at the last moment
when he was about to lose what little remained of the Riminese territory.

Passerini added the new argument that the continued goodwill between
Sforza and Sigismondo militated against the alleged murder. But his real
novelty lay elsewhere, in his tone of cool secular reasoning devoid of
moral denunciation. He refused even to quote the accusation of Pius II,
and he pointedly contrasted the civic virtues of Sigismondo's regime with
those of the papal administration. "His subjects loved him," said Passe-
rini, "because he eased their burden of taxes, because his government,
however harsh or disaster-prone, was considerably more humane than the
one that weighed on the nearby lands subjected to the Church, and be-
cause, splendid and magnificent in all that he did, he made Rimini flour-
ish in letters, sciences, and arts."[63]

Moroni and Passerini suggest how a civic and national "frame" altered
the terms in which discussion of the alleged murder took place, bringing
into play issues that extended far beyond the antiquarian confines of Rim-
inese history. Inside Italy, discussion of Polissena's murder assumed pre-
cise contours against a background that made each judgment political,
tied to the programs and vicissitudes of the Risorgimento. Outside, the
tendency was quite different, principally through the influence of Jacob
Burckhardt's epoch-making work, *Die Kultur der Renaissance in Italien*
(1860). So much has been written about this book, with its intense and
moving evocation of the birth of a culture—and with good reason, so
central has it been to the self-conception of European civilization—that
it would be pointless to attempt to add anything here. Suffice it to sketch
a few points relevant to our purposes. One is the political background to
Burckhardt's conception of the Renaissance, a story long known through
the diligent researches of Werner Kaegi. Its main elements are Burck-
hardt's role as editor of the *Basler Zeitung*, his militant journalism against
extreme right and democratic left on behalf of the moderate right (the
traditional ruling class of Basel), his utter defeat in the 1844 crisis over
reintroduction of the Jesuits, and his decision in 1845 to quit as editor
and journey to Italy.[64] Burckhardt's whole outlook was reshaped: the con-
servative who had accepted some liberal exigencies was transformed into
a man to whom political life was repugnant and modernity a horror. Dis-
dainful of mechanism, the rise of democracy, the growth of new and vocal
masses, Burckhardt saw in the Italian Renaissance a flight from time and
the concretization of an ideal of European civilization. It was the opposite
of the view within Italy. For contemporary Italians the Renaissance was a

site for debate on how to recuperate the cultural heritage for the present, how to integrate the artworks of the past into the fiber of a new state; for Burckhardt the Renaissance was a refuge from the present, and his aim was to depict a world in which, as the famous title of his first chapter puts it, the state was transformed into a work of art. His achievement was to renew and popularize, in a complete and harmonious portrait, the grand myth of the Renaissance as the formation of the "whole man," a new human "type" charged with rebellious and individualistic implications, a form of historical existence presented as exemplary for the course of civilization. He painted a moving tableau of great individuals, a marvelous spectacle of elect minorities who assumed the mysterious role of creative forces for collective history, whose innovative capacity shone in their repudiation of the past, their exaltation of the individual conscience and the force of will. Within this tableau the figure of Sigismondo Malatesta occupied a unique, exemplary position. He was presented as the crowning example in Burckhardt's chapter, "The Furtherers of Humanism." His court epitomized "the highest spiritual things," a stage where "life and manners . . . must have been a singular spectacle." Indeed, his entire family was distinguished as the concluding specimen for the chapter, "The Petty Tyrannies," and Sigismondo was specifically invoked to exemplify the twin aspects united in the "whole man" of the Renaissance: "Unscrupulousness, impiety, military skill, and high culture have been seldom so combined in one individual as in Sigismondo Malatesta." To be sure, he was also "a monster": "It is not only the Court of Rome, but the verdict of history, which convicts him of murder, rape, adultery, incest, sacrilege, perjury, and treason, committed not once, but often." But the moralistic strictures hardly concealed Burckhardt's admiration for the "type" he was tracing.[65] Indeed, within the logic established by Burckhardt, such "crimes" were not objects for moral reproval, but signs of that potent individualism at the core of the "Renaissance man," a type who embodies an ethical emancipation from (both outside and against) constraints and authorities transmitted by a world already exhausted. Burckhardt, then, turned Sigismondo into an exemplary figure who was charged with broad philosophical and ethical implications, who incarnated the lost unity and wholeness of the Renaissance man, who was equally capable in art or war, in contemplation or action. His success was staggering. The book was translated into French by Geiger (1876), into Italian by Valbusa (1877), and into English by Middlemore (1886). Sigismondo had become a figure of European stature—and for European civilization. This tradition, too, would influence Pound.

Aside from Burckhardt, three other agencies altered the grounds for assessing the alleged murder of Polissena. One appeared in the interval between the publication of Burckhardt's work (1860) and Passerini's (1869). It was the reading room of the Bibliothèque Nationale in Paris, constructed between 1865 and 1868. Its architecture registered all the new forces governing the production of knowledge—sixteen iron columns, all exposed, carrying nine domes of faience and glass. Such institutions (the British Library was another) radically changed the ways in which bibliographic components of specific traditions could interact. Spatio-temporal considerations and affiliations were displaced.[66] Consider all the books we have just discussed—both editions of Pius II's *Commentarii* (1584, 1614), all the editions of his *epistolae* containing the bull (1473, 1481, 1487), all the early editions of Simonetta (1482, 1486, 1490, 1544, 1545), the Muratori editions of Simonetta and the Rimini chronicle (1732, 1729), Clementini (1617, 1627), Amiani (1751), Mazzuchelli (1759), Battaglini (1794), Moroni (1852), Burckhardt, and Passerini.[67] All were now available in a single building to a wide public of scholars, writers, publicists, and historians (see table 2). Here was a reading space of unimaginable potency. Little wonder that Pound would do much of his research for the Malatesta Cantos amid the slender iron columns of the Bibliothèque Nationale.

Books and manuscripts were the domain of the new centralized library. Documents were entrusted to another institution emerging during the same period, the archive, designed to serve a public of scholars and contribute to the writing of national history. Such an idea was relatively new, and inevitably there were problems in execution. An example is the archive of Milan, where the two unpublished documents from Sforza were housed. The Milanese archive had been created when the city was under Austrian domination, and its earliest directors had instituted a system of archival organization based on the principles of Ilario Corte, a rationalist system derived from the encyclopedic principles of the Enlightenment. Accordingly original collections, formed in an organic historical-administrative unity, were dismembered and reorganized according to a series of topical ideas. The first director of the archive after Italian unification elected to continue and articulate the Corte system. The second found the situation so hopeless that he chose not to alter it. But by 1900 the disaster had become glaringly apparent through contemporary advances in archival theory and practice in Germany which, especially through the Florentine school of Guasti, were already well known in Italy. Only in 1907 when Luigi Fumi was appointed director at Milan was there an effort to undertake a systematic reconstruction of the original collections within the limits that the intervening alterations had already imposed.[68] Not surprisingly, during his tenure both the original documents by Sforza were to be rediscovered, and Fumi himself would uncover the crucial minute of 1462.

Contemporary with these developments was the spread of a third insti-

Table 2

Works in the Bibliothèque Nationale, Paris (BNP)

Author and Title	Catalogue général	BNP Shelf Mark
Amiani	vol. 2 (1900), 956	K. 188–189
Battaglini	vol. 8 (1901), 732	YC. 935
Litta/Passerini	vol. 98 (1930), 1027	Rés. 329–338
Mazzuchelli	vol. 111 (1931), 685–86	K. 15896, Z. 12382
Mittarelli	vol. 116 (1932), 64–65	Q. 386
Moroni	vol. 119 (1933), 1072–75	H. 578
Muratori (ed.), Cron. mal.	vol. 121 (1933), 988	K. 40
Muratori (ed.), Simonetta	vol. 121 (1933), 988	K. 46
Pius II, Comm., 1584	vol. 136 (1936), 933	H. 3117
Pius II, Comm., 1614	vol. 136 (1936), 933	H. 362
Pius II, Epist., 1473	vol. 136 (1936), 944	Rés. H. 940
Pius II, Epist., 1481	vol. 136 (1936), 944	Rés. H. 936
Pius II, Epist., 1487	vol. 136 (1936), 944	Rés. H. 937
Pius II, oration: see Mittarelli	—	—
Simonetta, 1480	vol. 371 (1948), 371	Vélins 723, Rés. K. 67
Simonetta, 1486	vol. 371 (1948), 371	Vélins 1172, Rés. K. 66
Simonetta, 1490	vol. 371 (1948), 371	Vélins 724, Rés. K. 68
Simonetta, 1543	vol. 371 (1948), 371	K. 8878
Simonetta, 1544	vol. 371 (1948), 371	K. 8828
Soranzo, "Cessione"	vol. 175 (1949), 310	K. 1340
Soranzo, "Missione"	vol. 175 (1949), 310–11	K. 1346
Soranzo, "Sigla"	vol. 175 (1949), 310	K. 1341
Soranzo, "Fallito"	vol. 175 (1949), 310	K. 1342
Soranzo, "Invettiva"	vol. 175 (1949), 310	K. 4609
Soranzo, Pio II	vol. 175 (1949), 310	K. 4611
Yriarte, Un Condottiere	vol. 229 (1980), 37	K. 143

Note: References to the Catalogue général are by volume, year of publication, and column. Shelf marks are listed as given in the catalogue. This list includes all the works that have been discussed in chapter two, as well as others that will be discussed later with reference to Pound's reading in the Bibliothèque Nationale.

tution that affected the culture of writing and reading, and so the socio-historical terms for discussion of the alleged murder. It was the railroad. The unification of Italy prompted a boom in railroad construction. In 1861 railroads had covered only 2,273 km; between 1861 and 1901 the rail network was expanded to cover 16,451 km (annual growth averaging more than 370 km). And Rimini was among the first towns to be affected, for it was located along the Bologna-Ancona line. Within a decade the railroad had utterly transformed the local economy, turning the small fishing town and agricultural market into a bathing resort and center of tourism. In 1843 Rimini had witnessed the construction of the first bath-house on the coast, a simple structure of wood; by 1870 it was contem-plating a regulatory plan to control the feverish building activity devour-ing the coastline. In 1872 appeared the Riminese Kursaal, in 1876 the Istituto Idroterapico, in 1907–08 the Grand Hotel. On the average two new hotels were constructed per year, and by 1900 tourism had become the dominant factor in Riminese economic life.[69] German and English tourists annually invaded the town, pursued "hydrotherapy," and toured monuments from the Roman and Renaissance past. Rimini boasted the oldest triumphal arch in Italy, its Roman bridge had been built by Tiber-ius, and it housed the "first" church built in the style of the Renaissance! It was healthful and historical, salubrious and edifying—the perfect tour for the liberal bourgeois. As Burckhardt turned Sigismondo into a figure of European civilization, the bathhouse and the railroad carved his niche in a historicist museum both real and imaginary, a stopping point in the cultural itinerary of elite bourgeois travel.

With the spread of railroads and the growth of elite tourism, Sigis-mondo was integrated into an ancillary institution that emerged with these: travel books and guidebooks. The Baedeker enterprise, which be-gan with a simple guidebook to Coblenz in 1829, soon developed into a cultural phenomenon that educated the bourgeois traveler in a character-istic tone—sure, precise, and posed. The new institution not only af-fected content and style, it required a specific size, format, and system of distribution. As early as 1837 Bernhard Tauchnitz began his series of pocket-sized paperbacks in English; these were designed to be sold at Continental railway station bookstalls, and were easily recognized by the green paper bindings and convenient size. Complementary to the guide-book was another type of book, the large-format deluxe travel volume. This was meant to be perused at home after a journey (or perhaps in lieu of one); it recounted a leisurely tour and presented hundreds of engrav-

ings that depicted favorite scenes with an aura of the antique and roman-
tic, recalled beloved views and filling the mind with "historical" images,
just as one filled a room with souvenirs.[70]

The debate on Polissena was now sited in a configuration of travel
practices, historiography, and book morphology—a *mentalité*. In 1874
John Addington Symonds, whose views on the murder we have seen,
published his *Sketches and Studies in Italy and Greece*, a work intersect-
ing with all the traditions we have considered. Rimini, his first sentence
explained, was alluring because of its combination of baths and antiqui-
ties, nature and history. Here the elite spirits of the Renaissance had first
pulsed with "a pantheistic feeling for the world," had experienced "the
charm and mystery which the Greeks had imaged in their Pan, . . . the
feeling of a hidden want." Here the city's ruins disclosed "something
infinitely charming in the crepuscular moments of the human mind."[71]
Through 1914 a new edition of *The Sketches* appeared every four years.
Meanwhile, in 1883 Symonds was asked by Tauchnitz to prepare a one-
volume selection culled from the *Sketches* and another work. He selected
"the more picturesque pieces" and adapted them to "the use of travelers
rather than of students," indicating his awareness of the railway's audi-
ence; the abridged edition took up only 312 pages, was packaged in the
familiar green paper binding, and was available at railroad bookstalls
throughout the Continent. Here was culture in a handy format! Bernard
Berenson bought a copy, had it bound in half-leather, and gave it to the
American painter Stuart Davis, a gift to "help him recall his first days in
Italy."[72]

Between 1875 and 1910 the cultural itinerary of elite travel became
increasingly stable. In 1878, for example, Charles Yriarte published *Les
Bords de l'Adriatique et le Monténégro*, a deluxe travel book embellished
with 257 wood engravings. For Rimini he offered tips on wine, typical
foods, restaurants, and prices; and of course he guided the reader to the
monuments of the past, each illustrated with an engraving. Yet he regret-
ted that the church of San Francesco was "rather little known, when all
is said and done" ("assez peu connue en somme") and promised to return
in another volume.[73] He did so in his 1882 biography of Sigismondo,
complete with 200 illustrations, the work that synthesized the late Ro-
mantic legend of the church of San Francesco and Sigismondo. By 1906,
when F. H. Jackson traced exactly the same tour of the Adriatic coast
(another deluxe travel book, 119 illustrations), he could claim that the
places he described were "very little known to English people, except for

a few towns such as"—and the pairing is significant—Rimini and Ra-
venna.[74] Together Rimini and Ravenna had come to be essential stops of
an itinerary both real and psychological—places of elite tourism, stages
in the construction of a historicist *mentalité*. Jackson's book, subtitled *An
Architectural and Archaeological Pilgrimage*, suggests how the cultural
journey had acquired a quasi-religious character. It is no accident that
Pound's haunting evocation of the Tempio in Rimini (at the end of Canto
9) modulates into an elegiac allusion to the sarcophagi "such as lie
smothered in grass" in Ravenna.

The cultural itinerary overlapped with a specific configuration of
genres: history, travel writing, and art history. Nearly every writer who
wrote about Rimini worked in all three, and several treated the city on
more than one occasion. Symonds treated the city once in his *Sketches*,
and again in numerous discussions in his six volumes of Renaissance
history. Yriarte included the city in his travel book and devoted a volume
to Sigismondo himself. Jackson published both his travel book and a
historical study of *True Stories of the Condottieri* (1903), the first contain-
ing a chapter on Rimini, the second a chapter on Sigismondo. Edward
Hutton wrote a historical novel on Sigismondo in 1906, then wrote a
travel book in 1913 that included a chapter on Rimini. Beltramelli's
Temple of Love was listed as a travel book, and Beltramelli served as a
traveling editor for the *Corriere della sera;* he also wrote several works on
contemporary events.[75] Moreover, all these authors (except Beltramelli)
wrote extensively on art history.[76]

This constellation of genres and institutions diffused the interpretive
frame outlined by Burckhardt among literate, well-traveled circles. Sig-
ismondo became a cipher for bourgeois culture. Insofar as the Tempio
drew on ancient architectural models and yet retained a distinctive style
of its own, liberal culture could view it as a mirror of its own formation of
elite historicism, its own evolution from a class supposedly without cul-
ture to one immersed in historicist reconstructions. (In architectural his-
tory one need only recall the massive demolition projects in Paris after
1851, Vienna after 1860, Florence after 1865, Rome after 1870, and the
historicist constructions built in the new zones.) Burckhardt had turned
Sigismondo into a "type" exemplary for the course of civilization, and
assessing his accomplishment and failure became an occasion for reading
the ambiguities of civilization itself. The symbolic struggle over the
crimes of Sigismondo was a locus for reflection on the price of the bour-
geois ascendancy, the cost entailed in the appropriation of the riches of

the past by the new educated man. Indeed, since the documentary corpus was stable throughout the period 1860–1910, data played only a minimal role in shaping the view expressed by any individual writer. What mattered was an entire outlook on the history of Western Europe.

Symonds indicated one way to treat the figure of Sigismondo and the

Figure 13. Charles Yriarte (1832–98). Journalist, author, art historian, and cultural bureaucrat, Yriarte wrote a biographical study of Sigismondo Malatesta, *Un Condottiere au XVᵉ siècle* (Paris: Jules Rothschild, 1882), that synthesized the Romantic interpretation of the church of San Francesco. Pound's copy of the book is filled with 150 marginalia and submarginalia. Reprinted from *Gazette des Beaux-Arts*, ser. 3, vol. 19 (1898), p. 431.

question of his crimes. He transplanted the Burckhardtian conception of the Renaissance into Anglophonic culture, but tempered its radical ambiguities with faith in the "liberal" doctrine of civilization's continual progress. The Renaissance was a transitional phase between the darkness of the Middle Ages and the enlightenment of modern science, and therefore its violence could be dismissed as a regrettable but necessary feature in a moment of historical change. At times he turned to conventional moral denunciation:

> Sigismondo Malatesta was one of the strangest products of the earlier Renaissance. To enumerate the crimes which he committed within the sphere of his own family, mysterious and inhuman outrages which render the tale of the Cenci credible, would violate the decencies of literature. A thoroughly bestial nature gains thus much with posterity that its worst qualities must be passed by in silence. It is enough to mention that he murdered three wives in succession. [77]

Symonds's control of tone was perfect: both respectful of "the family" and yet titillating ("mysterious and inhuman outrages"). The ambivalent linkage of violence and culture was not resolved, but softened by a moralism that never relinquished its apparent sympathy and fascination.

More important was the work of Charles Yriarte (1832–98; see figure 13), in part because it influenced so many others (especially Pound), and in part because it originated in his personal experience with every aspect of the rise of liberal dominance. As a journalist he had covered Garibaldi's heroic landing in Sicily in May 1860, leading to the overthrow of the Bourbons and the unification of Italy. He had traced the campaign as it spread into the peninsula, stayed in Naples with Dumas at Chiatamone, and even collaborated on his *Independente*. He had been a prominent figure in the new institution of the bourgeois newspaper, associated with *Le Monde illustré* (founded 1857) and *La Vie parisienne* (founded 1863), and it was through the newspaper that nineteenth-century Europe turned Italy into the site of a practical experiment in its philosophy of history: its belief that man, fundamentally good, would recover his lost virtues as soon as he had been freed from despotism. All these forces intersected in his study of Malatestan Rimini. He understood fully Burckhardt's assessment of Sigismondo, and both cited and quoted it. [78] He adduced vast quantities of documentation from archives in Florence and Siena (archives organized by the school of Guasti), though not surprisingly he failed to find either of the missing documents in the Milan archive (where the Corte system was intact). He studied extensively in the

Bibliothèque Nationale of Paris, where he consulted its copies of Clementini, Battaglini, Mazzuchelli, and Passerini, all but the last extremely rare. He drew on experiences garnered while writing his 1878 travel book with its chapter on Rimini.[79] Yriarte, in short, was the man in the black coat—riding the railways constructed by liberal Europe, studying in its centralized national libraries, perusing its archives, writing its travel and art history books—and in the contradictory portrait of Sigismondo depicted in the writings of Passerini and Burckhardt he found an ambiguous mirror of himself, a monstrous and uneasy double. How could he confront the nexus of civilization epitomized in the alleged murder of Polissena? The answer is not surprising. He was utterly baffled.

Yriarte compared the accusation with another charge, also widely diffused: that Sigismondo had murdered his first wife, Ginevra. In the earlier case he was prepared to accept Passerini's arguments for innocence, since there were only suspicions. But the second left him nervous, and his fears were sharpened by a needless error: he thought that Polissena had died in June 1450, not 1449, a date that preceded the legitimation of Isotta's children by only a few weeks—suggesting cold calculated murder. He considered the evidence furnished by Clementini very damning, especially his designation of the exact instrument of crime—a little cloth.[80] The charge by Pius, even if "tainted by prejudice," was also a formal accusation, and the chronicle of Alessandro (which he assumed was genuine) confirmed it fully. To be sure, Passerini's arguments did have some weight, but not enough to convince him once and for all. If nothing else, the charge was "more probable" than the one about Ginevra, and one had to concede that the character of the man lent itself to such accusations.

But to concede the possibility of guilt raised another problem. Having mistakenly dated Polissena's death to 1450, he was obliged to face a ghastly possibility suggested by its "coincidence" with the legitimation of Isotta's children. For if their legitimation had been undertaken with her knowledge and consent, was it possible that she had also instigated the murder? In effect this question merely disguised another. Insofar as the church of San Francesco had become an emblem of civilization, and Sigismondo an exemplary figure whose energy had realized it, the place of Isotta as the source that had inspired the work became fraught with tension. Isotta had come to embody disinterested beauty and knowledge, the love of which was thought to inspire genuine cultural activity. Could it be, instead, that the monument of civilization had really been inspired by crude yet cunning opportunism? Could the monument of culture really be no more than a monument of barbarity? It could not. Yriarte took extraordinary pains to dissociate her from the crime, an effort that would be repeated by every writer who followed him. Yriarte reasoned that if Isotta had spurred her lover to commit the crime in order to legitimize her children through marriage, then surely he would have married her shortly thereafter; instead, as several documents showed, the two had not married until much later.

> It is quite remarkable, and the circumstance redounds to the honor of Isotta, that not one historian or chronicler, invoking the famous axiom *is fecit cui prodest,* has accused the mistress of Sigismondo with complicity in the crime. It would seem that the ruler of Rimini, free of every shackle, should have wished to marry Isotta immediately; yet we see that six years later he had not yet fulfilled the wish of his mistress. Therefore, if we must maintain the accusation of murder, we must make it his responsibility alone.

It was love that had led to the construction of civilization, love that had probably driven Sigismondo to commit a savage crime—but it was disinterested love for a pure and disinterested object. Lacking the civic commitment and energy that had driven Passerini, Yriarte's quixotic treatment disclosed the ambiguities that were invested in the bourgeois defense of cultural activity as it turned increasingly conservative.[81] Confused and doubtful, he salvaged what seemed most essential.

Every writer between 1882 and 1910 depended directly or indirectly on Yriarte, and since his view of the murder charge was ambiguous, it could lend itself to either interpretation. The Italian historian Pasquale Villari, who wrote the article on Rimini for the 1886 edition of the *Encyclopaedia Britannica,* followed Yriarte's mistaken dating of her death in 1450 and the effort, based on this, to link the murder charge with the 1450 legitimization of Sigismondo's child by Isotta:

> Such being the nature of the man, it is not astonishing that, as his ardour for Isotta increased, he should have little scruple in ridding himself of his second wife. On the 1st June 1450 Polissena died by strangling, and on the 30th of the same month Isotta's offspring were legitimated by Nicholas V.
>
> It is only just to record that, although Malatesta's intrigue with Isotta had long been notorious to all, and he had never sought to conceal it, no

one ever accused her of either direct or indirect complicity in her lover's crimes.

These sentences were repeated without change in the major revisions of the *Encylopaedia Britannica* published in 1911 and 1929 (eleventh and fourteenth editions).[82] As with Yriarte, the effort to absolve Isotta is combined with an increasing note of moral denunciation.

English writers tended to be more eager to assert Sigismondo's innocence. One suspects that they, at the height of the Empire, were less likely to view civilization as an unhappy business. Consider the 1903 comments of Frederick Hamilton Jackson: "It was reported that he poisoned his first wife Ginevra d'Este, and strangled his second wife Polyxena Sforza, but neither the Marquis d'Este nor the Duke of Milan considered that the accusation was well founded, for they continued on good terms with him."[83] Even more adamant was the denial issued by Edward Hutton in his 1906 novel. The accusation so alarmed him that he abandoned his pretense of fiction and addressed it *propria voce* in a footnote: "There is not, so far as I can find, a tittle of evidence against Sigismondo." His comments indicated the extraordinary diffusion of printed source materials achieved by the central libraries. He referred to Yriarte's opinion of Clementini, quoted Clementini himself, and offered his own translation of Battaglini as conclusive evidence. In his 1913 travel book, Hutton addressed the subject again:

> It is asserted that he murdered his three wives; but as soon as we begin to sift the evidence we find that there is not enough to hang a dog. . . . As his second wife he married Polisenna [*sic*] Sforza, the sister [*sic*] of the future Duke of Milan, who also died mysteriously, but without any real suspicion falling upon Sigismondo, at any rate in Rimini.[84]

Outside England, writers were more inclined to believe the charges. Consider André Maurel, who wrote a series of guidebooks to the "petites villes d'Italie," reprinted in thirteen editions between 1906 and 1920. His chapter on Rimini recounted the familiar charges without flinching: "Marié deux fois, à Ginevra d'Este et à Polyxena Sforza, il empoisonne ses deux femmes." Needless to say, Maurel had mixed up the charges a bit. Others, such as Ermolao Rubieri, the author of a biography on Francesco Sforza, also accepted the accusations without hesitation.[85]

Intellectual life was gravitating toward the massive libraries of the metropolitan powers; those who remained in peripheral cultural zones were left behind, rendered irrelevant unless they could assimilate the themes and techniques governing the wider discussion. Paradoxically, then, the local tradition of Rimini—which still contained unseen documentation—grew increasingly moribund. In 1880, for example, Luigi Tonini (director of the city library) published a detailed chronicle of Sigismondo's life. He had access to the unpublished manuscript of Gaspare Broglio, a source with important testimony, and even cited it explicitly. But he then rehearsed the usual sources: he quoted the anonymous chronicle, referred to Pius II, cited Clementini, then paraphrased Battaglini and accepted his account that Polissena had died of the plague. Like Clementini and Battaglini before him, he had published his book at his own expense; but now it was not received by a local patriciate integrated into a wider institutional network of knowledge, and so the work was utterly ignored.[86]

As for Antonio Beltramelli, writing in 1912, he never addressed the charge directly. He dismissed the first two wives as "miserable creatures who pass a little time at the court of Rimini and die without having known joy," for in the Nietzschean schema informing his work, true joy was known only to the elect. At one point he fused them into a single person, Ginevra Sforza (instead of Ginevra d'Este and Polissena Sforza). Sigismondo's guilt was irrelevant, but of course Isotta's innocence demanded comment: "She lived at his side a long time, and yet not once was she charged with having had part in the crimes that he committed."[87]

It was on the eve of the Great War, the first of the two twentieth-century conflicts that forever clouded the concept of civilization, that the last and decisive stage of the debate on the murder of Polissena was enacted. It lasted from 1910 to 1922, as if constituting a frame on the war itself. It was inaugurated by a long article published in three parts in 1910 and 1911 by Giovanni Soranzo.[88] The series appeared in a review of local history, *La Romagna*, a form of publication suggesting Soranzo's contemporary affiliations. Born in Padua in 1881, Soranzo had been teaching at a local school in Rimini since 1906. He felt acutely his distance "from a significant center of studies," evidently aware that centralized institutions for research were dominating intellectual life of the time. Thus, Soranzo understood the larger historiographic environment; he traveled to Milan to work in the archive, and could assimilate his findings to current discussion. Indeed, he was eager to make his name, advance his career, and leave Rimini: already in 1905 (at age twenty-four) he had published his first book; in 1907 he announced the discovery of an important quattrocento chronicle; in his 1910–11 articles he displayed his mastery over all the materials available to him in Rimini.[89] Through his work and the controversy it aroused, the two letters from Francesco Sforza reappeared for the first time after 450 years.

Soranzo attempted a frontal assault on the oration of Pius II recited by del Benzi in 1461. The individual charges were "insufficiently proved or plainly unjust," and he hoped to "render less severe and less unjust the judgment of modern historians on the figure of Sigismondo Malatesta."[90] His method was rigorously historicist and positivist, based wholly on documentary sources. First, he demonstrated that Sigismondo was absent from Rimini when Polissena died, and so could not have committed the crime himself, as asserted in the two accounts of Pius II.

Second, he discovered and published the forgotten 1461 letter from Sforza, the first new document to appear in several centuries. Soranzo, it is clear, willingly sought testimonies that might disprove his own claims. Now he had to confront its vague yet potent allusion to having been offended by Sigismondo "in le carne et sangue." He rejected it because identifiable political motives explained and disqualified its testimony. He also dismissed the charges of Simonetta: the aulic historiography of his work was transparent, and it had been written in a period when the disgrace of Sigismondo made it too opportune to repeat the charges—particularly at a court in Milan. Thus he eliminated four of the five documents accusing Sigismondo.[91] But as yet he had only cast doubt on the extant testimonies; now he had to construct a persuasive alternative account to prove Polissena's death by other causes.

Soranzo tried to show that Polissena had died of the plague. His most important witness was the seventeenth-century historian from Fano, Vincenzo Nolfi, who had written that Polissena died "in that influenza that was also felt in Rimini."[92] He noted that one of Nolfi's claims—that Violante (wife of Sigismondo's brother) had left Cesena in April 1449 for Fano because the plague was raging there—was verified by council records of Fano. If Nolfi was accurate with details of this sort, he could be presumed accurate for his other claim about Polissena. Soranzo added the testimony of Simonetta himself, who had conceded that public opinion attributed Polissena's death to the plague, though Simonetta had charged it was due to falsification by Sigismondo. Soranzo was also the first scholar to consider the testimony of Gaspare Broglio, a counselor of Sigismondo Malatesta. Broglio had mistakenly given the year of Polissena's death as 1448, but for the same year he had also noted that Rimini was subject to a "terribellissima moria" ("truly terrible pestilence").[93]

Soranzo also committed an important error, however. He was too eager to link the documented plague of April 1449 in Cesena with the death of Polissena two months later on 1 June; and as a result he attributed to Nolfi a statement actually made by Amiani (1751), a far less reliable source, that Margherita d'Este had left Rimini on 2 June after seeing Polissena die—a claim that could be disproved.[94] And this was a key point in his argument. Without it, one could say only that the plague had been circulating throughout the region in this period; it was a plausible, not a persuasive candidate for the cause of death. Nor could one place more than limited faith in Nolfi's testimony, since it dated from two centuries later.

Soranzo adduced one last argument based on another contemporary document that also had not been brought to light before, the *condotta* of 1451 between Sforza and Sigismondo, pledging Sforza to pay the debt remaining on Polissena's dowry. He argued that nothing could have induced Sforza to undertake this pledge if he had had a well-founded suspicion of murder, and likewise that Sigismondo would hardly have insisted upon receiving the debt if such rumors had been circulating, since prudence would have dictated that he let the matter be forgotten.[95]

Soranzo's articles generated a controversy. There were two replies, one by Luigi Fumi in 1913, another by Gregorio Giovanardi in 1914. Fumi, we have seen, was director of the Archivio di stato of Milan and was engaged in trying to reorganize the earlier archival collections, those pertaining to the Sforzas. This activity brought to his attention the last of the five original documents that accused Sigismondo of having murdered Polissena, the minute of 23 August 1462 by Sforza that contained the most detailed form of the charges. Fumi published it for the first time, and argued that it confirmed the accusation by Pius II.[96]

In 1914 a second article appeared, one by Gregorio Giovanardi, a Franciscan brother who resided in the monastery associated with the sanctuary of the Madonna delle Grazie at Covignano, three kilometers from Rimini. In the sacristy of the church were some religious relics, a few bones and a skull stored in a little glass box. Giovanardi set out to vindicate the local belief that these were the sacred remains of Polissena's confessor, murdered by Sigismondo. He began by publishing a photo of the little box and bones—an inauspicious beginning. He pressed on, citing Fumi's recent article as support for his own views. Yet his major testimony lay elsewhere, in an unpublished and little-known chronicle that offered a gruesome account of the murder and the martyrdom. It was

the "Chronicle of Alessandro," the seventeenth-century forgery. Giova-
nardi not only accepted its authenticity, but argued that it was corrobo-
rated by all the martyrologies and ecclesiastical chronicles deriving from
Pius II, which, of course, were its sources and not its confirmation.[97]

Soranzo replied to both articles in 1915. His reply to Fumi was the
more important. Once more he laid out the immediate context of the 1462
minute and argued that it was merely "an able pretext" to secure Sforza's
aim of having the papal troops help the king of Naples. He noted, too,
that it had never been delivered, though he did not insist on this point.[98]
And in the same article he replied to Giovanardi, marshaling the philo-
logical evidence necessary to dismiss the false chronicle as a mere for-
gery. Its moment of glory had been brief indeed.

Giovanardi was undeterred. He pursued his plan to publish the entire
chronicle, quarreling with Soranzo in its footnotes.[99] Soranzo replied
once in 1917 and again in 1921.[100] But by then the debate was ending,
for in 1920 another scholar published extracts from a last and quite un-
expected source. It was a previously unknown miscellany (or *zibaldone*)
by Nicodemo Tranchedini (1411–89), Sforza's most trusted ambassador,
who had served in Florence between 1447 and 1450, when he had se-
cured Medici support for Sforza's bid to conquer Milan and been a party
to every detail of his political machinations. In his last years he had
assembled a loose collection of memoirs and historical notes, among
which was a genealogy of the illegitimate children of Francesco Sforza.
The genealogy contained a simple statement recording Polissena's death
and its cause: "Hec Pulisena . . . mortua est peste in anno 1451, Ari-
mini."[101] Although it erred by two years in assigning the death to 1451,
its testimony about the cause of death was decisive independent support
for Soranzo's thesis. The genealogy was published a second time in 1921
as the appendix to another work by Tranchedini, and in 1924 another
scholar linked the passage with the centuries-long debate on Polissena
and the recent conflict among Giovanardi, Fumi, and Soranzo. Further,
he offered an independent examination of the "Chronicle of Alessandro"
and dismissed it as "a petty forgery" ("una meschina falsificazione").[102]

For mainstream scholarship, that apparently ended the debate. Writ-
ing around 1953, P. J. Jones summarized subsequent consensus when he
noted: "It is probable that Polissena died of plague, then prevalent in
Central Italy." It was the laconic epitaph to a petty political maneuver
and a great romantic legend.[103] Yet what had been altered between 1910
and 1920 was not solely a philological problem, but an entire culture; for
with the Great War the hegemony of the liberal bourgeoisie entered a new

state of crisis. The debate about Polissena did not so much vanish as take on life in new forms.

Strange Shadows on You Tend

He envied the Renaissance, wrote Ezra Pound five months before he first saw the Tempio Malatestiano, "a period when the individual city (Italian mostly) tried to outdo its neighbour in the degree and intensity of its civilization, to be the vortex for the most living individuals." The comment is intriguing: its syntax sweeps effortlessly from "civilization" to "the most living individuals," from a social complex to an elect minority assigned a mysterious role as its creative force. "Civilisation is made by men of unusual intelligence," he had written in 1917, stating an assumption that not only conditioned his reflections on art and society but also had practical consequences for study of the past. To write history entailed a study of personality and sensibility, an exploration of the characterological depths that animated cultural development. Describing his research on Sigismondo to one correspondent, he expressed interest in "forming an historic rather than a fanciful idea of his character." To another he declared the object of his studies more bluntly: "la vie intime at Rimini."[104] Such aims inevitably required him to assess the charge that Sigismondo had murdered Polissena.

When Pound began his studies, he did not possess a narrative chronology that surveyed the development of Malatestan historiography. The order in which he encountered testimonies neither replicated their development nor proceeded backward from recent discussion to earliest testimonies in a kind of mirror image. Instead it was subject to particular constraints imposed by geography, institutional affiliations and resources, disposable time, and ideological premises. His first steps retraced the routes of a generation matured before the experience of the war, pathways formed by a network of institutions that had dominated the discussion from 1860 to 1910—elite tourism, bourgeois historicism, travel books. In February 1922 he announced that he and Dorothy were planning to tour central Italy for the first time. A month later he purchased his Baedeker for the journey.[105] Meanwhile he also took reading notes ($N\alpha$) as part of his intellectual preparation for the journey, and here too he turned to the heritage left by previous generations, consulting the works of Symonds and probably Burckhardt. When, in May 1922, he saw the church of San Francesco for the first time and wished to know more, he purchased a travel book by Antonio Beltramelli, *Un tempio d'amore* (1912).[106]

A month later at Sirmione on the Lago di Garda he composed Drafts *A* and *B*, sketches for a single Malatesta Canto. Draft *A* includes his first effort to confront the question of Polissena's murder, and it directly reflects his earliest sources. Pound, for example, reports that Sigismondo married four wives and killed the three prior to Isotta—the tradition that had evolved from Pius II (1461) to Foresti (1485–1581) to Sansovino (1582) to Symonds (1874). He states that Sigismondo had "4 wives"; that he had "lost or mislaid" three wives prior to Isotta; that Isotta (presumed the fourth) had been "patient, thru an ordeal of 3 wives" preceding her; and that their names were "Carmagnola, Ginevra, Polissena"—all claims obviously derived from Symonds (see the passage quoted in the preceding section). His stress on Isotta's patience and fidelity, on the other hand, stems from Beltramelli, who had emphasized her steadfast devotion to the wayward Sigismondo. Pound believed that Sigismondo had murdered Polissena, though apparently (here also influenced by Beltramelli) he questioned whether he had also murdered his first wife, Ginevra.[107]

Pound's interest in Polissena intersected with other thematic, historical, and ideological issues. In Draft *A*, for example, it is related to the issue of her father, Francesco Sforza, whom Pound was posing as the antagonist opposite Sigismondo Malatesta:

> *With shifty Sforza against him*
> *Sforza, Francesco, that gave*
> *him a wife, his daughter,*
> *in September,*
> *Stole Pesaro, in October,*
> *Sold the Milanese to Venice in November*
> *S Stood with the Venetians at Christmas =*
> *Condottiere to the Milanese in the spring[.]*

His earliest plan for a single Malatesta Canto, as indicated by a note near the end of this draft (line 98), was simple: "*Sigismund* = or Francesco." It called for a contrast between Sforza's concentration on affairs of state and Sigismondo's patronage of "art," between the transient and the eternal.

While still in Sirmione, Pound also assembled three sets of notes. In one (*N1*) he listed topics that he wished to explore further, among them Polissena:

d[aughter]. ~~Franc[esco]~~
Polisena. d[aughter]. ⟨*bastard*⟩ *of Francesco Sforza.*

Though its source is not clear, the note registers growing interest.[108] But to pursue it required concrete research. After sketching a list of topics, Pound began his reading notes proper (*N1*, notes 2.2, 5–31), all based on Heinrich Leo's *Storia degli stati italiani* (1840, 1842).[109] From this he assiduously recorded names, dates, battles, treaties—the sort of information that teems in Leo's exquisitely political history. But he wrote nothing about Polissena, whose murder Leo never mentions. For such details, the kind that might reveal "la vie intime," Pound would have to turn elsewhere. Consequently he assembled a second group of notes (*N2*), this time using Leo's footnotes to cull bibliographical information for future research. Some were directly relevant to the issue of Polissena. One, for example, reads (*N2*, 9): *Chronica Riminesi.*[110] Leo, of course, was citing the city's anonymous chronicle from the fifteenth century as published by Muratori in 1729—the only edition published before 1922, and so also the only edition available to Pound. (As a result, Pound would miss the rich footnotes of the modern edition, published in 1924, which recorded the recent debate among Soranzo, Fumi, and Giovanardi.)[111] Others also noted sources pertinent to the murder accusation, for example (*N2*, 6): *Pio II Aeneas Silvius Piccolomini. letters.* Or again (*N2*, 11): *Clementi[ni].* *"Istoria de' Malatesta."*[112] Both these books were difficult to locate. The editions of Pius II were incunabula, the volumes of Clementini extremely rare.[113] Yet evidence suggests that Pound intended to buy them if possible, for above his list he wrote: *Small cheap vols. = (5 l[ire].).* And a week later another aide-mémoire was added to the same manuscript, consisting of directions for finding the bookstore of the Milanese publisher Ulrico Hoepli, written when Pound paused in the city in late June en route to Paris.[114] But such books were available only through the rare book market, and Pound was obliged to wait until he was back in Paris and could consult them in the Bibliothèque Nationale. As a stopgap measure he left a standing order at Hoepli for any works concerning Sigismondo Malatesta or Malatestan Rimini.

Pound returned to Paris on Sunday, 2 July 1922. Though he soon informed one correspondent that he planned to read "contemporary commentators" on the Malatestan vicissitudes, the first weeks of July left him little time to pursue his studies.[115] Only during the second half of the month did he begin frequenting the Bibliothèque Nationale: by 17 July he was perusing a medieval chronicle of Ancona,[116] and by 19 July beginning Pietro-Maria Amiani's history of the city of Fano (1751), reading that he described the next day in a letter: "This big book on Fano seems to think he [Sigismondo] was merely engaged to the Carmagnola; the Este girl ⟨*his second.*⟩ was one of a lot of quadruplets, two of whom died."[117] Pound was beginning to sense that a mistake had arisen regarding the number of Sigismondo's wives, and that his engagement to the daughter of Carmagnola had never issued in marriage (though Pound still referred to Ginevra d'Este as "the second," rather than "first" wife). But this was just the beginning.

Amiani's was not the only work that Pound was reading. On 21 July he informed his wife of another discovery:

> I shall write to Neumayer [the London bookseller]; but can you go into Ellis, Bond St., Quairitch [*sic*], just by your club, and Sunderland or Sutherland (branch office Piccadilly) ⟨*near Wing.*⟩ (haven't their precise addresses), and ask them for, or ask them to track
>
> > Yriarte "La vie d'un condottiere italien au XV siecle"
> > pub. in 1882 (in Paris, editeur I think ⟨,⟩ Rothschild,
> >   now out of business, and book epuisé.
>
> No rush, just when you happen to be passing the shops.[118]

Pound, it is clear, had discovered Yriarte's 1882 biography of Sigismondo. Since as yet he did not own a copy, he took reading notes ($N\beta$) on it from the copy in the Bibliothèque Nationale. The notes were vague and perfunctory, provisional measures until his own copy arrived from London.[119] Meanwhile, eager to make headway on his poem as well as his research, he revised his initial Drafts *A* and *B*, creating a single canto into which he could later integrate new information as it arrived. The result was Draft *C1*, a version that minimizes historical data and stresses hieratic links between the cultures of medieval Provence and Malatestan Rimini. The procedure entailed certain limits: details were slighted, and when he revised the passage on Polissena, he repeated the material from Draft *A* but omitted her name (*C1*, 24–26):

> *married three wives   who died* =
> > *or were buried* = *or* ~~rejected~~ ⟨*sent home*⟩ =
> *X   ,   Y   ,   Z   .*

A few days later he revised this version, producing Drafts *C2* and *C3*. Once more he touched upon the death of Polissena: but for the first time he no longer spoke of her as the "third" wife, or of "three wives" preceding Isotta; now their legal status was left unspecified and new details about their lives were added:

> La Carmagnola, repudiated,
> Ginevra d'Este, died in the swamp, con voce di veleno,
> Francesco's daughter, died in the swamp, con voce di veleno[.]

This was a novel assertion, the claim that both Ginevra and Polissena had "died in the swamp." It stemmed not from a tradition concerning Polissena, but a particular subtradition concerning Ginevra, the first wife, which is so distinctive that there is little doubt that Pound was also reading a third book in Paris, Edward Hutton's 1906 novel.[120] Hutton vigorously denied the traditional accusation of murder, and his denial was now juxtaposed with the conflicting accounts of Amiani and Yriarte (the latter attributed the allegations about Ginevra to "une sourde rumeur" that had arisen immediately after her death). Pound was beginning to entertain doubts about the time-worn charges. In *C3* they are no longer reported as events, but as allegations spoken by a chorus of rumor—vague, accusatory, and foreboding.

Pound's researches changed radically after he finally obtained his copy of Yriarte's book on 3 August 1922.[121] His intense reading of the book is registered in numerous forms: 150 entries of marginalia and submarginalia in his own copy of the book, over 120 reading notes collected in six manuscripts, and eight draft fragments translating various poems that Yriarte had attributed to Sigismondo (on the poems see chapter 3). One marginal marking regards the charge that Sigismondo had poisoned his first wife, Ginevra d'Este:[122]

> L'histoire se fait l'écho de ces soupçons; Aeneas Sylvius Piccolomini, que devint le Pape Pie II, admet le crime; il en a fait un des chefs d'accusation du procés instruit au Vatican contre celui qui avait été son capitaine général. Fra Filippo de Bergame, un contemporain, dans son *"Supplé-*
>
> ?! *ment aux chroniques,"* n'hésite point à regarder Malatesta comme coupable; et enfin Clementini, historien austère, partage aussi cette croyance.

By now Pound was plainly sceptical about the charge regarding the first wife, Ginevra; and though he entered nothing opposite the passages concerning Polissena, it is clear that his doubts were growing.

Yet much of Yriarte's importance for Pound lay less in his specific arguments or discussions—which were confused and confusing—than in his vast mélange of citations and references to earlier authors. The pace of Pound's research was accelerating. Through Yriarte he rediscovered the major history of Rimini published by Cesare Clementini in 1617 and 1627. He also recorded the correct title of Pius's *Commentarii*, came upon Battaglini's biography of Sigismondo (1794), and noted carefully that a copy of Mazzuchelli (1759) was available at the Bibliothèque Na-

tionale in Paris (BNP).[123] Finally, he was deeply intrigued by references
to the mysterious chronicle of "Alessandro" (though for reasons more
connected with Isotta than with Polissena).[124] And except for the chron-
icle of pseudo-Alessandro (published only in a journal not available at
the BNP), he would eventually read all these works. But because he
never attempted to collate the various accounts of Polissena's death, or
any other event among the many connected with Sigismondo, he devel-
oped only a limited sense of the relations among various testimonies—
their historical evolution, their chronological and ideological interaction.
Instead he sought an account that would coincide with his own intuitions,
and as the month of August 1922 wore on, he began to find it.

Spurred by Yriarte's citations, around the second week of August
Pound began reading Clementini's history of Rimini, using the copy con-
served in the BNP. Among his papers is a BNP call slip ("bulletin de
commande") from 1922; it is filled out by Pound and registers the BNP
shelf mark for volume 2.[125] Once more Pound was taking extensive notes,
and not surprisingly one concerned the death of Polissena:

> *Polixena dies.*
> *2 June 1449.*
> *1ST September*
> *Sigismundo ⇌ governatore of Venetian armies*
>
> *⇌*
> *don't attack Francesco Sforza*
> *Francesco Sforza gets Milan ⇌   friends with Sigismondo afterwards ⇌*
> *[because of some natural sympathy]*
> *Suspended judgment.*
> *Sforza enters Milan. 26 February 1450.*

(The square brackets are Pound's.) The note offers several novelties. One
is small, yet significant: for the first time Pound spells the name of Polis-
sena with an *x:* Polixena. The spelling is clearly his own invention, for
Clementini always spells it with a double *s*. Indeed, glancing back at all
the passages cited earlier in this chapter, one sees that *every* document
contemporary with Polissena spelled her name with one *s* or with two.[126]
The issue is not, of course, whether Pound's spelling is "correct" accord-
ing to prescriptive rules or the actual practice of quattrocento writers, but
rather that it makes an implicit claim to mimic quattrocento practice
when it is really an invention by Pound. In miniature, yet concretely,
such a passage manifests the way in which Pound adopts the trappings of
positivist fidelity to primary sources even when engaged in a reading of

much later, quite secondary sources. In all subsequent writings he would spell the name this way.

More important, Pound notes Clementini's report of two related charges: Simonetta's, that Sigismondo had avoided battle with Sforza in 1449 for fear of reprisal; and another writer's, that the two condottieri had acted in collusion, as demonstrated by their amicable relations in later years ("friends with Sigismondo afterwards").[127] He then inserts his own speculation, "because of some natural sympathy," and finally reaches a conclusion partly his own and partly his interpretation of Clementini's ("suspended judgement"). It is a comment that indicates a larger shift in his reading of the Malatestan vicissitudes, a shift that stemmed from still further researches.

Pound's notes on Clementini extend over a period of several weeks; they are contained in six sets, and cover hundreds of entries. They record not only numerous historical incidents and anecdotes, but also his daily work in the Bibliothèque Nationale—and the growing pressure of incompatible interpretive demands. Much of this pressure stemmed from a single book, Giovanni Soranzo's monograph, *Pius II and Italian Politics in the Struggle Against the Malatesta (Pio II e la politica italiana nella lotta contro i Malatesti,* 1911). When Pound had visited the Hoepli bookstore in Milan (30 June or 1 July) he had left a standing order for materials connected with Rimini, an order that yielded its first results on 21 July: "Hoepli has found a book on ole Sforza, and got the one on the politic of Pio II contra i Malatesti."[128] Pound swiftly confirmed his order for Ermolao Rubieri's two-volume biography of Francesco Sforza, and Soranzo's monograph, both of which reached him eight days later, on 29 July: "Three vols. on Sig. arrived this a.m. from Milan, one evid. exc., but apparently mostly political; nothing yet about la vie intime at Rimini."[129] Pound was just beginning to read Soranzo's book, as his letter indicates ("nothing *yet*"), and evidently he took considerable time to complete it. He was a slow reader; it was not until 28 July, for example, that he had "finished the S[igismondo]. part in the two big vols. on Fano" by Amiani, meaning that he had read only some eighty pages in eight days.[130] Also, his social life at this time was especially full, typically leaving only a few hours in the afternoon to read. And his reading of Soranzo overlapped with his reading of the other book sent by Hoepli, Rubieri's biography of Sforza. Both books, however, were altering his view of Sigismondo's career. Rubieri, on the one hand, offered a sympathetic account of Francesco Sforza that blurred the dichotomy essential to Pound's initial conception of the story, *Sigismund* ⇌ *or Francesco,* as he reported to one correspondent soon after its arrival: "Francesco Sforza, whom I had first cast for the villa[i]n seems also to have had good reason for etc. etc. At any rate I have had some interesting hours of research or at least reading. . . ."[131] Soranzo, on the other hand, offered a different dichotomy that reshaped his entire conception of Sigismondo's fate. One can sense its first effect among the reading notes that Pound began taking (ca. 10 August) as he started perusing Soranzo in earnest. Among them is one on the oration delivered in January 1461 by Andrea Benzi, a crucial source for the murder allegation:[132]

16 January '61 ⇌ *A. Benzi invective*
denied the temporal power

Implicitly, Pound no longer assesses the allegation in relation to Francesco Sforza, but in relation to the ideological motives of Pius II. This change, which occurred gradually throughout the month of August, was accelerated when Pound became aware of Soranzo's earlier articles from 1910–11, references that he followed up while reading Clementini at the BNP. In the middle of his notes on Clementini (ca. 25 August) appears a sudden rupture: in large letters that consume the entire page, Pound records the 1910–11 articles and their BNP shelf mark.[133] His eagerness is almost palpable. Their effect, in combination with Soranzo's book, was decisive; on 29 August he wrote to his wife: "Have been doing more Sigismondo. Most of the crimes seem to be in an accusation drawn up by papal lawyer when Pius II wanted to grab Rimini for his nephew."[134]

Soranzo, we have seen, had dismissed all the accusations, stressing that every testimony adduced by Pius "derived from *malicious gossip* that was current among the vulgar, or from *public rumor,* very instable grounds for accusation" (italics mine).[135] Influenced now by Soranzo and Clementini, yet still responsive to the tradition that he had already registered in his earlier drafts, Pound needed time to resolve his doubts. In early September he wrote another draft (*D1*) welding together all the conflicting views. It contains three passages that treat the alleged murder of Polissena. One suggests the critical influence of Soranzo: here the charges are rehearsed in their traditional form, echoing his earliest drafts, but are prefaced by a crucial comment about their origins—they are "slander."[136]

all this in a welter of slander
"con voce di veleno" ~~when~~ Ginevra dies,

"with a bit of pillow he done it", ⟨*thus in*⟩ Polixena's case,
And ~~la Carmignola's~~ ⟨*the*⟩ dot? ⟨*for la Carmagnola refunded ⇋ no ⇋*⟩

Another passage attempts to integrate Polissena's death into a chronolog-
ical structure derived from his reading of Clementini, placing it after
Sigismondo's victory over Alfonso of Aragon in 1448:

> and, he beat Aragon, with a smaller army,
> and dr[o]ve him out of the Florentine land,
> ~~and Polixena died next June,~~

And a third reverts to the earlier structure, treating all three women to-
gether:

> Carmagnola, dead in Venice, Este's girl, dead, with suspicions,
> ⟨Frank⟩ Sforza's daughter, third shot of Sigismondo's.

Clearly this was confusing, and as an alternative he attempted another
draft that was a straightforward and crude verification of his notes on
Clementini:[137]

> (Polixena died that June)
> And September
>   he is the Venetian's chief,
> and hesitates:
>   Francesco is unattached.
> (with rumour . . .
>   say for a natural sympathy,
> some say from fear (Polixena's death ~~being~~ unsolved)
> ~~but~~ or from simple error, misjudging the temper of the Milanese.
> And in cold February, Sforza ~~enters~~ ⟨*is in*⟩ Milan.

Here Pound attempts to develop a tonal counterpoint emphasizing dis-
crepancies between the terse narrative ("Polixena died that June") and
the untrustworthy modulations of rumor ("say for a natural sympathy" or
"some say from fear"). He wants to report the charges, yet underscore his
growing disbelief in them. But the effect is too blurred, and he must try
again. One solution is a narrative that stresses the limitations of its point
of view, highlighting the narrator's subjectivity by localizing him as fully
as possible. In Draft *E* he tries this, selecting Sigismondo's brother as the
narrator:

> Polixena died about then
> and the next year in September, my brother signed with the Venetians, (49.)
> but missed fire somehow,

perhaps a mere error, they said he was scared of Francesco.
          ~~the two always~~
But at any rate he didn't attack.
          And ~~papa~~ wattlenose
took Milan. ⟨*cold February.*⟩ 1450,
He cd. always win in an intrigue.

Though it eliminates authorial speculation about "natural sympathy" between Sforza and Sigismondo, the new draft is also weak, at once too specific and too vague. The tone is colloquial and local ("missed fire," "at any rate," and "papa wattlenose"), whereas the report vanishes in a fog ("*about* then," "perhaps," "they said").[138] The problem was much deeper, and had to do with with the structural position of Polissena in the drama of civilization.

Pound encountered difficulty in altering his treatment of Polissena for reasons embedded in his work from the outset. Already in Drafts *A* and *B*, he had taken views of the Malatestan story that were essentially incompatible. In one (*B*) he had presented the subject in ethical-religious terms centered on the church of San Francesco, its status as a "temple of love." In the other (*A*) he had emphasized a more secular, basically political, conflict between Sigismondo and Sforza, terms less charged with moral resonance and less amenable to a holistic view of "civilization" such as Pound wished to suggest. Soranzo's work provided a means of mediating these polarities. His arguments that the traditional charges were false, among them that of murdering Polissena, transformed the cast of characters, so that the antagonist opposite Sigismondo was no longer Sforza, but Pius II. In particular, Soranzo's claim in *Pio II* that the pope had been motivated by self-interest enabled Pound to reconsider the Malatestan story through the prism of the nineteenth-century experience with capitalism and materialism, the experience that had reached its culmination in the Great War. Consider a draft fragment from October 1922:

> Then replied Pio Secundo, ⟨*speaking like*⟩ like the shits in our ⟨*own*⟩ day,
> Not that he wanted land for his family or that
>   Sigismundo was a murderer, but
> that he disprized the religion, and was guilty of heresy
>   a religion (a bag of lies)
> [. . .]
>   religion. (i.e. papal monopoly)

Here the effect of Soranzo's arguments on Pound is striking.[139] It enables him to retain the dichotomy that had repeatedly structured earlier debate about the charges, yet to invert the evaluation that had attached to its poles. Until now liberal culture had seen a reflection of itself in the secular reasoning and self-interest that it attributed to Sigismondo, and which it invoked in his defense against the accusations transmitted by ecclesiastical tradition. Now, however, it is Pius II—by rights the voice of spiritual orthodoxy—whose accusations are unmasked to reveal secular and material interests ("he wanted land for his family"), notwithstanding their religious terms ("that he disprized the religion"); while it is the mundane and courtly culture of Rimini, accused of nurturing an amoral sensualism, that turns out to be charged with spiritual values—the kind of values Pound had discerned in Provençal poetry: "a cult for the purgation of the soul by a refinement of . . . the senses" (*SR*, 90). In other words, the structural role of each figure has been shifted, and the effect is ambiguous: the monument of civilization is conserved, yet also assumes an accusatory dimension. Or in slightly different terms, its very conservation is effected *by* its transformation into a site of resistance *against* the liberal understanding of it. The vicissitudes of Sigismondo are no longer ambiguities in the genealogy of bourgeois culture, but a rebellious and contestatory gesture directed against it. And this gesture is both dehistoricized and rehistoricized. On the one hand, it is merged into a timeless war of spiritual vision against material interest; on the other hand, it is offered as a drama that defines the crisis of contemporary Europe ("in our own day"). In effect, the secular reading of the monument established by liberal tradition is retained, and in this respect preserved, but it is also invested with spiritual values that turn it into a rebellious critique of the very culture that engendered it.

At the crossroad of these conflicting impulses stands the figure of Polissena Sforza, and hence arise Pound's difficulties with the passage concerning her. In the liberal understanding, denial of the murder allegation meant an affirmation of civic and secular culture, and its natural collocation was therefore a worldly setting in which human activities proceed by rational and identifiable motives—the struggle for territorial gain and dominance epitomized in the shifting alliances between Sforza and Sigismondo, in which their continued amicability underscores a common understanding of how the game is played. But in the reformulation articulated by Pound, denial of the murder charge is welded to a rejection of the purely secular culture of liberal man, and its natural collocation becomes the terrain of the sacred, the church of San Francesco itself. The subsequent revisions all tend to bring the report of Polissena's death closer and closer to a report of the Tempio's construction, as emerges in a draft produced in November:

```
        and he began building the tempio,
    And then Polixena died,
    and my brother missed fire somehow
    it was for the Venetians,
                against ~~old~~ Sforza ~~at~~ by Brianza
    and he went over the Adda, and worried Francesco
    but without ever really attacking,
    and the old fox nipped into Milan.
                                In February of '50
```

Pound, by now, was convinced that he understood the charges concerning Polissena.[140] When he revised the entire sequence of three cantos between 10 December 1922 and 5 January 1923 (Draft *W*), the new passage on Polissena followed the previous version verbatim, merely executing the changes he had indicated earlier (cancellation of "old" and substitution of "by" for "at").

On 5 January 1923 Pound left Paris for Italy. After staying in Rapallo for a month, he made brief trips to Pisa (7–11 February) and Orbetello (12–15 February), and then Rome (15–16 February). On 17 February he submitted his request for admission to the Vatican Archive.[141] He began working there in earnest on Monday, 19 February: his notes for that day show him reading the 1614 edition of Pius II's *Commentarii*, the one that omitted the charges about Polissena. More important was his reading of the oration recited by Benzi in 1461, as printed in its only edition by Mittarelli (1779); it is his last contact with a primary source for the murder of Polissena:

> *strangled Polixena*
> *"although no cause for death was found afterward."*
> *(Sigismondo on other side of the peninsula.)*
>
> =
>
> *H Good franciscans had heard*
> *~~his~~ confession, and he then*
> *tortured them* ⤟
>
> ==   ==
>
> *~~Demanded a secret marriage~~*
> *Sigismondo demanded*
> *secrets not only of wife but*
> *of other women*
> *   from Franciscans.*

It was his most extensive examination of a primary source, and it shows how thoroughly he had internalized the arguments Soranzo had leveled against the charges raised in the oration.[142] Against the claim that Sigismondo himself had committed the deed, Pound immediately points out that Sigismondo was known to be elsewhere. It is Soranzo's 1910–11 argument and suffers from the same weakness as before: not taking into account the other letter of 1462, it cannot address Sforza's charge that the murder was actually committed by an accomplice. But for Pound, it is clear, by now the issue was closed.

Pound left Rome on 1 March, and for the next six weeks he continued his tour of Italian archives and libraries: Florence, Bologna, Modena, Cesena, San Marino, Pennabilli, Fano, Pesaro, Urbino, Rimini, Ravenna, Venice, and Milan.[143] In Rimini, on 23 March, he examined the 1487 edition of Pius II's *Epistolae*, which contains the bull incorporating the earlier oration (*Discipula veritatis*). This time he recorded nothing about the alleged murder; all that he wanted he had already noted in Rome.[144]

In Milan, between 9 and 13 April, Pound also examined some thirty-five letters in the Archivio di stato, though he never encountered the minutes of 1462 from Sforza to Ottone del Carretto, whose existence remained unknown to him. Also while in Milan, Pound sought to pay tribute to the man whose arguments had so affected his understanding of the Malatestan vicissitudes, especially his view of the alleged murder of Polissena. In Rome he had secured a letter of introduction to Giovanni Soranzo, who was now teaching at the Università cattolica of Milan. Pound planned to visit him, but apparently failed, missing perhaps his last opportunity to come across the minute of 23 August 1462. Still, one may wonder whether encountering it would have made any difference; the weakness of Soranzo's arguments could be detected only by a close collation of its sources in Amiani and Nolfi, a project that Pound was scarcely disposed to undertake at this late date.[145]

In the course of his travels Pound also wrote several draft fragments incorporating the new materials he had encountered in his research. From 15 to 18 March he was in Pesaro and Fano, cities that had been a part of the Malatestan domains, and momentarily he entertained an entirely new passage on the question of Polissena's death:

> *She was Frank Sforza's daughter*
> *and Fred Urbino had married her sister*
> *and I had married her sister—*
>
> =
> *and they ~~had~~ cashed in the dot*
> *~~and~~ S Gismondo's second wife*

and his first ~~old~~ an Este ⚊
of the old Sultan Nicolò
⚊ *quasi una famiglia*

The new fragment reverted to the earlier narrative structure in which the story was told by Sigismondo's brother, Novello, and it reflected Pound's growing familiarity with genealogical details gleaned from his studies.[146] But it was left stranded when, about a week later as Pound was momentarily unoccupied in Rimini, he reverted to the Watson typescript, or *W*, the typescript previously prepared in Paris. Returning to *W* meant that Pound could no longer introduce new materials at will, and instead was obliged to focus on changes of detail and nuance. His cumulative revisions were entered on Draft *X*. As before, the passage on Polissena was prefaced by a brief allusion to the church of San Francesco, but now there was much less effort to link her death with the desultory conduct of the 1449 campaign against Sforza:

> and it "saved the Florentine state"
> (rem eorum saluauit)
> And he began building the tempio,
> And then Polixena died, Polixena Sforza,
> ~~and old Visconti, and the~~
> And that year the Venetians sent down an ambassador
> saying, speak to him humanely. And old Visconti
> Finished his run. . . .

Not much later Pound added two layers of light revision to this entire draft, in blue ink and pencil,[147] when he came to the line on Polissena he concentrated solely on its style (alterations in blue ink are indicated by [b]; alterations in pencil by [p]):

And ~~then~~[b] Polixena ⟨~~Sforza~~⚊⟩[b] ⟨*his second wife*⟩[p] died, ~~Polixena Sforza,~~[b]

A few days after this he typed up a "final" version that would incorporate both layers of revision; now he altered the line that preceded the one on Polissena:

> And he ~~began buil~~ was ~~bul~~ building the TEMPIO
> And Polixena his second wife, died,

To this typescript Pound added one last set of alterations, which punctuated the aside on Polissena more explicitly and closed the sentence:[148]

> And he ~~began buil~~ was ~~bul~~ building the TEMPIO
> And Polixena⟨,⟩ his second wife, died, ⟨.⟩

It was not until the proof stage that Pound made three final changes. In the line that announced the Tempio's construction he restored his original reading ("began building") in place of his revision ("was building"); to the same line he also added a comma after "TEMPIO" to eliminate ambiguity concerning the object of the verb "building"; and in the line that reported Polissena's death, he changed the initial letter of "and" from upper to lower case. The making of the line on Polissena was finished:

> And he began building the TEMPIO,
> and Polixena, his second wife, died.

In its final version, the sentence posits a counterpoint of beginning and perishing, a contrast between the Tempio's birth and Polissena's death, between Sigismondo's active creation and Polissena's passive submission to the laws of nature. It epitomizes a dichotomy central to the Malatesta Cantos and to Pound's thought, a dichotomy informing his concept of civilization, his reading of the Malatestan vicissitudes, and his practice of historical study. At its center is an assumption implicit in his characterization of the Renaissance: "a period when the individual city . . . tried to outdo its neighbour in the degree and intensity of its civilization, to be the vortex for the most living individuals." Civilization, for Pound, consists not in a network of institutions or web of social structures, but in the constructive activity of "the most living individuals," or "men of unusual intelligence." Social institutions may be its necessary or material causes, but they are never sufficient ones. Beyond them is always a core that is fundamental, irreducible, and independent of social considerations or historical attributes, a core that resides in the mysterious creative force of an elect minority, and that Pound sometimes terms "unusual intelligence," "genius," or often, "intensity." The value of this force is secured through its links to metaphysical and anthropological premises: it is assumed that change, dynamics, and innovation are essential characteristics of the universe, and that their reflex is a creative impulse innate in human life and oriented towards the furtherance of life's dynamics (even if embodied in only a handful of individuals). Its function, therefore, is essential, but it is also abstract and in this sense resistant to more concrete aims. Responding to a basic need of the human situation, it is its own justification and is not required to meet more mundane notions of pragmatic function. When Pound touches on Sigismondo's motives for constructing the church of San Francesco, he can only praise what he terms its "beautiful inutility." [149] The church is not viewed as an expression of conventional piety or dynastic glorification culminating in the rule of Sigismondo; it has no content at all, in the ordinary sense. Rather it marks the patron's "intensity" and status as one of "the most living individuals." Its real significance consists not in culturally sanctioned meanings (orthodox devotion, say, or dynastic propaganda), but in the fact of its having been invested with meaning by Sigismondo, an act whose value is finally indistinguishable from the drives and motivations of his personality: whence Pound's wish to study "la vie intime," to form "an historical . . . idea of his character."

It is in this single act alone—"he began building"—that Sigismondo's career acquires meaning, articulates its raison d'être, and is consecrated by virtue of its essential harmony with the imperatives of life: "make it new." And it is this act that constitutes the ground of his difference from Polissena. For her life conforms not to the universal imperatives of change and creation, but to socially sanctioned codes of conduct. It is, in this sense, an existence wholly secular in character, one that neither hears nor heeds the call for innovation. The major moments of her life follow the paths set by established institutions: her marriage to Sigismondo obeys the laws of state, not the drives of Eros; their children are born from dynastic necessity, not individual passion. In the end the report of her death registers less a change in her existence and more the state in which it was passed. What at first sight appears to be a denial of the charge that Sigismondo murdered Polissena turns out to be something more, a reversal of the accusation. It is not Sigismondo who violated the sacred imperative of life, but Polissena, who simply "died."

The Whited Sepulchre

The Malatesta Cantos were first published in July 1923 in the fourth issue of T. S. Eliot's *Criterion,* a quarterly whose total circulation numbered six hundred copies.[150] Eighteen months later they appeared in the first collected edition of *The Cantos,* titled *A Draft of XVI. Cantos.* The volume was a deluxe edition issued in Paris in ninety copies and available only by subscription. (On this edition see chapter 3.) Five years later, in 1930, a second collected edition was published, this one also issued in Paris in an exiguous number of copies (212).[151] Such numbers suggest its appeal to a small, prosperous cultural aristocracy, one largely familiar with the cultural monuments surveyed in its imagined tour. Consider the publisher of the 1930 edition, Nancy Cunard, daughter of the shipping magnate Sir Bache Cunard. Her income derived from a trust fund, enabling her to travel throughout the Continent and experience the artistic heritage of a specific cultural itinerary. The routes, by now, will be familiar: in autumn 1922 she was in Italy, and in her contemporary letters to Pound she requested his advice on which monuments to visit in each city of the peninsula, including Rimini and Ravenna. Cunard, in return, purchased books for Pound and transcribed materials intended as resources for his composition of the Malatesta Cantos.[152] In February 1923 she met with him in Pisa, where they visited a bust once thought to represent Isotta degli Atti.[153] Publisher and poet, in short, moved in a homogeneous world of elite tourism and understood the shared premises of bourgeois historicism.

It was a decade after their composition and initial publication that the Malatesta Cantos became more widely accessible. In 1933 *A Draft of XXX Cantos* was published in one thousand copies in the United States, fifteen hundred copies in England, the first collected edition by a mainstream publisher. In part it traced a cultural historical shift in process: initially *The Cantos* had been formed at a conjuncture of elite tourism and the historicist tendency of high bourgeois culture, the heritage of leisured readers acquainted with a specific geographical and cultural itinerary. Rimini, after all, had steadily attracted German and English tourism since 1860, and interest in the city's monumental heritage was a staple of English bourgeois cultural life in the period 1880–1914. The English audience still dominated plans for the 1933 edition, comprising 60 percent of its anticipated readership; yet to some degree it epitomized a world already vanishing in the wake of the Great Depression, one that would perish forever after World War II. The premises of elite historicism that had nourished the production of *The Cantos*, even if the work had also contested their ideological underpinnings, were the common property of a shrinking cultural collectivity.

When the Malatesta Cantos were republished in the next (or fourth) collected edition of 1948, they appeared in a world utterly transformed. The new edition was initiated by an American publisher, New Directions, and the Anglo-American ratios of its anticipated readership were reversed: 64 percent American, 36 percent English. Equally important, the sixty-two-year-old poet was confined in St. Elizabeths hospital in Washington, D.C., having been declared mentally unfit to stand trial on charges of treason. The trajectory of the Malatesta Cantos was converging with the salient events of twentieth-century history, World War II and the Holocaust. It was also converging with a massive spatio-temporal and sociocultural shift, the new dominance of an American readership that stemmed from increasingly heterogeneous social strata. These trends were further accelerated by the massive expansion of higher education in

the postwar years. The new editions were a vast quotation of the earlier
texts, but the relationship of frame and inset was no longer anchored in a
set of shared pragmatic implications, a body of conventions and interests
derived from a common cultural formation. For new readers the issues
raised by the Malatesta Cantos were far less familiar. To many they
seemed alien or simply exotic, and most found themselves lost in a laby-
rinth of references. Each reference, moreover, was now doubled: what
had vanished was partly a certain familiarity with a background of knowl-
edge and beliefs about specific events between 1440 and 1460; but it was
partly the sociocultural premises that had nurtured that familiarity, the
very preconditions for constituting the original events into "facts."

Well-intentioned readers sought to aid one another by providing an-
notations for *The Cantos*. But their plans were formulated at a specific
moment in scholarly history, the apogee of New Criticism, when the idea
of annotations was suspect indeed. The result was a problematic heritage
epitomized in commentaries on the line about Polissena Sforza. The first
set of glosses appeared in 1955, prepared by Robert Mayo (then at North-
western University) for a journal printed in mimeographed copies (telling
testimony of Pound's status at that time); its crude typography spilled
across the page:

> 57. Polixena—the natural daughter of Count Francesco
> Sforza (v. lines 16–29, gloss). Polissena died in 1449,
> and Sigismondo was accused by Pius II and others of stran-
> gling her. This charge received some general credence. The
> circumstances of her death were highly dubious, and she
> had by some years outlived her usefulness. Moreover, it
> would be telling revenge upon her father, Sigismondo's
> former ally (v. the quotation from Hutton, in the gloss
> which follows). Pound's spelling of Polissena's name is an
> "antique" form.

In the next entry was the promised quotation from Hutton (brackets are
Mayo's):

> men have not hesitated to say that the reason why Sigis-
> mondo did not attack Sforza on the Adda in December [1449]
> was to be found in this [alleged] murder [of Polissena],
> asserting that he feared if he fell into Sforza's hands he
> would pay for it with his life (p. 196).

It was Simonetta's old charge (ca. 1475), though without indication of its
genesis or transmission.[154] These had now been obscured, erased by the
misleading reference to Hutton.

A second volume of annotations for Pound's work appeared in 1957, the *Annotated Index to the CANTOS of Ezra Pound* by Edwards and Vasse.[155] Now the format was typescript pages printed by photographic reproduction at the University of California Press, leaving a ragged right margin to signal the project's (and the poet's) equivocal support:

```
[Sforza, Polissena]: 8/32; 9/35: d. 1449, natural daughter
   of Francesco SFORZA; in 1441 Sigismondo MALATESTA married
   her to cement his alliance with Sforza; eight years later
   she died, believed to have been poisoned by Sigismondo.
```

In 1980 a third set of annotations for *The Cantos* was furnished by Carroll F. Terrell, again published by the University of California.[156] The new work sported an elaborate format of double columns justified right and left:

23.   Polixena: Polissena Sforza, natural daughter of Francesco Sforza. Sigismondo married her barely a year after the death of his first wife in return for her father's promise to help him regain Pesaro. In the following year she bore Sigismundo a son who died in his first year. Sigismondo abandoned her for his successive mistresses Vanetta Toschi and Isotta degli Atti. When the plague was ravaging Rimini in 1449, she fled to the Convent of Scolca in the hills where she choked to death one night and was hastily buried in an unmarked grave; it may thus be inferred that she fell victim to the plague. Ten years later Pius II accused Sigismundo of having strangled her [cf. 8:26, 40; 10:23].

The annotations, inevitably, were characterized by numerous discrepancies and omissions. The earliest suggested that the murder charge might be true (its author apparently knew neither the Soranzo articles of 1910–11 nor the subsequent debate) and ratified the implicit suggestion that the spelling "Polixena" was "an 'antique' form" (though without having checked a single testimony). The second rehearsed the charge that Polissena had "been *poisoned* by Sigismondo," although the more typical version was that she had been strangled. The third, however, was especially curious. It claimed a special status for its historical range and depth, and even credited one scholar with "correct[ing] a number of errors" in the earlier annotations, asserting that she "possesse[d] information known only to her."[157] In practice, however, it proved remarkably misleading. Nothing in the 1441 marriage contract warranted its claim that Sforza had "promise[d] to help" Sigismondo "regain Pesaro" when he married Polissena. (Indeed, since Pesaro was "lost" only in 1445, it would have required unusual clairvoyance to issue a promise of this sort in 1441.) No primary document stated that Polissena had "fled to the Convent of Scolca in the hills," or that she had died there. (Both were fabrications by Yriarte in 1882, subsequently transmitted to others.)[158] No quattrocento document transmitted the time of death so precisely ("one night"), specified its manner so nicely ("choked to death"), or reported an interment so heart-rending ("buried in an unmarked grave"). On the contrary, the anonymous chronicler of Rimini had recorded a lavish funeral, held in Rimini at the church of San Francesco, conducted by a bishop and attended by all the clergy of the town—just a ghoulish exercise, suggested the modern annotators. However insignificant in themselves, the mistakes in all three were symptomatic of a larger failure to maintain a critical distance from the subject; instead, scholars tended to replicate assumptions and priorities suggested by the poem, to internalize and represent its stylistic hierarchies as historical verities. The process extended to the most minute details: every annotation reported the date when Polissena "died," but none could indicate the year of her birth. And it affected the treatment of larger questions. Reflecting Pound's view that Pius II was responsible for Sigismondo's demise, the annotations excoriated the dead pope: "his references to Sigismondo were characteristically vulgar," reported one; his style was "pompously distended" with "rhetorical excesses," chided another.[159]

Some mistakes, plainly, were a result of scholars grappling with a confusing mass of heterogeneous materials that presented formidable problems at the basic level of conducting research. The overall pattern, however, was less a consequence of specific problems with local tasks than of assumptions about what the task was, presuppositions about scope, focus, relevance, and procedures that stemmed from the New Criticism. New Criticism, to be sure, has always been a problematic term: as used here it designates neither a school nor a homogeneous group, but a set of critical attitudes and practices often shared by the wider community of modern literary studies; it is used, therefore, in a weak rather than a strong sense. In some cases the annotators explicitly stated their premises. Vasse and Edwards, for example, explained their aims by invoking I. A. Richards's concepts of denotation and connotation:

> Annotations have been kept brief. We have wanted to give the basic information, not Pound's use of that information, in order to let *the poetry demonstrate its own purposes*. This is a guide to the poem, not a substitute for it. We have sought to establish the denotative center. (My italics.)[160]

Another was equally forthright. He sought to facilitate "literary criticism," which meant "to consider the work . . . as an object of art." This aim, however, was endangered by the "extraordinary and wide-ranging fields of reference" embedded in *The Cantos*, fields "quite outside the tradition in which literary scholars have been trained.[161] At best, "fields of reference" were a blemish that the cosmetics of annotation could dissemble; at worst they were a potential source of instability encroaching on the aesthetic domain, the "object of art." The annotation was intended to restore the proper boundaries by consigning them to their place in the background—making them harmonize with "the tradition in which literary scholars have been trained," a tradition based on the binary opposition between content and form, extrinsic data and intrinsic language. The annotation was intended not to provide "facts," but to defuse their troublesome presence by containing them in an illusory immutability. Only so could the poem "demonstrate its own purposes," assume its true status as an "object of art," and harmonize with "the tradition in which literary scholars have been trained." Naïve positivism was not an antagonist of New Criticism, but its complement and precondition. What threatened either one was something more complicated, more fractured and complex: history and text in an unstable dynamics of transmission privileging neither the imperatives of the present nor the immutability of the past. Here, in this reciprocal economy of exclusion, New Critical theory recapitulated the premises of Pound's work in a more important sense, one converging with the formative moments of modern textual and literary studies.

We can, for our purposes, identify three moments that occur in the life of any work—production, transmission, and reception.[162] Literary criticism, both in theory and in practice, has primarily focused on the first and third of these moments. Production has been the domain of historical criticism in many and various forms: classical philology, the hypertrophied studies on sources and influences dominant from ca. 1890 to 1940, Marxist inquiries into the social origins of works, studies of authorial composition, and more recent genetic studies. Reception, on the other hand, has been the preferred province of hermeneutical meditations, reader-response theory, or more recently *Rezeptionsästhetik*. From these viewpoints transmission has appeared as a problem only and yet precisely by its absence. Systematically excluded by the premises of the dominant modes of formalist, intrinsic, and hermeneutical studies, it has also been touched upon only rarely by historical studies, which have either dismissed it as an antiquarian fetish or tacitly assumed that it was a problem resolved by earlier theory. The motives for this view derive from historicism's origins in classical textual studies and in a series of ideological assumptions built into the discipline at its formative moments.

Our ordinary notions of transmission derive from the heritage of textual criticism formulated in the nineteenth century. That history is well known and need be reviewed only briefly here.[163] Textual criticism grew out of classical scholarship, and its great achievement was the Lachmann method. Its aim was "to produce a text as close as possible to the original," and to do so it elaborated a theory of transmission characterized by two features. On the one hand transmission was assumed to be remarkably simple: "copies made since the primary split in the tradition *each reproduce one exemplar only.*"[164] The premise derived from the historical circumstances peculiar to classical texts. The manuscripts studied by classical scholars stemmed primarily from the early Middle Ages, a culture of writing largely characterized by steady constriction, homogenization, and impoverishment of the means of written production. This was a graphic culture alien to that of the classical world, when writing had been a function of manifold agencies, institutions, and social classes; when its practitioners comprised notarial and legal bodies, the vast state apparatus, commercial and mercantile corporations, and large numbers of literate city dwellers who had formed a heterogeneous public; and when its productions had been an ensemble of rolls, papyri, tablets, and epigraphs of every sort. What classical scholars of the early nineteenth century found everywhere was one and the same, the ubiquitous codex, the mute messenger bearing alien news from a culture of writing much richer and more complex. To account for this they postulated a simple mode of transmission: a single scribe who copied a single codex, a picture of unrelieved uniformity. This assumption was incorrect in two ways. First, it turned out to reflect poorly the actual practice of medieval transmission, which in fact had often involved recourse to multiple manuscripts, collation, and emendation based on such consultation—all points that would prove the undoing of the classical theory, applicable in its pure form only to a very restricted group of traditions, such as that of Lucretius. But second, the assumptions about transmission were raised from a historical observation to a theoretical premise, one that would have unfortunate effects when absorbed into the developing studies of modern literatures. For modern literatures, the historical circumstances of transmission were precisely the opposite—ever increasing proliferation, heterogeneity, and complexity in the means, forms, and agencies of transmission. Yet the motives for this assumption were profoundly ideological, and were inseparable from a second feature of classical theory.

Classical theory assumed, not incorrectly, that all transmission entails corruption, or in its more specific formulation, that "each scribe consciously or unconsciously deviates from his exemplar, i.e. makes '*peculiar* errors'."[165] By tracing the interrelations between various moments of corruption, it proposed to discern families of manuscripts with common ancestors, and so to reconstruct a path back toward the lost original or the closest possible form of it. Transmission, in this schema, occupied an ambivalent place: since it entailed corruption, it would have to leave traces of its own workings; these traces would permit one to establish the history of their emergence, and on this basis to eliminate them. In theory, then, transmission was devoid of intrinsic value; its only worth consisted in the extent to which it corresponded with the moment of origin or production, the lost text to be recuperated. On the other hand, transmission could be redeemed; it could be instrumentalized and transformed into its own solution. Transmission stood at the heart of the classical theory, yet the object of that theory was to erase it.[166]

The aim of classical theory was to construct an "ideal text," a term suggesting the latent Platonism and idealism it harbored. Its assumptions were also incorporated into the discipline's historiography, producing a standardized account, which runs as follows. Classical scholarship is first dominated by clever Italians (the "docti Itali" of Lachmann's scorn) with a pernicious penchant for stylistic niceties and conjectural criticism, or *emendatio;* then it is given the scientific foundation of *recensio* with the advent of the Lachmann method, a development that examines the text with the criterion of mechanical recension. All this plays familiar motifs of the nineteenth century: the triumphal march of science, materialism, and mechanism over the prostrate bodies of speculation and conjecture. In reality the situation was more complicated, and in some respects antithetical to the standard portrayal. The "ideal text" was always that—one that did not in fact exist. It was merely a hypothetical construct, based on a theory historically commensurate with a limited and atypical corpus of textual traditions. The effect of this theory was to dematerialize the actual manuscripts that transmitted the works in question, to substitute for these the hypothesized Ideal, and to relegate the discordant testimony to the apparatus at the bottom of the page, marginalizing it in a most literal sense. In practice it offered the scholar-reader a text stripped of exactly those signs that registered the intervenient mediations which, ironically enough, had been essential to its preservation.

The material form of the new critical edition rehearsed exactly the same motifs with great thoroughness: exegetical criticism was banished, and the scholar-reader was free to engage in a "pure" encounter with the Ideal.

Seen thus, it becomes apparent that the tradition of hermeneutical criticism was not an aberrant development directed against philology, but its logical and perhaps inevitable corollary. Hermeneutical reflection merely theorized an extant historical (or in one sense, antihistorical) practice. Whereas classical philology sought to reproduce a moment of "pure" production and origin in the past, an ideal freed from all signs of intervention and mediation, hermeneutical criticism postulated a "pure" reception in the present, one that would be equally free of sociohistorical context, of mediating institutions and transmission.[167] Thus, historicist philology was the precondition for hermeneutical speculation, for only the mystified immutability of the ideal text enabled one to introduce the new problematics of psychologistic instability centered in the mind of the reader and in language. Ideal text (constructed through the "scientific" method of "mechanical" recension) liberated the reader-scholar from the labor entailed in an encounter with earlier scripts and inscriptures; mediation was no longer registered in half-uncial or *cancelleresca*, but in "language" and "mind." The stability of an ideal text, in turn, precipitated the formation of a series of ideal texts constituting a canon or tradition of Western civilization—a mental itinerary recapitulating and yet idealizing the works that had attracted the interest of nineteenth-century philologians.[168] The linkage of these concepts recurs in every variant of the hermeneutical tradition down to the present, as one can see in remarks by Geoffrey Hartmann when he urges that the object of criticism is the establishment of a "suspensive discourse" that seeks to "hold it in mind" in a "hermeneutics of indeterminacy."[169] What has vanished is the inscripture that is held in hand, and with it an array of institutions and sociohistorical structures that have shaped and channeled one's access to it. Those are now mystified as text and "great books." Now the sole form of mediation, says Hartmann, is the "grammar imposed by language or by those special and influential closetings of language which every 'great book' fosters."[170] Hermeneutic and formalist theory converge with "historicist" practice in their effort to marginalize and negate the forces registered by the fact of transmission.

Bracketing transmission from consideration effectively erases fundamental dimensions of graphic culture: the material character and social nature of the dynamics operative in every act of writing, forces denied by idealist concepts of production and the hermeneutics of reception. The concreteness and specificity of every inscripture (epigraph, codex, document, pamphlet), the determinacy of its diffusion, preservation, and accessibility—these testify palpably to the intervenient agencies grounding the dialectic of the present and the past. Transmission dissolves the illusion of independence erected around both production and reception, and shows that neither is conceivable apart from the living, social praxis of human beings. It refutes equally the historicist desire to isolate the past in an idealized, alien autonomy and the hermeneutical effort to subject it to a transcendental "reading" in an eternal present of "suspensive discourse." In contrast, transmission is directed toward an imagined future, pervaded by purpose and intentionality, by the manner in which human agency exploits it in specific settings.

The logic of modern literary studies has found it necessary to erase transmission, only to find that, like metaphor in philosophy, it has become our "white mythology"—the thing one is trying to exclude, which by this very effort turns out to be the hidden center of a contaminated order.[171] Consider two cases from the landmark essays in New Criticism. One is Allen Tate's acclaimed interpretation of Emily Dickinson's poem, "Because I Could Not Stop for Death," which dates from 1931. Tate cites the poem in full and urges that it be considered "one of the greatest in the English language." Its special beauty lies in its unity and precision: "Every image extends and intensifies every other," and what appears to be "a heterogeneous series" is fused "into a single order of perception." Yet as one critic has recently shown, Tate's remarks are based on the 1924 edition by Martha Dickinson Bianchi, which lacks an entire stanza of the poem and has seven other major variants of phrasing, many of which were corrected in a 1929 edition.[172] Equally revealing is the famous essay, "The Intentional Fallacy," by Wimsatt and Beardsley (first published in 1946). It begins with an epigraph taken from Congreve, employed to suggest the argument Wimsatt will advance. But as another critic has demonstrated, Wimsatt quotes from a contemporary edition of Congreve that was remarkably corrupt; indeed, another version of the passage, one proofread by the poet himself in 1710, was so different that it urged a reading diametrically opposed to the arguments of Wimsatt.[173]

The failure to take transmission into account has not vanished with the decline of New Criticism, but remains central to literary study's quotidian interpretive activity. Consider two examples from recent criticism on the Malatesta Cantos, the first by Michael Harper, a Marxist critic committed to historicism, the second by Christine Froula. Harper seeks to defend

Pound's historiography in the Malatesta Cantos. He argues that Pound "built on documents" and "returned to the primary material," but offers as evidence only Pound's use of the "Notes, Documents et Commentaire" in the work of Charles Yriarte—from 1882! These, of course, are not primary sources, but published transcriptions (and often barbarous ones at that). He terms Yriarte's work "an excellent model for the historian," notwithstanding evidence known for sixty years that Yriarte's attributions and arguments were seriously flawed (see chapter 3).[174] And on this basis he strives to defend "Pound's accuracy" as a historian, to rebut the charge that he "distorts or ignores the facts"—here is that fateful word again—and to demonstrate that "Pound is correcting the historical record." Finally, after alluding to the murder charge regarding Polissena, he concludes that Pound's portrait of Sigismondo is generally accurate, and in support of this he adduces the 1974 study by P. J. Jones, a historian who "has come to conclusions very similar to Pound's."[175] Yet the more complicated dynamics of transmission show something slightly different. Jones, in his preface, states that his work was originally written "some twenty years ago," or around 1953, a chronology essential to assessing his reference to increasing circumspection in "modern opinion" about Sigismondo Malatesta. For as an example he cites the 1910–11 articles by Giovanni Soranzo—exactly the same articles that Pound was reading in the Bibliothèque Nationale in 1922. Jones, in other words, has not reached "conclusions very similar to Pound's"; he has merely read the same secondary study by Soranzo. Indeed, he has done more, for he has compared it with the conflicting views of Fumi (1913) and Giovanardi (1915–21) as well as the replies by Soranzo, none examined by Pound. And all these authors are cited by him in his footnote to the very passage quoted by Harper.[176] Here is the white mythology of transmission: the process is no longer noticed and is taken for the proper "fact."

Similar operations occur in Christine Froula's study of Pound's writing practices, a work informed by an uneasy mix of post-structuralist and hermeneutic motifs. She argues that the Malatesta Cantos "embody" Hayden White's thesis that historical thought is always "the captive of the linguistic mode in which it seeks to grasp the outline of objects inhabiting its field of perception," recapitulating the hermeneutic stress on "language" and "mind" as the sole forms of mediation that govern our understanding of the past. The remark, however, takes on a curious aspect as she approaches her conclusion: "Pound's portrait of Sigismundo [is] . . . accurate in its general import." For her conclusion, it turns out, is based on the same source as Harper's: "In a more recent revisionary history,

The Malatestas [*sic*] *of Rimini*, Philip J. Jones concurs with Pound's view
that the pope's vilification of Sigismondo was politically inspired rather
than founded in fact." And her footnote not only cites Jones again, but
also Harper.[177] Indeed, in a later version of this argument, the claim is
formulated in even stronger terms: "more recent historians, such as
Philip J. Jones, *have followed Pound's lead.*"[178] Once again it is the white
mythology of transmission.

Instances from such diverse critical styles—New Criticism, Marxism,
post-structuralism—indicate that the neglect of transmission is not iso-
lated or occasional, but a structural feature in modern literary studies.
For nothing suggests that discussion concerning the Malatesta Cantos (or
the line on Polissena) is especially unrepresentative of recent critical
practices. On the contrary, the line is remarkable only for its prosaic
commonness, attracting discussion that typifies the array of critical prac-
tices brought to bear on ordinary problems. And yet these instances
merely corroborate what was apparent from theoretical arguments, that
the premises of modern literary studies systematically exclude the fact of
transmission from consideration.

As such a phrase—"the fact of transmission"—suggests, transmis-
sion converges at critical points with the problem of fact. We tend, unfor-
tunately, to think of fact in terms inherited from traditional historicism as
"something that really occurred or is actually the case," or as "a datum
of experience, as distinguished from the conclusions that may be based
upon it" (*O.E.D.*). Fact, in this view, is a site where language achieves an
especially transparent representation of events or states that are granted
a primary position within a hierarchy of knowledge. Yet insofar as we
accept the general post-structuralist attack on the search for origins, we
are leery of the foundational primacy accorded to fact. And if we are more
responsive to the force of post-structuralist theory, we distrust the binary
oppositions informing and overlapping with this notion: between experi-
ence and inference, information and interpretation, referential and other
uses of language; or on a more extended level, between unity and prolif-
eration, uniformity and diversity, totalization and difference. In respond-
ing this way, however, we may fail to perceive that our uneasiness stems
as much from our own preconceptions as from anything in the nature of
fact itself. For facts of the past are typically constructed not through any
set of transparent signs, but through transmissive histories that are ex-
tremely intricate and complex. Reconstructing those histories is seldom
a straightforward return to origins, but rather a negotiation of discrepant
communicative functions in precise and historically specific contexts.

And yet if so, why is our everyday notion of fact so inadequate, and our distrust of it so profound?

When we use the term *fact*, we seem to refer to a highly synthetic story recounting some event in the past. But this is somewhat misleading. What is referred to is less an original event than an understanding or consensus (provisional and subject to revision) about the intersections that appertain to various testimonies, documentary and material—an understanding that is the outcome of sets of manipulations, some our own, others already undertaken in the construction of the original testimonies. Such a consensus is always subject to constraints imposed both by the range of testimonies transmitted from the past (number, kind, spatio-temporal configuration) and by present-order conditions affecting consensus formation and its articulation (e.g., access to testimonies, ideological and pragmatic interests, transferential relations to the object of study, institutional-disciplinary assumptions about value, or simple exigencies of narrative and stylistic economy).[179] (Examples abound in the history of the charges regarding Polissena.) A fact, then, consists only partly in the synthetic narrative or assertion that is its most typical form, for informing this is also a multiplicity of heterogeneous histories that have occurred in public and institutional spheres characterized by inequalities in power and whose transmission has been irregular and uneven, occurring as a discontinuous series of events that extends far beyond their origins into unforeseen futures. (This historical dimension, it should be added, breaks with both the closed past of naïve historicism and the eternal present of hermeneutical reading.) Or to put it differently, we can better understand the constitution of fact if we conceive it less in terms of an unsophisticated notion of reference to events, and more in terms of reference to communicative conditions, to the sets of procedures governing how testimonies can interact, or more simply, the dynamics of transmission.

What is required, in other words, is a view of fact that is tied less to the representation of the past than to the possibilities of the future.[180] Factual consensus, we need to see, is constituted in the historical and/or conceptual creation of procedural conditions that enable various testimonies to engage in dialogic exchanges differing from those envisioned by their producers. This interaction generates patterns of meaning that transcend, however modestly, the intentionality of their makers. Fact, in some genuine sense, is less a return to origins than a departure from them; less a moment when the "text" is consumed in the logics of its production than a moment when it is freed from them. No single document from the quattrocento, for example, actually says, "On 1 June 1449, Polissena Sforza died, probably of the plague that was then prevalent in central Italy." That synthetic assertion is constituted only in a dialogic exchange of multiple testimonies, and even its most basic components are articulated in discrepancies and their conjunction with other testimonial fields. Consider just the date, which is variously reported as 1448 (Broglio), 1 June 1449 (the anonymous *Cronaca*), 2 June 1449 (Clementini), sometime before autumn 1449 (implied by Simonetta), 2 June 1450 (Yriarte), and 1451 (Tranchedini)—all reports that interact in the light of still others informing us about the motives and the general and specific kinds of reliability typical of each witness. Fact, on this view, is preeminently social in character, and its sociality is grounded in possible futures (conjunctures of transmission) in which more ideal speech situations (transmissional dynamics) can temper the inequalities and asymmetries that shaped the genesis of the original testimonies. It epitomizes, therefore, a dialogical refinement of understanding that in some genuine sense can be called processive.

But what about the synthetic assertion or story that represents a given consensus? Post-structuralist theory, as is well known, has forcefully reminded us, first, that every representation of something (an event in the past, say) is constituted by both a temporal and spatial gap, and second, that since representation can never be full, all acts of representation produce an "other" that is excluded or "marginalized." The synthetic assertion typical of factual statements, for example, does not fully represent the diverse histories or procedural conditions informing a consensus, and surely one "other" that it tends to exclude is doubt or degrees of uncertainty. Of course we can always indicate reservations in our assertions by qualifiers ("Polissena died, *probably* of the plague . . ."), but this only displaces the problem: even our qualifier does not *fully* represent our exact shade of doubt, much less the tangle of testimonies of which our doubt was, in some sense, already a representation. We can, however, also turn the post-structuralist argument against itself, and argue that its representation of representation is itself only partial, that its initial premise—that we really expect representation to be *full*, to be *absolutely* transparent—itself misrepresents the limited expectations that we normally bring to assertions of fact. Indeed, it is because our expectations *are* so limited that we have created various procedures designed to supplement assertion at the point of both production and reception. We use footnotes, for example, not (as often thought) in order to amass "facts" that "prove" our point, but in order to specify in abbreviated form the transmissive dynamics that inform an exchange of testimonies—a kind of moral record of the communicative conditions we have constructed. Or we observe conventions of reading, such as the so-called doctrine of charity, which asks us to place the most generous construction possible on any specific moment within a given discourse—a procedure clearly based on the premise that every representation is so partial as to require the supplement of readerly sympathy. (Perhaps it is the failure to observe this procedure that makes many post-structuralist accounts seem oddly mean-spirited, as if we were asked to admire the critic's cleverness in "exposing" the author's self-deception.) Such procedures, and others that can be readily imagined, hardly suggest that we are too complacent in our view of synthetic assertion or narrative representation, but that we are all too aware of their limitations. To be sure, that awareness is always susceptible to erosion, to unreflective assumptions of linguistic transparency and unwarranted premises about the cognitive status of narrative structures, but if we manage to keep a sense of their limits and their purely pragmatic uses, we can produce accounts sufficiently probing and self-critical.[181]

I have tried to argue that fact is better understood less as a crude correspondence between present assertion and past event than as the formation of a consensus through the construction of a space that is counterfactual with respect to the original circumstances. This space creates conditions of transmission and dialogic exchange that are less hierarchical, less liable to distortion than those of the original speech situations. It is important to underscore the social and dialogic dynamics of this consensus, which echoes analogous dimensions in the object of its attention, and which does not reduce tensions in the originals but engages them in a productive exchange. This is important, because it contrasts so starkly with the model of understanding that largely informs modern literary studies, its assumption of a single reader who confronts a single "text." It is a paradigm of "reading" radically flawed, one that categorically brackets fundamental questions about who is reading what, how, when, where, and why; one that systematically precludes, in other words, a dialogic encounter among heterogeneous phenomena as a condition of critical understanding. Its object of study (in New Criticism, for example) is "the individual work of art *clearly set off* from its antecedents in the mind of the author or in the social situation, as well as from its effect in society" (italics mine). Its reader (in post-structuralism) is "the reader [who] is without history, biography, psychology."[182] Whatever the specific theoretical allegiances, the premises of modern literary studies converge in their impulse to preclude any alterity suggesting a social world that poses resistances to the shaping power of the imagination, whether that power be assigned to the work (New Criticism), to the critic (post-structuralism), or to the "text" (deconstruction). The core of being in the work of "literature," the monument of culture, must lie beyond or be independent of social codes and historical attributes, must be discernible *as such* only insofar as it is freed of those dimensions, only insofar as it departs from them forever.

That, finally, is why we dislike the word *fact:* it offends our cherished conception of the imagination's power, threatens "the work . . . as an object of art," imperils "a suspensive discursive" that seeks to "hold it in mind." It suggests that history may be more than just an inert "text" awaiting the whims of our "reading," that it may retain a measure of in-dependence, or exert its own constraints upon our deliberations, perhaps even "reading" us as much as we "read" it. Its encroachments, therefore, must be continuously blocked, its name perpetually draped in quotation marks, "fact," as though this curious form of ritual magic might ward off what is, for modern literary criticism, the Evil One—the social and his-torical world, which, like Polissena, must be perennially declared "dead" in order to secure the sacred terrain of literature. And yet the particulars of that world, like those of transmission, seem always to reap-pear.

In writing his line about the death of Polissena, Pound himself was not merely reporting an event, but also registering the conditions that had grounded his conception of the issues at stake. The line on Polissena, after all, would be understood poorly if considered solely in its referential or representational function; no one would dispute its literal claim that Polissena "died," since it would be true whatever the circumstances of her death. Clearly its prosaic yet emphatic report acquires meaning only when viewed against the play of fractured traditions that informed and inform it: the accusation that she was murdered by Sigismondo; ideolog-ical motifs assimilated to the charge before the moment when Pound was writing in 1922–23; even the array of annotations and histories that have continued until now, and continue here with these very words. Adopting a purely referential frame of discussion, one might conclude that his re-port was accurate in its general import, its implicit denial of the murder allegation. Even so, the conclusion would be superficial. At the most basic level, Pound's decision to reject the murder allegation was based solely upon his reading of Giovanni Soranzo's 1910–11 article, a study not without flaws: it mistakenly attributed to Nolfi a claim made by the later and less reliable Amiani, and it offered no account of the most damning and particular formulation of the accusation, the 1462 letter by Sforza. To be sure, after the letter was published by Fumi (1913), Soranzo argued persuasively (1915) that its motives were suspect; and after "the chronicle of pseudo-Alessandro" was adduced by Giovanardi (1914), he demonstrated convincingly that it was a petty forgery. But Pound himself was unaware of the later studies by Fumi, Giovanardi, or Soranzo, just as he was unaware of the "Genealogy" by Nicodemo Tranchedini published in 1920 and 1921. Why did he fail to locate these studies? And why was he so eager to believe Soranzo?

Pound's ignorance—the term carries no pejorative connotation here—of the later studies resulted partly from the material form of their transmission and preservation. Soranzo's 1910–11 article was printed not once, but twice: first as part of the journal in which it appeared, then as an independent offprint (or *estratto*) with its own pagination. It was the second form that reached the Bibliothèque Nationale in Paris, where under BNP cataloguing procedures it was given independent author, title, and subject listings—just as if it were a book. Pound, in other words, could locate this work easily because the way in which it was transmitted and preserved made it far more accessible. This was not true of the other studies. Giovanardi's article of 1914 was published in a journal not received by the Bibliothèque Nationale.[183] The other articles by Fumi (1913) and Soranzo (1915, 1917, and 1920), as well as the "Genealogy" by Tranchedini (1920), were not published as independent offprints, but only as integral features in scholarly historical journals.

The Bibliothèque Nationale, to be sure, received (and still preserves) the relevant volumes of these journals, and consequently they were available to Pound in 1922. But the context of Pound's reception offered few resources that could have guided him to them: he did not work in a university setting that offered a network of colleagues with expertise in various fields who could counsel or advise him, and the avant-garde milieu in which he moved was indifferent or hostile to the historical subject matters that attracted him. In January 1922 Pound suggested to one acquaintance that he design the decor for Pound's recent opera on the poet François Villon (1431–63), a contemporary of Sigismondo Malatesta; Jean Cocteau, who was also present at the conversation, "giggled all the time" because he thought it "quite ridiculous" that anyone should be interested in "the Middle Ages."[184]

Still, it is true that Pound was capable of great perseverance when he wished to learn something. In February 1923, for example, he managed to visit a leading art historian in Rome who furnished him with information about unpublished manuscripts and inscriptions regarding the Tempio and Isotta (see chapter 3). But between Isotta and Polissena there was a difference: in part Pound simply assumed the subject was less important, and in part he found that Soranzo's study of 1910–11 discussed the accusation in terms that converged with his own reading of the Malatestan vicissitudes. Since Soranzo's study was written *before* the recovery of the 1462 letter by Sforza, it laid all the blame for the accusation on Pius II. Seen thus, it was an instance of the Christian falsification of history, a hypocritical accusation issued partly to mask the nepotistical ambitions of Pius, but primarily to facilitate a wider program to suppress a neopagan culture that Pound regarded as exemplary for the progress and renewal of European civilization. Indeed, it is this contrast that informs his final decision to place his "denial" of the charge directly after he invokes the monument of the neopagan culture:

> And he began building the TEMPIO,
> and Polixena, his second wife, died.

In contrast, knowledge that the charge originated not in Rome but in the Sforzescan chancery tends to dissolve the ideological dichotomy that attracted Pound; it becomes less charged with ethical resonance, more an instance of petty politics as usual. But that knowledge could be generated only by a more careful examination of the interaction between origins and transmission.

As for his failure to uncover the 1462 letter by Sforza while in the archive of Milan, it too is explained by a convergence of ideological interests and institutional forms of transmission. Since the minute was directed to Sforza's ambassador at the papal court, it was classified under the archival series pertaining to "Rome." Pound's researches, however, were so concentrated on the figure of Sigismondo, seen in quasi-heroic isolation, that he examined only documents housed in the series for "Romagna." Other documents did not interest him. Nor was he eager to seek out alternative testimonies that might contradict or conflict with his preferred views. Here his practice was only a variant of his reading of Soranzo's article; nothing among his seven hundred pages of notes for the Malatesta Cantos suggests that he compared the article with any of its sources, examined it for potential contradictions, or sought to locate alternative accounts.

Pound's lack of interest in seeking alternative testimonies and conflicting accounts did not stem from a lack of energy or from intellectual inca-

pacity. Clearly he possessed both in abundance and expended them lav-
ishly when so inclined. Rather, it stemmed from theoretical premises: the
intransigent individualism that shaped his conception of subject matter
("the most living individuals") also informed his view of critical under-
standing. He increasingly integrated this individualism into a neo-
idealist notion of knowledge. For Pound, a historical problem was
grasped in an intuitive apperception by the observer, the validity of which
was secured by "sensibility" and personality, not a dialogic exchange of
heterogeneous testimonies. If contradictory testimonies existed, the "se-
lection" of one over another would be adjudicated on the basis of another
intuitive apperception. If a "selection" had once been made and was
contested by contemporaries, that conflict could be resolved only by fur-
ther appeal to "men of unusual intelligence." Talent or genius ("inten-
sity") both authorized the initial choice of one testimony over another and
adjudicated any ensuing conflicts. If, in a worst case scenario, many
contemporaries declined to assent to the decisions of "men of unusual
intelligence," Pound maintained a supreme confidence that their intui-
tions would ultimately be warranted by the approbation of later historiog-
raphy, a consensus achieved by processes it was unimportant to specify.

> A signed letter [having cited an example from the quattrocento] proves
> what the writer wanted the recipient to believe on such and such a day.
> But the clarity of an idea remains among the ASCERTAINED facts. The
> definition of an idea, as observed *by someone who understands the events
> of the day*, may shed more light on the historical process than many vol-
> umes. [My italics.][185]

In the "personality" and "sensibility" of "someone who understands"
Pound discerned a source for assessing the relations of conflicting testi-
monies, and what it grasped was "an idea," an essential notion at the core
of a period's vital life that was itself "a fact" that would inevitably be
ratified.

It was only in this deferred form that the future played any role in his
conception of critical understanding. Otherwise Pound's view tended to
stress the present and the value of judgments made by its most talented
individuals. Both emphases appear with particular force in remarks from
A Guide to Kulchur (1938): "We do NOT know the past in chronological
sequence, but what we know we know by ripples and spirals eddying out
from us and from our own time" (*GK*, p. 60). Or again:

> It does not matter a twopenny damn whether you load up your memory
> with the chronological sequence of what has happened, or the names of

protagonists, or authors of books, or generals and leading political spou-
ters, so long as you understand the process now going on, or the processes
biological, social, economic now going on, enveloping you as an individ-
ual, in a social order. (*GK*, pp. 51–52)

Such ideas have obvious affinities with the general tendency of herme-
neutic criticism to stress the constituent role of the present in historical
understanding, and they have come to seem increasingly attractive to
literary critics eager to consummate the holocaust of "fact." Christine
Froula, for example, quotes the second passage above in order to com-
ment approvingly that "it is historical 'process' and not isolated facts
which Pound aims to represent in *The Cantos*. . . . " [186] Yet it is difficult
not to suspect that these remarks offer another case of the white mythol-
ogy of transmission.

Pound's views on history emerged out of the widespread revolt against
positivism that appeared at the turn of the century.[187] One work that fo-
cused this revolt was an essay by Benedetto Croce, entitled "History Sub-
sumed under the Concept of Art," a work that has rightly been called "the
manifesto of anti-positivism in Italy." [188] Its appearance was greeted with
a review by Giovanni Gentile, then a young professor of philosophy in
Florence, who praised Croce for having overturned the traditional rela-
tionship between historians and the events that were the object of their
research. Rather than looking outside themselves, in a nonexistent ar-
chive, historians were to search within themselves, within their own
imagination and sensibility. Croce had already entered the road that
would later permit him to affirm that history is always contemporary, a
statement much like Pound's emphasis on history as an understanding of
"the process now going on." Gentile concurred, "It is manifest that it is
impossible to speak of facts, as pure facts, as brute facts, if not as an
abstraction, as an ideal content, which it will never be possible to find or
catch in actual reality external to the spirit [or mind]." And he added,
"[Facts] are such for us insofar as they are represented in spirit [or mind];
and inasmuch as we can discuss or philosophize about them, inasmuch
as they have already been received and elaborated by spirit itself.[189]

The intimate relationship between Gentile's remarks of 1897 and
Pound's of 1938 is sufficiently clear and needs no elaboration here. Yet
the relation between their lives deserves some remark. In the years fol-
lowing 1897, Gentile became an increasingly important and well-known
figure in Italian philosophy, noted especially for his views on logic (which
interested Eliot) and educational reform (which were applauded by
Yeats).[190] Within days of Mussolini's arrival in power in late 1922, he was

named minister of education. In May 1923 he accepted honorary membership in the Fascist party. By 1925 he had become a dominant figure in the intellectual life of the regime, and in April that year he presided over the "Convention of Fascist Culture" in Bologna (at which Antonio Beltramelli delivered his lecture on intercultural understanding), where he drafted its principal document, "The Manifesto of Fascist Intellectuals." He went on to become the regime's quasi-official philosopher, guiding its intellectual policies and directing production of its major intellectual project, the *Enciclopedia italiana*. For the encyclopedia's article on "Fascism" he wrote the opening section on "The Philosophical Bases of Fascism," personally approved and signed by Mussolini (and until recently also attributed to him). When the regime collapsed in 1943, Gentile remained faithful to his principles and elected to follow Mussolini northward, as did also Pound. On 15 April 1944, as he stopped his car before the gateway to the villa at which he was staying, three men approached him and asked if he was Giovanni Gentile, and when he nodded, one pulled out a pistol and shot him repeatedly at point blank, screaming that he was killing not the man, but his ideas.[191] In "The Pisan Cantos," Pound voices his distaste for those who "assassinated Henriot [a broadcaster for radio Vichy] and Gentile."[192]

As for Pound, the outline of his own biography and its tragic vicissitudes are all too well known. My point, rather, is to call attention to the way in which Froula's claims validate the shared premises of Gentile and Pound with little sense of their historical context, assimilating them to her own attacks against "the possibility of historical objectivity."[193] Her work, in this respect, recapitulates the structures that we have seen at work in the genesis of the line on Polissena: it dissolves the distance between the past and the present (between its own setting and that of its subject), evades the give and take of heterogeneous testimonies whose dialogic encounter permits a social reconstitution of intentionality, and erases the intervenient layers that must also be a part of the subject of critical attention. Her practices are typical of the text-centered and intrinsic theories informing the hermeneutical tradition, and typical of a tendency to instrumentalize the work at hand only to affirm the critical modes that currently dominate literary studies. And yet, having surveyed the complex histories shaping the composition and transmission of the Malatesta Cantos, we may want to view them somewhat differently.

The line on Polissena Sforza is typical of many that appear in *The Cantos*. It is carefully understated, assuring us that its information is unimportant and the death of Polissena Sforza inconsequential. And within the logic of *The Cantos* this is true: Polissena seems a "misera creatura," as Antonio Beltramelli called her, one who is not to be numbered among the higher specimens of mankind. Unlike Isotta, for example, she receives no honor, inspires no monument, evokes no "temple of love." She does not contribute to civilization, as it was defined by Pound in 1922, "a vortex for the most living individuals." For Polissena is not to be counted among these; she simply "died." Her passage from life receives less stress, less vigor, than a chronicle of the weather in a certain year: "One year floods rose" (as one of the Malatesta Cantos begins). Like weather, she is reduced to a transient and peripheral object within *The Cantos*, relegated to the status of background—a kind of fact, mentioned only as a stage screen serving to set off the monumental figures, the "canon of grand monuments" parading before us at Pound's behest, exemplars of the imagination's shaping power. His report of her death effaces her, and her life, as surely as it erases the complex of mediating forces that grounded its own making. Yet oddly, in this particular sense Polissena also seems to acquire new significance for us, to become a figure for the dynamics of transmission, the interjacent agencies and institutions that condition all aspects of the written environment. She speaks not only of the past but, like transmission, of the future.

To suggest that Polissena becomes a figure is to use the word in a double sense, as both *emblem* and *conspicuous appearance*. For Polissena can be seen as an emblem, a figure of all the forces that are effaced or consigned to the amorphous ground of *The Cantos*, and by extension, of modern literary studies. As literary studies experience a renewal of interest in history, they may find it imperative to reconstitute that ground as a conspicuous appearance, as a distinct figure. Such criticism will no longer confine its attention solely to the traditional monuments of the canon, but will also undertake to study the larger written environment as a central component of its interest. Or to put this in different terms, criticism will have to sharpen its delineation of the hitherto amorphous ground to the point where it becomes a figure itself, bearing in mind the implications of works such as Fernand Braudel's in social and economic history, where the traditional "figures" making "events" are displaced by "la longue durée." The synthetic surveys executed by Braudel, to be sure, emerge from a rigorous tradition of detailed studies executed by two generations in the *Annales* school, a heritage that contrasts starkly with the lack of systematic disciplinary support for historical studies within literary criticism of recent decades. Still, it may be an opportune moment for microhistories that reconstitute the contextual ground around determinate points within the familiar monuments, that lucidly reconstruct the dynamics of transmission informing both their production and reception, even as they unsettle these latter categories by exploring their reciprocal relationships within a contradictory network of uses, including our own. Such studies will not, to be sure, lead to a utopian renovation of literary criticism, or resolve problems that are ultimately inseparable from much wider social and institutional questions. Still, they may at least remind us that the past and its works are never given, pure, or stable objects knowable outside the documentary and material forms or apart from the institutional apparatuses and historical processes that transmit them, encoding their appropriations by subjects. They may also remind us that the intervenient layers and agencies that always mediate historical understanding are not solely the passive instruments of "text," "language," or "discourse," but also exert their own constraints on the formation both of cultural works and of the exegetical labors performed by readers of every sort, past or future.

We may, of course, prefer to ignore those constraints or pretend they are of no consequence—impulses that doubtless go far to explain our almost visceral distrust of fact as a notion that threatens basic assumptions of modern literary studies, even as it resists our efforts to erase it from the texture of our deliberations. But doing so will only curtail the terms of our exchange with the past, indeed eliminate it as an authentic possibility by trivializing the past into a simulacrum of the present. A more self-critical interaction with the problematics of fact, on the other hand, may go far toward enabling us to achieve a less reductive and less unilateral definition of literary criticism, one that addresses more forthrightly the delicate issue of how subjects relate and have related to objects of the past, historical and cultural, and how they might relate to them in a possible future. For every fact, in the conditions that ground its formation, points as much to the future as it does to the past. The future, to be sure, may seem rather remote when we consider the death of Polissena Sforza so long ago in 1449 or the network of contradictory uses that have gathered around that event. Still, in the course of its transmission the death of Polissena became inseparable from the life of Isotta degli Atti and the monument of culture she had supposedly inspired—inseparable, finally, from a vision and a history of civilization. Could it be that civilization is somehow bound up with the transmission of some little fact? With even a single letter? Or with forms of moral imperative in the discrimination of such minutiae? That remains to be seen.

Desperate Love: Isotta and the Monument of Civilization

Ecco qui ad attestare il seme

non ancora disperso dell'antico dominio

questi morti attacati a un possesso

che affonda nei secoli il suo abominio

e la sua grandezza.

Behold them here, brought to bear witness

to the seed, still undispersed, of the ancient dominion,

these dead attached to a possession

that sinks into the centuries its abomination

and its grandeur.

Pier Paolo Pasolini, *Le ceneri di Gramsci*

And when ye shall hear wars and rumors of wars, be ye not troubled: for such things must needs be; but the end shall not be yet.

Mark 13:7

Ma dimmi: al tempo de' dolci sospiri,

a che e come concedette Amore

che conosceste i dubbiosi disiri?

But tell me: in the time of sweet sighs,

how and by what occasion did Love

lead you to know such doubtful desires?

Dante Alighieri, *Inferno,* **5**

When Dr. Johnson prepared the fourth edition of his dictionary in 1772, he refused to admit the word *civilization*. It was too recent a coinage, he thought. Within a century, however, the term had become an essential point of reference for debate about the nature and progress of Euro-American culture. *Civilization*, D. C. Gilman recognized in 1898, was a new word introduced scarcely a century before, and it meant "the highest welfare of mankind." President of the first American graduate school from 1876 to 1892, Gilman felt that the center of any advanced civilization was a university, "the highest school."[1] Others, however, increasingly disagreed. In 1889 Edward Carpenter published *Civilisation: Its Cause and Cure*, a title that revealed both how problematic and compelling the concept had become. Carpenter had abandoned his university position at Cambridge to found a utopian community at Millthorpe, and his book predicted the coming of a new and glorious post-Christian man:

> The meaning of the old religions will come back to him. On the high tops once more gathering he will celebrate with naked dances the glory of the human form and the great processions of the stars . . . or in the open, standing uncovered to the Sun, will adore the emblem of the everlasting splendour which shines within.

Carpenter's views were respectfully discussed among intellectual circles of the period. A book of 1910 cast him alongside Nietzsche as one of "three modern seers," and the pairing was not infrequent.[2] A deep primitivism, evidenced by Carpenter, and a radical individualism, looking to Nietzsche, were key components in a vague yet potent ideal for a new civilization that emerged in inchoate, often contradictory, forms during the period between 1900 and the Great War. It was a utopian aspiration that emphasized a direct rapport with instinct and the self, inimical to the institutionally grounded notion of civilization implicit in Gilman's re-

157

marks. And as often as not, it located its intellectual genealogy in the Renaissance as imagined by Burckhardt.

Burckhardt's view of the Renaissance offered a moving tableau of great individuals, a spectacle of elect minorities who had assumed a mysterious role as the creative force for collective history; their innovative capacity shone in their repudiation of the past, their exaltation of the individual conscience and the force of will. Their activity had shaped the modern world, and it constituted a form of historical existence exemplary for the course of civilization. It was a paradigm understood, and further articulated, by Burckhardt's younger colleague at the university of Basel, Friedrich Nietzsche:

> The Italian Renaissance contained within it all the positive forces to which we owe modern civilization: liberation of thought, disrespect for authorities, victory of culture over the darkness of ancestry, enthusiasm for knowledge and the knowable past of man, unfettering of the individual, a passion for truthfulness and an aversion to appearance and mere effect (which passion blazed forth in a whole host of artistic characters who, in an access of moral rectitude, demanded of themselves perfection in their work and nothing but perfection); indeed, the Renaissance possessed positive forces which have up to now, *in our contemporary modern civilization*, never been so powerful again. Despite all its blemishes and vices, it was the golden age of this millennium.

This passage from *Human, All Too Human*, translated into English in 1909, appeared when Nietzsche's work was the focus of intense discussion in England. The Renaissance man was being transformed into the paradigm of the "free spirit" envisioned by Nietzsche, a harbinger of the future. "The great task of the Renaissance," what Nietzsche had defined as "the complete growing-together of the spirit of antiquity and the modern spirit," had been left incomplete, blunted by the Reformation and the Counter-Reformation.[3] In this light the exemplary figures sketched by Burckhardt acquired new urgency—among them Sigismondo Malatesta, the crowning example in Burckhardt's chapter "The Furtherers of Humanism," whose court had epitomized "the highest spiritual things."[4] As Pound would write in 1938, here was a type of cultural life furnishing an "example of civilization" in every branch of activity, above all in its consummate monument: the church of San Francesco, the Tempio Malatestiano. Pound was perhaps recalling Nietzsche's millennial evaluation when he wrote: "The Tempio Malatestiano is . . . the apex of what one man has embodied in the last 1000 years of the occident."[5]

All this suggests the enormous burden of psychic and cultural significance that pivoted on the figure of Isotta degli Atti; for in Burckhardt's words, it was "in *her* honour and as *her* monument that the famous rebuilding of San Francesco at Rimini took place—*Divae Isottae Sacrum.*"[6] In the Malatesta Cantos, Isotta's role is underscored by the structural position of all the passages that treat her, each located at a critical point within the sequence of four cantos. The first appears midway in the introductory Canto 8, a hint of her centrality to all the action that follows. The second appears at the end of Canto 9 (the second of the four cantos), the midpoint of the entire sequence—again signaling her role at the work's thematic center. In addition, a third important passage appears only in the 1925 edition of *The Cantos*, which has been entirely omitted in previous discussion. We need to examine each of these carefully: we must consider the kinds of testimonies they represent, and how they were constituted into testimonies at all. Then we can consider why recent criticism has failed to assess them adequately, and whether this failure offers insights into the nature and function of criticism in our time. At stake, after all, is not only our understanding of the Malatesta Cantos, or the entire project of *The Cantos*, but the fate of "civilization." This is what depends on the desperate love of Sigismondo for Isotta.

The Honor of Italy

Canto 9, the second of the four Malatesta Cantos, concludes with a curious tract of thirteen lines:

> *"et amava perdutamente Ixotta degli Atti"*
> *e "ne fu degna"*
> > *"constans in proposito*
> *"Placuit oculis principis*
> *"pulchra aspectu"*
> *"populo grata (Italiaeque decus)*
>
> "and built a temple so full of pagan works"
> > i.e. Sigismund
> and in the style "Past ruin'd Latium"
> The filigree hiding the gothic,
> > with a touch of rhetoric in the whole
> And the old sarcophagi,
> > such as lie, smothered in grass, by San Vitale.

The lines resonate with a note of epiphanic importance, an urgent self-consciousness of style.[7] Two are given in Italian, then four in Latin, suggesting the author's familiarity with original sources, and thereby the veracity of his claims. Then both language and tone are abruptly altered: seven lines of elegiac English trace an incantatory and typically Poundian movement toward stillness, toward the hieratic conclusion where scarcely a verb ripples the calm. The structure is simple: the first six lines regard Isotta degli Atti, the next seven concern the church of San Francesco, or the Tempio Malatestiano, forming a diptych that recapitulates the romantic interpretation of the Tempio. Isotta has inspired the construction of the church of San Francesco, a "temple of love" that simultaneously expresses the neopaganism of the Renaissance ("so full of pagan works").

The six lines treating Isotta refract a variety of sources. The briefest is the phrase "Italiaeque decus," which concludes the series. For the moment we can render this: "and the honor [or *decus*] of Italy." The word *decus*, however, requires further attention. In classical Latin *decus* covered a range of meanings: ornament, grace, embellishment, splendor, glory, honor, dignity. It was a favorite word with Cicero in his orations, who sometimes used it as here, in apposition to a person.[8] Vergil, too, used it to address illustrious persons both *in propria voce* and in "fictional" discourse, twice in the *Eclogues* and five times in the *Aeneid*.[9] In *Aeneid* 11, 508, for example, *decus* appears in a speech by Turnus, who is about to thank the warrior-princess Camilla for her offer of help, and who addresses her, "O decus Italiae virgo" (O maiden, the honor of Italy).

Vergil's locution lies behind the reappearance of this phrase many centuries later in several testimonies connected with the court of Sigismondo Malatesta, in particular a group of medals and inscriptions that refer to Isotta degli Atti as "decus Italiae." The phrase's Vergilian origins suggest that the inscriptions were authored by the poet and humanist Basinio da Parma, who labored in Rimini from 1449 until his death in 1457.[10] Basinio's familiarity with Vergil was thorough and intense, apparent in almost every line of his neo-Latin epic celebrating the deeds of Sigismondo.[11] Moreover, in a verse epistle directed to Sigismondo, Basinio addresses him as "Ausoniae decus" (the honor of Ausonia, i.e., Italy). Little wonder that Basinio, known to have written other inscriptions for the Malatestan court, should deem it appropriate to honor Isotta with nearly identical phrasing, "Italiae decus," a usage that recalled his address to Sigismondo, invoked the authority of Vergil, and tacitly compared her with Camilla, the noble princess of Vergil's masterpiece.[12]

Basinio's epithet, "Italiae decus" (or in neo-Latin, "Italie decus"), appears on two portrait medals of Isotta degli Atti, cast in bronze and signed by Matteo de' Pasti.[13] In one the legend on the obverse reads (with points in the form of flowers):

· ISOTE · ARIMINENSI · FORMA · ET · VIRTUTE · ITALIE · DECORI ·

In the other the obverse shows the same text ("To Isotta of Rimini, [who is] the honor of Italy for her virtue and her beauty"), but with regular points.[14] In addition, there is a second group of medals that portray Isotta; these, although unsigned, are also universally attributed to de' Pasti. (The lack of a signature is thought to indicate that he was responsible for the model, but did not directly supervise the casting.)[15] A third group of medals of Isotta, also unsigned, carries a different inscription entirely, much shorter and without the phrase "Italie decus":

· D · ISOTTAE · · ARIMINENSI ·

Further, in two cases these latter medals portray an image of a book, clearly referring to a collection of poetry composed for Isotta by Malatestan court poets and known as the *Isottaeus*.[16]

All but one of the medals bear the date 1446, supposed to commemorate the beginning of Sigismondo's rapport with Isotta. The medals themselves, however, were clearly produced at a later date. De' Pasti's presence in Rimini is first documented only in 1449, and other testimonies confirm that his labors began subsequently. The evidence is furnished by archaeological studies that have enabled scholars to trace a rudimentary though revealing chronology of his medals; it is based on the Renaissance practice of burying deposits of coins and medals to commemorate the completion of fortresses or monumental buildings. For example, the deposit at the fortress in Verucchio dates from 1449, and it contains only specimens of a medal portraying Sigismondo, clearly one of de' Pasti's earliest works for the court. The deposit in the chapel of San Sigismondo, the first portion of the church of San Francesco (i.e., Tempio) that was reconstructed, dates from its dedication in 1452; it also contains no medals of Isotta—a curious omission for a building where Isotta was supposed to be "the true and only ruling divinity." In contrast, the deposit at the base of the Torrione in Senigallia, which dates from 1455, is the earliest to contain medals bearing Isotta's image. The evidence leaves little doubt that the public exaltation of Isotta began only after 1452, quite some time after the death of Polissena Sforza, Sigismondo's second wife, in June 1449.[17] The date is important, for late Romantic scholarship assumed that the inscriptions registered the date of the medals' production, not a retrospective commemoration. According to this view, the medals had been made while Polissena was still alive, and they demonstrated the passionate character of Sigismondo's love for Isotta, desperate love that flouted public convention and epitomized the victory of private passion over public constraint, of self-fulfillment and instinct over convention and conformity.

One figure who precipitated the romanticization of de' Pasti's medals was Charles Yriarte (see figure 13), whose study of the Riminese court was published in 1882. It appeared when a feverish interest surrounded the Italian medals of the Renaissance, interest that fueled a massive production of scholarship and staggering increases in prices on the art market. Major studies of the medals were published by Friedländer (1880), Heiss (1881), and Armand (1883–85), all deluxe volumes with hundreds of illustrations.[18] Simultaneously, prices soared: medals that had sold for several hundred francs only a few years before, noted one critic in 1883, would now fetch three or four thousand; and the same year a medal attributed to Sperandio, a medalist of the second rank, fetched the amazing price of 9,500 francs.[19] This complex of mixed motives also informed Yriarte's work. As art critic and historian, he assessed the authenticity and "aesthetic value" of works; as Sir Richard Wallace's consultant and purchasing agent for Renaissance artworks, he helped amass a private collection considered the most valuable in the world when Wallace died in 1890. (In 1897 his widow bequeathed it to the English nation, creating the Wallace Collection in London.) How these activities influenced his treatment of the medals related to Isotta is hard to specify. Wallace had bought two of the de' Pasti medals in 1866 and 1869, and perhaps another purchase was in the air in 1882 when Yriarte made a curious attribution, one that later affected Pound.[20]

Yriarte, in his study of the Riminese court, published an engraving that represents a medal of Isotta; it appears on page 142, above a caption reading "Isotta de Rimini—Médaille de Matteo da Pasti (1446)." It shows the obverse of one of the signed medals (of course the signature is not illustrated, since it appears on the reverse).[21] This engraving has been identified as the source of Pound's phrase, "Italiae decus."[22] Nor is this supposition unreasonable. Of the three engravings given by Yriarte, only this one shows the inscription:

· ISOTE · ARIMINENSI · FORMA · ET · VIRTUTE · ITALIE · DECORI ·

However, two discrepancies distinguish the inscription shown in the engraving and the phrase used by Pound. One is the use of *decus* instead of *decori*, though this can be explained by changes in the syntactic context. The other is orthographical, the presence of an extra letter *a* in Pound's phrase; for the engraving reads *ITALIE*, while Pound writes *Italiae*. This suggests that Pound did not copy the phrase from the engraving, but from some other source.

Besides his remarks accompanying the engravings, Yriarte offered a second treatment of the medals when he surveyed the iconography of Isotta degli Atti. This time, however, he mentioned not only de' Pasti, but also the greatest of all the medalists, Pisanello:

> We know of eight medals of Isotta, seven by Matteo da Pasti and an eighth by Pisanello. Of the seven by Matteo, only one is dated 1447 and the other five are dated 1446. Apart from one that depicts an open book, commemorating the collection of poetry written for her, none makes allusion to any special events. In one case she appears in profile, with the inscription: *Isottaei. Ariminensi. forma.—et. virtute. Italiae. decori.* . . . The only medal by Pisanello also shows her in profile with the same hairstyle as in the medals by Matteo; on the reverse is depicted Sigismondo, in armor.

Yriarte introduces several errors in reporting the inscription on the de' Pasti medal; perhaps the most important occurs when he "corrects" the Latin to make it conform with classical usage, changing the genitive from *ITALIE* to *Italiae*.[23] It was this last alteration that apparently influenced Pound, who transcribed the inscription not from the engraving, but from Yriarte's discussion introducing the "corrected" classical form. Yet this raises another question: if Pound was copying from Yriarte's discussion here, and if this was notable for claiming that a medal of Isotta had been produced by the great Pisanello, is it possible that the poet mistakenly associated the inscription with the medal supposedly by Pisanello?

Yriarte's claim that Pisanello had made a medal of Isotta was controversial. The medal, depicting Isotta on one side and Sigismondo on the other, had long been known, and only a year earlier it had been dismissed by Heiss as a late and worthless forgery. To defend his attribution, Yriarte claimed that he had come upon another specimen of the medal in the library at Cesena (a city formerly ruled by Sigismondo's brother), where it was found "chained to the wall alongside other Malatestan medals." In effect, argued Yriarte, its contiguity with medals known to be authentic was proof that it too was authentic.[24] Though it was a silly argument, it apparently intrigued Pound. Pound obtained his copy of Yriarte's book on 3 August 1922, and not much later he entered two markings in the margin opposite Yriarte's defense of the medal, on page 150:

1.—Cette médaille du Pisanello est extrèmement rare. On en connaît un exemplaire
dans la collection Taverna de Milan, aujourd'hui musée municipal, et on a cru longtemps
qu'on avait, postérieurement au XVᵉ siècle, accolé un revers de Matteo da Pasti à une
face de Sigismond; mais nous en avons trouvé une seconde à Cesena, dans la biblio-
thèque, où elle est enchaînée au mur à côte des autres médailles des Malatesta. On
pourrait donc croire qu'elle est du temps; cependant M. Heiz, dans son intéressante
publication *les Médailleurs de la Renaissance*, 1881 (Rothschild, Paris), persiste à voir
là une médaille faite avec deux faces d'autres médailles déjà connues à une époque pos-
térieure.

Pound, we can see, was intrigued by the location of the two specimens of
the pseudo-Pisanello, one in Milan and one in Cesena.[25] Indeed, he was
anxious to recall this information: later, on a blank leaf at the back of his
copy he also entered an index meant to remind him of his most important
markings, and among his notations is this one:

medal   150

Clearly it refers to the medal allegedly by Pisanello, and to the two mark-
ings Pound had entered opposite the footnote on page 150 in his copy of
Yriarte.[26]

The index was probably made in November or December 1922, when
Pound was preparing for a trip to Italy that he planned for early 1923. In
February his travels began, and on 10 March he sent a postcard to his
wife Dorothy, postmarked from Cesena, which reported, "Amiable librar-
ian has showed me most of what he can lay his hands on."[27] The librarian
was Manlio Torquato Dazzi, then its director and later good friend of the
poet. Evidently he must have shown him the medal mentioned by Yriarte,
the medal supposedly fashioned by the great Pisanello, and indeed the
"bronze disc" must have impressed him deeply; fifteen years later he still
remembered it affectionately when he praised the features of Malatestan
culture that he considered perfect "Examples of Civilization": "You get
civilization in the seals. I mean it was carried down and out in de-
tails. . . . The Young Salustio [referring to an epistolary seal that depicts
Sallustio de' Malatesta] is there in the wax *as Isotta and Sigismundo in
the bronze discs of Pisanello*" (italics mine).[28] Pound fully accepted
Yriarte's ascription of the medal to Pisanello. And yet by 1938 he was
perhaps the last person who still did. The attribution, already contested
by Heiss in 1881, was rejected by Armand in 1883, and rejected again
by G. F. Hill in 1905. By 1917 it was considered "a well known for-
gery."[29]

Appreciating how Pound acquired his knowledge of the pseudo-
Pisanello and the inscription linked with it permits us to understand how

he employed this material in his early manuscripts. Pound first refers to the inscription in Draft Fragment *b*, a typescript composed between 11 and 15 August 1922, which shows him working closely with arguments and information given by Charles Yriarte.[30] The material regards the biography of Isotta, and one passage (lines 18–24) echoes a crucial claim that Yriarte had advanced, that Isotta was unable to read or write.[31] It is in this context that the phrase "Italiae decus" makes its first appearance:

> Italiae decus, diva Ixotta, knew or did not know,
> read or could not read, was herself a writer,
> was ignorant,
>   cheat, dither, and cheat,
> lies blocked over with lies, loose phrases,
>   and the fragment . . .
>   the real, the onrush.

Against the charge that Isotta "was ignorant," "could not read" or "did not know" how to write, Pound vents his exasperation and anger. He lashes out at Yriarte, damning his suggestions as "lies blocked over with lies, loose phrases." And to rebut them he makes two significant maneuvers. First, he sets forth terms evoking an idealist, vitalist vision of history, phrases asserting the superior understanding of spirit over the apparent quibbling of the philologian: "the fragment" and "the real, the onrush" (23–24). But this is not enough, for Pound lives in the wake of the positivist cultural hegemony and must forestall the charge that his assertion of spirit is an illusion devoid of historical consequence. As a historical refutation, therefore, he cites the testimony of the Malatestan court itself: its claim that Isotta was "diva Ixotta" (a goddess, in his interpretation of *diva*), its testimony that she was "Italiae decus," the honor or glory of Italy. Could such terms, he asks, have been elicited by a woman who was illiterate? The phrase "Italiae decus," however, evokes not just the documentary report of contemporaries, but the transcendent testimony of art via its association with the medal allegedly by Pisanello; one could find no higher testimony to the ethical and spiritual worth of Isotta, no surer proof than this exquisite "example of civilization."

In its earliest appearance, the phrase "Italiae decus" serves to rebut Yriarte's charge that Isotta was illiterate, while on an ideological plane it lends a patina of historicity, concreteness, and reality to the neo-idealist vision that animates Pound's understanding of the Malatestan vicissitudes, an understanding that grants them an exemplary status in the drama of civilization unfolding now, in 1922. Here, as in the final version of the poem, it epitomizes his view that Isotta is the real inspiration for the cultural flowering of the Malatestan court, a view that legitimates a wide program of cultural renewal in the modern world. An investigation of its philological underpinnings, however, reveals something more complex and ambivalent: the words from the inscription are a pedestrian citation from Vergil, executed by a humanist bureaucrat discharging his duties; the drama linked with its date has disappeared, for all the genuine medals of Isotta (those by de' Pasti) were made several years after the death of Polissena Sforza; the orthography (*Italiae*) no longer testifies to the authority and authenticity of primary sources, but to the "corrected" version concocted by Yriarte and adopted by Pound; and the medal supposedly by Pisanello is a late and worthless forgery. "Civilization," it turns out, is constructed upon curious foundations.

Worthy of This Love

"et amava perdutamente Ixotta degli Atti"
e "ne fu degna"

In the dead of night, the Venetian triremes lay at anchor in the waters of Ancona. Commanded by the doge himself, they stood ready to embark at dawn on a new crusade to deliver Constantinople from the infidel Turks, an expedition advancing under the personal guidance of the pope. Meanwhile, in his room in the episcopal palace, beside the cathedral of San Ciriaco and overlooking the harbor, the man who had dreamt of this moment was dying. "Pray for me, my son," he murmured, "for I am a sinner." Jacopo Ammanati was deeply moved. He knelt alongside the bed of the dying pope, Pius II, and he wept. The pope placed his hand on the head of Ammanati and added: "Be good, son; and pray for me." They were his last words; some two hours later he expired, still attended by Ammanati.

Ammanati was one of a handful of people whom Pius II requested to stay with him the night of 14–15 August 1464, and his letters and commentaries make up the only eyewitness account of the event.[32] They testify to the ties that bound the two men, and they make him a figure of interest for students of Ezra Pound: not because Ammanati was involved in the struggle between Pius II and Sigismondo Malatesta, though this is a central subject in the Malatesta Cantos, but because he authored several lines that reappear—much altered, it is true—in *The Cantos*. They have never been identified as his. How did this come about?

Jacopo Ammanati was born in 1422 in Lucca, son of a prominent family with roots in Pescia. He studied first in Pescia, then in Ferrara under Guarino Veronese, and then in Florence under Leonardo Bruni and Carlo Marsuppini, concentrating in rhetoric and poetry. He possessed a thorough grounding in humanist culture and close acquaintance with the bureaucratic circles of the chancery and secretariat. As the papal court was lodged in Florence more or less continuously from 1434 to 1443, he also gained access to the circles of the Curia, becoming secretary to Cardinal Domenico Capranica. Thereafter he rose steadily through the ecclesiastical bureaucracy: in 1455 he was named *apostolicorum diplomatum scriptor* by Calixtus III, and in 1458 his post was confirmed upon the election of the new pope, Pius II.

Ammanati's career took shape at a particular moment in ecclesiastical history. In the aftermath of the conciliar movement's collapse, the papacy had regained the prerogatives of a temporal power, and increasingly it was administered under the structures prevalent in the typical Italian *casato* (extended family). But this posed difficulties for a pope like Pius II, who stemmed from a modest family with limited social connections; Pius was forced to create an artificial *casato* or house, and to do so he made liberal use of the device of adoption.[33] One of his adopted sons was Ammanati, thereafter known as Ammanati-Piccolomini. His devotion to Pius was total, and he even took up citizenship in Siena (Pius II's native city). Ammanati's career advanced steadily. In 1460 he was nominated bishop of Pavia; in late 1461, after having reorganized the ecclesiastical troops disordered in a defeat by Sigismondo, he was named a cardinal. During the next three years he consolidated his role as the most trusted confidant of Pius II. However, with the election of Paul II in 1464, Ammanati's fortunes seriously declined. Disregarded in the new Curia, he retreated to the humanist studies of his youth, gathering a distinguished group of scholars around his house in Rome. Though he returned to active participation in the papal administration under Sixtus IV, his role was no longer so central or his interest in affairs so intense. In later years he often returned to Pienza, the little town in which Pius II had been born and which he had begun to reconstruct as a perfect "Renaissance city" before his untimely death. There Ammanati's own palace still stands across from that of his adopted father. He died on 10 September 1479.[34]

At his death Ammanati left behind several unpublished writings. One was a collection of his correspondence; another was his *Commentarii*, a discursive narration of contemporary events. Ammanati had played so pivotal a role in the church that both were essential documents for the period's history, and in 1506 they were published together for the first time by Giacomo Gherardi da Volterra, Ammanati's former secretary. In 1614, when a second edition of Pius's *Commentarii* appeared in Frankfurt, the two works by Ammanati were issued together again, this time as a continuation and supplement to the work of Pius, included in the same volume. And as such they were transmitted to subsequent generations.

Ammanati's *Commentarii* continued the homonymous work of his protector. It resumed the narrative in June 1464, where the earlier work stops, and it pressed forward to November 1469. Among the events of this period was the death of Sigismondo Malatesta in October 1468, and here Ammanati mentions for the only time the name of Isotta degli Atti:

> But in those days it happened that Sigismondo, who had returned to Italy from the Peloponnesian war on behalf of the Venetians exhausted by incessant ill health, departed from this life in Rimini, having entrusted custody of the city and its fortress to his wife Isotta whom, earlier as a kept mistress, later as his wife, he had desperately loved ["perdite amaverat"].[35]

About Isotta and Sigismondo he said no more—not a word. Clearly he had never seen Sigismondo and Isotta together, and the occasions when he might have met or spoken with Sigismondo were rather limited.[36] Such facts only confirm what is already obvious from Ammanati's tone and style—his report of Sigismondo's love is a modest rhetorical device, an incidental comment to flesh out his only mention of Isotta, a way to explain her identity before proceeding to the narrative of Rimini's fate under her brief rule. Its terms ("quam . . . perdite amaverat," had loved desperately) were a conventional formula of humanist prose, a result of their place in the history of Latin. In ancient Latin the adverb *perdite* (desperately) appears with the verb *amare* (to love) as an expression of common speech on four occasions (once each in Terence and Plautus, twice in Catullus), and with the synonymous verb *ardere* one time more (in Terence). It also appears connected with other verbs in Cicero, Quintilian, pseudo-Quintilian, and Apuleius—in short, always in works by authors recovered and reevaluated by humanist philology.[37] In the period around 1470, when Ammanati was writing, to use the expression *perdite amare* indicated less a specific content than a familiarity with works congenial to humanist tastes, and an adherence to the conventions of humanist neo-Latin.[38] When Ammanati characterizes the rapport between Sigismondo and Isotta, he does not wish to describe the depth of their passion, but to use a formula applicable to love outside of marriage; he wishes to note the violation of decorum, that most humanist value, entailed in marrying the woman who had earlier been one's mistress, and therefore he applies a conventional phrase from ancient Latin for the description of illicit or improper love. His exact contemporary, Giovanni Simonetta, also characterizes Sigismondo's love for Isotta with almost the same expression, "perdite adamare."[39] And both authors expressly describe Isotta as "the kept mistress," as the "pellex."

Ammanati's remarks about Sigismondo and Isotta began to attract attention after their inclusion in the 1614 edition of Pius II's *Commentarii*. In 1718 they were quoted by a Riminese scholar writing about the church of San Francesco; this reintegrated them into the repertory of local scholarship on Sigismondo and, most likely, brought them to the attention of Gianmaria Mazzuchelli, author of a biography of Isotta published in 1756.[40] Mazzuchelli cited Ammanati's passage in its entirety and incorporated it into a crucial argument.[41] Sounding a note of pre-Romanticism, he sought to show that Isotta was worthy of Sigismondo's affection, that she was not only beautiful, but endowed with the highest intellectual and spiritual gifts. As evidence he assembled testimonies from three sources: a late and worthless chronicle (ca. 1650); a passage from the local historian Cesare Clementini (1627); and the quotation from Ammanati. Now the passage by Ammanati acquired new importance: it showed that "there was no one . . . whom Sigismondo trusted more than her," and it demonstrated "the power she held over the spirit of Sigismondo"—power so overwhelming "that she was capable of leading him near the end of his life to repentance for his wayward ways and his sins." This claim was buttressed by a footnote to the late chronicle that reported that, thanks to Isotta, Sigismondo had finally repented.[42] In only a few lines, Mazzuchelli had transformed the shape and function of the passage by Ammanati: a terse aside within a historical narrative had become consummate testimony to the inspiring, redeeming power of love.

From Mazzuchelli, Ammanati's remarks were transmitted to Gaetano Moroni, the ecclesiastic whose vast encyclopedia was published in 1852 (see chapter 2, pp. 98–100). Now the tendencies announced in Mazzuchelli's work were accentuated, exaggerated, and refunctioned. Moroni adopted Ammanati's phrase, "perdite amaverat," translated it into Italian, and wove it into the fabric of his own work. Isotta was all but canonized:

> It is reported that Sigismondo was led to love Isotta desperately ["ad amare perdutamente Isotta"] not only for her singular beauty, but for the excellent gifts of her mind cultivated by her in every type of study, refining itself in the contemplations of philosophy, nurturing itself in the pasture of history, and happily drawing delight from poetry.

These were high spiritual gifts indeed, and according to Moroni they yielded a happy harvest: "it is said that Isotta put Sigismondo back on the path of virtue." Her benign influence, moreover, had issued in the salvation of the wicked condottiere, who had breathed his last "with sincere repentance" ("con sincero pentimento").[43] The effect was to turn Isotta into a figure of exquisite spiritual power set against the crude materialism of her mate (a contrast reflecting Moroni's view of the choices facing contemporary Italy). This contrast shapes all subsequent usage of the passage by Ammanati.

The most startling transformation of the passage by Ammanati occurs three decades later at the hands of Charles Yriarte (1882), who taps both Mazzuchelli and Moroni for his portrait of Isotta in his study of the Riminese court.[44] In his account the dogmatic content of Moroni is attenuated and obscured, while its religious foundations are retained, secularized, and reinvested in the sphere of cultural production. The "fine arts," epitomized in the figure of Isotta, assume a civilizing and redemptive function; the spiritual and the worldly converge in the exemplary unity of "the whole man" imagined by Burckhardt, unity now embodied in Isotta.[45] On the one hand "she [is] virtue itself" (p. 155), a space of autotelic disinterestedness; on the other hand, she is "no less capable in affairs of the heart and the senses than in affairs of politics" (p. 156). Here the discrepancies of bourgeois cultural life are resolved in an uneasy synthesis of idealism and mundanity, reconciling the ideal of disinterestedness with the pursuit of self-interest, the imperatives of "art" with the demands of the market. Because, however, such a synthesis stands in patent contradiction to contemporary social practice, because it is purely conceptual and devoid of actual foundations in the present, its validity can and *must* be corroborated in the past, in the domain of history. On the character of Isotta, says Yriarte, "there is not a discordant note in all the testimonies of history, from contemporary chroniclers to the most recent historians" (p. 155). The love that she inspires *must* be both real and historically verified, and the decisive evidence, odd as it might seem, becomes the passage by Jacopo Ammanati—and yet O how transformed:

> One may object to the testimonies of the paid poets who deified Isotta in their encomia, but one is forced to bow before the judgment of Sigismondo's severest judge and cruelest enemy. Pope Pius II has written: "He loved Isotta desperately, and she was worthy of this love." ["Il a aimé éperdument Isotte et elle en était digne."]

Yriarte transforms the passage from Ammanati in three ways: first, he renders it in French; second, he attributes it to Pius II rather than to Ammanati; and third, he adds a new clause that appears nowhere in the original, "et elle en était digne"—"and she was worthy of this love."[46] The attribution to Pius II also charges it with new significance: it ratifies the spiritual and historical reality of the values embodied by Isotta because it derives from the most hostile source imaginable, "the judgment of Sigismondo's cruelest enemy." It was the ne plus ultra of historical evidence.

Enter Antonio Beltramelli, the author of *Un tempio d'amore* (1912).[47] Beltramelli drew nearly all his information from Yriarte (although he never mentions his name), whose portrait his account both accentuated and deformed. The secular idealism of Yriarte is invested with new tensions from the sensualism of D'Annunzio, the egoism of Stirner, and the rebelliousness of Nietzsche.[48] When he treats the marriage of Isotta and Sigismondo, he depicts it as the fulfillment of their mutual devotion to an ideal existence set against the conformity and pettiness of the world around them. But to secure the purity of Isotta as its repository and incarnation, he must absolve her of any complicity in the charges of murder that stained Sigismondo, and to this end he adduces the passage originally written by Ammanati so long ago, but in the version created by Yriarte (pp. 50–51):[49]

> She lived a very long time at the side of Sigismondo, yet not once was she accused of having had a part in the crimes that he committed. Pius II, the historian who never spares a charge against Sigismondo, indeed who surpasses every limit, writes: "Sigismondo loved Isotta desperately, and she was worthy of this love." ["Sigismondo amò perdutamente Isotta ed ella ne era degna."]
>
> The words of the enemy ["la parola del nemico"] could not be clearer in their concision. Isotta is pure when she exits from the life of her time, through which she passed loving and suffering, noble and larger than human.

Here is the crowning testimony, "the words of the enemy" invoked to show that the animating ideal embodied by Isotta is neither fiction nor delusion, but historical fact, and thus a concrete point of reference for the modern world mired in materialism.

Pound probably purchased Beltramelli's work when he first visited the church of San Francesco in May 1922, and a month later he used it while writing his earliest drafts for a single Malatesta Canto (see chapter 1, pp.

31–33). But after his return to Paris in July he consulted the book only sporadically. Now he wanted to master facts in the crudest sense— names, dates, battles—and for this purpose Beltramelli offered little help. Only after he had studied other authors, only when he felt that his fund of information was sufficient, or even overwhelming—only then did he return to Beltramelli, sometime in late October.[50] By now Pound was concerned that readers might lose their way among the masses of data he was accumulating.[51] Beltramelli was useful at this point because he offered a perspective, an ideology that was also congenial to Pound's own views. Now the passage from Ammanati makes its first appearance in a draft fragment:[52]

That is to say he "ruled" and "loved"
Questi principi regnavano ⟨*governaron*⟩ savi⟨*a*⟩ment⟨*e*⟩, says Leo (Henrico)
and the offices were given to men of talent,
xxxxx⟨*tutti gli*⟩ uffic⟨*i pubblici*⟩ ad uomini di talento,
    find metric permitting the words.
        ⟨"⟩regnavit⟨"⟩, ⟨"⟩e⟨*d*⟩ amava perdutament⟨*e*⟩""
            Ixotta degli Atti ɵ, ⟨"⟩
sister of Alberto ⟨*Antonio*⟩, whose court yard was selciato
paved (vide . . . Genari,)
                e ne fu degna,
she was worthy of his affections, says Pio Secundo,
le parole del nemico

And on the verso of the same draft fragment, Pound added:

His enemies words (from the brochure of Beltramelli[).]

The draft fragment was clearly provisional, a sketch to be fleshed out later.[53] In mid-December 1922 he typed a massive, cumulative revision of all the earlier work, in which the quotation from Ammanati/Yriarte/ Beltramelli assumed a more definitive form, including quotation marks:

    "et amava perduta Ixotta degli Atti"
    e "ne fu degna"

A few days later he retyped this, correcting the erroneous *perduta* to *perdutamente* in the course of making numerous alterations to the entire draft. Thereafter the two lines were never changed.

For Pound, as for Beltramelli, the quotation from Ammanati (which we may call "pseudo-Pius") serves roughly the same function as did the allusion to the inscription from the medal by pseudo-Pisanello. It offers a historical verification of the reality—and realizability—of the idealist aspirations invested in the figure of Isotta; it testifies to their power to elicit a novel and exemplary form of cultural life, an "example of civilization" whose monument is the construction of "a temple of love." It is compelling because it comes from "Pius II," because *his* claim cannot be motivated by self-interest (unlike that of the court poets), and because his theology and office demand that he should not legitimate a secular and sensual idealism grounded in *this* world.

And as it turns out, he does not, for the passage is not by Pius II at all. The question, to be sure, is not merely which source is "correct." That question interests us only insofar as it leads to another: *how* has this passage been legitimated as a testimony to and for a specific form of civilization? The stages of that development are clear enough: the passage of pseudo-Pius becomes a "testimony to civilization" via a process that strips it from its use-context, erases its social settings, and brackets intervenient processes of transmission. Still, Pound's place in this evolution might be justified by the press of specific circumstances and motivations, or even by the pervasive sense of crisis and dislocation after the Great War. Yet something different takes place when the same process is replicated through uncritical assent to tacit paradigms of intellectual activity—as has surely happened when thirty-five years of scholarship always reproduces what Pound apparently believed: that these lines are a quotation from Pius II. It says much about modern literary studies that thirty-five years could not induce one scholar to read an edition of Pius II's works to verify whether any such "quotation" might be found. It raises, moreover, a theoretical question: if literary studies since roughly 1940 have been dominated by intrinsic and formalist conceptions that reject the notion of intentionality, why is it that scholars have consistently replicated Pound's intentions with such precision? Is this instance anomalous, or does it recur elsewhere?

A Little Chronicle

"constans in proposito
"Placuit oculis principis
"pulchra aspectu"
"populo grata

In a little box of cedar and glass, housed in a monastery on the hills of Covignano outside Rimini, lie some bones and the skull of a man whose name is unknown. The skull is stained, suggesting that he met a violent death. Who killed him? With what instrument, and with what motives?

"The certainty of death is attended with uncertainties," wrote Thomas Browne; and certainly it is uncertainty that surrounds the fatal passage of this anonymous figure. Around 1650, however, an effort was made to lend him an identity and his life a meaning, when an unknown yet zealous monk from Rimini forged a chronicle that reported that the Covignano relics were the mortal remains of the confessor to Polissena Sforza, murdered by Sigismondo Malatesta for refusing to divulge her confessional secrets. The stain on the skull, the chronicle said, had been left by a burning helmet that Sigismondo shoved over the sacerdote's devout though recalcitrant head—visible proof of martyrdom. The chronicle was said to have been written by "fra Alessandro of Rimini."

The chronicle of pseudo-Alessandro is mentioned in print for the first time in the biography of Isotta that Gianmaria Mazzuchelli published in 1756 and again in 1759, entitled *Notizie intorno ad Isotta da Rimino*. Mazzuchelli acknowledges that he learned about it from Giovanni Bianchi, a resident of Rimini, who had also warned him that some people questioned its antiquity and authenticity. But Mazzuchelli elects to cite it often in the course of his study, especially in a passage praising Isotta's intellectual and spiritual gifts and their effects on Sigismondo (pp. 36–37):

> But Sigismondo never considered the idea of displeasing his Isotta, who had also become his strongest source of support within Rimini itself. *Erat haec*, thus is she described in the Chronicle of Rimini, *pulchra aspectu, plurimis dotibus locupletata, foemina belligera, fortis, & constans in proposito, grata populo, & placita oculis Principis, ex qua nonnullos habuit filios, & filias, inter quos Pandulphum, & Lucretiam.* [She was ... of pleasant features, richly endowed with many gifts, a valiant woman, strong, firm in her resolve, dear to the people, and pleasing to the eyes of the prince, by whom she had several sons and daughters, among them Pandolfo and Lucrezia.]

Mazzuchelli goes on to adduce the passage by Ammanati that we have just studied, which, like that of pseudo-Alessandro, serves as contemporary testimony to the virtues of Isotta.[54] Under the guise of this new function, the chronicle was launched into the world.

Mazzuchelli was the principal source for Charles Yriarte's chapter on Isotta, as we have seen, and since Mazzuchelli quoted the chronicle of pseudo-Alessandro and the passage from Ammanati in the same discussion, it was only natural that Yriarte should link them still more closely. Yriarte puts the two passages together on page 155 (the lineation follows

Yriarte's, in order to register the exact tenor of Pound's marginal marking, discussed below):

> La chronique de Rimini[1] l'a caractérisée ainsi: "Erat hæc pulchra aspectu, plurimis dotibus locupletata, fœmina belligera et fortis, et constans in proposito, grata populo et placita oculis principis." Pour une maîtresse de prince, ce sont là des qualités de premier ordre. . . .

Yriarte also gives a footnote regarding the chronicle (Yriarte's lineation is indicated by a solidus):

> I.—C'est une chronique du XVe siècle conservée à la Gambalunga de Rimini et / qu'on attribue à Alessandro da Rimini.

His treatment of the passage by pseudo-Alessandro is identical with his use of Ammanati; it testifies to the redemptive and civilizing powers embodied in Isotta, a view that would remain uncontested for three decades.

In 1910–11 Giovanni Soranzo published a major study that explored all the charges traditionally leveled at Sigismondo, among them the accusation that he had murdered his second wife, Polissena Sforza.[55] In reply, Gregorio Giovanardi in 1914 angrily defended the time-worn accusation. He based his argument on the chronicle by pseudo-Alessandro, with its explicit report of Polissena's murder.[56] To parry this, Soranzo examined the document itself, publishing his results a year later, in 1915.[57] Methodically and meticulously, Soranzo demonstrated that it was a forgery from the seventeenth century, its testimony worthless. His article appeared in an important scholarly review, a journal that was received by the Bibliothèque Nationale of Paris, where Pound did much of his research for the Malatesta Cantos in 1922. But Pound never came across it; his knowledge of the chronicle stemmed wholly from Yriarte.[58]

Pound obtained his copy of Yriarte's book on 3 August 1922. Almost immediately he began entering an elaborate sequence of marginalia and submarginalia to signal subjects that had caught his eye. Three regard the chronicle of pseudo-Alessandro. One is a vertical double bar in pencil, entered in the margin opposite the quotation of the pseudo-chronicle on page 155:

> La chronique de Rimini[1] l'a caractérisée ainsi: "Erat hæc pulchra aspectu, plurimis dotibus locupletata, fœmina belligera et fortis, et constans in proposito, grata populo et placita oculis principis." Pour une maîtresse de prince, ce sont là des qualités de premier ordre . . .

Another is a kind of bracket with a double bar, located on the same page in the margin opposite footnote 1:

I. —C'est une chronique du XVᵉ siècle conservée à la Gambalunga de⎤⟋
Rimini et qu'on attribue à Alessandro da Rimini.

The third appears in an index, which Pound assembled on a blank leaf at the back of his copy, and it too registers his interest in the topic:

> *155   Chron. di Alex. Rim—Gambalunga*

The index, probably made in November or December of 1922, was intended to serve as a resource for Pound's researches in Italy in early 1923.[59] However, nothing among his notes from Rimini (made in March) suggests that he actually examined the chronicle. Perhaps Pound lost interest: in Rimini he was seeking unpublished sources, not consulting ones already well known, and by now his own version of the passage from the chronicle was firmly established as part of the Malatesta Cantos.

Already in late August 1922 Pound wrote a draft fragment that drew on the Isotta passage from the chronicle as reported by Yriarte:

> Isotta
> placita oculis principis
> locupletata dotibus plurimus [*sic*]
> foemina belligera populo grata
> constans in proposito, belligera et fortis,
>   aspectu pulchra[.]

Initially the passage is only another fragment stored among the masses of data accumulating in his notes.[60] Pound does not integrate it into a fuller context until a few months later in October 1922. When he discovers the quotation from Ammanati/pseudo-Pius in Beltramelli, it reminds him of the fragment based on pseudo-Alessandro, and he attempts a new version that merges them (the passage below is continuous with the one given above on p. 172):

> constans in proposito, populoque grata,
>   a trueth teller, in favour ~~xxx xxx~~ with the p[e]ople,
> bellig[e]ra, fortis, who ruled Rimini in his absence,
> and kept out the intriguers, save Roberto
>   her stepson.

Below this he adds two autograph notes on a theme that especially interests him:

> *She kept her word*
> *(the people liked her)*

From this point on the two passages are forever linked. In a subsequent autograph draft he adds the allusion to Landor ("past ruin'd Latium") that appears in the final version. Later, in mid-December, he undertakes the massive revision culminating in the Watson typescript, in which the passages from pseudo-Pius and pseudo-Alessandro appear just as they are in the final version of Malatesta Cantos.[61]

The reception of these lines in modern scholarship has followed a curious pattern. Critics have consistently reported that they stem "from a fifteenth century chronicle of Rimini."[62] (Two writers, it is true, have stated that the line "constans in proposito" derives from Horace, testifying to the cultural attainments of clerics in both the seventeenth and twentieth centuries.)[63] Still, as we consider the testimonies rehearsed at the close of Canto 9, we may feel a certain malaise. If Isotta stands at the center of the Malatesta Cantos, if it is really she "in whose honour and as whose monument" was constructed "the apex of . . . the last 1000 years of the occident," and if these are the testimonies that corroborate the reality of that vision, we may begin to suspect that the foundations of "civilization"—both Pound's and modern criticism's—rest on somewhat curious grounds. Out of six lines only a hemistich was written during the lifetime of Sigismondo or Isotta; only one and a half lines can be considered contemporary testimony, and even these are conventions of humanist rhetoric or pedantic borrowings from the classics. Still, perhaps this is only an isolated aberration, and we should investigate further.

Lyrical Center

Lyra:
"Ye spirits who of olde were in this land
Each under Love, and shaken,
Go with your lutes, awaken
The summer within her mind,
Who hath not Helen for peer
        Yseut nor Batsabe."

Midway through Canto 8, the first of the Malatesta Cantos, a lyrical fragment bursts into view: it is rendered with delicacy and ease, like clear water after the muddy specifications of the contract between Sigismondo and the commune of Florence, a few lines earlier. It is a love poem. Placed here, it articulates the thematic axes elaborated in the rest of the sequence. First there is the material surrounding it, depicting an external and objective world of public activity: its dominant values are practical, self-interested, and useful, or directed toward the accomplishment of a specific goal (a telos, usually economic in character). This fills the foreground of the principal characters' activity, generating the confusing contracts and official letters of public life. Then there is the aesthetic domain epitomized in the lyric poem, an internal and subjective world reserved for more authentic states of consciousness; its reigning values are love and the disinterested contemplation of beauty, activities that are autonomous, autotelic. This deeper reality is ignored by most, and only glimpsed by Sigismondo at moments such as this, when a return to basics generates the harmonious order and simplicity of the little poem. The dichotomy is also structured in sociohistorical terms: social, political, and economic dimensions command the field of attention, consuming most of the canto and most of the characters' lives, while the aesthetic dimension is a fragmentary insight granted only to the individual, and granted only when a character sheds his specifically historical attributes, becoming no longer a specific subject (e.g., Sigismondo) but a voice of bare essentials ("Lyra"). But within the structure of this canto, presumed to be homologous with a deeper structure of reality, the love poem is also the midpoint, the center that organizes the otherwise heterogeneous and disparate activity. It is a poem for Isotta, scholars have told us. It is for her that the monument of civilization is constructed; and *only* because it is *for her* can the poem, and by extension the church of San Francesco, be "a temple of love," be something more than just another building constructed for practical or ideological motives shared by contemporaries. Here is the consummate testimony at the core of Pound's entire project.

Poems allegedly written by Sigismondo are first mentioned by Ezra Pound in Draft *C3* (line 60), written between 3 and 10 August 1922, a draft that adopts motifs and phrases derived from Yriarte's book, *Un Condottiere au XVe siècle*, which Pound received on 3 August.[64] The earliest mention of them is a terse memorandum, an autograph addition to the typescript draft, to which Pound has later added a large *X* to draw further attention to it:

Sono venuto a mal passo. **X**

The referent is clear: Pound is citing, apparently by memory, the opening line of a poem attributed to Sigismondo by Charles Yriarte, "Soccorrime per dio, ch'io so' a mal porto," or in some variants "sono al porto" (loosely translated, "Help me, for God's sake, for I'm in evil straits"). The poem is long (130 lines in Yriarte's transcription), and is filled with images drawn from ancient mythology, medieval romance, and biblical story, lending it an air of genteel erudition.[65]

THE EIGHTH CANTO

THESE fragments you have shelved
(shored).
" Slut!" " Bitch!" Truth and Calliope
Slanging each other sous les lauriers:
That Alessandro was negroid. And
      Malatesta
Sigismund:
          Frater tamquam
Et compater carissime: *tergo*
    . . hanni de
    . . dicis
    . . . . entia
Equivalent to:
      Giohanni of the Medici,
      Florence.
Letter received, and in the matter of
      our Messire Gianozio,
One from him also, sent on in form and with all due dispatch,
Having added your wishes and memoranda.
As to arranging peace between you and the King of Ragona,
So far as I am concerned, it wd. give me the greatest possible pleasure,
At any rate nothing wd. give me more pleasure
      or be more acceptable to me,
And I shd. like to be party to it, as was promised me,
      either as participant or adherent.
As for my service money, perhaps you and your father wd. draw it
And send it on to me as quickly as possible.   Piero della
And tell the *Maestro di pentore*   Francesca
That there can be no question of his painting the walls for the moment,   Petrus de
As the mortar is not yet dry   Burgo
And it wd. be merely work chucked away
      (buttato via)
But I want it to be quite clear, that until the chapels are ready
I will arrange for him to paint something else
So that both he and I shall get as much enjoyment as possible from it,
And in order that he may enter my service
And also because you write me that he needs cash,
I want to arrange with him to give him so much per year
And to assure him that he will get the sum agreed on.

Plate 1. Henry Strater, artist, and William Bird, publisher: first page for Canto 8 of *A Draft of XVI. Cantos* (Paris: Three Mountains, 1925). Reprinted from Ezra Pound, *A Draft of XVI. Cantos* (Paris: Three Mountains, 1925), p. 27.

HESE fragments you
(shored).
" Slut!" " Bitch!" 7
Slanging each other
That Alessandro wa
Malatesta
Sigismund:
Frater i
Et compater carissin
. . hanni d
. . dicis
. . . . entia
Equivalent to:
Giohanr
Florenc
Letter received, and

Plate 2. Henry Strater, decorative capital and headpiece for Canto 8 of *A Draft of XVI. Cantos* (1925), shown in actual size. The Gothic windows behind the Roman arches in the church of San Francesco have been altered. Now they are given illustrations, and the entwined letters *S* and *I* are inserted into the trefoil, furnishing a key for reading the series of Malatesta Cantos that follows. Reprinted from Pound, *A Draft of XVI. Cantos*, p. 27.

THE ELEVENTH CANTO

grādment li antichi cavaler romanj
davano fed a quisti annutii
And he put us under the chiefs,
        and the chiefs went back to their squadrons:
        Bernardo Reggio, Nic Benzo, Giovan Nestorno,
        Paulo Viterbo, Buardino of Brescia,
                Cetho Brandolino,
And Simone Malespina, Petracco St Archangelo, Rioberto da Canossa,
And for the tenth Agniolo da Roma
        And that gay bird Piero della Bella,
And to the eleventh Roberto,
And the papishes were three thousand on horses, dilly cavalli tre milia,
And a thousand on foot,
And the Lord Sigismundo had but mille tre cento cavalli
And hardly 500 fanti (and one spingard),
And we beat the papishes and fought them back through the tents
And he came up to the dyke again
And fought through the dyke-gate
And it went on from dawn to sunset
And we broke them and took their baggage
        and mille cinquecento cavalli
E li homini di Messire Sigismundo non furono che mille trecento
And the Venetians sent in their compliments
And various and sundry sent in their compliments;
But we got it next August;
And Roberto got beaten at Fano,
And he went by ship to Tarentum,
I mean Sidg went to Tarentum
And he found 'em, the anti-Aragons,
        busted and weeping into their beards.
And they, the papishes, came up to the walls,
And that nick-nosed s.o.b. Feddy Urbino
Said: "*Par che e fuor di questo . . . Sigis . . . mundo.*"
" They say he dodders about the streets ·
" And can put his hand to neither one thing nor the other,"
And he was in the sick wards, and on the high tower
And everywhere, keeping us at it.

Plate 3. Henry Strater, artist, and William Bird, publisher: first page for Canto II of *A Draft of XVI. Cantos* (1925). Reprinted from Pound, *A Draft of XVI. Cantos*, p. 42.

ELE

grādment li antichi cavaler ı
davano fed a qui.
And he put us under the chie
and the chiefs went back
Bernardo Reggio, Nic Benzo,
Paulo Viterbo, Buardino of Bi
Cetho Brandolinc

THE T

Plate 4. Henry Strater, detail from decorative capital and headpiece for Canto 11 of *A Draft of XVI. Cantos* (1925). The armaments echo Yriarte's claims about the entwined letters *S* and *I*. Reprinted from Pound, *A Draft of XVI. Cantos*, p. 42.

Plate 5. Henry Strater, detail from headpiece for Canto 10, *A Draft of XVI. Cantos* (1925)., Several scenes in the pediment and frieze of the classical temple rehearse the motif of the entwined letters *S* and *I*. Reprinted from Pound, *A Draft of XVI. Cantos*, p. 37.

Plate 6. Henry Strater, detail from the headpiece to Canto 10, *A Draft of XVI. Cantos* (1925). In the center is a knight riding right, and on the caparison of his horse are the entwined letters *S* and *I* (compare the knight in figure 19), echoing the belief that Sigismondo obliged his soldiers to wear the device into battle as a token of his love for Isotta degli Atti. Reprinted from Pound, *A Draft of XVI. Cantos*, p. 37.

Plate 7. Henry Strater, detail from the headpiece to Canto 10, *A Draft of XVI. Cantos* (1925). The illustration shows Sigismondo Malatesta being burned in effigy in a ceremony performed on 27 April 1462: on the chest of the effigy are the entwined letters *S* and *I*, turning Sigismondo in a martyr for "the temple of love" and a forerunner of a new, post-Christian era (note the citation of Christ's crucifixion in the outstretched arms). Reprinted from Pound, *A Draft of XVI. Cantos*, p. 37.

And the old row with Naples continued.
And what he said was all right in Mantua;
And Borso had the pair of them up to Bel Fiore,
The pair of them, Sigismundo and Federico Urbino,
Or perhaps in the palace, Ferrara, Sigismund upstairs
And Urbino's gang in the basement,
And a regiment of guards in, to keep order,
            For all the good that did:
"*Te cavero la budella del corpo!*"
El conte levatosi:
            "*Io te cavero la corata a te!*"
And that day Cosimo smiled,
That is, the day they said:
            "Drusiana is to marry Count Giacomo . . ."
(Piccinino) un sorriso malizioso.
Drusiana, another of Franco Sforza's;
It would at least keep the row out of Tuscany.
And he fell out of a window, Count Giacomo,
Three days after his death, that was years later in Naples,
For trusting Ferdinando of Naples,
And old Wattle could do nothing about it.

                    Et:

. . . .

NTEREA pro gradibus basilicæ S. Pietri
ex arida materia ingens pyra extruitur in
cujus summitate imago Sigismundi collocatur
hominis lineamenta, et vestimenti modum adeo
proprie reddens, ut vera magis persona, quam
imago videretur; ne quem tamen imago
falleret, et scriptura ex ore prodiit, quæ
diceret: Sigismundus hic ego sum
Malatesta, filius Pandulphi, rex proditorum,
Deo atque hominibus infestus, sacri censura
senatus igni damnatus;
                    scripturum
multi legerunt. deinde astante populo, igni
immisso, et pyra simulacrum repente flagravit.
                    Com. Pio II. Liv. vii, p. 85
                    Yriarte, p. 288.
. . . .

So that in the end that pot-scraping little runt Andreas
            Benzi, da Siena
Got up to spout out the bunkum

Plate 8. Henry Strater, artist, and William Bird, publisher: second page for Canto 10 of
A Draft of XVI. Cantos (1925). Opposite a passage from the *Commentarii* of Pius II,
which is set in small capitals to establish an effect of gray uniformity, one sees the
device composed of the letters *S* and *I*, which soars over the page like a defiant gesture.
Reprinted from Pound, *A Draft of XVI. Cantos*, p. 38.

Plate 9. Henry Strater, inset illustration for Canto 10 of *A Draft of XVI. Cantos* (1925). The design is based on a heraldic device with a long tradition in the Malatesta family, which was used in a commemorative medal by Pisanello. The Pisanello model, in turn, was reproduced in an engraving published by Charles Yriarte in *Un Condottiere au XVe siècle*, the source of Strater's rendering (compare figures 20, 21). Reprinted from Pound, *A Draft of XVI. Cantos*, p. 38.

The poem is a *capitolo ternario*, which is to say, written in *terza rima* in hendecasyllabic verse. It is transmitted by several manuscripts, including one in the Vatican Library, ms. Vat. Lat. 5159, where the poem is explicitly ascribed to "Sigismundus Pandulphus Malatesta."[66] This was the manuscript consulted by Yriarte. Though it is conserved in the Vatican Library, Yriarte claimed that he had found it "in the Vatican's secret archives" ("dans les archives secrètes du Vatican," p. 139)—a rather different place. The manuscript is a collection of poems from the middle and late quattrocento, but Yriarte claimed to have uncovered it "among the administrative papers regarding the military captains of the State of the Church" ("parmi des papiers administratifs que se rapportent aux capitaines généraux des États de l'Eglise," p. 139). In short, more inept fictions to enhance the drama and color of his narration, contrived in the same spirit as his rewriting of the quotation from Ammanati. Yriarte accepted the ascription given by the Vatican manuscript without question and never examined other documents in order to control its testimony. He was, in fact, convinced that the poem was written by Sigismondo Malatesta. But attribution was only the beginning.

Of all the poems attributed to Sigismondo, said Yriarte, this was "the most characteristic of his works" ("la plus caractéristique de ses oeuvres," p. 139). It also had special historical significance, a "capital importance . . . for the history of art in Rimini" ("importance capitale . . . pour l'histoire de l'art à Rimini," p. 141 n. 1). It furnished the "key to the enigma" ("la clef de l'énigme," p. 218) of the bas-reliefs that fill the interior of the church of San Francesco. Since the poem had clearly been "written by Sigismondo in honor of Isotta" ("poésie écrite par Sigismondo en l'honneur d'Isotta," pp. 218–19), its many references to mythology furnished a code for unraveling the enigmatic iconology of the Tempio's sculptures. "Each of its stanzas explains to us the subject of one of the bas-reliefs sculpted by Agostino di Duccio in one of the chapels of San Francesco" (p. 141, n. 1).[67] The mythological images of the poem, said Yriarte, had been rendered as designs by Matteo de' Pasti, and in turn his designs were "translated into marble" by Agostino di Duccio.

Matteo translated them into designs made on wax tablets or with chalk . . . and Agostino di Duccio translated into marble his master's compositions. Of that we have no doubt whatever.

The sculptor, who flatters his master and his lord, and who is delighted with these strange representations, extracts from the marble, one by one, each of the symbols and constellations which Sigismondo has invoked [in his poem].[68]

The poem stood at the very core of the "temple of love," proof that the church of San Francesco was a poem in stone, the material expression of Sigismondo's desperate love for Isotta degli Atti.

The *capitolo ternario* was not the only poem that Yriarte attributed to Sigismondo. He also claimed to have discovered four more. One he had found in a manuscript in Florence, three others he had encountered in the collection of Apografi Bilancioni, papers left by the lawyer and bibliophile Pietro Bilancioni (1808–77) on his death and purchased by the library of Bologna in 1878.[69] Among these was a *serventese* beginning, "Alto signor, dinanzi a cui non vale," copied from a Florentine manuscript now in the Biblioteca Nazionale (hereafter BNF).[70] Indeed, in the BNF manuscript it was explicitly attributed to Sigismondo: "Opus magnifici et potentis domini domini Sigismundi Pandulfi de Malatestis factum 1445." Unfortunately, since Yriarte knew only the testimony of the illegible transcription from the Apografi, he could print just six lines from it, one of which he rendered (p. 394):

> Quale Elena è egualea te o quale Isolta.[71]

It is this rendering that would later serve Pound for his own adaptation:

> ["]Who hath not Helen for peer
> Yseut nor Batsabe."

(The concluding reference to Batsabe, or Bathsheba, however, derives from the other poem or *capitolo ternario*.) But apart from this one line, Pound's lyrical fragment is based entirely on the *capitolo ternario*, the central text for Yriarte's claims about the Tempio.

Yriarte's claims were diffused rapidly and widely. Only four years after the publication of his book, the 1886 edition of the *Encyclopaedia Britannica* contained an article on Rimini, which, describing the church of San Francesco, included the declaration:

> The bas-reliefs of one of the chapels represent Jupiter, Venus, Saturn, Mars, and Diana, together with the signs of the zodiac. And these subjects are derived, it appears, from a poem in which Sigismondo had invoked the gods and the signs of the zodiac to soften Isotta's heart and win her to his arms.[72]

The explanation also became a standard feature in authoritative guidebooks. The 1900 Baedeker for Italy, reviewing the church of San Francesco, described "the planets and other fantastic representations from a poem by Sigismondo in honour of his mistress." The 1908 edition of the Baedeker repeated this verbatim.[73] Other genres were also affected. In

1906 Edward Hutton published a novel on Sigismondo's life that treated the poem extensively. Hutton quoted and translated it in its entirety, lavishing nine pages on the mysteries of "those sculptures so wonderfully setting forth the verses of Sigismondo." He concluded, perhaps with more truth than he realized: "And truly, who can tell all the wonders of the place?" Yet even this was not enough for Hutton; in a later passage he described Sigismondo's soldiers following him on a hard military campaign, all the while singing the poems written for Isotta: "and his soldiers followed him, singing through all that desolate, silent country, as I have heard, the poems he had made in praise of Madonna Isotta."[74] In 1913 Hutton also published a guidebook to the province of Romagna: once again he described the "bas-reliefs by Sperandio, illustrating, as I think, a poem by Sigismondo in honour of Isotta," and reported that "all these subjects are taken from one of Sigismondo's poems." And Hutton was not alone. Without the love poems we might never have had that felicitous work by Antonio Beltramelli, *A Temple of Love* (1912), whose very title nodded to what by now was an established tradition.[75]

Pound, we have seen, read all these works. His interest in the poems ascribed to Sigismondo was intense and unremitting: it began with the memorandum appended to *C3* in August 1922, after he had received his copy of Yriarte, and it continued throughout his research in Italy in 1923. His labors amassed a documentary corpus of remarkable dimensions and complexity: (1) marginalia and submarginalia made in his copy of Yriarte, (2) typescript bibliographical or reading notes drawn from Yriarte, (3) drafts and draft fragments based on Yriarte's transcriptions, and (4) reading notes from and transcriptions of manuscripts and secondary sources consulted in Italian libraries in the spring of 1923.

His reading of the poems attributed to Sigismondo assimilated them to three subjects that especially interested him: the culture of neopaganism (as he understood it), the culture of Provençal poetry, and the project of writing his own poem. Consider a verse's development. In August, in his own copy of Yriarte, he draws a bracket and line opposite Yriarte's claim that the *capitolo ternario* is "la plus caractéristique" of Sigismondo's works.[76] Next, in September, his reading notes show him attracted by Yriarte's remark that at one point the poem addresses itself "to aged king Solomon, who, 'vanquished by the love of a pagan, worships idols on his knees.'" Pound duly records: "Solomon lover of pagan bent the knee."[77] His reading note is then followed by draft fragments that translate and paraphrase the same line about Bathsheba from the *capitolo ternario*. The outcome is the enigmatic reference to "Batsabe" that we see in the completed version of the Malatesta Cantos. For Pound it suggests a chain of resonant analogies: Solomon's submission to Bathsheba prefigures the love of Sigismondo for Isotta; his worship of gentile gods foreshadows the neopaganism that Pound believes has been expressed in the Tempio; and both events rhyme with a transition that Pound awaits and half-expects in his own age, a turn from the monotheism and sexual repression allegedly characteristic of bourgeois culture to a new paganism that would celebrate the vital powers of human sexuality and creativity, a new age when, as one contemporary wrote, man would "reunite the passion and the delight of human love with his deepest feelings of the sanctity and beauty of Nature."[78]

As another example, in his own copy of Yriarte, perhaps sometime in mid-August 1922, Pound makes two markings opposite the transcription of a sonnet, "O vaga e dolce luce, anima altera." Both are submarginalia that earmark two lines of the poem for further attention.[79] The lines describe the grass and flowers bending before the feet of the beloved as she walks over them, eager to be pressed by her tender feet and "rustled by her cerulean mantle." A few weeks later he translates these lines in a draft fragment that is buried among his reading notes from Yriarte:

> And the new grass bends, the flowers bend before you,
>   hoping your feet will press them,
>   moved by your bel mantel d'indi.

One part of his rendering, "bel mantel d'indi," is curious, since it lacks any analogue in the original, which instead reads "ceruleo manto." Plainly it stems from a line in an entirely different poem by Arnaut Daniel, a line Pound had translated and discussed in his 1912 essay "Psychology and Troubadours":

> She made me a shield, extending over me her *fair mantle of indigo*, so that slanderers might not see this. [Italics mine.][80]

In the 1912 essay Pound had argued that one could understand this line in two ways: either as "a conceit" or as a "historical" practice reported by the poem. Both were "obvious" and perhaps valid interpretations, but ultimately "less satisfactory" than a third view, "a visionary interpretation" that regards Provençal poetry as the expression of "a cult . . . for the purgation of the soul by a refinement of, and lordship over, the senses." Now, ten years later, this understanding of Provençal poetry and culture informs his translation of the sonnet attributed to Sigismondo, as the "ceruleo manto" is assimilated to the "bel mantel d'indi" from Arnaut

Daniel. The transformation recapitulates Pound's belief that a vital thread of cultural continuity links the culture of medieval Provence with quattrocento Rimini; the mantle of indigo becomes the emblem of a cultic vision, and Malatestan Rimini its spiritual heir.[81] These lines, considerably elaborated by Pound in later draft fragments, were not included in the final version of the Malatesta Cantos—not because Pound had changed his view, but because it had already been made sufficiently clear when he depicted Guillaume IX of Poitiers (at the end of Canto 8) riding up from Spain with musical instruments that forecast the flowering of Provençal poetry, instruments that reappear in the lutes mentioned in the poem of Sigismondo: "Go with your lutes, awaken | The summer within her mind."

That Sigismondo had written poetry suggested comparisons between his activities and Pound's; and if the poem represented the core of the building's inspiration, his labors on the Tempio might be seen as analogous with Pound's on his poem. In Draft *D2*, for example, Pound compares his trials in writing *The Cantos* to those of Sigismondo in building the church of San Francesco:

> ~~Chien de metier,~~
> ~~hop[e]lessness of writing an epic,~~
> ~~chien de metier,~~
> ~~hop[e]lessness of building a temple,~~
> in Romagna, in a land teeming with cattle thieves[.]

These lines are swiftly canceled in a subsequent layer of autograph revisions (as the transcription shows). Pound, however, continued to invoke the analogy throughout his life, sometimes ironically or playfully, but always with undisguised pleasure in the comparison. In 1925, when the first edition of *The Cantos* was printed by William Bird, Pound expressed his approval of the printing by citing a line from the chronicle of pseudo-Alessandro: it was "a bhloody ghood job, after awl your night sweats," he said, adding enigmatically, "Placuit occulis."[82] As Isotta had pleased Sigismondo, so the deluxe edition of *The Cantos* had pleased Pound: *The Cantos*, so this implied, was his true Isotta, its text his genuine love. Yet the same analogy could suggest different axes of emphasis: in 1938, for example, he praised Sigismondo for having appreciated good art immediately, dismissing the rival ruler of nearby Urbino, Federigo d'Urbino, as a wealthy collector who had acquired only "the seconds." Federigo "was his Amy Lowell," said Pound, referring to the wealthy poetess who had replaced Pound as the leader of imagism in late 1914. The implied analogy was all too obvious—Ezra and Sigismondo had been men ahead of their time, enjoying "the firsts," while Amy and Federigo had been mere latecomers.[83] Their sensibilities had constructed the "temple of love" and the "epic of love," monuments to the vital powers of human creation and sexuality. And in 1958, shortly after he had been released from St. Elizabeths Hospital and had returned to Italy, Pound informed his daughter that he wished to build a small temple on the summit of a nearby mountain—a desire inseparable from his appreciation of "the Malatestan temple" and of analogies between himself and the Renaissance condottiere.[84]

Like Luigi Orsini and other writers of guidebooks, Pound also implied or stated that the church of San Francesco was a poem in stone.[85] In Draft C3, for example, he suggests that Provençal culture had been characterized by song alone, in contrast to Malatestan Rimini (C3, 40):

> but here Rimini, the voice, the stone[.]

Elsewhere in the same draft he celebrates the building for having captured "life in a setting, and the word made stone" (C3, 58.1), a phrase rehearsed in different terms a few weeks later when he admires the Tempio as "a song caught in the stone."[86] Thus, while a common cultural psychology links medieval Provence with Malatestan Rimini, the quattrocento city is portrayed as having gone further, as having materialized the visionary content of song in its public monument. The distinction between the public and private realms is inverted, or simply vanishes: the public realm is privatized, the private publicized. It is the love poem that structures the external objective world of public activity, the aesthetic that informs the social, political, and economic fields; it is the private, ideal, and subjective world that is materialized as "stone." Such a burden of cultural desire pivots precisely on the attribution of this poem to Sigismondo, the belief that it is written by him for Isotta, the conviction that the Tempio expresses its subjects and themes—a burden that helps explain Pound's conduct in Italy a few months later.

With the exception of a few modest variants, Pound completed his adaptation of the poems attributed to Sigismondo by mid-December 1922. A few months later, when he went to Italy, he examined all the manuscripts that Yriarte had indicated as his sources—and no others. Pound was not searching for evidence to test or control the claims of Yriarte, assertions that he found congenial and wished to believe himself. Instead he sought manuscripts that could only confirm them. Further, whenever he actually examined a manuscript containing the poems, he never transcribed the document's own readings, but always the readings of the published transcriptions that he was also consulting simultaneously. He clearly examined, for example, Riccardiana ms. 1154, containing a series of sonnets by Sigismondo; yet his transcriptions coincide in every case with the modernized readings of the Bilancioni edition of 1860, not with the manuscript itself.[87] Again, it is certain that he examined BNF Palatino Capponiano 152—a manuscript that contains the *capitolo ternario* (though without an explicit attribution to Sigismondo)—yet once more all his readings coincide with the published transcriptions of Palermo, who had attributed the poem to Sigismondo for the first time in 1860, rather than with the manuscript itself.[88] Clearly his interest lay elsewhere. He regarded the manuscripts with a more romantic eye, as physical entities imbued with evocative powers. They were ethnographic objects endowed with an aura of authenticity, and he derived an essentially "aesthetic" pleasure from this "unmediated" experience with the documents produced by a culture that fascinated him. When it came to the poems, he was engaged not in research, but in erudite tourism— engaged in this way, however, because he was disinclined to discover anything that might contradict the center of his whole work.

Alas, the fatal blow to Yriarte's claims about the poems had already been struck a decade earlier, in 1911. In that year Aldo Francesca Massèra had published the first part of his study on the Malatestan court poets, a preliminary step toward his planned biography of Isotta degli Atti. His critique was cool, clear, devastating, and showed that every poem attributed to Sigismondo by Yriarte was the work of another author. Yriarte had failed to examine other manuscripts to control the testimony of his sources. Thus, it was true that the *serventese* that had been copied by Bilancioni and published by Yriarte was, as Yriarte had noted, explicitly attributed to Sigismondo Malatesta in BNF Palatino Capponiano 152. However, already in 1741 one scholar had noticed that the same poem was attributed to Carlo Valturi in another manuscript, the famous Codex Isoldiano in Bologna, a contemporary collection of Italian poetry from the mid-quattrocento with far more authority than the manuscript in Florence. The attribution to Sigismondo in the Florentine manuscript represented an error typical of later collections, which frequently assigned works by lesser known writers to others more famous or better known, often their patrons. And Valturi, of course, had been a minor poet at the court of Sigismondo. But the worst fate was reserved for the *capitolo ternario*, the poem that had been "the most characteristic" of Sigismondo's works, the "key to the enigma" of the Tempio. In this case there were eleven other manuscripts that attributed the same poem to Simone Serdini, a Sienese poet who had enjoyed close relations with Rimini and its rulers.[89] Unfortunately, Serdini had died in 1419 or 1420, making it unlikely that his poem referred to Sigismondo Malatesta (then three years old), Isotta degli Atti (then not yet born), or the Tempio Malatestiano.

The effects of Massèra's critique were felt only slowly. In its 1911 edition, the *Encyclopaedia Britannica* reprinted its 1886 article on Rimini with exactly the same claims about the *capitolo ternario* and the Tempio.[90] In his guidebook of 1913, Edward Hutton also repeated all of Yriarte's assertions. Even when authors no longer mentioned Yriarte's specific claims, the analogy between the church and a poem was retained or asserted still more vigorously, as in the guidebook by Luigi Orsini (1915, reprinted 1927), which compares the building with "a poem of indestructible beauty, uniting all the tenderest harmonies of art and of feeling." It is, says Orsini, a "hymn to immortal Beauty and infinite Love."[91]

These views were close to those of Pound himself. Apparently he never came across the Massèra article, even though it was published in a journal for the study of Italian literature that enjoyed wide recognition (comparable to that of the *Publications of the Modern Language Association* at the same time) and ample diffusion (the Bibliothèque Nationale held a copy of every issue). Still, Pound's eagerness to accept the authenticity of the poems by pseudo-Sigismondo may seem understandable, however strange or objectionable to our later tastes. More puzzling is the case of scholars who have always reproduced what Pound believed, that the poems were authentic works of Sigismondo Malatesta, and who have never questioned the veracity of these claims—even though Massèra's article demonstrating this error was published in 1911. It is an unhappy record: Mayo (1954), Moramarco (1978), Kearns (1980), Terrell (1980), Harper (1981), Cookson (1985).[92] And it is a record of remarkable consistency and duration. One begins to sense a pattern emerging, a curious pattern indeed.

The Missing Letter: Why?

So far we have examined the constitution of two passages. The first appears at the end of Canto 9, in six lines. It comprises three testimonies: an inscription associated with a medal by pseudo-Pisanello, a passage from the chronicle by pseudo-Alessandro, and another passage partly composed by Ammanati, partly concocted by Yriarte, yet generally attributed to Pius II. The second appears at the midpoint of Canto 8, also in six lines. It contains one phrase from a poem by Carlo Valturi, and five lines from a poem by Simone Serdini, or "pseudo-Sigismondo." These are Pound's most extended treatments of Isotta, but not his only ones. The first edition of *The Cantos* (1925) included a third passage, which has disappeared from all subsequent editions, consisting of only two letters: *S* and *I*, entwined with one another. Despite its brevity, it received a curious typographical treatment: apart from the book's title and decorative capitals at the beginning of each canto, this symbol was printed larger than any other word in *The Cantos*—the biggest letters in the entire text—and in two colors, red and black. What did it mean, and why was it given such privileged treatment?

The entwined letters *S* and *I* appear in numerous testimonies linked with the court of Sigismondo Malatesta. Poets of the court, for example, mention the sign on several occasions in their poems. Yet because its meaning was conventional and easily understood, none of them pause to explain it. Gaspare Broglio, lieutenant and counselor to Sigismondo, also uses it frequently in his manuscript chronicle, and at one point he explicitly states that it refers to *Sigismondo*. This practice was not uncommon in the mid-quattrocento: rulers often used the first two letters of a name to form an abbreviation, a device found in contemporary medals and inscriptions throughout the courts of northern Italy. Only when this practice was no longer widespread did its meaning become a mystery.[93]

The first to suggest that the sign might mean something other than Sigismondo was Giuseppe Malatesta Garuffi (1655–1727), alternately professor, librarian, and priest in Rimini.[94] Driven by local patriotism to defend Sigismondo against the charges raised by ecclesiastical chronicles following Pius II, Garuffi sought to demonstrate the "quite deep affection" ("ben grande affezione") of Sigismondo for Isotta, and as evidence he adduced the sign, explaining, "And for this reason he wanted to cipher her name together with his own in this fashion, as appears in various marbles, ⚭ which is to say, *Sigismundus Isotta*." Garuffi also admitted it might stand only for Sigismondo's name. Indeed, in a second discussion he acknowledged that this was more likely, since it was "an ancient custom to write names with the first two letters in majuscules." Ultimately, however, it was Garuffi's first and more romantic suggestion that would triumph.[95]

The sign was next mentioned in 1756 when Gianmaria Mazzuchelli discussed it in his biography of Isotta. Mazzuchelli cited Garuffi, recited both interpretations, then leaned toward the amorous one: "And this is rather likely."[96] Still, contemporaries were not so easily swayed. Gian

Battista Costa (1700–67), also writing in 1756, never even entertained
the amorous reading; he reported coolly that the sign was used by Sigis-
mondo "in order to indicate his name."[97] But Costa's view vanished with
the dawn of Romantic culture. In 1789 another author, Battaglini, as-
serted unequivocally that Sigismondo had formed the sign "profiting from
the similar beginning of the letters S and I in his name and in that of his
young lover." The sign, he said, indicated "that in all his deeds he had
no goal other than to honor this woman [Isotta]." This he repeated in
1794, adding that Sigismondo also carried the sign on his armor when-
ever he went into battle.[98]

Battaglini's opinion was supported by Nardi in 1813, and reported
without discussion by Symonds in 1874.[99] But it was Yriarte, of course,
who integrated the Romantic interpretation of the sign within a global
view of the Tempio. At one point he even reversed the sign's significance,
so intent was he on the figure of Isotta; for him it was no longer Sigismon-
do's sign, to which Isotta's had been attached, but "celui d'Isotta, enlacé
au chiffre de Sigismond." For Yriarte the sign was crucial evidence for
his claim that the church of San Francesco was a monument to Isotta, or
to Sigismondo's love of her.[100] After 1885 his interpretation became stan-
dard, repeated in one work after another: the 1886 *Encyclopaedia Britan-
nica*, Premoli (1898), Hutton (1906), Arduini (1907), Albini (1908), the
1911 *Britannica*, Beltramelli (1912), Maurel (1920)—to name only a
few.[101] The generic ubiquity is remarkable: guidebooks, travel books, en-
cyclopedias, plays, novels, scholarly studies, popular historiography.
Consider the engraving by Lodovico Pogliaghi that appeared in Francesco
Bertolini's history, *The Renaissance and the Italian Signorie* (1897). (See
figure 11.) It epitomizes the iconography of an entire generation: Sigis-
mondo kneels before the fair Isotta, gesturing toward the monument that
he has dedicated to her and their love. Surrounding them are his attend-
ants, who hold aloft Roman banners bearing the sign $.[102]

The fatal blow to the Romantic interpretation of the sign was adminis-
tered in 1909 when Giovanni Soranzo demonstrated the fallacies in its
arguments.[103] His evidence was clear. First, not a single contemporary
testimony could be adduced in favor of the Romantic reading. Second,
Gaspare Broglio had explicitly stated that his own use of the sign always
referred only to Sigismondo. Third, it was a common practice among the
quattrocento courts of northern Italy to abbreviate someone's name by
using its first two letters, while not a single instance could be found of
combining two persons' names to form an independent device. Fourth,

and most important, contemporary documents nearly always spelled the name of Isotta *not* with the letter *I* but with the letter *Y*—as *Ysotta* or *Yxotta*.

Soranzo's proofs were not refuted, but were instead evaded. The central figure in devising a stratagem to conserve the Romantic interpretation of the sign was Corrado Ricci, an important art historian, who wrote a fundamental work on the Tempio Malatestiano, published in 1924. Ricci argued that the simple, historically verifiable reading of the sign was only its official, public meaning ("il significato ufficiale"), while behind this stood an equivocal meaning ("il significato equivoco") alluding to Sigismondo and Isotta. And Sigismondo, he claimed, had deliberately created the sign for this equivocation.[104] Ricci's argument was obviously weak: it offered no evidence to prove its claim about Sigismondo's creation and it evaded the damning argument that contemporary documents almost never spelled Isotta's name with an initial *I*. Such weaknesses, however, fulfilled their own ends, since their purpose was to create a claim that by its nature could be neither proved nor, if one believed it, refuted—a perfect Romantic "argument." Yet what was really at stake? Why did it matter so much to Ricci and to others like him? And equally important, since Ricci's work was not published until 1924, a year *after* Pound had composed and published the Malatesta Cantos, how should we account for Pound's interest in reasserting the late Romantic reading of the sign? For in 1922–23 Pound could have understood this argument only if he had met with Ricci himself, or someone associated with him. And thereby hangs a tale . . .

Antonio Beltramelli's book on the "temple of love" (*Un tempio d'amore*, 1912), which Pound probably purchased in Rimini in May 1922, contained Pound's first encounter with the entwined letters *S* and *I*. Like Yriarte, on whose work he drew heavily, Beltramelli viewed the sign as belonging more to Isotta than to Sigismondo. "From that time on he made the device of Isotta his own, a device that he would never abandon, and his chivalrous gesture deliberately surpassed the limits of courtly custom."[105] Beltramelli's reading of the sign was clearly a "hard" interpretation, one that turned the sign into a rebellious gesture against convention, and one that synchronized with the restless temperament of Ezra Pound in the summer of 1922.

Its effects, I think, are registered in Pound's second encounter with the Romantic interpretation shortly after 3 August 1922, when he received his own copy of Yriarte's book (1882). Among the marginalia conserved in his copy are three concerning the letters *S* and *I*. One, especially important, is a brief note opposite Yriarte's discussion of the sign on page 146. Pound, it is clear, was dumbstruck when Yriarte expressed surprise at how frankly Sigismondo had displayed his passion for Isotta by using such a sign:

> Sigismondo gave her public testimonies of his attachment and, even while his second wife was still alive, never carried any other device except hers in festivals, tourneys, and public ceremonies. He had his cipher enlaced with hers, and on his seals, on his arms, on the armor of his soldiers, on the walls of monuments, on the friezes of churches, on the frontons of altars, he declared publicly that his destiny was linked with that of his lover.

Opposite these lines, in large letters, Pound commented:

Prov[ençal]. *customs*. *Y*[riarte]. *ignorant of middle ages*

Pound, in other words, endorsed the Romantic interpretation of the entwined letters, yet felt that it was too weak, too soft in its understanding of the sign's significance: the cipher derived from "Prov[ençal] customs" that had miraculously survived or been revived in Rimini in the love of Sigismondo for Isotta. Pound, in short, advocated an interpretation that was not only "hard"—it was the hardest imaginable.[106]

Yet if Pound was so interested in the sign as to write two marginalia and one reading note about it between 1 August and ca. 15 September, how can we explain the apparent absence of any reference to it in his drafts, or even in subsequent notes? The answer is clear. On 29 July he had received his copy of Soranzo's book; by late August its footnotes were directing him to all of Soranzo's articles issued before 1911 and conserved as offprints in the Bibliothèque Nationale of Paris (BNP). For Soranzo, we have seen, routinely sent offprints of his youthful articles to the BNP, where they were catalogued with separate author and title listings just as if they were independent monographs. Once Pound had found one, he could locate the rest quite simply by using the author listing in the BNP catalogue. Locate them he certainly did: his notes and letters show that he read—and attempted to purchase—every article written by Soranzo and held in the BNP. With one exception: the article on the sign.[107] Pound, it would appear, disliked it intensely. Still, the study was not without its effects; its influence is registered not positively, but negatively in the abrupt cessation of reference to the entwined letters *S* and *I* after mid-September 1922.

This provisional solution to the question of the sign was really no solution at all. The problem was inescapable, in fact, for every time that Pound wrote Isotta's name he was obliged to confront the question of how to spell it. If its most common spelling by her contemporaries was *Ysotta* or *Yxotta*, and not *Isotta*, each act of writing her name threatened the Romantic interpretation of the cipher. It is precisely this problem that recurs in Pound's manuscripts during the period between late August 1922 and January 1923. For on several occasions Pound actually copies—from a photographic facsimile of Isotta's only known letter to Sigismondo—the contemporary spelling of her name, which begins with *Yx*, or *Yxotta*. Repeatedly, however, he alters the reading of the first two letters from *Yx* to *Ix*. Whether consciously or not, he "corrects" the reading of the signature in a way that eliminates the troublesome presence of the letter *Y*; at the same time, though, he retains the letter *x* instead of the more typical *s* because it lends his claims a patina of authenticity, an air of erudite familiarity with primary sources.[108]

The issue of the sign might have disappeared altogether had it not been for a series of curious events that happened to Pound in the spring of 1923, when he went to Italy to examine archival and documentary materials preparatory to final revisions on his poem. Pound arrived in Rome on 16 February, and on his first day in the city took a walking tour of the imperial forums. While strolling amid the ruins, by chance he met with Giacomo Boni (1859–1925), a distinguished archaeologist who was directing the forums' excavations. A Venetian who had studied in Venice, Pisa, Austria, and Germany, Boni spoke several languages, including English, and was renowned for an exemplary career in ancient archaeology: he had unearthed the houses of Sulla and the Gracchi on the Palatine hill (1913), and had discovered the "mundus" or heart of the original city of Rome founded by Romulus (1914). Sixty-two years old in 1923, Boni was a cordial conversationalist. "Have met several amiable literati—also Giacomo Boni, chief of the scavators who lives up on the hill inside the forum enclosure," Pound wrote to his mother a week later (24 February 1923).[109] Their conversation may be easily imagined, a typical exchange between people meeting for the first time. Boni, of course, must have asked Pound about his business in Rome; and Pound must have replied that he had come to the city in order to do research on Sigismondo Malatesta. Boni was amazed by an odd coincidence: one of his closest colleagues was working at that very moment on a major study of the Tempio Malatestiano. Would Pound like to meet him? He would be only too

Figure 14. Corrado Ricci (1858–1934). Director of Antiquities and Fine Arts for Italy from 1906–19 and nominated a "Senator of the Kingdom" on 1 March 1923, Ricci was the author of *Il tempio malatestiano*, a monumental study of the church of San Francesco published in 1924. His friend Giacomo Boni suggested that he had "copied some mysterious secrets" regarding the building's meaning, and provided Ezra Pound with a letter of introduction to him in February 1923. Reprinted from R. Istituto d'archeologia, *In memoria del Com. Corrado Ricci* (Rome: R. Istituto d'archeologia, 1935), frontispiece.

happy, he replied. Boni graciously offered to furnish a letter of introduction, and Pound thankfully accepted. The letter, remarkably enough, is still conserved. It is addressed to Corrado Ricci.

Il Com. Dottore Corrado Ricci
Palazzo Venezia

The text reads:

Dear Ricci,
*   Ezra Pound, the American arch-arch-critic, wishes to meet you in order*
to know better, with your help, that Sigismondo, of whom you have doubt-
less copied some mysterious secrets.
*   In any case, when you meet him in person you will be capable of recog-*
nizing that he is very learned and productive.

Very affectionately yours,
Boni[110]

Corrado Ricci (1858–1934) was born in Ravenna (see figure 14). His career was a steady ascent through the ranks of the cultural bureaucracy: he served as director of the galleries of Parma (1893–96) and Modena (1897), and as superintendent of monuments in Ravenna (1898). In this latter post he initiated a major cycle of restorations to the church of San Vitale (so that the church and nearby mausoleum, which Pound so deeply admired, owed much to Ricci's labors). His career advanced: director of the Brera in Milan (1899–1903), director of the Royal Galleries of Florence (1903–6), and finally director of antiquities and fine arts for all of Italy (1906–19), in which position he gave unstinting support to the excavations of the imperial forums in Rome, the activity conducted under Boni's direction. Meanwhile Ricci produced a torrent of scholarly works on art history and literature, acquiring a distinguished reputation. In 1923 he was sixty-four years old, renowned for his scholarship, admired for his administrative abilities, and universally praised for his warmth and generosity. His apartment was located in Piazza Venezia in the heart of Rome, only steps away from his office in Palazzo Venezia, the elegant quattrocento building still overlooking the city's core. But things in Ricci's office had recently changed: when Benito Mussolini had come to power a few months earlier, he had chosen the Palazzo Venezia for his center of command, a sign of his will to change the course of Italian society, a site from which he could address the masses thronging below.

In February 1923, Benito Mussolini had been in power for less than four months. His seizure of power had been the result of many compromises. His party was small and in some respects weak, and its membership was able to furnish few of the qualified personnel necessary to administering the government. Mussolini turned to professionals outside the party, to nationally respected figures qualified by training, in order to execute broad reforms that would symbolize the regime's ability to impose change while maintaining order. Eventually they might be assimilated into the party, furnishing Mussolini with an instrument against the more volatile elements at the party's base, whose violence threatened to undermine the new government's claim to establish order; meanwhile they helped place the new government on a national level, above the petty interests of faction and party.[111] In his first ministry, for example, he selected Giovanni Gentile as minister of education (1 November 1922), an independent whose appointment was approved even by opponents of the regime as staunch as Gaetano Salvemini. But only six months later, on 31 May 1923, Gentile accepted membership in the party, eventually becoming a major force in the party's intellectual life.[112] It was with similar intentions that Mussolini courted Corrado Ricci.

On 1 March 1923, two weeks after his meeting with Pound, Ricci was nominated a Senator of the Kingdom, one of Italy's highest honors. On 11 April he was appointed president of the Commissione Centrale per le Antichità e Belle Arti. On 6 May he was named president of the Casa di Dante, among the nation's most prestigious cultural institutions. The next year, in 1924, Mussolini lent a sympathetic ear to his plan to demolish the impoverished housing that had gathered around the imperial forums during the centuries, opening grounds for the construction of a massive thoroughfare that would link ancient Rome with the renewal of modern Italy—a project that resulted in the Via dell'Impero, constructed under Ricci's direction. In late March 1925 Ricci participated, together with Gentile and Beltramelli, at the Convention of Fascist Culture held in Bologna, which issued the "Manifesto of Fascist Intellectuals" penned by Gentile. And in subsequent years his role in the cultural politics of the regime continued to grow. In February 1933 he gave the inaugural lecture for the annual courses at the Fascist National Institute of Culture in Rome (Istituto nazionale fascista di cultura); his talk was introduced by Achille Starace, the Party Secretary and Mussolini's right hand. Also in attendance was the president of the institute, Giovanni Gentile. (His lecture, incidentally, surveyed the regime's archaeological achievements, stressing recent discoveries at the Temple of Venus Genetrix in Rome, the goddess whose "feast," in Pound's view, "[had] survived as May Day" and nurtured the cultural achievements of medieval Provence and the Malatestan court.) On his death in 1934, it was reported that Mussolini "knew him intimately and appreciated his deep learning and indomitable energy."[113]

In early 1923 Ricci was hard at work, putting the finishing touches on his magisterial study of the Tempio Malatestiano. The book was the outcome of a lifelong interest in the church. Already in early 1907 he had given a lecture on it in Rimini. A short while later he had received a letter from the journalist Antonio Beltramelli, who informed him that he too was preparing "a lecture on Rimini, and more especially on the Tempio and on Isotta," and inquired if Ricci could send him a copy of his recent talk. A few weeks later Beltramelli thanked him for "the gift of your magnificent lecture"; it had been "a most agreeable and inspirational guide to me," he wrote, and Ricci would easily see that Beltramelli's talk showed "*many reminiscences* of your very beautiful piece." The lecture was Beltramelli's first sketch for his book, *A Temple of Love*, issued in 1912.[114]

Ricci's work on the Tempio, meanwhile, continued throughout the years. In 1912 he supervised a complete restoration of the church's interior, in which every funerary stone from the eighteenth and nineteenth centuries was removed, the whitewash on all the chapel walls was stripped, and the "original" deep blue frescos were "recreated." (This was the purified "monument" that Ezra Pound would see in 1922.) Contemporaneously with the restorations, Ricci also conducted an archaeological study of the building that yielded numerous significant discoveries—among them, a remarkable find related to the tomb of Isotta degli Atti. Ricci had decided to remove the bronze plaque bearing the well-known inscription, and beneath it he uncovered another, previously unknown and earlier, inscription carved into the sepulchre's marble. This discovery, along with many others, Ricci had kept to himself for ten long years, waiting until the news could be released together with all his other finds in a definitive study of the Tempio.[115] In February 1923 only one person, Corrado Ricci, had ever seen the earlier inscription on Isotta's tomb—a fact that sheds unexpected light on a single leaf of paper found among Pound's manuscripts for the Malatesta Cantos. For it contains a transcription of both the earlier and the later inscriptions, and a brief explanation in Italian of their chronological relationship (see figure 15). After giving the text of the earlier inscription in Latin, it reads: "*This original inscription in the marble of Isotta degli Atti's tomb in the Tempio Malatestiano of Rimini was covered with a bronze plate on which is written this second inscription:* [followed by text of later inscription in Latin]." There is no doubt that it was written by Corrado Ricci, and that he gave it to Ezra Pound when the poet visited him in February 1923.[116]

That Pound and Ricci discussed the inscriptions on the tomb of Isotta is suggestive, for the topic was pivotal to the Romantic interpretation of

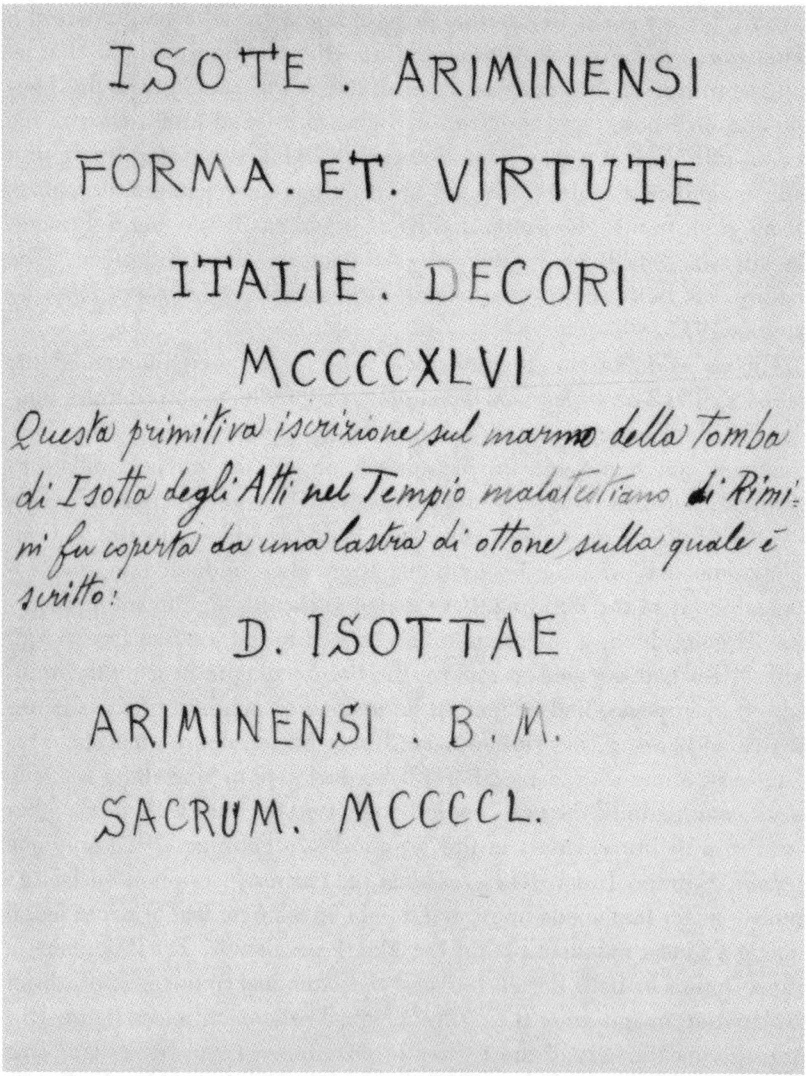

ISOTE . ARIMINENSI
FORMA. ET. VIRTUTE
ITALIE. DECORI
MCCCCXLVI

Questa primitiva iscrizione sul marmo della tomba di Isotta degli Atti nel Tempio malatestiano di Rimini fu coperta da una lastra di ottone sulla quale è scritto:

D. ISOTTAE
ARIMINENSI . B. M.
SACRUM. MCCCCL.

Figure 15. Corrado Ricci, transcription of the original inscription on the tomb of Isotta degli Atti, given by him to Ezra Pound when the two men met in February 1923. From original manuscript in Beinecke Library, Yale University.

the church as a "temple of love." Here was the heart of their conversation, we may surmise: historical moments that were crucial for understanding the church of San Francesco. Did they also discuss the cipher with the entwined letters *S* and *I*? How can we doubt it? Would Pound have failed to raise a question so crucial, a question that had obviously puzzled him, with a man so knowledgeable about the church as Ricci, a man who knew about hidden inscriptions, a man who had "copied some mysterious secrets" about the building that had become the very icon of Pound's poem? What better occasion? Yes, surely the question arose, and the name of Soranzo was mentioned. Why else would Pound report to his mother, in the same letter of 24 February that mentions Boni, "[I] have discovered that Soranzo still exists."[117] Obviously the name of Soranzo had arisen in conversation with Ricci—had arisen because Soranzo had authored the article disputing the romantic interpretation of the letters *S* and *I*. Quite clearly Pound and Ricci discussed the entwined letters; and after having explained his position regarding the sign, perhaps Ricci concluded with the same words that he would use in his book of 1924: "Therefore let the poets and rhetoricians continue in their sentimental exercise. The sign was supposed to signify *Sigismondo* only to popes and notaries."[118]

Pound's encounter with Ricci helps explain a curious moment that occurred in the last stages of his journey in Italy, when he found himself in Rimini, poring over archival documents related to Sigismondo and Isotta. Here were documents written in the very city where Isotta had lived, written by notaries who were her exact contemporaries—testimonies eminently worthy of credence for the spelling of her name since their legal validity depended precisely on such minutiae. And imagine Pound's joy when he came upon a previously unpublished document concerning Isotta degli Atti herself, buried among the *rogiti* (notarial deeds) of the notary Francesco Paponi. The *rogito*, dated 27 July 1452, records her purchase of a piece of land from Ghirardo di Cristoforo da Rimini and Giovanni di Angelino. At the head of the *rogito* is a minute summarizing the document: "Magnifice domine Ysotte | de Actis | emptio | completum per manum Rodulfi." ("Purchase on the part of the magnificent lady Ysotta degli Atti, executed by Rodolfo.") Line 5 of the document records their sale of the property to the "magnifice et generose domine Ysotte filie quondam nobilis viri Francisci de Actis." (To the "magnificent and noble lady Ysotta, daughter of the late nobleman, Francesco degli Atti.") Pound surely saw one of these, for his own note carefully registers the folio number of the *rogito*. And yet twice he wrote her name as *Isotta*, with the letter *I*. Whether deliberate or careless, Pound's error had the convenient result of eliminating the dissonant testimony. Moreover, he was also aware of another testimony no less important, the manuscript chronicle of Gaspare Broglio, which he also examined when in Rimini. Since Pound tended to make diplomatic transcriptions, his notes from Broglio register every instance when he encountered the chronicler's use of the abbreviation ẛ to represent *Sigismondo*, showing that Pound copied the sign three times in contexts where its meaning was unequivocal. [119] In the light of this and the other evidence so far adduced, Pound's decision to alter the spelling of Isotta's name forms a coda to a pattern of evasion too frequent to be the result of mere chance: when confronted with testimonies that threatened to undermine the romantic interpretation of the sign ẛ, Pound proved adept at devising stratagems for not discerning their significance.

Pound returned to Paris around 11 April 1923, and managed within days to complete a final version of the Malatesta Cantos. Though he was obliged to dash off a translation for Horace Liveright immediately afterward, he was jubilant, and the effect on his work was catalytic: he plunged into a massive revision of all the earlier cantos, then swiftly finished five more to follow the Malatesta sequence. [120] The result was the completion of *The Cantos* in their modern form, and at its center stood the complex of cultural aspirations informing the Malatesta Cantos. Plans were now set in motion to produce the first publication of his magnum opus in book form, and not surprisingly, Pound intervened actively to ensure that the volume would match his expectations. The decision was taken to produce a deluxe volume with decorative capitals and illustrations, and an illustrator was selected—a twenty-four-year-old American named Henry Strater.

Why Pound selected him is unclear. Strater (1896–1988) was young, had accomplished little, and was breezing through life on a trust fund endowed with profits from the family business, a snuff factory in New Jersey. He had studied at Princeton, served in France with the Red Cross during World War I, then remained in Europe to study art. By the spring of 1922 he was in Paris, and by the fall he had scored his first success at the Salon d'Automne: a jury including Braque had selected his *Nude with Black and White Fox Terrier* to hang alongside works by Vuillard and Foujita. Although the painting is lost, we can surmise its characteristics from two contemporary works: his portrait of *Margaret Strater in Red* (1922) and his *Little Nude by a Table* (1925) (see figures 16, 17). Both show him using taut draftsmanship to delineate static, classicizing forms that are rendered in a muted palette—a formula that clearly appealed to

Figure 16. Henry Strater, *Margaret Strater in Red* (1922). The painting shows the sober colors and classicizing forms of Strater's work at this time. Museum of Art of Ogunquit, Permanent Collection.

Figure 17. Henry Strater, *Little Nude by a Table* (1925). It was probably a similar paint-ing by Strater that attracted attention at the Salon d'Automne in mid-1922, leading to his first meeting with Ezra Pound in July. Museum of Art of Ogunquit, Permanent Collec-tion.

the sober neoclassical taste prevalent in Paris after the war.[121] Strater's
sudden success earned him entry into new circles, and by the autumn of
1922 he had met Pound:

> After I sent in that painting to the 1922 salon I became the latest young-
> ster to become a local celebrity and some girl took me to Pound's open
> house. And he served tea in little cups with no handles, little Chinese
> cups. And I was feeling like a fool with these little cups with no handles,
> and next to me I saw this young guy who was good-looking, so I said to
> him, "Weak stuff." And he said to me, "Sure is." And with that he reached
> into his pocket and drew out a hip flask, and we took a swig. So then he
> said to me, "Whaddya do in this town for exercise?" And I told him that I
> did some boxing, and that was how I met Hemingway. After that we both
> became acquainted with Pound. That was the first time.[122]

In January 1923 he met with Pound in Rapallo, where they were joined
by the endocrinologist Louis Berman; as Pound reported to his father,
"Berman also here, and a lunatic ex-athlete called Stretter [*sic*], who
plays tennis rather better than the gland-sleuth."[123] Pound's report (note
the spelling of Strater's name) suggests that their acquaintance was fairly
casual. But Strater's memories of this period evoke a much warmer ca-
maraderie.

> Oh well by that time we [Strater, Pound, and Hemingway] were all bud-
> dies. He was writing the last of his cantos then, and was thinking about
> how to print them. He wanted it illuminated . . . he wanted it to be
> brought out in illuminated form. So he said to me, "Will you do it?"
>   I said, "Hell no!"
>   He said, "I don't know anybody else to do them." And he kept at it and
> persuaded me. I had done a great deal of training in life-size drawing, and
> I thought maybe I could learn something by trying my hand at these small
> drawings. Later on he had me meet Bill Bird [the publisher].

Pound viewed their collaboration a bit differently. In 1924 he would claim
that Strater had been not reluctant, but "grateful" for the opportunity to
work on the project: "I got him out of a slough, he trembled—he was
grateful 'for a chance'—*then*."[124]

Pound had taken the initiative in soliciting Strater's participation and
in originating the idea for a monumental presentation of his own work.
Clearly he dominated every aspect of their collaboration.[125] His domina-
tion sprang partly from psychological factors: Pound was aggressive and
self-confident, while Strater confessed to having "a horrible inferiority
complex about my work."[126] Other motives were social. Pound was older
by a decade, a respected poet who had published many books and se-

cured a firm though controversial reputation, while Strater was virtually unknown, his portfolio small. Success, he understood, might depend on the approval of someone like Pound, who wrote contemporary art criticism and had important connections in London and Paris. Pound's domination of the project extended to details of design; when he found something he disliked after Strater had left, he wrote to one friend, "I jumped H. for this [i.e., "the rotten uphill arrangement of perspective"] in his earliest attempts at design."[127] If Pound endeavored to exert such extensive control over minutiae of design, an area where the artist's autonomy is customarily sacrosanct, we may imagine how thoroughly he dominated Strater in the choice of subject matter. Indeed, as Strater later recalled, the difficulties of *The Cantos* made this a necessity: "He was in the tradition of Browning—ob-fus-cu-tra-tion! So I would occasionally get together with him and have him translate it for me. I'd say, 'What the hell is this?' And he'd explain it." Pound must have explained things carefully indeed, cajoling and coaxing, urging and prompting. He even lent Strater his own copy of the book that had so influenced his work on the Malatesta Cantos, Yriarte's *Un Condottiere au XVᵉ siècle*, and he specified the illustrations that Strater was to adopt as models for his work on *The Cantos*.[128] The illustrations in *A Draft of XVI. Cantos* represented not Strater's artistic impressions, but Pound's understanding of his own work. And that understanding was a "hard" reading, for the illustrations in *A Draft of XVI. Cantos* contain five representations incorporating the cipher with the letters *S* and *I*.

The first illustration appears in the headpiece to Canto 8, at the outset of the four Malatesta Cantos. It serves as a visual preface that furnishes guidelines for decoding the text to follow. (See plates 1, 2.)[129] The illustration depicts several church windows: these are shaped like Gothic arches which, however, are also framed by a second set of round, or Roman, arches. It is the side of the church of San Francesco (see figures 3, 4), and is plainly based on Yriarte's engraving of the same subject (see figure 18). There is a discrepancy, however, between Strater's illustration and its source: the engraving in Yriarte renders the stained glass only as a dark shape, without any specific images, while Strater furnishes a scene for each window. The first window shows a conventional representation of the fall of Lucifer. But the second is unusual: it shows a man and a woman facing each other, both kneeling, and with their hands uplifted in prayer toward the heavens. The object of their worship, however, is not God: above the woman is the horn of the young moon, and above the man, a bright sun. The suggestion of neopagan worship is clear, accentuated

Figure 18. Probably by Paul Laurent, an engraving published in Charles Yriarte, *Un Condottiere au XVe siècle* (1882). It depicts one of the Gothic windows seen behind the Roman arches in the church of San Francesco (compare figures 3 and 4), and it served as the model for Henry Strater's illustration of the same subject in the headpiece to Canto 8 (pl. 2). Strater used Pound's own copy of the Yriarte work, lent him by Pound in the summer of 1923. From Charles Yriarte, *Un Condottiere au XVe siècle* (Paris: Jules Rothschild, 1882), p. 257, fig. 143. Reproduced courtesy of the Beinecke Rare Book and Manuscript Library, Yale University

by the couple's apparent abandon; for as Edward Carpenter had written, describing the new man of the post-Christian era:

> The meaning of the old religions will come back to him . . . he will cele-
> brate with naked dances the glory of the human form and the great proces-
> sions of the stars, or greet the bright horn of the young moon . . . or in the
> open, standing uncovered to the Sun, will adore the emblem of the ever-
> lasting splendour which shines within. [130]

The couple, one assumes, is also meant to suggest Sigismondo and Isotta, who no longer worship God, but instinct in themselves. The illustration, in effect, recapitulates the two poles of the Romantic interpretation of the church of San Francesco: it is a monument to neopaganism and a monument to the passion of Isotta and Sigismondo—"a temple of love." Further, it recapitulates the tension in Ricci's notion of a *significato ufficiale* and a *significato segreto* in the sign ⚵, for above the moon and sun are conventional images of the Holy Father and the Virgin Mary, forcing the viewer to decide which is the real object of their worship. Yet an attentive observer will have few doubts: in two of the windows one also sees the entwined letters *S* and *I*, the secret cipher—and it is with this understanding that the reader is to interpret the poems that follow.

The sign ⚵ also appears twice in illustrations of heraldic devices and weapons. In the headpiece to Canto 11 is depicted a shield that bears the entwined letters *S* and *I* (see plates 3, 4), a choice of subject matter that reflects the marginalia and notes that Pound had made while reading Yriarte: in particular, a marginal entry earmarking Yriarte's claim that Sigismondo forced his soldiers to wear the entwined cipher whenever they went into battle, as well as a typescript note that tersely recorded: "(later. S and I on the shields)." [131]

In the headpiece to Canto 10 the sign again appears in a military setting, this time a sequence of scenes arranged within the pediment of a stylized classical façade (see plate 5), the whole derived from another illustration in Yriarte's book (see figure 19). [132] The sequence presents a panoramic view of the siege and assault of a castle, with different incidents represented by discrete scenes, each showing a single moment of battle. One scene shows a knight on a cantering horse, riding right and lifting his lance into the air, its pennant tossed by the wind (see plate 6). The knight has obviously been copied from a figure depicted in the Yriarte illustration, as is evident from the plume trailing from his helmet. (Strater probably made a tracing, since the knight appears in reverse to the original; Yriarte's knight is at the bottom of figure 19, in the foreground.) On the caparison of his horse we see the entwined *S* and *I*, which appear twice.[133] As before, the illustration echoes Yriarte's claim that Sigismondo obliged his men to wear the device as a token of his love for Isotta, a claim that has been filtered through Ricci's arguments about the sign's *significato equivico*.

The entwined letters *S* and *I* appear two other times in illustrations for

Figure 19. Process reproduction of an eighteenth-century engraving, printed in Charles Yriarte, *Un Condottiere au XVᵉ siècle* (1882). The reproduction is taken from an engraving made in 1794, itself taken from a miniature in a Renaissance manuscript of an epic by Basinio de Parma that celebrates the deeds of Sigismondo. (The original manuscript remained lost until the 1950s.) In the foreground, bottom right, is the figure of a knight, which served as the model for Henry Strater's illustration in the headpiece for Canto 10 (see figure 20). From Yriarte, *Un Condottiere au XVᵉ siècle*, p. 170, fig. 85. Reproduced courtesy of the Beinecke Rare Book and Manuscript Library, Yale University

Canto 10. The context is dramatic, indeed stunning. But to appreciate it, we must return for one moment to the fate of Sigismondo Malatesta. Sigismondo, as we saw earlier, was forced to halt construction on the Tempio because of a lack of funds, for by 1460 his economic situation was precarious indeed. His imprudent decision to assist efforts to unseat the king of Naples had involved him in plans that threatened the entire balance of power that prevailed within the peninsula. The major powers responded as major powers are wont to do: they let him hang. And hang he did—almost literally. By law the Malatesta family were not the rulers of Rimini, but only vicars appointed by the church; now the resurgent papacy was looking to reclaim its land. It was the beginning of the long process that led to the formation of the papal state that ruled central Italy until 1860, and Sigismondo was among its earliest victims. The church joined with Naples in waging a ferocious campaign against Sigismondo's little dominion, and in customary fashion it also invoked its array of spiritual arms as well. On 27 April 1462 Sigismondo was formally deprived of his dominions and condemned to hell for countless crimes—many of them rather poor fabrications, such as the murder of Polissena Sforza—against the laws of God and man. The ceremony was accomplished with theatrical flair, as three effigies of Sigismondo were burned in public squares in Rome to symbolize his infernal fate.[134] Of course, an event like this offered perfect material for the late Romantic interpretation of the Tempio. Seen thus, Sigismondo's fate seemed a result less of crass political considerations than of ideological war between orthodox Christianity and incipient neopaganism, between the church of God and the temple of earthly love.

The last two illustrations of the sign ᛯ are designed to present exactly this view. The first appears in the headpiece to Canto 10, within the frieze of the stylized façade (see plate 7): it shows Sigismondo being burned in effigy, and on his chest we see the entwined letters S and I, suggesting that Pius II has condemned him for his desperate love of Isotta. Sigismondo is portrayed as a martyr to the cult of life, human sexuality, and the creative powers it embodies.

The second illustration in Canto 10 is bolder still (see plates 8, 9). It appears not in a headpiece or tailpiece, but in a special illustration set within the body of the text—one of only two such illustrations in all *The Cantos*.[135] It shows a shield, and above it a helmet surmounted by a crested elephant's head. This emblem, a heraldic device of considerable antiquity in the Malatesta family, had been adopted by Pisanello in his famous medal of Sigismondo (see figure 20), while Pisanello's rendering, in turn, had been reproduced twice in the engravings that embellished Yriarte's study of Sigismondo (once on the title page, once on p. 80; see figure 21). From here, once again, it had served as the basis for Strater's illustration for Canto 10. Yet within *The Cantos*, the traditional device bursts into sight at a crucial point within the text, placed opposite Pius II's narration of how Sigismondo Malatesta was burnt in effigy on the day of his excommunication. The typographical context is eloquent: Pius II's oration is set in small capitals, producing long files of uniform gray, while

Figure 20. Antonio Pisano, il Pisanello, reverse of commemorative model of Sigismondo Malatesta (Hill, no. 33), commissioned ca. 1455. Sigismondo is shown completely armed, standing between a shield with his decorative monogram (right) and a helmet with crest (left). An engraving of this medal, published by Charles Yriarte, served as the basis of an illustration in Canto 10 of *A Draft of XVI. Cantos* (1925) (see plates 8 and 9). From Giovanna de Lorenzi, ed., *Medaglie di Pisanello* (Florence: Museo Nazionale del Borgello, 1983), p. 25, fig. 10R. Reprinted by permission.

across from it stands the defiant sign—with the letter *I* inked in flaming red. Seeing this, who can forget the words of Ricci, which he may also have addressed to Pound: "The sign was supposed to signify *Sigismondo* only to popes and notaries."

Placed in this context, the sign becomes a key to Pound's entire argument in the Malatesta Cantos, and by extension throughout *The Cantos*. Sigismondo Malatesta had been destroyed by the forces of ecclesiastical orthodoxy because he embodied "the cult . . . of the senses" that had

Figure 21. Probably by Paul Laurent, an engraving reproduced in Charles Yriarte, *Un Condottiere au XVᵉ siècle* (1882). The engraving represents a medal by Antonio Pisano, il Pisanello, and was adapted by Henry Strater for his inset illustration for Canto 10 in *A Draft of XVI. Cantos* (1925) (compare plates 8 and 9, figure 20). Reprinted from Yriarte, *Un Condottiere au XVᵉ siècle*, p. 80.

once reigned in Provence, that had once been manifested in a cipher such as this. But in opposition to the decayed authority of orthodoxy, Pound reclaims and reasserts the secular spirituality that had lived in Provence and Malatestan Rimini, spirituality charged with shades of vitalism and aestheticism, sensuality and voluntarism. Pound vindicates the cultic martyr that Sigismondo has become, strikes a blow of posthumous vengeance as he flaunts the hermetic symbol in the face of the persecutor, damns the blindness of materialism and positivism by displaying the sign whose meaning is hidden from the figures of orthodoxy ("popes") and the ignorant middle classes ("notaries"), a meaning perceptible only to the "aristocracy of emotion." Here the sign takes on extraordinary weight, epitomizing the entire project of *The Cantos*—to discern and write the counter-history of secular vitalist spirituality, as well as to place that spirituality at the core of a new ethical culture in the twentieth century.

It is disconcerting to consider the treatment of the sign at the hands of modern literary studies. Although it has not been reprinted since the first edition of 1925, scholars have nevertheless managed to replicate Pound's own views about it without prompting. Since 1955 it has been consistently reported that the sign is important for understanding the Malatesta Cantos, that its meaning is the one established by the Romantic interpretation and by Pound—Sigismondo and Isotta. As the standard commentary on *The Cantos* puts it: "[Sigismondo's] love for her is celebrated all over the Tempio by the intertwined initials *S* and *I*." Not once has a dissenting testimony been raised.[136]

The Last Judgment

The August sun beat the ruins into stillness. Over two hundred bombings had destroyed or rendered uninhabitable 80 percent of the housing in Rimini, and the danger posed by the collapsing buildings had provoked a massive exodus. The streets, choked with rubble, were deserted. The ghostly quiet was punctuated only by the blows of artillery sounding in the distant hills, as the front drew nearer.

The outcome of the battle could not be foreseen. For months he had pursued his labors in the city alone, virtually its last inhabitant. Each day he registered the results in a diary: which works had been saved, which lost for ever—Roman epigraphs, medieval inscriptions, the extent of damage to various monuments. In June, on a bicycle threading his way among the debris, he had taken a few boxes of archaeological materials from the museum to a secret place in the mountains where Carlo Luc-chesi, the city librarian, had fled months before to conserve what he could of the rarest manuscripts and books. A few days later, in another bombing, the museum had been pulverized. Originally it had been the Franciscan monastery attached to the nearby church of San Francesco, and ten years earlier it had been converted into the city museum. Its foundations went back to the Middle Ages. The church itself, miracu-lously, had been spared, though by now it hardly mattered: earlier bomb-ings in December 1943 and January and March 1944 had already dam-aged it severely. The roof was gone, the apse annihilated; the walls of the façade had buckled, and at some points were bulging by as much as half a meter; several of the arches had cracked. The building was threatening to collapse. (See figures 22–24).

Earlier in the day, 16 August 1944, it had struck him that he could save one last object menaced with theft or depredation by the soldiers of either side. With the help of a local worker who had also remained in the city, Augusto Campana went to the great hall of the city's medieval com-mune, erected in 1204, and dismounted a huge painting from its wall. Together the two men carried it outside and placed it in a wheelbarrow; they braced it against their shoulders and pushed it through the streets choked with rubble. It was a medieval fresco from the 1300s, rediscov-ered after the earthquake of 1916 and transferred to canvas. It depicted *il giudizio universale*, the Last Judgment: the dead, it showed, were rising from their graves, soaring heavenward to be weighed in the scales of justice, while angels were descending earthward to greet them, some with fiery swords, others with palms. In the center was an empty space for-merly occupied by a portrait of the Redeemer; only his left hand re-mained now, issuing a gesture of disseevered blessing against the indigo background. At last the two men reached the main piazza: opposite them, in the piazza's center, they saw a crude wooden gallows, two stubbed poles stuck in the ground and connected by a beam at the top. From it were suspended three corpses, partisans who had been hanged and left as a warning by the retreating German forces. The two men dared not pause. They braced their shoulders against "The Last Judgment," pushed it across the barren piazza, and took it to its hiding place in a nearby cellar. In the piazza, silence reigned. There was no one now to hear the remote, almost inaudible, echoes of the voices that had filled this space, four centuries before, celebrating the marriage of Polissena Sforza with jousting and races. Then, emerging from the dark ruins of a building on the other side, a thin, bespectacled figure advanced gingerly into the

Figure 22. Church of San Francesco, Rimini, 1944. Allied bombings in late 1943 and early 1944 destroyed most of the church's roof and all of its apse. When Pound read about the building's destruction he began to write Cantos 72 and 73. Reprinted from *Bollettino d'arte* 35 (1950), pp. 176–84.

sunlight. It was the local optician and photographer, Gino Severi, camera in hand. Alone, in the empty piazza, he raised his camera, took careful aim, and photographed the horrible scene before him (see figure 25). [137]

The destruction of Rimini was reported in various newspapers, among them *Il Secolo XIX* of Genoa. Its editor-in-chief, Mario Rivoire, had been appointed to his post shortly after the creation of the Republic of Salò in September 1943, part of the government's effort to control the press by placing trusted supporters in key positions. Already in November that year the Ministry of Popular Culture had begun urging newspapers to stress the destruction of cultural monuments wrought by the "terrorist bombers" of the English and Americans. [138] On Sunday, 4 June 1944, *Il Secolo XIX* published an article entitled, "Il tempio malatestiano di Rim-

Figure 23. Church of San Francesco, Rimini, 1944; the right side of the building, second arch. Damage from the bombings had caused deep cracks in the walls, threatening to prompt the collapse of the deep arches, and at some points the walls had buckled by as much as half a meter. "Broken are the arches, burnt are the walls / Of the mysterious bed of the divine Ixotta . . ." (Canto 72). Reprinted from Emilio Lavagnino, *Fifty War-Damaged Monuments of Italy* (Rome: Istituto Poligrafico dello Stato, 1946), p. 97, fig. 167.

Figure 24. Church of San Francesco, Rimini, 1944; the apse. A single bomb annihilated the apse of the church, leaving it mere rubble. Reprinted from Lavagnino, *Fifty War-Damaged Monuments of Italy*, p. 96, fig. 164.

ini," and above it a "kicker" reading: "I monumenti che il nemico ci distrugge" ("The Monuments the Enemy is Destroying"). It reported the bombings of Rimini and the Tempio's perilous condition. A copy of it came into the hands of Ezra Pound, then living in nearby Rapallo (fifty kilometers from Genoa) and a frequent reader of the Genovese newspaper in which he had published an article only two months before.[139] Pound was shocked, moved, angered. The report suggested irreparable harm to the monument that had come to represent his life's work. In the wake of his reading he began to compose two cantos, numbered 72 and 73, which were excluded from all collected editions of *The Cantos* from 1948 through 1986. In 1987 they were printed as a sort of appendix at the back of the volume; late in 1989 they were moved to their "proper" place following Canto 71.[140]

Both cantos are written in Italian. One presents a phantasmagoria of voices lamenting the conditions of wartime Italy. The first voice belongs to Filippo Marinetti, the futurist poet; the second to Manlio Torquato Dazzi, the former director of the library in Cesena who had shown Pound the medal by pseudo-Pisanello in the spring of 1923. Then a third voice begins to speak (lines 84 ff.). His identity is unclear and the narrator inquires whether he is Sigismondo, his suspicions raised by the speaker's remarks about Rimini (lines 108–12):

Figure 25. Luigi Severi, photograph of Luigi Nicoló, Adelio Pagliarini, and Mario Cappelli, hanged on 16 August 1944 in the central piazza of Rimini. After the war the piazza was renamed La Piazza dei Tre Martiri (Piazza of the Three Martyrs); for centuries it had been known as the Piazza of Julius Caesar, based on the belief that Caesar had stopped here to harangue his troops shortly after crossing the Rubicon in 44 B.C. From Rimini, Biblioteca Civica Gambalunga, *Archivio fotografico*.

> Rimini burnt, and Forlì destroyed,
> Who shall see again the sepulchre of Gemisthus
> Who was so wise, even if Greek?
> Broken are the arches, burnt are the walls
> Of the mysterious bed of the divine Ixotta. . . .

Momentarily the speaker evades the question, but later he identifies himself as Ezzelino, the famous medieval tyrant of northern Italy who was the subject of a neo-Latin tragedy by the prehumanist scholar Albertino Mussato (1261–1329), a work that Dazzi had translated into Italian (1914).[141] As the three figures converse, central questions of identity and history unfold in the psychic space articulated by the destroyed Tempio—a space that engenders a frightening hallucination.

In the second canto, or Canto 73, the speaker is identified from the outset as the spirit of Guido Cavalcanti, the famous medieval poet (ca. 1250–1300). But Cavalcanti, too, identifies himself in terms of his asso-

ciation with Rimini, specifically his recent encounter with a spirit whom
he met while passing near the war-torn city (lines 33–47):

> I passed by Arimino
> > and I met a gay spirit
> Who sang as if enchanted
> > with joy!
> She was a young country girl
> A bit stocky yet lovely
> > and she held by the arm two Germans
> And was singing,
> > singing of love
> > > without need
> > > > of going to heaven.
> She'd led the Canadians
> > to a mine-field
> Where was the Tempio
> > of the beautiful Ixotta.

Cavalcanti then explains (lines 54–57):

> The Canadians were coming
> > to 'mop up' the Germans,
> To demolish what little remained
> > of the city of Rimini.

Raped by a troop of Canadian soldiers not long before, she encounters a
second group of Canadians who have lost their way at the edge of the city.
They ask her for directions to the road leading to Bologna, a pivotal target
in the Allied offensive. She deliberately conducts the soldiers to a mine-
field "along the shore" of the Adriatic near Rimini, where twenty of the
soldiers and herself are killed when a mine, set by her brother the day
before, explodes. The only survivor is one of two German soldiers whom
the Canadians had earlier taken prisoner. "What splendor!" Cavalcanti
remarks as he reports the blast, commending her spirit to the "Glory of
the fatherland." He concludes (lines 105–110):

> What a beautiful winter!
> > In the north the fatherland is being reborn,
> Yet what a young woman!
> > what young women
> > > what young men
> are wearing the black [uniform]!

The story narrated by Cavalcanti is situated at a highly particular point
in the war. On 21 September 1944, the city of Rimini was occupied by

troops of the First Canadian Infantry Division and the Greek Brigade, both units of the British Eighth Army. Upon entering the city, the Greek soldiers hoisted their native flag over the town hall—this explains the otherwise cryptic reference to the Byzantine philosopher buried in the Tempio, Gemistos Plethon, "who was so wise, even though he was Greek"—while the Canadians attempted to secure the town. The incident narrated by Cavalcanti, then, occurs on 21 September, as the first Canadian troops are passing through the abandoned city.

Italian newspapers in the north of Italy, still under German control, had closely covered the campaign for Rimini, considered vital to the Allied advance. The invasion of Normandy in June and continued Russian gains were boding ill, and the loss of Rimini might presage a complete collapse of the German front in Italy. As it turned out, the loss was far less eventful, as a tenacious German defense organized by Kesselring effectively stalled subsequent advances until late autumn, when the Allies finally called off the attack altogether (28 October). This, of course, could not be foreseen in the last week of September, when a defeat threatened to demoralize a citizenry already indifferent at best. At first newspapers in the north simply denied the loss altogether: *Il Corriere della sera* (in Milan) for 24 September issued a front-page article headlined: "Rimini Still in German Hands." Only the next day did a single sentence, buried amid praise of the German defense along the Adriatic sector, contain a veiled admission of the city's loss, and even this was counterbalanced by other reports that grossly exaggerated the casualties inflicted on the Allies: "45,000 Dead for a Few Kilometers" declared the same *Corriere* of 25 September, describing the combat near Rimini. Equally important, however, was a vigorous effort to rouse the morale of a citizenry either hostile to the Germans and Mussolini's puppet regime or, if part of the tiny minority still sympathetic to Mussolini, increasingly resigned to defeat. Newspapers instrumentalized patriotic motifs to demand the ultimate in self-sacrifice from everyone: it was better to die with pride than live with the humiliation of defeat. It was in this context that the *Corriere* published, on 1 October 1944, a strange account headlined "The Heroine of Rimini," with a "kicker" reading, "Italian Blood." (For a transcription and translation, see appendix 3.) It recounts the same incident rehearsed in Canto 73, coinciding in so many details as to leave no doubt that it was Pound's source. It is, of course, a transparent fabrication; no such incident ever occurred.[142]

Pound, it must be assumed until it can be shown otherwise, did not know that the story was a counterfeit. Presumably he felt that he was transmitting an accurate record of exceptional courage that might inspire demoralized Italians to resistance against the Allies. Still, he also alters the newspaper account significantly: in his narration every crucial step depends on associations with the Tempio Malatestiano of Rimini. Its "broken arches" epitomize the destruction of a form of civilization specifically linked with the late Romantic interpretation of the building, which is described as "the mysterious bed of Ixotta." The Canadian troops are portrayed as agents of cultural rape—their "literal" or physical rape of the young girl merely externalizes the motif of cultural violence—whose aim is "to demolish what little remains of Rimini," to violate "the mysterious bed of Ixotta." The young girl's suicidal deed is consummated in a mine-field specifically sited as "Where was the Tempio | of the beautiful Ixotta." Her sacrifice of the self is described as an act of "pure love" ("per puro amore," line 76), and her deed turns her into a second Isotta, a figure who promises another Renaissance of the fatherland and the fascist dream—"*rinasce* la patria."

Inevitably these passages force us to ponder the ambivalent itinerary Pound had traced in the twenty-two years since that moment when, about 15 May 1922, he first saw the church of San Francesco. The view presents a series of painful contrasts. In 1944, the tranquility of the Adriatic shore is imagined only as the site of a mine-field: how different since he and his wife Dorothy had walked the beaches so many years ago; how innocent the 1922 postcard she had sent her mother from Rimini: "[We] walked on the sea shore this afternoon, & saw lots of boats with those yellow & red patterned sails. Had very fresh fish dinner—."[143] It was also in Rimini in 1922, we recall, that Pound purchased a copy of Antonio Beltramelli's book, *Un tempio d'amore*, with its curious report supposedly quoted from Pius II, "And she [Isotta] was worthy of this love"— a passage copied by Pound and transmitted in the final version of the Malatesta Cantos, a passage to which Beltramelli had added another claim: "Isotta is pure when she exits from the life of her time, through which she passed loving and suffering, noble and larger than human." Yet if the inspiring figure of Isotta is the epitome of "love" and "purity," and if she is the model to whom the country girl of 1944 is assimilated when her destructive deed is characterized as one of "pure love," then clearly we confront a core of ideas that is profoundly ambivalent. What sort of love is this? How has it led to the constitution of such a "monument to civilization"?

Such questions are disquieting because they concern more than the psycho-biography of Pound, as the tradition of scholarly exegesis that we have traced makes very clear. Modern literary studies have maintained every "fact" requisite to viewing the Tempio as a specific type of "monument to civilization." Pound offers not one historical claim regarding Isotta that has not been repeatedly ratified by Anglo-American scholars of literature since 1955: that the lyrical fragment of Canto 8 is a poem written to her by Sigismondo; that the closing lines of Canto 9 offer authentic and contemporary testimonies to her worth (an inscription from a medal associated with the Malatestan court, a quotation from a quattrocento chronicle by one "Alessandro," or a passage from the *Commentarii* of Pius II); or that the entwined letters *S* and *I* represent Sigismondo and Isotta (even when the cipher has not been reprinted in any edition of *The Cantos* since 1925). It is inadequate to dismiss these practices only as poor scholarship or copying for the sake of convenience; this only labels rather than explains them. For "convenience" in these cases is a specific form of activity in relation to historical materials, which it is "convenient" to dispatch in this manner. It is inadequate, too, to argue that there was no evidence indicating the problematic character of the "traditional" attributions. The lines attributed to Pius II offer an egregious example: they are cited by Pound in Italian, leaving it unlikely that they derive from Pius (whose works are all in Latin) or Yriarte (whose work is in French) without some mediating agency. Yet when faced with recalcitrant evidence so elementary in nature, scholars have elected to ignore it. What is at stake is something more: the tradition of scholarly exegesis on these passages represents the local and concrete forms of systemic disorders in the dominant practice of literary studies since roughly 1950. At their center is a corpus of premises and procedures that literary studies share with Pound's operations in constituting the text of *The Cantos*— shared assumptions and inclinations that result less in critical scholarship and more in an uncritical replication of authorial intentions, validating the poem's own claims and central emblems.

The desperate love of Sigismondo for Isotta degli Atti cannot be maintained on the basis of the testimonies adduced by Pound and affirmed by literary critics in his wake. Perhaps it was never the issue at all. The desire enciphered in the letters *S* and *I* was less the passion of Sigismondo for Isotta, more the desperate love of Ezra Pound for another "Isotta" whose ambiguous charms were invented partly by Euro-American culture at the turn of the century and partly by Pound. To define this figure is not easy. In several crucial respects it embodies only a corpus of common antipathies related to class and socioeconomic developments, antipathies formulated in Corrado Ricci's derisive reference to "popes and notaries"—those who could never perceive the true significance of the sign. Figures such as Pound, Ricci, and Beltramelli deeply distrusted the urban, industrialized masses that became so noticeable in the late nineteenth and early twentieth centuries, and felt only hostility toward the positivist ethos and materialism characteristic of the middle classes—surely this is the group tartly dismissed as "notaries." They were skeptical of the conservative leadership that represented parliamentary democracy, orthodox piety, positivist philosophy, and capitalist growth—the leadership epitomized as "popes." Against this they posited an elite of the spirit (Pound's "aristocracy of emotion") that would be cultivated and yet retain the vitality of popular culture, existing in an imaginary unity with the "people." Thus the tendency to admire a figure such as Sigismondo, "the whole man" who embodies both popular vigor and aristocratic refinement, who figures their own desire for "Isotta."

Yet the ambivalent charms of "Isotta" encompassed not only aversions, but also a core of positive aspirations that, though vague, were capable of attracting a wide consensus. In contrast to the moribund authorities of science and religious orthodoxy, they sought a secular spirituality—at times charged with hints of vitalism (Pound's "the real, the onrush" in Draft *C1*) or sensuality and voluntarism (Pound's "lordship over the senses" and "a cult stricter . . . than that of the celibate ascetics"). Above all they posited an idea of man as primarily characterized by his active role in the world and a view of knowledge that rejects the conception of experience as a kind of mirror of nature or reality, and regards it instead as the active life of man as organizer and constructor of all data. "To philosophize," as Giovanni Gentile wrote in 1906, "is not to understand books, but to seek to live fully, to know what life is . . . it is not pure speculation, but also action."[144] Or as Pound epitomized his ambitions in an early draft (ca. 1917) for *The Cantos*, it was time to reclaim "the spirit," or "the flow, the pulse, the surge, . . . the uncontrolled, indecorous, actual living."[145] Meaning, in this view, is no longer located either in reality (a point of origin or production) or in the cultural system (transmission), but in the act of investing these with meaning, or in a *pattern* of meaning-acts, "the pulse, the surge." (Its source is what would be traditionally viewed as its point of destination or reception). Value is not found or received, but made.

Sigismondo's construction of the Tempio, or his creation of the entwined sign, therefore becomes an exemplary type of man's active creation; he acts not in conformity with conventional motives of piety or dynastic aggrandizement, or with meanings grounded in the cultural system, but in harmony with an inborn drive deemed basic to the human condition, whose exercise is elicited by "Isotta." And it is here that one sees the paradoxical status of Sigismondo in relation to history. Sigismondo discovers true being insofar as he sheds his historical traits, insofar as his constructive activity is at the same time a refusal to accept culturally (and therefore historically) given values; yet the *fact* of his having done so is what turns him into a concrete historical resource for the crisis of contemporary civilization. He is, in other words, the historical exemplar of an ahistorical form of life. And this exemplary status is established through, even as it also exhibits, a specific dynamics of cultural transmission. Sigismondo's form of life, the cipher, the Tempio itself— all share a common pattern, a shedding of historical attributes (habits, conventions) and meanings of the cultural system, in order to lay bare something other: an inborn drive that is more basic, a meaning (*significato equivoco*) that stands apart from everyday language and institutional discourse (*significato ufficiale*), a privileged site that is essentially autonomous, private, and opposed to the illegitimate constraints of the public sphere.

How these dynamics of transmission converge with social processes can be illustrated by the opening passage from Draft *C1* of the Malatesta Cantos (from mid-July 1922), also notable for being the earliest poetic response to *The Waste Land:*

> *"These fragments" you "have shelved"*
>   *against your ruin.*
> *And Malatesta?*
>   *Sigismundo Pan. filius.*
> *The broken arch* ⇌
>   *spoils of Ravenna*[.]

Citing one of the last lines of *The Waste Land*, this passage draws an analogy between Eliot and Sigismondo, both of whom have abstracted a "fragment" from the past and deployed it to create a cultural monument. The analogy is articulated through a reference to the "broken arch," or so-called Arch of Augustus in Rimini, a commemorative gate that issues from the city at the point where the ancient via Aemilia met the via Flaminia. It is the oldest gate of its type in Italy, built in 27 B.C. to commemorate the Augustan reconstruction of the roads after the civil wars and so to publicize the *pax augustana*. Scholarly discussion has always assumed that it served as a model for the "triumphal" arch in the main doorway of the Tempio, often considered its most singular architectural innovation (see figure 2).[146] Sharing this belief, Pound assimilates the "broken arch" to the "fragments" used by Eliot in *The Waste Land*, stressing the difficulty of wresting its genuine beauty from surroundings deemed degraded and sordid. Yet to a modern reader the analogy may seem curious: the gate, after all, stands isolated in a lovely piazza, quite free of any surroundings that might be termed squalid. In 1922, however, its situation was different, and Pound's emphasis marks a precise intersection between perceptual and social processes. When he saw the gate of Augustus in 1922, it was engulfed by the surrounding buildings which, in the course of the centuries, had grown up around it. Its transformation from a commemorative gate into a triumphal arch, and from a static support for local housing into a monument of culture, took place only in 1937 when the regime demolished every building that circumscribed it, creating the ample piazza where it presently stands in solitary splendor. Even more, the regime also destroyed the two towers that flanked it, which went back to the original Roman construction and were evidence of its use as a commemorative gate within the city walls, rather than an isolated arch.[147] To create a monument of civilization, in other words, the regime divested the gate of its historical traits, the features that registered its use-value both in the events of its production and in subsequent transmission. Likewise, the "fragment" of modernism is abstracted from its surroundings and turned into a monument of culture; and likewise, the "text" of modern criticism is forged in a shedding of its historical-cultural attributes: the "text's unity," as Barthes observes in a remark that inaugurated the post-structuralist era, is located "in its destination . . . in the reader [who] is without history, biography, psychology." And likewise, the monuments of the canon are abstracted to become "literature"—by a categorical demolition of the surrounding graphic and social environment, both contemporary and subsequent.[148]

Corrado Ricci's treatment of the sign made up of *S* and *I*, as we can see now, anticipates the central premises of modern literary criticism. At Ricci's hands the sign is severed from all its social and historical dimensions: those are deemed extrinsic, parts of the contaminated orders of "merely" public or social meaning; while the sign achieves true being only insofar as it diverges from this, only insofar as it departs from the realm of the everyday, the social, the institutional. Such claims seem so familiar because they have become the staple of modern literary studies, as one sees by considering Paul de Man's urbane observation that "the statement about language, that sign and meaning can never coincide, is what is precisely taken for granted in the kind of language we call literary. Literature, unlike everyday language, begins on the far side of this knowledge." De Man, in this passage, seeks to establish cognitive grounds for the familiar premise of aesthetic autonomy, the idea that one particular category of cultural works enjoys a special status in relation to all others. To do so he must abstract it from the sordid surroundings of "everyday language" and "history," from what he terms "empirical reality . . . a reality from which it [the sign] has forever taken leave."[149] As for Ricci, so also for de Man, semiotic plenitude is achieved only through historical emptiness. The monument of "literature" or "the sign" is secured by the demolition of the testimonies registering the events of its production and transmission, and by its elevation to a separate ontological domain. Geoffrey Hartmann is surely right when he observes, "Deconstruction is, in this respect, a defense of literature."[150] De Man's procedures, we can see, resemble Pound's treatment of the lyrical fragment in Canto 8, or the regime's treatment of the gate of Augustus. "Literature" and the "sign" are explained and conserved, but at a cost that may strike many as too high, since the epistemological claims become only abstractly affirmative, even as the terrain of cultural engagement shrivels to nothing.

De Man's remarks appear in the course of his seminal essay, "Criticism and Crisis," which begins by citing a series of lectures delivered in 1935 by Husserl, "The Crisis of European Humanity and Philosophy." De Man identifies a contradiction between Husserl's view of philosophy as self-interpretation that eliminates "the tendency of the self to hide from the light it can cast on itself" and his categorical assumption that philosophy is the historical privilege of Europeans. He takes for granted that contemporary readers will dispute this privilege, pausing briefly to note "the pathos of such a claim at a moment when Europe was about to destroy itself." Elsewhere, too, de Man admits to his consciousness of "reading this text with the hindsight that stems from more than thirty years of turbulent history."[151] Yet he evinces no interest in his own remarks, and instead proceeds to instance Husserl for his thesis about "the structure" of blindness and insight inherent in any rhetoric. This is curious, since de Man himself is clearly conscious that his insight into the "pathos" and structure of the Husserlian discourse is grounded in a chronological discrepancy: in 1935, after all, it could not be *assumed* that "Europe was about to destroy itself" or that it would experience "more than thirty years of turbulent history." Such observations derive their force by virtue of events that could be but dimly imagined then, when they pertained to a future that had not yet occurred. Indeed, his passing remarks show that his insights stem from the historical discrepancy he leaves otherwise unattended, not from the rhetorical structure and intrinsic methodology he so deftly explains. His actual practice is more telling: there will always be descriptions, such as de Man's, of events in 1935, which depend upon accounts of events that took place long after 1935. Only when those later events have occurred can we give such descriptions, and without them our account may remain seriously inadequate. Our knowledge of the past, as Arthur Danto has pointed out, is grounded in our knowledge (and ignorance) of the future.[152]

De Man enacts this in making his observations on Husserl, but withdraws from its demands when he articulates their theoretical foundations. And yet paradoxically its demands are felt acutely in our current reading of de Man's work: when he remarks on "the moment when Europe was about to destroy itself," we ponder his statement in the light of recent disclosures about his wartime involvement with the collaborationist newspaper *Le Soir;* and when he notes "the hindsight that stems from more than thirty years of turbulent history," we sense that our reading is grounded in our knowledge of a future that the recent disclosures have realized, and that are now a part of our past. The reconstitution of de Man's intentions, like Ricci's or Pound's, we see, does not consist wholly in achieving congruence between sign and meaning (the view de Man attacks), but in the creation of procedural conditions that enable various testimonies to engage in dialogic exchanges differing from the logic of their production. Insofar as the future is always incomplete, those exchanges are characterized not by absolute plenitude, but by pragmatic adequacy. It is in the future, which is to say in the dynamics of transmission, that intention is always emerging.

Drawing on Wittgenstein and Danto, Jürgen Habermas has observed:

> It is proper to the grammar of a language game not only that it defines a form of life but that it defines a form of life as one's own over against others that are foreign. . . . For this reason, the limits of the world that it defines are not irrevocable; the dialectical confrontation of what is one's own with what is foreign leads, for the most part imperceptibly, to revisions.[153]

To confront "what is foreign"—the heterogeneous testimonies of history, the world that informs cultural works, both past and future—is a task that has been largely evaded by literary studies in our time. Conceiving of cultural works solely in terms of their linguistic status severed from all sociohistorical terms, recent criticism has effected few "revisions" indeed. The exclusions already encoded in the notion of "literature" have been only ratified by concepts of the "sign" or the "text," which categorically preclude structures of falsification by "foreign" or historical testimonies that have been cast forever outside the disciplinary purview.

It is in this sense, we see, that the reception of Pound's work has replicated his intentions—not only at an explicit propositional level, but at the level of constitutive maneuvers. The arch of triumph is such—can be such—only because the towers that once indicated its purpose as a gate, or the houses that once registered its later engagements, have been demolished. The enciphered letters S and I are constituted only over against the letter Y, the letter that must never be written. The poem attributed to Sigismondo is such only because other manuscripts with "foreign" testimonies are precluded from consideration, just as the testimonies to the worth of Isotta are validated only by erasing the events of their transmission. Pound turns out to be an ambivalent mirror of our critical practices; like de Man, he is our *hypocrite lecteur*. The late Romantic view of the Tempio in Rimini is less the construction of an aberrant mind than the monument of modern "literature," a construction testifying to the desperate love not only of Sigismondo, or of Pound, but of an entire culture. When we contemplate the nightmarish scenario imagined in Canto 73 as an outgrowth of the cantos of 1922—the cantos that are distinguished for modern critics solely by their technical innovation of incorporating prose documents—we can say as Robert Lowell did of Mussolini: "He was one of us only, pure prose."

Fascism is the salient and central experience of Western culture in the twentieth century. As Gramsci so clearly intuited, its totalitarian spirit and monolithic appearance repeatedly obscured a series of stratifications in its midst; it was less an organic phenomenon with well-defined characteristics than a complex reality in continuous transformation. Its appeal to intellectuals from diverse backgrounds and nations—Yeats, Heidegger, Lewis, Céline, Pound, de Man, Beltramelli, Gentile, the scholarly Ricci—suggests its multiformity, the sheer diversity of its specific manifestations and implications. As Gramsci's companion, Tasca, perceived, it is not a subject for which it is sufficient to list its attributes, but the resultant of a complex situation from which it cannot be severed.[154] To say this does not exculpate Pound, or anyone else, by implying that environment, specific situations, or "causes" necessarily contained specific solutions, but it does require us to understand how these were reached, which were the alternatives and openings, which errors were made and why. How was it that a single letter could epitomize the utopian aspirations of scholars and poets, or that a chance encounter amid the ruins of antiquity could foreshadow the terrible ruins of modernity? Such questions can be addressed only by engaging in meticulous, highly specific accounts that are comprehensive—not totalizing—in their effort to create conditions of dialogic exchange that differ from those already transmitted to us, yielding revisions whose contents cannot be detailed in advance.

It will require years and years of minute research, far beyond the capacity of any single individual, before we can confront these questions, perhaps especially so in the United States, where the long domination of formalist and intrinsic modes of criticism has destroyed the most minimal premises for it. And it will require that we reject sincere but ingenuous moralisms, facile appeals to a contemporary consensus in the formation of which fascism itself has played a crucial part, or the allure of abstract coherencies beyond all reality—the concatenations of empty concepts assimilated to the play of "self" and "other" now so characteristic of literary studies. To confront the cultural heritage of the twentieth century will demand a reconception of the notion of literature and its changing relations to other forms of graphic-cultural life, a reconception in which the problematics of fact and transmissive processes will necessarily occupy a more prominent place, while the role assigned to the mediation of "text" will diminish in importance. Even when, as has begun to happen more recently, literary studies have explored nonliterary or historical materials, the result has largely been a collapse in favor of the "literary," a "textualization" of other generic or documentary forms that tacitly reaffirms the dream of totalization in the mastery of "reading." We have tended to "fictionalize" other disciplines, but we may need to "factualize" our own. Doing so will not provide the immutable substratum of "history" dreamed of by earlier generations, as opposed to the untrustworthiness of the work itself, but it may furnish points of reference for mapping the contradictory networks of uses (facts of quotation) in which works are constituted, or the diverse processes whereby they are transformed (the quotation of facts) amid specific use and exchange values. Inquiry into the relations among works and institutions will mean that we consider less production and reception than the dynamics of transmission.

Still, greater notice of these dimensions will not provide a unified or total solution to questions of history and literature, or fact and language, if only because the boundaries between them shift and dissolve, harden and soften too swiftly for any totalizing narrative to encompass. The study of transmissive dynamics may enable us to measure such changes more precisely, but there will still be arguments about their meaning. And such arguments, as Hayden White has lucidly noted, "cannot be justified by an appeal to the 'facts' of history, since it is precisely the nature of these facts and the determination of what they are fact *of* that are at issue." [155] Yet more attention to the processes of transmission may at least keep us alert to the shifting terms—both linguistic and social—under which our own discussions are conducted, conditions that shape the extent to which our own exchange with the past will be more probing and self-critical than it has been in recent decades. For in the future imagined in every act of transmission, we may find that we are forced to revisit the sites of our labors, a return in which our monuments will disclose all that we have buried, all that we have excluded in our deliberations—a "past" that does not "pass," the specter of our mixed vanities.

Coda

28 August 1963

Luigi Pasquini was born on 15 February 1897 in Rimini, in Borgo San Giuliano, a poor district of the city. His parents owned a *trattoria* frequented by the local fishermen. He was educated in Bologna, fought in World War I, then returned to Rimini, where he taught drawing and design in the local schools. His teaching career eventually took him to other cities in Italy and during the 1920s he began to write journalism. His first book appeared in 1936, a guide to his native province of Romagna, accompanied by his own illustrations (*Romagna per i lettori e veditori*). Others soon followed, novels and collections of his journalistic essays. In 1966 he suffered a heart attack; on 20 March 1977 he died in Rimini. After his death, his friends discovered a manuscript that he had worked on for years, reminiscences of his encounters with the great and not so great. Among them was a description of his only meeting with Ezra Pound at a concert in Rimini in 1963. [156]

Here he is, seated beside me in the nave of the Tempio Malatestiano: Ezra Pound, author of *The Cantos*, the magnum opus begun in 1917 and still unfinished, a work that begs comparison with the hundred cantos of Dante. This is the great American poet who emigrated to Italy, who broadcast his disdain for the American government throughout the war, who was locked in a hospital for the insane for twelve years, and who was finally released and returned to Italy.

Here he is. His hair is white, his beard short. He is tall, but a little stooped, as if gathered into himself. His eyes are blue, an aquamarine that scintillates with traces of light. And here he is, seated beside me: the man whose generosity was a legend when he lived in London and

Paris, who launched new poets and writers, who helped them financially (Joyce, Eliot, Hemingway)—who shaped a new literature. He is sitting here, in the celebrated temple of Sigismondo and Isotta, amid the bas-reliefs of Agostino di Duccio, within the monument that inspired some of his most lyrical passages in *The Pisan Cantos*—here, incognito, accompanied by his companion Olga Rudge—to listen to a symphony concert given by the Malatestan Philharmonic with help from the Viennese Sing-akademie.

The concert program has two parts: the first is Mozart's *Requiem*, a musical poem both agonizing and consoling; the second is Bach's triumphal *Magnificat* as interpreted by the young conductor, Antonio de Bavier. Yet the odd thing is what happens to me in the intermission.

When I reach him he is standing in the sacristy of the church, a tiny room that formerly housed its relics. Above the door is Piero della Francesca's fresco depicting Sigismondo Malatesta as he kneels before his patron saint. Pound is standing beneath it, surrounded by people.

I approach him slowly, nervously, until I am directly before him, face to face. I look him in the eye, and inquire: "Ezra Pound?"

He does not respond. He stares at me, silent, and his mouth hints at a thin smile.

I insist, and repeat his name. He gazes at me, arching his eyebrows for a moment, but says nothing.

I fear I must be mistaken and address my glance to the woman beside him. She peers up at him, then nods, reassuring me that it is him.

I offer him my hand, and he takes it in his own. I do not tell him my name, but I make clear that I know his books, that I have read some of the articles he published between 1938 and 1943 for the *Meridiano di Roma*, a literary weekly on which I collaborated. He understands, it seems. He gives a sign of assent, but continues to remain silent.

Our hands are still clasping each another. "This is the hand of the great American poet," I offer. ["La mano del grande poeta americano!"]

And at last his voice emerges, his first words, uttered in a tranquil Italian accent without a trace of an Anglo-American inflection: "I am not great." ["Non grande."]

Swiftly I reply: "—you are among the greatest." ["Grandissimo."]

But the conversation falters, and I grow uncertain. Through friends I had heard that he was living in Rapallo, but a stray remark from Miss Rudge indicates they have just come from Venice. I try to take up the topic: "Where are you living now: in Rapallo? Or in Merano with your daughter, or in Venice?"

He will not reply. He looks at me again, with a mocking gaze.

I persist: "Rapallo, Merano? Venice, Rome?"

Nothing. He is still silent, his gaze fixed on me, like someone playing a guessing game.

I press on: "So where are you living now?" I continue, "Where?"

At last he lowers his head, slowly, and puts his mouth next to my ear so that no one can hear us. His voice is a whisper, rasping: "I live in hell."

This leaves me bewildered. Here we are in a church, in a sacristy in fact (even if it is the sacristy of a paganizing temple)—in a place, in short, as far as possible from Erebus or the underworld of Lucifer. And yet he says we're in hell. I fail to understand and want to pursue it: "Which hell do you mean? The hellish tourism? The inferno of the war, here in Rimini? The hell of Rome? Of Italy? Of the world?"

He is silent again. At last he moves his hands: he places them before his stomach, and slowly lifting them to the level of his heart, as the traces of light in his pupils become like glowing coals, he whispers a suffocated scream: "Here is hell. Here."

*

The intermission is almost over. I have nothing to say, and we continue to stare at each other in silence. Meanwhile news of his presence has spread through the crowd, and I can hear voices whispering: "He is a great American poet. . . ." Photographers have arrived and are shooting pictures. But a bell indicates the end of the intermission, and everyone resumes his seat.

Pound is seated alongside the balustrade guarding the third chapel on the right—the chapel of the Zodiac. On the pilaster beside him is the bas-relief that depicts Cancer descending on the city of Rimini, shown as it was in the fifteenth century [see figure 8]. When the music begins, his head sinks, and he remains absorbed for the rest of the performance.

After the concert, he rises and gets ready to leave. The conductor has offered a car to take him to the train station, where he can catch the evening train returning to Venice, the city where he had published his first book of poems some sixty years before, *A Lume Spento* (*With Tapers Quenched*). Miss Rudge accompanies him, solicitous. I notice them leaving and escort them to the car, helping him as he slumps into his seat. His voice mumbles: "Outside . . . I'm outside of myself . . . outside of the world."

The doors are closed, and the car lurches into the evening.

APPENDIX ONE

The Chronology of the Manuscripts

Only five or six of the Malatesta manuscripts contain explicit indications of the date of their composition.[1] In dating them, three kinds of criteria have been used—historical, intrinsic, and extrinsic. Historical criteria refer to those elements of the document's content whose production can be collated with external documentation. An example is furnished by transcriptions from archival documents (even though none of these are actually edited here); these can only have been made in situ on a precise date that can be determined by archival administrative records or by Pound's own correspondence. Of course most items are less easily dated. Intrinsic characteristics are those referable to the content of the manuscripts under their formal aspects—drafts comprising only two cantos, say, versus drafts comprising three. Extrinsic characteristics are the identifiable elements of the material production of any document, such as paper, ink, typing ribbon, and so on. These characteristics help us to date many of the Malatesta notes and drafts, for we can collate them with the same features in Pound's correspondence during the same period, which thus serves as a control for the establishment of a chronology.

The entire composition of the Malatesta Cantos can be divided into two stages. The first begins with materials drafted shortly after Pound saw the Tempio Malatestiano for the first time around 15 May 1922. The earliest drafts and notes were written at Sirmione on the Lago di Garda in Italy between about 9 and 20 June 1922.[2] The rest of the first stage, however, took place in Paris, where Pound returned on 2 July 1922, and where he continued working until 5 January 1923, when he completed and sent off the Watson typescript, or *W*, a complete draft of the four Malatesta Cantos which he mailed to Dr. James Sibley Watson, Jr. (co-editor and co-publisher of *The Dial*). Thus, in stage one all the work except for the five "Sirmione Manuscripts" was done in Paris. In stage two, however, nearly all the work was done in Italy. Pound left for Rapallo on 5 January 1923, the same day that he mailed *W* to Watson, and in Rapallo he soon began revising it extensively. From 16 February until ca. 20 April he conducted a research tour of Italian libraries and archives, continuing to make additions or revisions to his poem in the light of the manuscript and documentary material he consulted. He returned to Rapallo, and at last went back to Paris, where around 18 May he sent off the final draft of the Malatesta Cantos to T. S. Eliot, submitting them for publication in *The Criterion*.[3]

The geographical settings for each stage of composition correspond with other more important differences, such as the nature of Pound's source materials and the kinds of evidence that survive to help reconstruct the chronology of composition. In the second or Italian stage, for example, Pound's main sources were primary manuscripts and documents. These he could consult only in libraries and archives, whose administrative records often enable us to date and reconstruct Pound's studies, and so also the corresponding revisions to the poem. There are also Pound's letters, inevitably more frequent because he was away from his home in Paris. In particular, he wrote notes and letters to his wife Dorothy almost daily when he was traveling alone during his research.[4] There are also Pound's notes on his consultations, more abundant because he was obliged to be attentive and thorough, since original manuscripts and documents could be consulted only in situ. Thus the second stage offers a considerable amount of external, historical evidence on which to base a reconstruction of Pound's activities and the chronology of composition.

The same is not true for the first or Paris stage. Here the most important resources for Pound were secondary, printed sources. Some books Pound purchased himself, including old or rare works obtained through antiquarian bookdealers. On these he took far fewer notes, simply because he owned them and could reexamine them at need; and because he could consult them repeatedly, their influence was also less precisely marked within the chronology of composition—less a precise moment, more a prolonged series of effects. Many books, of course, Pound also consulted in libraries, particularly the Bibliothèque Nationale of Paris; and predictably he took ampler notes on these materials. Yet we can date these notes and consultations only approximately because the Bibliothèque Nationale no longer preserves the "bulletins de demande de livre" from this period. Thus for this stage we must often establish the chronology of composition through internal evidence, the intrinsic and especially the extrinsic characteristics of Pound's own manuscripts. The latter can certainly tell us a great deal. Consider only the earliest materials for the

Malatesta Cantos, the Sirmione manuscripts, and how we might date
them.

The earliest materials for the Malatesta Cantos can be identified by the
kind of paper on which they were written. In a rough way Pound's choice
of paper reflected the circumstances of his life at this time. Since he
could not take his typewriter with him when he was traveling, he was
forced to write letters and other works by hand, and for this purpose he
preferred to use graph paper, perhaps because the close, fixed pattern of
lines helped to anchor his unsteady pen. Apparently he always (during
1922 and 1923) bought the same general type of graph paper, large
sheets measuring roughly 425 × 275 mm, with a printed pattern of hor-
izontal and vertical lines. At first glance all these papers look much alike,
but on closer examination they fall into distinct kinds. A few, for ex-
ample, bear particular watermarks or brand-names, but these are rare,
and most lack such easily identifiable features. All the papers, however,
were distinguished by the pattern of the printed graph lines, and in par-
ticular by the lines that were "horizontal" as they appeared on the sheet
and as Pound most frequently used them. These presented several iden-
tifiable characteristics. First, the lines varied in quantity from one kind
of paper to another, from twenty-seven to thirty-one. Second, even when
two kinds of paper had the same quantity of "horizontal" lines, these
varied either in their size as a block or in their place within the overall
space of the sheet. These variations resulted from a distinctive feature of
the type of graph paper that Pound preferred. Whereas most graph papers
have both vertical and horizontal lines running flush to the edges of the
sheet (and so filling uniformly the sheet's space with small quadrangles),
this type of graph paper had *only* the vertical lines running flush to the
sheet's edges. The pattern of horizontal lines stopped before reaching the
sheet's edge, and so created a discrete block framed at the top and bottom
by a margin of space without quadrangles, containing vertical lines only.
As a result the "horizontal" lines in this general type of graph paper had
two distinguishing characteristics: (a) an amount of space they occupied
as a block, and (b) an amount of space found at the top and bottom mar-
gins of the block (or the amount of space without quadrangles). The pre-
cise dimensions of these varied from one kind of graph paper to another,
making each identifiable. In one case, say, two kinds of paper both had
thirty-one "horizontal" lines, but in each the thirty-one lines took up
different amounts of space as a block, 231 mm versus 238 mm. In an-
other case, two kinds of paper both had twenty-eight lines occupying a
block of 212 mm, but each was distinguished by the amount of space at

the block's top and bottom margins—30 and 30 mm versus 34 and 28 mm. Thus the pattern of "horizontal" lines in each kind of paper presented distinctive features which we can quantify and arrange in a formula that reflects their order as seen on the sheet:

1. The "top" margin, given in mm (the larger of the two margins is always considered the "top" margin)
2. The block of "horizontal" lines (2.1) given first in mm and then (2.2) by the number of lines (between parentheses and always ranging between twenty-seven and thirty-one)
3. the "bottom" (or smaller) margin, given in mm

An illustration clarifies how this formula reflects the sequence of these features as they appear to the eye.

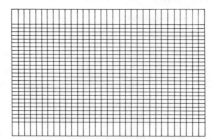

(1) the "top" or larger margin

(2) the block of "horizontal" lines

(3) the "bottom" or smaller margin

Using this formula we can classify the several hundred sheets of graph paper that contain notes and drafts for the Malatesta Cantos, and such classification makes clear that they are of ten kinds. This information is useful principally because Pound used the same kinds of paper for his correspondence, and since his letters are usually dated they furnish a key for establishing a chronology of many notes and drafts.

Consider the letters written by Pound from Sirmione in June 1922, dated 9, 16, 20, and 29 June.[5] All are written on a kind of graph paper measuring 420×270 mm, without a watermark or brand name, and with "horizontal" lines forming a pattern: 20.232 (31).18. This paper is found only in Pound's letters from Sirmione; it is quite different from the paper that he used both earlier (in Venice) and later (in Paris). Though the Venice letters (dated 28 and 29 May) were also written on graph paper, the paper has very different features.[6] It measures 435×275 mm; it has a watermark (entwined C and V amid ornamentation) and a brand name (Old Mora Mill); and of course it has an identifiable pattern of "horizontal" lines: 22.236 (31).15. Likewise, the letters from Paris are written on paper that is noticeably different, for when Pound was again at home he could use his typewriter and so he no longer had need of graph paper.

Instead he used ordinary typing paper.[7] Thus the paper used in Pound's Sirmione letters has distinct and identifiable features, and if these are collated with their counterparts among the papers used in the various notes and drafts of the Malatesta Cantos, matching features appear in four manuscripts—two drafts and two groups of notes. These manuscripts conserve Pound's earliest work on the Malatesta Cantos.[8]

Extrinsic characteristics (such as paper or typewriter ribbon) of Pound's manuscripts usually furnish the crucial evidence for establishing a chronological outline for the first stage of composition, running from June 1922 to January 1923. Yet often the outline gains in detail if supplemented with evidence furnished by the manuscript's intrinsic characteristics, or by historical evidence. Once more the Sirmione manuscripts offer an example. Pound's letters from Sirmione extend from 9 June to 29 June 1922. Before 9 June the only letter we have from Pound is dated 29 May, a date that therefore would offer the most conservative *terminus post quem*. For conceivably Pound might have bought the kind of graph paper found in his Sirmione letters already on 30 May, and so have used it for composing the earliest Malatesta drafts during the period 30 May to 9 June, when he wrote his first letter on this kind of paper. Yet this is unlikely for two reasons. First, one of the drafts (*B*) contains a distinct reference to a variety-show performance that took place in Verona between 1 and 6 June, and we know that Pound visited Verona with T. S. Eliot between about 31 May and 2 June. Second, Pound's letter of 9 June makes no reference to recent composition.[9] In contrast, his letter of 20 June reports on his recent accomplishments with manifest pride. So it is much more likely that Pound only began composing after 9 June, and that this stands as the most reasonable *terminus post quem*. Less difficult to specify is the *terminus ante quem*. Pound announced on 20 June that he had "blocked in" four cantos, that one of these was "the 'Hell' canto," and that he was "at work" on this "Hell" canto that very moment. But nine days later on 29 June he reported to Agnes Bedford that he had written "four, probably five" cantos—one more than reported on 20 June. Further, he noted that "two of them [are] unprintable, dealing with modern life"—a description that can have referred only to the same "Hell" canto, sufficiently expanded now to constitute "probably" two cantos.[10] This indicates that Pound had continued working on the "Hell" material from 20 June to 29 June; and if so, it must have been before 20 June that he had already finished his drafts for a Malatesta canto. Thus the earliest versions of the Malatesta Cantos were composed between 9 and 20 June 1922.

Pound's Travels in Italy, 1922

Accounts of Pound's travels in Italy in 1922 have been flawed in elementary matters of geography and chronology, and his meeting with T. S. Eliot in Verona has been largely neglected by most biographers.[1] This appendix traces his travels in 1922, sketches his activities during the same period, and surveys the documentary basis of the information.

In March 1922, before leaving Paris, Pound was involved in four projects: his reading and publicization of Louis Berman's book, *Glands Regulating Personality;*[2] a plan to create a lifetime endowment in support of T. S. Eliot, known as Bel Esprit;[3] correspondence regarding the publication of Eliot's *The Waste Land* as well as editorial planning of Eliot's new review, soon to be named *The Criterion;*[4] and negotiating rights to translate two books by Paul Morand, a French author whose second collection of short stories, *Ouvert la nuit*, was published in the last days of February 1922 and greeted with critical acclaim.[5] All these affected his journey to Italy in various ways.

Pound, together with his wife Dorothy, left Paris for Italy on March 27.[6] He took the train to Genoa, then on to Rapallo. To his father he wrote a postcard dated "Genoa 29 March" and bearing on its recto the mark: ALBERGO ITALIA | *Unico Sul Mar* | RAPALLO. He was "supposed to go to Carrara day after tomorrow," he said, and later he planned to "try the one [i.e., the Hotel Royal Aquila] at Pisa."[7] Presumably he followed this plan; if so, he went to Carrara on 31 March, where he stayed perhaps a day, and on 1 April continued down the Ligurian coast to Pisa.

On 4 April he traveled to Siena, arriving in the evening.[8] Almost immediately he wrote to John Quinn: "Just got here in high wind—believe the place will be charming when I get time to look at it." His note to Quinn had been prompted by receipt of a letter from Jeanne Foster, Quinn's companion, who had worriedly described Quinn's increasing ill-health due to overwork and nervous exhaustion. Pound, therefore, was inviting Quinn to take a vacation, and he suggested that they meet at the Lago di Garda later in the course of his journey: "Now my schedule is Venice by end of May & Lago di Garda by 7 or 15th of June."[9] When he replied to Jeanne Foster the next day, he reiterated these plans; and in a third letter, also to Foster, written on 23 April, he stated yet again that he would "probably" be in Venice "at the end of May."[10]

His stay in Siena lasted 4 April to ca. 1 May and is well documented. On 6 April Pound wrote to Scofield Thayer, editor of *The Dial*, requesting permission to reprint his translation of a short story by Paul Morand that had appeared eight months earlier in *The Dial*.[11] A few days later Pound received a letter or telegraph from Victor Llona, a literary agent in Paris who had been negotiating a deal for Pound to translate Morand's two collections of short stories. The event was reported in a letter of 11 April to his father: "Have had an order for translations of Morand—at least Llona says go ahead it will be O.K., so I am damaging this end of my vacation in hope of clearing *the other*."[12] Pound buckled down to work. To prevent interruptions, he hit upon the curious expedient of pretending that he had died; the plan obliged him to solicit the collaboration of his family and friends and yet to reassure them the rumor was untrue. To his father on 12 April he wrote: "If you hear a rumor of my demise please DO NOT contradict it." And to John Quinn he wrote the same day: "If you hear a rumour of my death, don't be disturbed[,] but *fer* Gawd's sake DONT CONTRADICT IT. I shall be dead to the world." For Pound, however, perhaps nothing was closer to death than silence, and so it was hardly long before he wrote to Jeanne Foster: "I am dead. This is communicated from the world of spirits."[13] For the rest of April the translations consumed his time in Siena.[14] Only on 23 April did he pause to write a lengthy letter to Scofield Thayer, explaining his views about the publication of *The Waste Land* and assuring Thayer of his regard for *The Dial*.[15]

Pound finally left Siena around 2 May. He went to Cortona, and from there continued southward to Perugia. Upon arrival he wrote to John Quinn a letter dated "Perugia 6 May" and postmarked 6.5.22 PERUGIA. "Magnificent place this Perugia," he exclaimed.[16] Nor was Quinn the only person to receive correspondence from Perugia: Pound sent a letter to Jeanne Foster that stated that he was writing from Perugia, a letter whose envelope is postmarked 6.5.22 PERUGIA; and on the same date he also sent a postcard to Scofield Thayer dated "Perugia 6/5/22" and postmarked 6.5.22 Perugia.[17] (In some accounts it is reported that he was in Venice at this time).

To his various correspondents Pound traced his itinerary very clearly. Reiterating his invitation to Quinn to join him in Italy, he urged him to take the route he had just completed: "Damn it, you've got to take off some time and look around a little. Easy—no distance by motor. Siena, Cortona, etc. What's the sense in your not having it?" He also announced his plans for the future: "Start for Assisi, and thence up Adriatic coast next week."[18] And in a postcard to Scofield Thayer he was still more specific: "Will go to Assisi on Tuesday" (or May 9).[19]

Pound probably followed his plans. After three or four days in Perugia (5/6 to 8 May) he set out for Assisi on 9 May. There he must have seen the array of cultural treasures assembled to commemorate St. Francis— the basilica with its fresco cycles by Giotto and his successors that make the town one of the world's most important centers of medieval art. As early as 1910, in *The Spirit of Romance*, Pound had recorded his interest in St. Francis; and only two months later, in July, he would contrast the medieval saint with Sigismondo Malatesta in his notes for the Malatesta Cantos (*N4*, note 4).

As in Perugia, Pound probably stayed in Assisi for several days. Around 11 May he headed southward to Spello, where he no doubt stopped to observe the Renaissance frescoes of Pinturicchio. The next day he turned westward toward the Adriatic coast and the city of Ancona. There he probably stayed for only two days before taking the train that goes northward, hugging the shoreline, to Rimini. He and his wife Dorothy probably arrived in Rimini on 14 May. After visiting the Tempio Malatestiano, Dorothy purchased a postcard that depicted the backside of a sculpted putto standing on a balustrade in the church's interior, and when she sent it to her mother she affectionately called the putto a "chars" (a family name for cats and sort of tutelary household spirit): "Good marble one, this CHARS—with several gay companions. Will write from Ravenna when we've been to post. Going on tomorrow—Walked on the sea shore this afternoon, & saw lots of boats with those yellow & red patterned sails. Had very fresh fish dinner—Written on Monday [15 May], posted later."[20]

As Dorothy indicated to her mother, the Pounds left Rimini on 16 May ("tomorrow"), and traveled to Ravenna, where they stayed until 20 or 21 May. Pound especially admired the so-called Mausoleum of Galla Placidia, a small chapel of the fifth century located in a little field behind the great Byzantine church of San Vitale. Later he would describe the weathered tombs, half-covered by grass, flanking the path that leads from the church to the mausoleum. In the mausoleum itself he felt the suggestive power of the sunlight that filters through the alabaster pane of its window, tracing the orange-colored stars in the deep-blue mosaic of the vaults— emblems of time's passage, art's power, and the turn of imperial fortunes epitomized by the demise of Byzantine Ravenna—images he would invoke in early drafts of the Malatesta Cantos.

Pound probably arrived in Venice on 20 or 21 May (a weekend), too late to receive several letters that were waiting for him at the post office (this explains why his correspondence does not resume until 22 May). But when he wrote to his father on Monday, he took a moment to recapitulate his itinerary in its exact order: "Have had fine trip. Cortona, Perugia, Assissi [sic], Spello, Ancona, Rimini, Ravenna." He was also pleased with their accommodations in a deluxe hotel on the Grand Canal, a rarity made possible by the generous terms of his recent contract with Liveright: "We are blowing ourselves for a fortnight—rooms on G[ran]d. Canal. next door to Hotel Danieli. Balcony six feet away from it.—can't go on indefinitely. But Sirmione [at Lago di Garda] is cheap enough to balance it."[21] Meanwhile, there was business to attend to. Victor Llona had sent him a contract for the Morand translations, and Pound signed and dated it (22 May).[22]

After several days in Venice Pound received either a letter or telegram from T. S. Eliot that prompted a small yet important change in his itinerary. The document itself no longer exists, so far as I know, and its contents can be reconstructed only by Pound's subsequent actions. Yet those actions themselves must be reconstructed through indirect references in two contemporary letters. One is a letter from Pound to Kate Buss, dated 4 May 1922.[23] It contains a brief but significant remark by Pound: "But as Eliot is again ill—and I hope by now in Italy—I shall probably start turning over funds [from the Bel Esprit Project] to him very soon, even before a definite subsidy can be secured." This indicates that Pound, by 4 May, already knew of plans by Eliot to come to Italy at some point soon. The plans grow clearer when viewed against the background of another letter, this one to Agnes Bedford, dated "28 May | Hotel Savoia | Venice."[24] Bedford was a close friend who had moved into Pound's flat in London when he left the city in late 1920; Pound, when he was away from his home in Paris, would have correspondence sent to his former address in London, then have Bedford forward it to him en route. His note, therefore, regards a letter he anticipated receiving from John Quinn, a reply to his invitation to meet in Italy:

> Did you get a card from Ravenna asking you to send Quinn's letter re-
> enveloped & registered to Venice[?] If it hasn't gone send it s.v.p.
>   Fermo in Posta   Verona
> (registered) IF you *mail* it before midnight of May 31st; otherwise to
>   Fermo in Posta   *Sirmione* Lago di Garda

The note to Bedford clarifies two points. First, Pound now intended to go to Verona, if only long enough to pick up his letter from Quinn. Verona, of course, is where one must change trains if traveling from Venice to Sirmione; but if Pound had intended only to change trains he would hardly have asked Bedford to forward the letter there. Clearly he intended to spend several days in Verona—at least two in order to allow for postal unpredictability, and more likely three or four. Second, the note indicates that the decision to go to Verona was recent, apparently made between ca. 16–20 May (when Pound had sent "a card from Ravenna") and 28 May, the date of this note. Most likely it was made that very day, prompted by Eliot's message. A few days later, probably on 30 or 31 May, Pound left Venice and joined Eliot in Verona for a period of three days (31 May–2 June, or 1–3 June).[25]

In Verona, Pound watched a performance of a traveling variety show, which he later described in Draft *B* and subsequent drafts (see p. 53–55). It is not possible to identify which performance he saw, though we know that single performances were given at 8:00 P.M. on the evenings of 1 June (Thursday), 2 June (Friday), and 3 June (Saturday).[26] In one draft (written when Pound was back in Paris), Pound juxtaposes the performance occurring inside the arena with a portrait of himself, Eliot, and two other companions sitting together outside:

> By the arena- you. Galla Placidia ⚌ the Roman. and myself ⚌
> inside it the footlights ⚌
>   the clowns- dancers ⚌
> performing dogs ⚌

This indicates a performance simultaneous with his meeting with Eliot, suggesting that both events occurred on 1 or 2 June.[27]

This meeting is one of two with Eliot in Verona that are described repeatedly by Pound in several drafts, and it is consistently located at an outdoor caffè within sight of the arena, or Roman amphitheater (*C1*, 100–101):

> *Thi and the Chinese empress* ⚌
> *and the arena behind them* ⚌[. . .]

Again (*C3*, 61–62):

> By the arena, you, Thomas amics, Galla Placidia, and the Roman;
> inside it the footlights, the clowns, dancers,
> performing dogs.

Or again (*C3*, 81–82):

> Ti and the Chinese empress, then,
> and the arena behind us [. . .]

At one point, another person also at the meeting addresses Eliot, who is referred to in the second person, with a mysterious speech and gesture (*C1*, 108–9):

> *digs into your powdered past* ⇌
> *   smells a⟨your⟩ soiled cuff lace*[.]

Or again (*C3*, 89–90):

> digs into your powdered past,
>   ~~smells~~ ⟨*sniffs*⟩ your soiled cuff lace[.]

These lines suggest a view of Eliot as overcivilized, associating him with habits and clothing from the eighteenth century. Written in July 1922 when Pound had returned to Paris, they were originally part of a single canto that treated Sigismondo Malatesta.[28] But the material seemed too extraneous, and it was not used until much later in two other cantos. The first is Canto 29, written around 1928:

> And another day or evening toward sundown by the arena
> (les gradins)
> A little lace at the wrist
> And not very clean lace either . . .

The other is Canto 78, written in 1945:

> So we sat there by the arena,
>   outside, Thiy and il decaduto
>   the lace cuff fallen over his knuckles
>   considering Rochefoucauld

Aside from the meeting at a caffè near the arena, Eliot and Pound also met at a second location, the caffè Dante, noted for its gilded decor and fin-de-siècle atmosphere. It is located in the Piazza dei Signori, quite far from the arena. This meeting concerned the editorial program to be followed by Eliot's new journal, soon to be named *The Criterion*, and Pound recalled it many years later in Canto 78, written in 1945:

> but the program (Cafe Dante) a literary program 1920 or
> thereabouts was neither published nor followed[29]

Pound and Eliot were not alone at their first meeting near the arena, but accompanied by two people. One is referred to alternately as "Thi" or "Ti" and as "Galla Placidia," names that are collapsed at one point into a single identity, "Ti, Galla's hypostasis" (*C3*, 77). As has long been known, this is the name by which Pound addressed Evelyn St. Bride Scratton, née Goold Adams (1883–1964). She was apparently present in Verona, and accompanied the Pounds and Eliot at the cafe.

The rendezvous between Pound and Bride Scratton had been under planning for some time. Already on 21 February, five weeks before Pound left Paris for Italy, Scratton had written to him:

> Found two letters [from you] with Matthew this morning, and am writing to the bank manager this afternoon to buy lire. Mrs. Sandeman writes: "I have not written because I cannot get an answer from Rome. I want to go there on May 2nd for a week and after that to Assisi or some place in the country for two or three weeks and in June to the Dolomites. Would Rome and Assisi do for you too?" What shall I say in answer?

Pound's reply is not conserved, but some of its contents can be deduced from another letter by Scratton, of 1 March 1922:

> Mrs. Sandeman can be managed as you say, quite well. But I'll have to say here that I'm going to Perugia and leave an address, in case of a wire being sent. To say "posta restante" would arouse a great deal of suspicion. Cook's [travel agency] says there is "Brufani's Grand Hotel" at Perugia. Hadn't I better give that?
>
> Am hoping to get away from England about April 30th. [. . .]
> I really do want to see you again and I love you.

And on a separate sheet of paper she added, "Don't you know how I am missing you? Shut your eyes and I will kiss them. You are stupid not to understand how much I want you. X I love you." Five days later (6 March) Scratton reported the outcome of her researches on travel arrangements to Italy: "They say here that much the cheapest route is the Mount Denis. One crosses Paris, and changes at Pisa and Florence for Perugia. Will find out from Cook's for certain when I am next in London." Scratton was also kept informed of Pound's travels, since her letter to him of 1 April is addressed to him in Siena. Whether or not they met in Perugia, as suggested by the previous letters, cannot be ascertained. There are no other documents for April or May 1922, and the next testimony is only an envelope postmarked from Milan on 21 June 1922, addressed in Scratton's hand to Pound in Sirmione, on the Lago di Garda—which shows that Scratton was in Italy at this time, no more. Pound appears to have replied to the letter it contained (his reply is also not preserved), since Scratton, in a letter written on 14 July when she was back in London, states, "Haven't heard from you since I was in Milan."[30] The letters, then, confirm the evidence of the drafts that Scratton met with Eliot, Pound, and his wife Dorothy in Verona.

After Eliot had left to return to England, probably on 3 June, Pound and Dorothy left Verona for Sirmione, on the Lago di Garda. On 9 June he wrote a brief note to John Quinn. As always he was pleased with the idyllic setting. It was a special place for him, as he had explained to Quinn before. "The Lago di Garda—Sirmione is where I always go to refit. [. . .] Lago di G[arda].—full of sulphur. You can either swim in the lake or take the hot baths. I have done both in different states of dilapidation."[31] Secure and at ease, Pound launched into new work on *The Cantos*. Eleven days later he wrote to John Quinn again, summarizing his accomplishments. "Have had busy spring. Translated 2 vols. of Morand in Siena, and have blocked in four cantos—(Including the 'Honest sailor,' which I hope I haven't spoiled). At work on the 'Hell' canto, chiefly devoted to the English."[32] Among these were Drafts *A* and *B* of the Malatesta Cantos. In the last days of his stay at Sirmione he assembled a set of reading notes to be used in revising these later.

On 29 June he wrote to Agnes Bedford that he was leaving soon for Paris: "shd[.] have left 5 days ago as the flies are beginning. Also, I want my typewriter. have 4, probably 5 cantos blocked out."[33] Pound probably left Sirmione the next day, stopping in Milan for two days before going on to Paris. His visit took up Friday and Saturday (30 June and 1 July). As always Pound was a whirlwind of activity once he found himself in a metropolis. He met Carlo Linati, who was associated with the "bodega" group; he "liked them and their gallery," urged them to "improve the quality of their expositions," and suggested an exhibition of work by Wyndham Lewis. He also pursued the idea with Enzo Ferrieri, head of the Libreria del Convegno, a bookstore that published a journal and also ran a gallery. Pound was impressed with both groups. "I think Milan is alive and worth using as a base of operation," he wrote two weeks later to Lewis, transmitting the exhibition proposal.[34] "Like Milan very much," he informed his father around the same time; and always eager to impress his parents with signs of status, he told them that the city housed "two group[s of] young men, shops with galleries for exhibits, ready to do what I tell 'em.[35] Finally, Pound also took a moment to stop by the famous bookstore of the publisher/bookseller Ulrico Hoepli, where he attempted to purchase works on Italian history connected with Sigismondo Malatesta.[36]

Pound must have taken the evening train that leaves from Milan, arriving in Paris sometime on Sunday morning, 2 July.[37] Though the weather seemed "quite cold" after the heat in Sirmione, the change was bracing: "Am feeling damned fit," he roared.[38] He was eager to resume work, and the clue to his future had appeared in his note to Agnes Bedford announcing the new cantos drafted in Sirmione: "I want my typewriter." The next ten months would be devoted to writing the Malatesta Cantos.

The Principal Source for Canto 73

The following article was published in the *Corriere della Sera*, 1 October 1944, p. 1. The text is given first in Italian, then in English translation.

Sangue Italiano

L'eroina di Rimini

Il Radiogiornale del Partito ha trasmesso, ieri sera, la seguente nota su un leggendario episodio della battaglia di Rimini, dal titolo: "L'eroina riminese".

La prima pattuglia nemica entra in Rimini da Porta Romana. Il lungo viale di platani che immette nel sobborgo XX Settembre con sullo sfondo le macerie della bramantesca chiesa della Colonnella taglia col suo rettilineo cumuli di rottami: tutto è diroccato, lo stadio civico, la chiesa di San Giovanni, le case, i palazzi, il convento dei Cappuccini, la chiesa di Santo Spirito. Sul quadrivio della via Flaminia, di dove si dipartono la via nazionale di San Marino, la via dei Trai e la via XX-Settembre, dondola un semaforo sospeso lassù a mezzaria non si sa come tra le rovine di ogni cosa all'intorno. La pattuglia canadese esita incerta sulla via da prendere. Il cielo è solcato dal rombo dei velivoli e delle cannonate che vengono dal mare, dalle colline e dalla parte opposta della città: crepitano in distanza le mitragliatrici, l'aria acre è velata di fumo e di polvere. All'intorno, in qualsiasi parte volgano lo sguardo, i Canadesi non scorgono se non calcinacci, non una casa in piedi: le macerie si stendono per chilometri: tutta la superficie di quella che era la vivace, elegante e ricca città adriatica è una sola immensa caotica distesa di pietre: a malapena si distinguono i tracciati di quelle che furono le vie principali.

Mentre la pattuglia sta per imboccare a caso via XX Settembre, un'ombra si muove dietro un cumulo di rovine: i Canadesi spianano le armi pronti a sparare. Non è un'ombra, è una donna, una giovane donna. Ella alza le mani e i Canadesi la circondano. Una granata cade sui ruderi dello stadio sollevando un nugolo di rottami. Il terriccio e la polvere entrano nella bocca e negli occhi. Alla deflagrazione la ragazza è rimasta immobile a braccia levate. Un Canadese le rivolge la parola in un gergo a base di francese. La ragazza si sforza di comprendere e alla fine riesce a capire la domanda del soldato. Costui chiede da che parte si vada per raggiungere la via Emilia. L'interpellata dopo un'impercettibile incertezza indica con la mano la via dei Trai. Il Canadese si consulta coi compagni e torna a guardare la ragazza.

Costei gli fa cenno col braccio invitandolo a seguirla. Il gruppo allora s'incammina. La ragazza, una popolana sui 18 anni, bruna, dalle membra forti e slanciate, lacera e sporca, cammina spedita. La lunga e dritta via dei Trai conduce in piazza Tripoli, al mare, non all'arco di Augusto e alla via Emilia. La pattuglia, composta di una ventina di uomini più due soldati tedeschi prigionieri, procede nel tragico scenario della città morta: i Canadesi tengono i fucili spianati, pronti a far fuoco: i due Tedeschi, al centro del gruppo, mostrano i segni della lotta nei volti e sulle uniformi, ma camminano marzialmente. La popolana li sbircia di sfuggita: pare ai Tedeschi che quello sguardo abbia un significato. Quale significato? La giovane riminese continua a camminare, gli alberi che fiancheggiano la via sono divelti, tronchi e fronde ingombrano il passaggio, giacciono sulle macerie delle case. La popolana si volge ancora a guardare i due Tedeschi, i quali questa volta sono loro a sorriderle.

Ancora pochi passi, poi un tremenda esplosione lancia in aria macerie e persone, avvolgendole in una nube di terriccio, di calcinacci, di informi rottami. Una pausa tragica. Un attimo di terrificante silenzio. Poi il gemito dei feriti. Un'uomo si raddrizza sulle natiche, si netta il sangue dal volto, si leva in piedi. È ferito ma salvo. I Canadesi sono morti in gran parte, sfracellati dallo scoppio. I rimanenti agonizzano. Agonizza anche la popolana, che ha avuto le gambe amputate e il volto ferito dalla formidabile esplosione. L'uomo che fra tutti è salvato, uno dei soldati tedeschi, si accosta alla moribonda: ella gli sorride con una smorfia e riesce a dire penosamente: "Sapevo che qui esisteva un campo di mine . . . perchè vi aveva lavorato mio fratello . . . vi ho condotto gli Inglesi perchè sono stata violentata da due Australiani . . . in una casa colonica dove ci eravamo rifugiati . . . ho seguito questa pattuglia . . . volevo vendicarmi . . . non sapevo come . . . La sorte mi ha favorito . . .".

L'eroina sta dissanguandosi; il suo volto diventa cadaverico. Il soldato tedesco non può fare nulla per lei se non raccoglierne l'ultima parola: "Ho vendicato il mio onore."

Il soldato tedesco si china sulla morente e la bacia in fronte. Quando risolleva il capo, la giovane eroina è spirata.

Questo ci ha raccontato il soldato tedesco dopo avere raggiunto i propri camerati all'altra estremità della città morta. Il soldato, che dopo un anno di soggiorno in Italia si esprime abbastanza bene nella nostra lingua, così ha commentato il suo racconto: "La ragazza non aveva indosso alcuna carta o qualsiasi documento di riconoscimento. Non ho potuto quindi sapere il suo nome". E si è rammaricato, il soldato tedesco, di non averglielo chiesto prima che ella spirasse. Il nome dell'eroina rimarrà sconosciuto forse per sempre, e così la storia di questa guerra ricorderà il leggendario episodio come quello dell'eroina riminese. Dell'anonima fulgida eroina riminese.

Italian Blood

The Heroine of Rimini

Yesterday evening the Radio-News of the Party broadcast the following report of a legendary episode in the battle for Rimini, with the title: "The Heroine of Rimini."

The first enemy patrol enters Rimini by Porta Romana. The long avenue of planes, debouching into the suburb "The Twentieth of September" against the background of the Church of the Colonella, built in the style of Bramante, cuts a straight line through the heaps of wreckage. Everything is in ruins: the town stadium, the church of San Giovanni, houses, buildings, the convent of the Capuchins, the church of the Holy Spirit. At the intersection of the Via Flaminia, where the road to San Marino meets the "Street of the Trajans" and the "Street of September Twentieth," a traffic light is dangling suspended in mid-air, like a miracle amid the ruins surrounding it.

The Canadian patrol, uncertain which road to take, hesitates. The air shudders with the rumbling of aircraft and the cannonades coming from the sea, the hills, the other side of the city. In the distance one hears the crack of machine-guns, and sees the acrid air dense with dust and smoke. All around them the Canadians see rubble, not a house left standing: the ruins extend for miles, and what had once been the panorama of a prosperous, elegant, and vivacious city is now an immense chaotic expanse of collapsed stones. The outlines of the main streets can scarcely be distinguished.

As the Canadians begin to enter at a guess the "Street of September Twentieth," a shadow moves behind a heap of ruins: they level their weapons, ready to fire. It is not a shadow, but a woman, a young girl. She lifts her hands into the air, and the Canadians surround her. A grenade falls on the rubble of the stadium, raising a cloud of wreckage. Dust and dirt fill their mouths, their eyes. The woman has remained immobile, her arms held high. One of the Canadians tries to interrogate her, posing his questions in a debased form of French. The girl strains to comprehend, and at last understands the soldier's question. He wants to know how they can reach the Via Emilia. After an imperceptible moment of hesitation she gestures toward the "Street of the Trajans." The soldier discusses it with his companions, then returns to examine the girl.

She gestures with her arm, inviting him to follow her. The group begins to move out. The girl walks swiftly. She is a commoner, dark, eighteen years old, with strong and slender limbs, ragged and filthy clothes. The long straight "Street of the Trajans" leads to piazza Tripoli, by the sea, not to the Arch of Augustus and the Via Emilia. The patrol, composed of some twenty men and two German soldiers taken prisoner, advances against the tragic backdrop of the dead city. The Canadians keep their rifles leveled, ready to fire: the two Germans, in the center of the group, show signs of battle on their faces and uniforms, but walk with martial vigor. The girl gives them a furtive glance: they are convinced that her look is a sign. Yet what does it mean? The young girl from Rimini continues to walk ahead. The trees flanking the road have been uprooted, and trunks and branches encumber their advance, sprawled over the ruins of the houses. The girl turns to look at the Germans again, and this time they smile back at her.

A few steps more: then a tremendous explosion launches ruins and bodies into the air, engulfing everyone in a cloud of dirt, rubble, shapeless wreckage. A tragic pause. A moment of terrifying silence. Then the groans of the wounded. One man lifts himself to his knees, wipes the blood from his face, rises to his feet. He is wounded, but alive. Most of the Canadians are dead, shattered by the explosion. The rest are dying. So is the girl, whose legs have been amputated and whose face disfigured by the explosion. The only man who has survived, one of the Germans, comes alongside the dying girl: she smiles with a grimace and says, full of pain: "I knew that there was a mine-field here . . . because my brother worked on it . . . I led the English here because I was raped by two Australians . . . in a farmer's house where we had fled . . . I followed this patrol . . . I wanted to avenge myself . . . no matter how . . . luck was kind to me. . . ."

The heroine is bleeding to death; her face grows cadaverous. The German soldier can do nothing to help her, except listen to her last words: "I have vindicated my honor."

The soldier leans over the dying girl and kisses her brow. When he raises his head, the young heroine has already expired.

This story was told to us by the German soldier after he had reached his companions on the other side of the dead city. After a year in Italy, he has learned to speak Italian well, and he commented on his own story in these words: "The girl had no identification or other documents on her, so I wasn't able to find out her name." He regretted that he hadn't asked her before she expired. The name of this heroine will perhaps remain unknown forever, and so the history of this war will have to record this legendary event as the episode of the heroine from Rimini. Of the anonymous, radiant heroine from Rimini.

Notes

Abbreviations

Published works by Ezra Pound are cited using the following abbreviations:

GK *Guide to Kulchur* (New York: New Directions, 1970; 1st edn., 1938).
LE *Literary Essays*, ed. T. S. Eliot (New York: New Directions, 1968; 1st edn., 1954).
SL *Selected Letters 1907–1941*, ed. D. D. Paige (New York: New Directions, 1971; 1st edn., 1950).
SP *Selected Prose 1909–1965*, ed. William Cookson (New York: New Directions, 1975).
SR *The Spirit of Romance* (New York: New Directions, 1968; 1st edn., 1910).

Reference to the *The Cantos of Ezra Pound* is made by the abbreviation ND70¹⁰ (New York: New Directions, 1970 edn., 10th printing 1986). After this, a specific canto is cited *in arabic numerals* (for the ease of readers who dislike the lengthy Roman numerals more often used) and thereafter the line number(s) within the canto. Thus a typical reference might be: ND70¹⁰ 8.54–57. It should be noted that the "10th printing" is actually a new edition: it includes Cantos 72 and 73 for the first time (placed as an appendix); it incorporates a new "conclusion" addressed to Olga Rudge; it adds new lines to "The Pisan Cantos," and sports new illustrations on the title page and frontispiece. Moreover, in October 1989 an "11th printing" was issued in which Cantos 72 and 73 were moved from the end of the volume to their "proper" place after Canto 71, thereby prompting a repagination of all the succeeding cantos. Since most readers still own the earlier editions, in which the pagination was unchanged from 1970 to 1989, I have elected not to cite from the newer 11th printing. It should also be noted that before assuming their "modern" form in 1925, thirteen of the first sixteen cantos were published in various versions and sometimes with different canto numbers. When these are under discussion, the canto number is given *in roman numerals*. The Malatesta Cantos, for example, were originally published as Cantos IX–XII, but in their modern form are Cantos 8–11.

References to collections in U.S. libraries are made with the following abbreviations:

BLSUNY, *PC*	Buffalo, Lockwood Library, State University of New York, Poetry Collection.
BLUI, *BP*	Bloomington, Lilly Library, University of Indiana, Bird Papers.
BLUI, *PM.1*	Bloomington, Lilly Library, University of Indiana, Pound Mss. 1.
BLUI, *PM.2*	Bloomington, Lilly Library, University of Indiana, Pound Mss. 2.
BLUI, *PM.3*	Bloomington, Lilly Library, University of Indiana, Pound Mss. 3.
CHH	Cambridge, Houghton Library, Harvard University.
NHBY, *BP*	New Haven, Beinecke Library, Yale University, Bird Papers.
NHBY, *DP*	New Haven, Beinecke Library, Yale University, *Dial* Papers.
NHBY, *PA*	New Haven, Beinecke Library, Yale University, Pound Archive.
NYPL, *MD*, JQP	New York Public Library, Manuscripts Division, John Quinn Papers.
NYPL, *BC*, JSWP	New York Public Library, Berg Collection, James Sibley Watson, Jr., Papers.

After the reference to the library and collection, further reference is made, as the case warrants, to (1) the archival series, (2) the box number, (3) folder number or title, (4) the specific site of a document within the file. A typical citation to an autograph draft of Ezra Pound reads: NHBY, *PA*, Series 5, Box 63, f. 2436.4 (formerly 46.4). The last numbers indicate that the document containing the draft is found in folder ("f.") 2436, that it is the sixth item (.6) within the folder, and that folder 2436 was formerly numbered folder 46 (allowing one to refer to previous scholarly discussion).

Reference is made to marginalia and submarginalia entered by Ezra Pound in his copy of Charles Yriarte, *Un Condottiere au XVe siècle: Rimini: Études sur les Lettres et les Arts à la cour des Malatesta* (Paris: Jules Rothschild, 1882), using the following abbreviation: NHBY, *Ymn*. Following the abbreviation (for "Yriarte, marginal notes"), further reference is made to the number of the note according to my enumeration of the 150 markings that can be securely ascribed to Pound. Since April 1989 the volume is in the Beinecke Rare Book and Manuscript Library of Yale University (NHBY), with the shelf mark: Za P865 +ZZ882 Y. Materials (clippings, calling cards, etc.) stored by Pound among the volume's pages are catalogued separately, with the shelf mark: Uncat. Za file.204. I wish to thank Mary de Rachewiltz for permitting me to consult this volume when it was in her possession, and to acknowledge her generous donation to the Beinecke.

Finally, archives and libraries in Italy are cited by the following abbreviations:

FAS	Florence, *Archivio di stato*
MAS	Milan, *Archivio di stato*
MaAG	Mantua, *Archivio Gonzaga*
RaAS	Ravenna, *Archivio di stato*
RaBC	Ravenna, *Biblioteca Classense*
RAS	Rimini, *Archivio di stato*
RBCG	Rimini, *Biblioteca Civica Gambalunga*.

Introduction

1. Clifford Geertz, *The Interpretation of Cultures* (New York: Basic Books, 1973), p. 9. Hereafter cited as Geertz. In these introductory remarks I quote from some historical sources that I later discuss at greater length; in such cases I do not furnish citations here, giving references only to works not discussed elsewhere.

2. This was first recognized in an acute study by Myles Slatin, "A History of Pound's *Cantos* I–XVI, 1915–1925," *American Literature* 35 (1963), pp. 183–95. For views contemporary with Slatin's see Donald Davie, *Ezra Pound: Poet as Sculptor* (New York: Oxford University Press, 1964), pp. 124–34; and Thomas Jackson, "The Adventures of Messire Wrong-Head," *English Literary History* 32 (1965), pp. 238–54. Brief but important discussions appear in Ronald Bush, *The Genesis of Pound's Cantos* (Princeton: Princeton University Press, 1976; rpt. 1990), pp. 247–49, and Michael André Bernstein, *The Tale of the Tribe* (Princeton: Princeton University Press, 1980), pp. 39–42. For studies after 1980 see Peter D'Epiro, "A Touch of Rhetoric: Ezra Pound's Malatesta Cantos" (diss., Yale University, 1981), published with minor revisions under the same title (Ann Arbor: University Microfilms, 1983); Marjorie Perloff, *The Poetics of Indeterminancy: Rimbaud to Cage* (Evanston, Ill.: Northwestern University Press, 1983; 1st edn., Princeton: Princeton University Press, 1981), pp. 175–89; Michael Harper, "Truth and Calliope: Ezra Pound's Malatesta," *Publications of the Modern Language Association* 96 (1981), pp. 86–103; Daniel Bornstein, "The Poet as Historian: Researching the Malatesta Cantos," *Paideuma* 10 (1981), pp. 283–91; Ben D. Kimpel and T. C. Duncan Eaves, "Pound's Research for the Malatesta Cantos," *Paideuma* 11 (1982), pp. 406–19; Akiko Miyake, "Ezra Pound's Defence of a Hero in 'Malatesta Cantos'," *Kobe College Studies* 30(1)(July 1983), pp. 15–45; Michael North, "The Architecture of Memory: Pound and the *Tempio Malatestiano*," *American Literature* 55 (1983), pp. 368–87 (rpt. with some changes in Michael North, *The Final Sculpture: Public Monuments and Modern Poets* [Ithaca, N.Y.: Cornell University Press, 1985] pp. 132–56); Richard Sieburth, "Dada Pound," *South Atlantic Quarterly* 83 (1984), pp. 44–68; Peter Makin, *Pound's Cantos* (London: Allen and Unwin, 1985), pp. 137–44; James Longenbach, *Modernist Poetics of History: Pound, Eliot, and the Sense of the Past* (Princeton: Princeton University Press, 1987), pp. 131–52. Other studies are cited throughout the text.

3. A list of eighty-one "Allusions to the Malatesta Cantos" is given by Peter D'Epiro, "A Touch of Rhetoric," pp. 238–43. However, D'Epiro misses several allusions, and treats the numerous references in Cantos 72 and 73 as only two allusions. For examples of the prose, see Ezra Pound, "[A Review of] *Stones of Rimini* [by] Adrian Stokes," *Criterion* 13 (1934), pp. 495–97, and *GK*, pp. [2], 115, 159–61, 194, 261, 301. The slides, which were purchased in the 1930s, are in the private collection of Mary de Rachewiltz. I wish to thank her for bringing them to my attention. The photographs, which adorned Pound's room

in St. Elizabeths Hospital in the 1950s, are housed in the Beinecke Rare Books and Manuscript Library of Yale University. The bas-relief of Isotta degli Atti is shown above Pound's desk in a photograph by Vittorino Contini, in Gianfranco Ivanuci (ed.), *Ezra Pound in Italy: From the Pisan Cantos* (New York: Rizzoli, 1978), fig. [12]. On the 1963 visit, which has not been previously mentioned, see chapter 3, pp. 226–28.

4. See Theodor W. Adorno, "Sociology and Empirical Research," in Theodor W. Adorno et al., *The Positivist Dispute in German Sociology* (London: Heinemann, 1976), pp. 68–86; rpt. in Paul Connerton (ed.), *Critical Sociology: Selected Readings* (Harmondsworth: Penguin, 1976), pp. 237–58, quotations from pp. 239–40. See Geertz, pp. 24–25.

5. See Hans-Georg Gadamer, *Truth and Method*, tr. Garrett Barden and John Cumming (New York: Crossroad, 1986; rpt. 1975 edn.), pp. 340–41, for example. An excellent survey of the critical issues at stake is offered by Martin Jay, "Should Intellectual History Take a Linguistic Turn?" in Dominick LaCapra and Steven L. Kaplan (eds.), *Modern European Intellectual History: Reappraisals & New Perspectives* (Ithaca: Cornell University Press, 1982), pp. 86–110.

6. See note 4. On the place of this concept in Adorno's work, see Martin Jay, *Adorno* (Cambridge: Harvard University Press, 1984), pp. 14–15, 22, 50–51, 138.

7. See Jerome J. McGann, *A Critique of Modern Textual Criticism* (Chicago: University of Chicago Press, 1983), along with two important essays: "The Monks and the Giants: Textual and Bibliographical Studies and the Interpretation of Literary Works," in Jerome J. McGann (ed.), *Textual Criticism and Literary Interpretation* (Chicago: University of Chicago Press, 1985), and "Shall These Bones Live?" in *Text* 1 (1984), pp. 21–40.

8. In English see Philip J. Jones, *The Malatesta of Rimini and the Papal State* (Cambridge: Cambridge University Press, 1974), chap. 7. Also important is the collection of essays (including one by Jones, "Le signorie di Sigismondo Malatesta") in P. J. Jones et al., *Studi malatestiani* (Rome: Istituto storico italiano per il medio evo, 1978). The most organic treatment of Sigismondo's life is still Francesco Gaetano Battaglini, *Della vita e de' fatti di Sigismondo Pandolfo Malatesta Signor di Rimino, Commentario*, in Basini Parmensis poetae, *Opera praestantiora nunc primum edita et opportunis commentariis illustrata* (Rimini: ex tipographia Albertiniana, 1794), vol. 2, pp. 257–699. Other works are discussed in the following chapters. On the church of San Francesco the indispensable work is still Corrado Ricci, *Il tempio malatestiano* (Rome-Milan: Bestetti & Tumminelli, n. d. [but 1924]; rpt. Rimini: Bruno Ghigi Editore, 1974). More recently, see Rudolf Wittkower, *Architectural Principles in the Age of Humanism* (New York: W. W. Norton, 1971; 1st edn., 1949), pp. 1–41; Charles Mitchell, "Il Tempio Malatestiano," in Jones et al., *Studi malatestiani;* Franco Borsi, *Leon Battista Alberti: L'opera completa* (Milan: Electa Editrice, 1980). Other studies of the church are discussed in the following chapters.

9. Nikolaus Pevsner, *Outline of European Architecture*, 7th edn. (Harmondsworth: Penguin, 1963), p. 189.

10. See Mitchell, "Il tempio malatestiano."

11. Giorgio Vasari, *Le vite de' più eccelenti pittori, scultori e architettori* (Novara: Istituto geografico De Agostini, 1967; 1st edn., 1550), vol. 2, pp. 138, 358–59, 414.

12. These traditions and other matters pertaining to interpretation of the church are discussed fully in chapters 1 and 3, where relevant references are furnished.

13. For a detailed statement of procedures, see Lawrence S. Rainey, "The Earliest Manuscripts of the Malatesta Cantos" (diss., University of Chicago, 1986), pp. 264–84.

14. Martin Jay, "Should Intellectual History Take a Linguistic Turn?" p. 96.

1. Production

1. Noel Stock, *The Life of Ezra Pound* (Harmondsworth: Penguin, 1974; 1st edn., 1970), p. 577.

2. Dorothy Shakespear Pound to Olivia Shakespear, [15 May 1922]; private collection. I am grateful to the owner for generously making this document available, as well as for constant help and encouragement.

3. Myles Slatin, "A History of Pound's *Cantos* I–XVI, 1915–25," *American Literature* 35 (1963), pp. 183–95; quotations are from pp. 189, 191.

4. Ezra Pound, *GK*, p. 159.

5. Marjorie Perloff, *The Poetics of Indeterminacy: Rimbaud to Cage* (Evanston: Northwestern University Press, 1983; 1st edn., Princeton: Princeton University Press, 1981), pp. 157, 177, 181. Also Richard Sieburth, "Dada Pound," *South Atlantic Quarterly* 83 (1984), pp. 44–68.

6. Peter D'Epiro, "A Touch of Rhetoric: Ezra Pound's Malatesta Cantos" (diss., Yale University, 1981), pp. 47, 61; later published with minor revisions under the same title (Ann Arbor: University Microfilms, 1983), pp. 12, 20.

7. Ezra Pound to John Quinn, 20 June 1922; NYPL, *MD*, JQP, Box 34, f. 4.

8. Pius II, *Commentarii*, ed. Luigi Totaro (Milan: Adelphi, 1984), pp. 366, 368. Unless otherwise indicated, all translations in this book are my own.

9. The same events are rehearsed in the same sequence in the following sections of Beltramelli's book and Draft *A:*

Beltramelli, pp. 31–39, on Isotta and wives:	lines 18–20
Beltramelli, pp. 41–43, on numerous battles:	line 21
Beltramelli, p. 43, on the campaign in Morea:	line 22
Beltramelli, pp. 46–48, on attempted murder:	line 23

10. On Isotta degli Atti see Augusto Campana, "Atti, Isotta degli," *Dizionario biografico degli Italiani*, vol. 4. (Rome: Istituto della Enciclopedia Italiana, 1962), pp. 547–56, who includes complete references to the antecedent literature and a sober discussion of the Romantic tradition.

11. Jacob Burckhardt, *The Civilization of the Renaissance in Italy*, tr. S. G. C. Middlemore (New York: Harper & Row, 1958; 1st edn. in German, 1860), p. 235.

12. John Addington Symonds, *Sketches and Studies in Italy and Greece*, 2nd ser. (London: Smith, Elder, 1898; 1st edn. 1874), p. 20.

13. Symonds, *Sketches*, pp. 14–15.

14. Pasquale Villari, "Rimini," *Encyclopaedia Britannica*, vol. 20 (Edinburgh: A. & C. Black, 1886), p. 558.

15. Karl Baedeker, *Italy: Handbook for Travelers*, 13th rev. edn., vol. 2: *Second Part: Central Italy and Rome* (Leipzig: Baedeker, 1900), p. 104. See also the same author and title, 1908 edition, p. 98. The reference is important because Pound apparently took a Baedeker along with him during the trip in which he first saw the Tempio Malatestiano. "[I] HAVE bought the Baedeker, so don[']t worry about that": Ezra Pound to Agnes Bedford, 16 March 1922; BLUI, *PM.2*, Bedford, 1922.

16. André Maurel, *Les Petites Villes d'Italie*, vol. 2: *Émilie–Marches–Ombrie* (Paris: Librairie Hachette, 1920), pp. 137–56.

17. Edward Hutton, *Sigismondo Pandolfo Malatesta—Lord of Rimini: A Study of a XV Century Italian Despot* (London: J. M. Dent, 1906), pp. 295–96. Pound had read the Hutton novel, but did not own a copy as of late August 1922: "I shd. like the Hutton volume if he [Friedrich Neumayer, bookseller in London] can find it." Ezra Pound to Dorothy Shakespear Pound, 29 August 1922; BLUI, *PM.3*, 1922.

18. Luigi Arduini, *Gli scultori nel Tempio malatestiano di Rimini* (Rome: Stabilimento danese, 1907), pp. 10, 12–13, 25.

19. Giuseppe Albini, "Sigismondo e Isotta: Poema drammatico in un'atto," in *La Romagna: rivista di storia e di lettere* 5 (1908), pp. 312–46; quotation on p. 344.

20. Pasquale Villari, "Rimini," *Encyclopaedia Britannica*, vol. 23 (Cambridge: Cambridge University Press, 1911), pp. 83–93. There are some modifications in the 1911 article, but they regard Roman Rimini and not the Malatesta material, which is unaltered.

21. Joseph Linskill, "Introduction," *Poems of the Troubadour Raimbaut de Vaqueiras* (Hague: Mouton, 1964), pp. 1–33. Readers should consult Linskill's arguments directly, due to the philological problems inherent in the lives of all the troubadours. Linskill's account differs in several respects from accounts that Pound would have known (Linskill cites all the antecedent bibliography and should be consulted for this as well), though the central feature of Raimbaut's role as a bridge between Provençal and Italian culture has long been recognized. The text of the poem by Raimbaut given in the present study is from Carl Appel, *Provenzalische Chrestomathie*, 2nd edn. (Leipzig, 1902), p. 52, no. 3—a standard text that Pound would have used as a student during his years of study of Provençal. All editions before that of Linskill in 1964 duplicated Appel's text.

One reason that Pound may have recalled the text so readily is the word *glaya*, sufficiently rare that it received the attention of Emile Lévy in his *Provenzalisches Supplement-Wörterbuch*, vol. 4 (Leipzig, 1904), p. 130, also citing Appel's edition. Pound visited Lévy in August 1911 and recounts a version of the visit in Canto 20. A few points about the poem cited by Pound should be also noted. It is an *estampida* or *estampie*, a lively rhythmical composition intended for either instrument or voice, which originated as a popular stamping dance. One of the five manuscripts that conserve Raimbaut's poem (Paris, Bibliothèque Nationale, fr. 22543) also offers a transcription of the musical setting. It was first discovered and published in 1896 (Restori), and reprinted in 1905 (Riemann), 1909 (Aubry), and 1917 (Lommatzsch). Musicologists agree that the melody "is one of the finest creations of European music," according to Linskill (p. 189); but it is not clear that Pound was aware of the transcription, despite his having worked on manuscript materials connected with Provençal poetry in Paris in 1912. For a fuller discussion and bibliography, see Linskill, pp. 184–90. It should be noted that Justin H. Smith (published in 1899 and consulted by Pound in 1912) was unfamiliar with the 1896 discovery of the musical setting and does not report it. "Kalenda Maya" has been recorded several times in recent decades by early music groups. These recordings include performances by Gerald English with the Jaye Consort of Viols (*The Jolly Minstrels*, Vanguard Cardinal [ves. 10049], 1969), Musica Reservata (*Medieval Music and Songs of the Troubadours*, Everest [3270], n.d.), and the Studio der Frühen Musik (*Chansons der Troubadours*, originally released as an LP record by Das Alte Werk, and now available on compact disc [Teldec, 1985]).

22. *SR*, p. 90. The lines first appeared in "Psychology and the Troubadours," published in *Quest* 4.1 (October 1912), an essay later incorporated into *The Spirit of Romance* as chapter 5 in editions published in 1932 and later. The 1912 date is significant because it is also when Pound was reading Justin H. Smith (see the discussion in the text).

23. Some attention to this question is given by Leon Surette, *A Light from Eleusis* (Oxford: Oxford University Press, 1979), pp. 34–41. However, Surette limits his research to "a rather precursory perusal" of several works by Joséphin Péladan, and does little to relate it to the cultural context contemporary with Pound.

24. Ezra Pound and Dorothy Shakespear, *Ezra Pound and Dorothy Shakespear: Their Letters 1909–1914*, ed. Omar Pound and A. Walton Litz (New York: New Directions, 1984), p. 129. Pound consulted Smith's volume in the spring of 1912 in preparation for a tour of southern France. After the tour he wrote the article cited in note 22.

25. Ezra Pound, *SL*, letter no. 263, p. 248, 24 September 1933: "Anybody who can penetrate the text-book ring wd. confer a blessing [on society]. Gaston Paris wrote text-books, and France had some sort of culture and amenity." For a survey of theories on the origins of courtly love, see Roger Boase, *The Origin*

and Meaning of Courtly Love: A Critical Study of European Scholarship (Manchester: Manchester University Press, 1977), chap. 2. On ideological dimensions of the scholarly tradition, see Maria Rosa Menocal, *The Arabic Role in Medieval Literary History* (Philadelphia: University of Pennsylvania Press, 1987).

26. Ezra Pound, *SR*, pp. 91–92.

27. Ezra Pound, "Terra Italica," *New Review* 1.4 (Winter 1931–32), pp. 386–89, rpt. in *SP*, pp. 54–60, quotation on p. 58.

28. "Yriarte book recd. from Neumayer," reads a note in Pound's hand on the envelope of Ezra Pound to Dorothy Pound, postmarked 3 August 1922; BLUI, *PM.3*, 1922.

29. Yriarte is surprised at the ubiquity of the entwined letters *S* and *I*, which he supposes indicate *Sigismondo* and *Isotta*. On the origins of this belief and its place in the historiographical tradition, see chapter 3, pp. 186–89.

30. Ezra Pound, *Ymn*, 32 (on p. 146 of Yriarte) and 35 (on p. 149 of Yriarte). The passage from Homer is *Iliad* III, 157, which Richard Lattimore translates: "Terrible is the likeness of her face to immortal goddesses." Pound also offers an abbreviated translation of this line in modern Canto 2: "And has the face of a god." Canto 2 was originally published as Canto VIII only a few months before the Malatesta Cantos were written. It was moved to its present position in May–June 1923. Further, Pound commented on this and the surrounding lines from Homer in an essay, "Early Translators of Homer," reprinted in *LE*, pp. 249–75, esp. pp. 250–51.

31. [Ezra Pound], "The Little Review Calendar," *The Little Review* 8.2 (Spring 1922), p. [2], with "Note to Calendar," p. 40. All subsequent citations are from these pages.

32. James Joyce to Ezra Pound, 30 October 1921; BLUI, *PM.1*, 1921.

33. Anonymous, *Cronaca malatestiana del secolo XV (AA. 1416–1452)*, part II, in Aldo Massèra (ed.), *Cronache malatestiane dei secoli XIV e XV (AA. 1295–1385 e 1416–1452)*, vol. 15 of *Rerum Italicarum Scriptores*, 2nd edn., ed. Giosuè Carducci and Vittorio Fiorini (Bologna: Zanichelli), fascicles 184 (1922) and 185 (1924), p. 121. Hereafter this is cited as *Cron. mal.* The same date is registered by Luigi Tonini, *Della storia sacra e civile riminese*, vol. 5: *Rimini nella signoria de' Malatesti* (Rimini, 1880; rpt., Rimini: Bruno Ghigi, 1971), p. 210. The same date also appears in Charles Yriarte, *Un Condottiere au XVᵉ siècle* (Paris: Jules Rothschild, 1882), pp. 189 and 195, but with the year mistakenly given as 1446. On his error see Corrado Ricci, *Il tempio malatestiano* (Milan-Rome: Bestetti & Tuminelli, n.d. [but 1924]; rpt., Rimini: Bruno Ghigi, 1974, with Appendix by Pier Giorgio Pasini), p. 236, n. 1.

34. Stock, *Life*, p. 311.

35. *Cron. mal.*, p. 135.

36. Roberto Valturio, *De re militari* (Paris: apud Christianum Wechelum,

1535; 1st edn., 1472), pp. 382–83. As the title indicates, the work is a discussion of military affairs, and its comments on the relics are decidedly incidental.

37. Francesco Sansovino, *Della origine, et de' fatti delle famiglie illustri d'Italia* (Venice: presso Altobelli Salicato, 1582), f. 235ʳ: "Et volle che'l primo di Maggio si facesse la festa di quel Santo ogni anno, e che si mostrasse sul pulpito al popolo le reliquie ch'erano in S. Francesco."

38. Cesare Clementini, *Raccolto istorico della fondatione di Rimino e dell' origine e vite de' Malatesti* (Rimini: Simbeni, vol. 1, 1617; vol. 2, 1627; rpt. in "ristampa anastatica," Bologna: Forni, 1969, in "Historiae urbium et regionum Italiae rariores," vol. 38), vol. 2, p. 378: "& ordinò ch'ogni primo giorno di Maggio si solenneggiasse la sua festa, e si mostrassero sopra il pulpito le Reliquie sante, ivi poste, & assegnate alla Città, accioche n'havesse particolar cura, dichiarando una per una di chi fossero, come anco oggidì si costuma." A comparison shows that the Clementini text derives from Sansovino.

39. I believe that I have read every available primary and secondary source within the relevant historiographical tradition. Of course the proliferation of texts in the late nineteenth and early twentieth centuries always leaves the possibility that I have missed one. Yet on the whole this is unlikely, since such sources constantly refer to one another. Also, examples exist showing that Pound sometimes fabricated an event when confused by some element within his own notes, and these examples are exactly contemporary with the composition of Draft *B*. Consider the history of a reading note made by Pound within a few days of Draft *B*, note 26 in *N1*. The note regards the 1460 battle of S. Fabiano between the Angevin forces under Piccinino and the Aragonese army under Federigo di Montefeltro. Pound's source is Heinrich Leo, *Storia degli stati italiani* (Florence: Società editrice fiorentina, vol. 1, 1840; vol. 2, 1842), translated by Eugenio Albèri and Adolfo A. Loewe from the original German work in five volumes, *Geschichte der italienischen Staaten* (Hamburg: Friedrich Perthes, 1829–37). The passage appears in Leo, vol. 2, p. 84, col. b. Leo reports that Piccinino is forced to retire from battle, but that the forces of Federigo are also so weakened that they retreat into the Marches, leaving Piccinino free to ransack the territory around papal Rome, ally of the Aragonese dynasty. Pound's note omits the dynastic struggle that is behind the battle; it also omits the retreat into the Marches; and it mistakenly converts "the Roman Territory" into the province of "Romagna." The result is a senseless battle waged by puppets with no one to pull the strings. And it bewilders even Pound when he later attempts to type up the note. Apparently confused, he fixes his attention on the invasion of "Romagna," the province that contains Malatestan Rimini. He reasons that the battle must somehow involve Sigismondo Malatesta, and "corrects" his former note by substituting Sigismondo's name for that of Federigo di Montefeltro. The outcome is a battle of Pound's own creation, for Sigismondo had not been present even as an observer at the battle of S. Fabiano. Likewise Pound invents

the consequence with Piccinino's invasion of "Romagna." The error is not without irony in historical terms, since only a month later in 1460 Sigismondo was to ally himself with Piccinino in supporting the Angevin revolt against the Aragonese dynasty. More important, the error is produced through reasoning informed by ideological motives. Since Pound wishes to portray his hero as a solitary victim, he is prompt to trace an accumulation of forces arrayed against him—hence his predisposition to record Piccinino invading "Romagna" rather than the "Roman territory." And in a second note among the same set of reading notes, Pound reverses Leo's meaning entirely (note 20), apparently through a misunderstanding of the Italian.

Another example is found in Draft *A,* again contemporary with the text of Draft *B.* In line 34 Pound describes Sigismondo Malatesta "thugging a Bishop." A few weeks later he refers to this incident again in a letter to John Quinn (Ezra Pound to John Quinn, 10 August 1922; NYPL, *MD,* JQP, Box 34, f. 4), in which he reports that "some authorities say it was Farnese and not [Sigismondo] Malatesta who raped the bishop of Fano." But the charge that Sigismondo had raped the poor bishop was never advanced by any "authority" other than Pound, for it was entirely his invention. It resulted from his misreading, or misunderstanding, his notes on two incidents that were recounted together by both Burckhardt and Symonds. The earlier version was Burckhardt's. Rehearsing various crimes attributed to Sigismondo, Burckhardt had remarked on "the most shocking crime of all—the unnatural attempt on his own son Roberto, who frustrated it with is drawn dagger." In the same passage he mentioned a second but unrelated incident: he speculated that "perhaps" Sigismondo had been motivated by "some magical or astrological superstition" in attempting to rape his son, then noted that a similar explanation had been advanced "to account for the rape of the Bishop of Fano by Pierluigi Farnese." (See Burckhardt, *Civilization,* p. 442). The two incidents were also reported together by Burckhardt's English imitator, John Addington Symonds. Symonds rehearsed what was rapidly becoming a familiar topos, the wickedness of the Renaissance, then wondered, "How far . . . were these dark crimes of violence actuated by astrological superstition? This question is raised by Burckhardt apropos of Sigismondo's assault upon his own son, and Pier Luigi Farnese's violation of the Bishop of Fano." (See John Addington Symonds, *The Renaissance in Italy,* vol. 1: *The Age of the Despots* New York: Henry Holt, 1888; 1st edn., 1876), p. 428 n. 1. Whether through Burckhardt or Symonds, the two incidents reached Pound, who fused them into a new incident of his own invention—Sigismondo Malatesta's rape of the bishop of Fano.

Both the stories Pound had merged were probably false. The alleged rape of Roberto by Sigismondo is reported solely by Giovanni Gioviano Pontano, writing some thirty years after Sigismondo's death. See Giovanni Gioviano Pontano, *De immanitate liber,* ed. Liliana Monti Sabia (Naples: Loffredo, 1970), p. 33, or chap. 17 according to the traditional division of the work. No historian seems to have believed it apart from Burckhardt and Symonds. The other incident, Pier-luigi Farnese's alleged rape of the bishop of Fano, was narrated by Benedetto Varchi, who placed the event in 1538. See Benedetto Varchi, *Storia fiorentina* (Florence: Salani, 1963), vol. 2, pp. 651–55; the text is easily found in other editions, since the incident constitutes the concluding episode of the work. The story enjoyed an immense *fortuna* within the tradition of scandalistic historiography until it was dismissed in 1905 by Raffaelo Massignan, whose patient and refined research has been accepted by all scholars since then. See Rafaello Massignan, "Pier Luigi Farnese e il vescovo di Fano," *Atti e memorie della R. Deputazione di storia patria per le provincie delle Marche* n.s. 2 (1905), pp. 249–304; the subsequent consensus is summarized by Emilio Nasalli Rocca, *I Farnese* (Varese: dall'Oglio, 1969), p. 63.

40. Antonio Beltramelli, *L'uomo nuovo* (Rome-Milan: Mondadori, 1923). Page references are given in parentheses within the text.

41. On this tradition see Renzo De Felice, *Mussolini*, vol. 1: *Mussolini il rivoluzionario* (Turin: Einaudi, 1965), pp. 3–4.

42. Ezra Pound, "Paris Letter, January 1922," *The Dial* 72.2 (February 1922), pp. 187–92; all quotations from pp. 191–92. Here also, less hermetically than in the *Little Review* calendar, Pound implies that the completion of *Ulysses* marks a revolutionary change in history, writing that "Voltaire was printed in Holland, and the Bourbons deliquesced: Ulysses on the schedule of Paris events" (p. 192).

43. John Quinn to Ezra Pound, 12 December 1920; BLUI, *PM.1*, Quinn.

44. Stock, *Life*, p. 298.

45. Ezra Pound to John Quinn, 11 April 1921; NYPL, *MD*, JQP, Box 34, f. 3. Ezra Pound to Agnes Bedford, 12 April 1921; BLUI, *PM.2*, Bedford, 1921.

46. Ezra Pound to Agnes Bedford, 10 June 1921; BLUI, *PM.2*, Bedford, 1921. Pound refers to his translation of Rémy de Gourmont, *Physique de l'amour;* the volume was issued over a year later, on 10 August 1922, by Boni and Liveright, under the title *The Natural Philosophy of Love.*

47. Thayer planned to arrive in Paris on 12 July 1921, according to Scofield Thayer to Ezra Pound, 8 June 1921; BLUI, *PM.1*. Descriptions of his meetings with Pound are given by John Quinn to Homer Pound, 29 November 1921, carbon; BLUI, *PM.1*, John Quinn 1921. Payment records from *The Dial* show that Pound received $305 during the period January–September 1922, which at an annual rate would yield slightly over $400 per year; NYPL, *BC*, JSWP, "Payments." This figure is about half the $750 per year Pound had earned during the year running from July 1920 to June 1921; for this figure see John Quinn to Wyndham Lewis 25 May 1921, quoted by B. L. Reid, *The Man from New York: John Quinn and His Friends* (New York: Oxford University Press, 1968), p. 491. See also his discussions on pp. 434, 435; see also Stock, *Life*, pp. 287–88. See also Ezra Pound to T. S. Eliot, carbon, 14 March 1922; BLUI, *PM.1*, Eliot. The letter makes clear that Pound's earlier services as "foreign editor and scout" for

The Dial had been eliminated; he had salvaged only the income from his own writings. (The material in the Berg Collection was formerly in the possession of Mrs. Nancy Dean Watson of Rochester, N. Y.: I wish to thank her for permission to examine the materials before they were consigned to the New York Public Library, and for her kindness and hospitality. I am also grateful to Ms. Dale Davis for facilitating access to the papers.)

48. Ezra Pound to John Quinn, 22 October 1921; NYPL, *MD*, JQP, Box 34, f. 3.

49. Ezra Pound to Agnes Bedford, 17 December 1921; BLUI, *PM.2*, Bedford, 1921.

50. Copy of Horace Liveright to John Quinn, 24 March 1922; BLUI, *PM.1*, Quinn. The contract is given by Stock, *Life*, pp. 309–10, taken from Charles Norman, *Ezra Pound: A Biography* (London: Macdonald, 1969).

51. Ezra Pound to "Grandmother" [Mary Weston], 3 February 1922; NHBY, *PA*, Series 2, Box 52, f. 1967.

52. See note 47.

53. Ezra Pound to John Quinn, 4–5 July 1922; NYPL, *MD*, JQP, Box 34, f. 4.

54. Ezra Pound to John Quinn, 4 April 1922; NYPL, *MD*, JQP, Box 34, f. 4.

55. On the enormous interest in this motif see Patricia Merivale, *Pan the Goat-God: His Myth in Modern Times* (Cambridge: Harvard University Press, 1969). Merivale assembles a vast range of material, integrating it through "mythological criticism" in the tradition of Douglas Bush. She seems to acknowledge the limits of this method in suggesting (p. vii) that a social critic of the future might also address "the key question: why was there, between 1890 and 1926, that astonishing resurgence of interest in the Pan motif, and that rich harvest of its varied possibilities?" I have drawn on her work throughout the discussion here and below. It should be noted that the phrase "Pan, Pan is dead!" acquired particular resonance through Elizabeth Barrett Browning's poem, "The Dead Pan," which repeated it with slight variations thirty-nine times, using it as a symbol for the transition from pagan to Christian culture. The late antique story is from Plutarch, *De defectu oraculorum*, and scholarly interest in it was as intense as the literary-cultural interest discussed here. Merivale indicates "upwards of sixty complete examples of such scholarly interpretations" between 1910 and 1916 (p. 239 n. 36).

56. See Merivale, *Pan the Goat-God*, pp. 177–93, who cites Gosse on p. 128, Brooke on p. 127, Amelia J. Burr on p. 122. It would require a heart of stone to pass up the occasion of quoting Teresa Hooley (?1921), who was as eager as Burr to subject herself to Pan: "Stamp, burn and pipe in me, Great Pan!" (also p. 122). Incidentally, the selection of works listed here is limited to those that cite Pan in the title, a very small portion of the total number of works concerning Pan.

57. The identification of Pan with the dying god of spring is advanced by Salomon Reinach in "La Mort du grand Pan," *Bulletin de correspondance hellénique* 31 (1907), pp. 5–19, reprinted in his *Cultes, mythes et religions*, vol. 3 (1908), pp. 1–15. Merivale convincingly shows that this interpretation stands behind Pound's use of the motif here and in several cantos as well. Her argument is supported by another instance in which Pound turns to Reinach, detailed in John Espey, *Ezra Pound's Mauberley: A Study in Composition* (Berkeley: University of California Press, 1955), pp. 78, 99, 101. His "vision" of Pan is reported in "Affirmations . . . I. Arnold Dolmetsch," in *The New Age* 16.10 (7 January 1915), pp. 246–47. It is reprinted in *Pavannes and Divisions* (1918), and *LE*, pp. 431–36.

58. For Pan in Germany see Aleida Assmann, "Pan, Paganismus und Jugendstil," in *Antike Tradition und Neure Philologien*, Hans-Joachim Zimmermann (ed.) (Heidelberg: Carl Winter Universitätsverlag, 1984). For Pan in France see Brian Juden, "Visages romantiques de Pan," *Romantisme* 50 (1985), pp. 27–40. No comparable study exists for Italy. One should note that Pan was also the object of attention in music in Mahler's Third Symphony and Debussy's *Prélude à l'après-midi d'un faune* and his piece for solo flute, *Syrinx*.

59. The definition of fascist cultural outlook is from Alice Yaeger Kaplan, *Reproductions of Banality: Fascism, Literature and French Intellectual Life* (Minneapolis: University of Minnesota Press, 1986), p. 3.

60. The evidence regarding this visit is extremely complicated; see appendix 2.

61. On Tontolini see Maria Bianchi, ["Memorie"], in Stefano de Matteis, Martina Lombardi, Marilea Somaré (eds.), *Follie del varietà: vicende memorie personaggi 1890–1970* (Milan: Feltrinelli, 1980), pp. 118–19, as well as the preface to that volume by Goffredo Fofi, pp. 9–12; *Enciclopedia dello spettacolo*, vol. 6 (Rome: Le Maschere, 1959), pp. 50–51; Mario Verdone, "Polidor, l'ultimo dei Guillaume," *Bianco e nero: rassegna mensile di studi cinematografici* 13.3 (March 1952), pp. 33–35, with photos on pp. 32, 49; e.r.r., "I comici 'muti'" (a review of "la Rassegna Retrospetiva del Cinema muto italiano, XIII Mostra Internazionale d'Arte Cinematografica di Venezia"), *Bianco e nero: rassegna mensile di studi cinematografici* 13.7–8 (July–August 1952), pp. 95–96; Manlio Cancogni, "Tontolini e Polidor ci insegnarono a ridere," *L'Europeo* 230, Anno VI n. 12 (19 March 1950), p. 7.

62. The figure of Tontolini/Polidor offers obvious analogies to the showman who narrates from his carnival booth in Browning's *Sordello*, an influential model for Pound when he began writing *The Cantos*; see Ronald Bush, *The Genesis of Ezra Pound's Cantos* (Princeton: Princeton University Press, 1976), pp. 75–86. In some respects he resembles the narrator/voice of *The Cantos*, an identifiable yet fictive character who presents, comments on, and intrudes into the scripted performance of the epic (or the complex of expectations associated

with the long poem). However, Pound chooses to ignore these possibilities and instead assimilates the performance to the viewpoint of a quasi-timeless ancient observer, a figure probably derived from his reading of *The Waste Land,* and if so perhaps fresh in his memory since Eliot was also àt the performance.

In later drafts of the Malatesta Cantos Pound gave increasing attention to the Tontolini show. In some cases he combined features of the performance with other impressions from his stay in Verona (his meeting with T. S. Eliot at the Caffè Dante) or his 1919 visit to Excideuil (where Eliot was also present). The entire complex became a sort of counterweight for the historical material of the Malatesta story. The effect was twofold: on one hand it hinted willfully at rich, hermetic analogies between the past and the present, between aspects of the Malatesta story and Eliot and Pound; on the other it bracketed the data of history within an abstract schema that denied the significance of the events themselves, reducing them to occasions for the stern gaze of the poet.

The last stage of Pound's dealings with the arena setting of Verona took place after he completed all of the Malatesta Cantos, probably between May and June 1923, when Pound was reshaping all the previous cantos. Pound took radical steps. He eliminated every reference to the performance in Verona, leaving only the detached and timeless observer in the arena, who watches an indeterminate, unspecified spectacle. This image he placed in the first canto that followed the Malatestas (now 12; see ND70[10] 12.1–4). Still later he added an anticipation of this image to the end of Canto 4; on this manuscript, labeled "Fragment xvi," see Christine Froula, *To Write Paradise: Style and Error in Pound's* Cantos (New Haven: Yale University Press, 1984), with transcription on p. 130, and description on p. 66. As a result, the arena image frames all of Cantos 5–11, or those that directly treat history. In effect this schema recapitulates the "envelope" device of Draft *B* itself, which frames the historical material on the church at the beginning (lines 1–5) and the end (line 15) with the image of the arena, but now it encompasses a much vaster tract of material. Echoes of the image also appear in Canto 21 and elsewhere.

63. For a general discussion and bibliography see Peter Jelavich, "Popular Dimensions of Modernist Elite Culture: The Case of Theater in Fin-de-Siècle Munich," in Dominick LaCapra and Steven L. Kaplan (eds.), *Modern European Intellectual History: Reappraisals and New Perspectives* (Ithaca: Cornell University Press, 1982), pp. 220–50.

64. NHBY, *PA,* Series 5, Box 63, f. 2436.12 (formerly 46.12).

65. William Butler Yeats, *Autobiographies* (Macmillan: New York: 1965), p. 129: "I thought that all art should be a centaur finding in the popular lore its back and strong legs." As Merivale shows (*Pan the Goat-God,* pp. 192–93), the centaur was another token used in place of Pan in the cultural debate described here. Pound himself makes use of it often, notably in his 1913 essay, "The Serious Artist" (*LE,* pp. 41–57, in particular p. 52): "Poetry is a centaur. The thinking word-arranging, clarifying faculty must move and leap with the enger-

gizing, sentient, musical faculties." To be noted also is the place of the centaur in the thought of H. D., described in her volume *Tribute to Freud* (New York: New Directions, 184), who refers to her lifelong fascination with Algernon Blackwood, *The Centaur* (London: Macmillan, 1912), on p. 161. Blackwood's volume closely follows the story of E. F. Benson, "The Man Who Went Too Far," another Pan story (1906); and Blackwood himself wrote *Pan's Garden* (1912).

66. Daniel Pearlman, *The Barb of Time: On the Unity of Ezra Pound's Cantos* (New York: Oxford University Press, 1969), pp. 17–30, quotation from p. 30.

67. Michael André Bernstein, *The Tale of the Tribe: Ezra Pound and the Modern Verse Epic* (Princeton: Princeton University Press, 1980), p. 107.

68. Hugh Kenner, "The Modernist Canon," in Robert von Hallberg (ed.), *Canons* (Chicago: University of Chicago Press, 1984), pp. 365–66. For Kenner this innovation is primarily formal in character: "That was a central modernist discovery, that distinctions between 'prose' and 'verse' vanish before distinctions between firm writing and loose; there is no more dramatic moment in the *Cantos* than the one that affixes to the poem's page scraps of so-called prose that have been extracted and Englished, with neither meter nor ragged right margins, from the contents of Sigismundo Malatesta's post-bag." For Bernstein, the device is linked with issues of subject matter as well: "The seemingly unobtrusive moment in Canto VIII, when the first series of historical letters is introduced into *The Cantos* and the personality of Sigismundo is shown by juxtaposing his prose instruction concerning a painter he wishes to engage with a lyric he writes for Isotta degli Atti *without privileging either medium*, represents one of the decisive turning-points in modern poetics, opening for verse the capacity to include domains of experience long since considered alien territory." See *The Tale of the Tribe*, p. 40.

69. "Quoted speech is not a necessary ingredient of poetry, which consists, instead, at its most basic level, in the kind of uniform discourse which Bakhtin says we would be wrong to look for in the novel," writes one scholar, reflecting this assumption. See Ann Jefferson, "Intertextuality and the Poetics of Fiction," *Comparative Criticism: A Yearbook* 2 (1980), p. 239.

70. Antoine Compagnon, *La seconde main ou le travail de la citation* (Paris: Seuil, 1979), p. 54. This is an exemplary study and should be consulted for its comprehensive exploration of quotation from several perspectives.

71. Roland Barthes, *Image, Music, Text* (New York: Hill and Wang, 1977), p. 146. Aside from the study of Compagnon (cited in note 70), more recent studies include Nelson Goodman, "Routes of Reference," *Critical Inquiry* 8 (1981), pp. 121–31; Marie-Laure Ryan, "When 'Je' is 'Un Autre'," *Poetics Today* 2 (1981), 127–55; Jacqueline Authier, "Paroles tenues à distance," in Bernard Conein, Jean-Jacques Courtine, et al. (eds.), *Matérialités Discursives* (Lille: Presses Universitaires de Lille, 1982), pp. 127–41; Meir Sternberg, "Proteus in Quotation-Land," *Poetics Today* 3 (1982), pp. 107–56; and Angelo Jacomuzzi, "La citazione come procedimento letterario," in *L'arte dell'interpre-*

tare: studi critici offerti a Giovanni Getto (Cuneo: Arciere, 1984), pp. 3–15. Three studies on quotation in the work of Pound are Philip Kuberski, "Ego, Scriptor: Pound's Odyssean Writing," in *Paideuma* 14 (1985), pp. 31–51; and the insightful essays by Michael André Bernstein, "Bringing It All Back Home: Derivations and Quotations in Robert Duncan and the Poundian Tradition," *Sagetrieb* 1 (1982), pp. 176–89; and "History and Textuality in Ezra Pound's Cantos 15–22," in Marianne Korn (ed.), *Ezra Pound and History* (Orono: National Poetry Foundation and University of Maine, 1985), pp. 176–89.

72. Jacques Derrida, *Spurs: Nietzsche's Styles,* tr. Barbara Harlow (Chicago: University of Chicago Press, 1979), p. 107, with a fuller meditation on the Nietzschean passage on pp. 122–43; hereafter reference to this work is given in parentheses within the text. An earlier version of the discussion is found in *Limited Inc.,* which is translated in *Glyph* 2 (1977), pp. 162–254. Translations here are my own, adapted from Harlow.

73. Derrida, "Living On: Border Lines," in Harold Bloom et al. (eds.), *Deconstruction and Criticism* (New York: Seabury, 1979), p. 78.

74. See Sylva Norman, *Flight of the Skylark: The Development of Shelley's Reputation,* p. 90 n. 14.

75. Peter Ackroyd, *T. S. Eliot: A Life* (New York: Simon and Schuster, 1984), p. 10. Recent actions by U.S. courts have eroded authors' right to make use of unpublished material. For example, in early 1990, the U.S. Supreme Court declined to hear an appeal by publishing company Henry Holt involving *Barefaced Messsiah,* a book by Russell Miller about L. Ron Hubbard, founder of the controversial Church of Scientology. In so doing, the Court upheld a lower court ruling that a book relying on unpublished writings may be blocked. New Era Publications International had attempted to suppress Holt's publication of the book, on the ground that it relied on Hubbard's unpublished writings and other material protected by copyright. See *Publishers Weekly* (9 March 1990), p. 10.

76. See Paul de Man, *Wartime Journalism, 1940–42,* ed. Werner Hamacher, Neil Hertz, and Tom Keenan (Lincoln: University of Nebraska Press, 1988), and Werner Hamacher, Neil Hertz, and Tom Keenan (eds.), *Responses on Paul de Man's Wartime Journalism* (Lincoln: University of Nebraska Press, 1988).

77. Jacques Derrida, "Living On," p. 81.

78. Dating of the decision to proceed with the *Endlösung* has been notoriously difficult. The "first official reference" to the project is made on 20 May 1941 by Goering, a second again by him on 31 July. See Martin Gilbert *The Holocaust: A History of the Jews of Europe during the Second World War* (New York: Henry Holt, 1985), pp. 152, 176. See also Arno J. Mayer, *Why Did the Heavens Not Darken? The Final Solution in History* (New York: Pantheon, 1988), who dates the crucial decisions as late as winter 1941–42, not long before the Wannsee Conference of 20 January 1942, in which the project was bureaucratically coordinated.

79. Charles Yriarte, *Les Prussiens à Paris et le 18 Mars* (Paris: Plon, 1871),

p. 1: "Là, et là seulement, se trouvent désormais les véritables éléments de l'histoire, et il n'est pas jusqu'à la langue heurtée en usage dans les télégrammes, surtout quand ils sonts écrits sous l'impulsion d'événements aussi pressants, qui n'ajoute, dans ces documents, à la vivacité des récits, et leur donne une couleur et une relief plus particuliers." Yriarte emphasized that he had initially planned a narrative "oeuvre d'historien," but that he rejected this on the grounds of impressionistic force: "mais nous n'aurions pu qu'affaiblir l'impression que nous avons ressentie en relisant, après huit mois, la succession des dépêches officielles, dont la plupart sont jusqu'ici restées secrètes" (p. 1).

80. On Baschet's life (1829 – 86) and works see Charles Dufay, *Un érudit au XIXᵉ siècle* (Orléans: H. Herluison, 1887). Baschet "discovered" the Venetian archives in the course of a diplomatic mission in 1852 and five years later published *Souvenirs d'une mission: les archives de la Sérénissime République de Venise*. A string of related works followed, including *La diplomatie vénitienne: les princes de l'Europe au XVIᵉ siècle d'après les ambassadeurs vénitiens* (1862) and *Les archives de Venise, histoire de la Chancellerie secrète* (1870). From here he went to new archives and libraries, including those of Paris and Mantua. His influence on Yriarte is documented in an unpublished letter from Yriarte to him, dated 13 October 1883, which accompanied Yriarte's gift of the 1874 book: "Voici le Patricien, je vous l'envoie sans la fragile enveloppe qu'il avait de chez Rothschild [the publisher]; pour ne pas le défaire je n'y écris pas de Dédicace, je le ferai chez vous. Vous savez que vous avez guidé mes premiers pas dans ce genre d'études, et ce livre vous doit beaucoups" (Bibliothèque de l'Institut de France, Ms. 2488). His phrase "le Patricien" refers to his own book *La Vie d'un Patricien de Venise au Seizième Siècle* (Paris: 1st edn., Plon, 1874; 2nd edn., Jules Rothschild, 1883). Its title page took pains to point out that the book was written "d'après les papiers d'État des Archives de Venise."

81. See Burton J. Bledstein, *The Culture of Professionalism: The Middle Class and the Development of Higher Education in America* (New York: W. W. Norton, 1976). For more recent remarks see Michael Warner, "Professionalization and the Rewards of Literature: 1875–1900," *Criticism* 27 (1985), pp. 1–28, with a survey of discussion since Bledstein at p. 27 n. 15.

82. Richard G. Moulton, *Shakespeare as a Dramatic Artist: A Popular Illustration of the Principles of Scientific Criticism* (New York: Macmillan, 1885; 2nd edn., Oxford, 1888), p. 25. Cited by Warner, "Professionalization," p. 14.

83. Cited in Stock, *Life*, p. 40.

84. Ezra Pound, "Provincialism the Enemy," published in three parts in *The New Age* 21 (1917) on 12, 19, and 26 July. Reprinted in *SP*, pp. 189–203; all quotations are from this edition, and appear in the text proper in parentheses. For a different reading of this essay see James Longenbach, *Modernist Poetics of History: Pound, Eliot, and the Sense of the Past* (Princeton: Princeton University Press, 1987), pp. 101–4, who argues that this essay "holds up" what he terms "the humanist ideal of the individual."

85. Pound does not state here whether this lack of personality is culturally or genetically determined. However, his later interest in the biological specula- tions of Louis Berman, *The Glands Regulating Personality* (1921), suggests that he regarded such differences as largely hereditary; see especially his letter to Felix Schelling of 8–9 July 1922, in *SL*, letter no. 189, pp. 178–82, and the carbon of his letter to Louis Berman of 1 March 1922, in NYPL *BC*, JSWP.

86. FAS, *Fondo Direzione Archivio di Stato*, Sopraintendenza vecchia, Busta 428 (1923).

87. NHBY, *PA*, Series 5, Box 63, f. 2432.1 (formerly 42.1). The original document is conserved in FAS, *Mediceo avanti il principato*, VIII, 212 (formerly 203, 196).

88. V. N. Voloshinov, *Marxism and the Philosophy of Language*, tr. Ladislaw Matejka and I. R. Titunik (New York: Seminar Press, 1973; 1st edn., 1930), p. 115.

89. Perloff, *The Poetics of Indeterminancy* (see note 5). Subsequent refer- ences are given in parentheses within the text, citing only the page number.

90. Ezra Pound to Henry Allen Moe, John Simon Guggenheim Foundation, 31 March 1925; NHBY, *PA*, Series I, Box 22, f. 848.

91. On Beltramelli's participation at the congress, see Emilio R. Papa, *Fa- scismo e cultura* (Venice-Padua: Marsilio, 1974), p. 165 for the program of the congress, pp. 161–62 for the signers of the manifesto. See his illuminating discussion of the entire affair, pp. 159–94. For Beltramelli's life and career, see R. Bertacchini, "Beltramelli, Antonio," in *Dizionario biografico degli italiani*, vol. 8 (Rome: Istituto della Enciclopedia Italiana, 1966), pp. 56–60. For the regime's tributes to Beltramelli on his death, see *Il Popolo d'Italia*, 16 March 1930, p. 3; the newspaper was founded by Mussolini and edited by his brother Arnaldo, whose elegy for Beltramelli appears on the same page.

92. Reprinted in Benito Mussolini, *Opera Omnia*, ed. Edoardo and Duilio Susmel, vol. 1 (Florence: La Fenice, 1957), pp. 275–76.

93. See Library of Congress, *National Union Catalogue, Pre-1956 Imprints* (London: Mansell, 1979), s.v. "Beltramelli."

94. See, for example, Carroll F. Terrell, *A Companion to the Cantos of Ezra Pound*, vol. 1 (Berkeley: University of California Press, 1980), p. 48; and Peter Makin, *Pound's Cantos* (London: George Allen & Unwin, 1985), p. 139.

95. *SL*, letter no. 252, p. 239, 18 February 1932.

2. Transmission

1. Jean Baudrillard, *Simulations* (New York: Semiotext(e) 1983), p. 2.

2. ND70[10] 96.96–97.

3. Christine Froula, *To Write Paradise: Style and Error in Pound's* Cantos (New Haven: Yale University Press, 1984), pp. 158, 160.

4. Marjorie Perloff, *The Poetics of Indeterminacy: From Rimbaud to Cage*

(Evanston, Ill.: Northwestern University Press, 1983; 1st edn., Princeton: Princeton University Press, 1981), pp. 183, 188.

5. Richard Sieburth, "Dada Pound," *South Atlantic Quarterly* 83 (1983), p. 57.

6. Froula, *To Write Paradise*, p. 168.

7. See Marjorie Perloff, "Response to Jacques Derrida," *Critical Inquiry* 15 (1989), pp. 767–76.

8. Alessandro Giulini, "Di alcuni figli meno noti di Francesco I Sforza," *Archivio storico lombardo* 43 (1916), pp. 31–32. See also Piero Parodi, "Nicodemo Tranchedini da Pontremoli genealogista degli Sforza," *Arcivio storico lombardo* 47 (1920), p. 339, quoting from a *Genealogia sforzesca*, or "Genealogy [of the Natural Children of Francesco Sforza]," prepared by Nicodemo Tranchedini (ca. 1411–86). The *Genealogia* was included by Tranchedini on folio 21 of his autograph *Zibaldone*, or "Miscellany," a manuscript formerly in the possession of Pietro Ferrari, who in 1911 first reported its existence and in 1920 furnished Parodi with a transcription of the genealogical portions, the source for his quotation:

> 1428, die. . . . nata est in Mortario agri papiensis Pulisena [*sic*] ex domina Johanna, cui impositum est tale nomen ob amorem quem gerebat ipse dominus meus dicte domine Pulisene [*sic*] Ruffe. Hec Pulisena [*sic*] data est nuptui Magnifico domino Sigismundo Pandulfo.

The same passage was reported a second time when the "Genealogy" was included as an appendix to Piero Parodi (ed.), *Un memoriale ignorato di Nicodemo Tranchedini da Pontremoli* (Abbiategrasso: Arti Grafiche B. Nicosa, 1921), on p. 17; and this last is also cited by Aldo Francesco Massèra (ed.), Anonymous, *Cronaca malatestiana del secolo XV (AA. 1416–1452)*, part 2 of *Cronache malatestiane dei secoli XIV e XV (AA. 1295–1385 e 1416–1452)*, in *Rerum Italicarum Scriptores*, 2nd edn., ed. Giosuè Carducci and Vittorio Fiorini, vol. 15 (Bologna: Zanichelli, 1922–24), fascicles 184 (1922; pp. 1–80) and 185 (1924; pp. 81–192), on p. 84 n. 6 Hereafter the text of this chronicle is cited as *Cron. mal.*, while the editorial portions by Massèra are cited as Massèra (ed.), *Cron. mal.*

In addition to Tranchedini's "Genealogy," another source that reports Polissena's birth is an anonymous fifteenth-century chronicle conserved in the Biblioteca Concina in San Daniele in Friuli, described by Piero Parodi in "La cronaca sforzesca della Biblioteca Concina di San Daniele nel Friuli," *Archivio storico lombardo* 47 (1920), pp. 541–44. Under the year 1428 it records that Francesco Sforza "ando per istantia a mortara e si li mori quella prima figliola che aveva chiamata polisena [*sic*]," and that while staying "in mortara ge naque una fiolla de madona Iohana [*sic*] chiamata Pulisena [*sic*] la quale poy fo moglie del S. Sigismondo pandolfo S. di Rimini" (both passages given by Parodi, p. 543).

9. F. Fossati (ed.), Pier Candido Decembrio, *Opuscula historica*, in *Rerum Italicarum Scriptores*, 2nd edn., vol. 20 (Bologna: Zanichelli, 1933–1943), p. 548, n. 1.

10. The contract is reported by Alessandro Giulini, "Di alcuni figli," p. 31 n. 6; also cited by Massèra (ed.), *Cron. mal.*, p. 84 n. 1. The original is located in MAS, *Archivio sforzesco avanti il principato*, Carteggio sforzesco, Potenze sovrane, Polissena Sforza. The 15,000 gold ducats indicates the importance that Sforza attributed to the union with Sigismondo. For the marriage of Polissena's younger sister, Drusiana, to the doge of Genoa (Giano Fegroso) just six years later, in 1447, Sforza offered a dowry of only 10,000 gold ducats. After Sforza had become duke of Milan (in 1450), however, the amount of a dowry increased significantly; when Drusiana was offered a second time to the powerful condottiere Giacomo Piccinino in 1464, the dowry was 35,000 gold ducats, aside from her own substantial possessions and furnishings. See Giulini, "Di alcuni figli," pp. 31–32. Drusiana's betrothal to him is mentioned by Pound in the Malatesta Cantos, ND70[10] 10.51–53, an account based on his reading of Giovanni Soranzo, *Pio II e la politica italiana nella lotta contro i Malatesti, 1457–1463* (Padua: Fratelli Drucker, 1911), pp. 73, 73 n. 4.

11. On Sigismondo's alliance with Sforza between 1441 and 1445 see Phillip J. Jones, *The Malatesta of Rimini and the Papal State: A Political History* (Cambridge: Cambridge University Press, 1974), pp. 186 –93.

12. Macerata, Archivio communale, *Riformanze del 1441, Consiglio di 3 settembre*, quoted by Giovanni Benadduci, *Della signoria di Francesco Sforza nella Marca e peculiarmente in Tolentino* (Tolentino, 1892; rpt., Bologna: Forni, 1980), p. 193 n. 2.

> Super litera Contutii Locumtenentis continenti in effectu qualiter Excellentis Comitis dederit suam inclitam filiam Polissenam magnifico et potenti domino Gismundo de Malatestis et debeat de proximo ire Firmum prefatus magnificus dominus Gismundus ad desponsandam ipsam et in eundo seu in reditu stabit in civitate ista, et voluntas Comitis est ut honorifice recipiatur.

13. *Cron. mal.*, p. 84.

14. *Cron. mal.*, p. 85.

15. Michele Rosi, *Della signoria di Francesco Sforza nella Marca* (Recanati, 1895), p. 82, doc. 204. Cited by Massèra (ed.), *Cron. mal.*, p. 86 n. 5.

16. *Cron. mal.*, pp. 86 – 87. Massèra's transcription reads:

> El nostro magnifico signore, signore miser Sismondo Pandolfo di Malatesti, menò per sua donna la magnifica madonna Pullisena, figliola del magnifico signore conte Francesco. La quale fo acompagnata da multi signuri e gentili omini cum grandissimi triumfi, e fo coverta la strada da Sam Bartolo per infina ala corte de panni de lana gentile. El segondo dì se fé in palazo una bella e famoxa festa e cum grandissimi triumfi, e foglie quasi tutte le donne de Arimino e citadini acti a festa: e fo facto uno solenne e bello e copioso convido. Ala qual festa el prefato nostro

magnifico signore fé cavalero misere Pero Gioanne da Cexena e donoglie una bella veste brocada d'oro e spada e speruni. El terzo dì, che fo adì primo de magio, fo fatta una bella giostra nel foro, e fo zostrato una peza de veluto azurro, la quale abe uno fameglio del nostro magnifico signore, chiamato Gioanne da Riva, perché a lui fo dato l'onore dela giostra. A dui dì de magio se partì la compagna dela ditta magnifica madonna, e ritornò in la Marca. Le noze fonno belissime, famose e sontuose, cum molto ordine e providimento.

17. One notes how conservative, traditional, and commonplace this celebration is in comparison with the May Day events of 1447, only five years later, as imagined by Pound. (See the discussion in chapter 1, pp. 42–45.) One later historian, incidentally, reports that Polissena was escorted to Rimini by three hundred people on horseback; see Pietro-Maria Amiani, *Memorie istoriche della città di Fano* (Fano: Stamperia di Giuseppe Leonardi, 1751; anastatic rpt., Bologna: Forni, 1967), vol. 1, p. 389.

18. *Cron. mal.*, p. 87:

Venne in Arimino el magnifico signore e capitanio conte Francesco, e capitanio e gonfallonero de santa Chiexa, et intrò cum sette stendardi, ciò è uno dela Chiexa, l'altro del papa Eugenio, l'altro de Sam Marco, l'altro de Fiorentini e tri altri agollupati. Et anco venne la sua donna magnifica madonna Bianca, figliola del duca de Millano, cum otto dongelle cum tutti cavalli bianchi, et erano tutte vestide de verde ad una liverea. E venne sotto el baldachino bianco cum gram trionfo, e fo coverta la strada tutta dala porta de Sam Giuliano per infina ala corte de panni bianchi, e fo fatta una bella festa cum balli e triumfi, e magni, famusi e solenni comviti. E cum lo prefato magnifico conte erano molte gente d'arme da pè e da cavallo de una bella e fiorita compagnia.

Pound imitates the chronicle indirectly in a well-known passage of the Malatesta Cantos, ND70[10] 8.99–113. But his acquaintance with the incident is partly via the baroque report of Cesare Clementini, *Raccolto istorico della fondatione di Rimino, e dell' origine e vite de' Malatesti* (Rimini: tip. Simbeni, vol. 1, 1617, vol. 2, 1627; rpt., Bologna: Forni, 1969, as vol. 38 in the collection "Historiae urbium et regionum italiae rariores"), vol. 2, pp. 324–25; and partly via his later consultation in March 1923 of the original manuscript of Gaspare Broglio Tartaglia da Lavello, published as *Cronaca malatesiana del secolo XV*, ed. Antonio G. Luciani (Rimini: Bruno Ghigi, 1982), where the incident appears on p. 83. Hereafter this is cited as Broglio. Both Clementini and Broglio copy from and elaborate on the account of the anonymous chronicle.

19. *Cron. mal.*, p. 91 (baptism); Massèra (ed.), *Cron. mal.*, pp. 72 n. 5, 91 n. 6 (Fra Bartolo and Ariminuccio Martini); *Cron. mal.*, p. 72 (baptism of Galeotto Roberto).

20. Aldo Francesco Massèra, "Amori e gelosie in una corte romagnola del Rinascimento (Per la biografia d'Isotta da Rimini)," *La Romagna* 13 (1916), p. 67 n. 2; *Cronaca del Anonimo veronese*, ed. Giovanni Soranzo (Venice: R. Deputazione di storia patria, 1915), p. 62; Luigi Tonini, *Della storia civile e sacra*

riminese (Rimini, 1848–82) vol. 5: *Rimini nella signoria de' Malatesti* (Rimini: tip. Albertini, 1880; rpt. Rimini: Bruno Ghigi, 1971), pp. 469–70.

21. Augusto Campana, "Atti, Isotta degli," *Dizionario biografico degli Italiani*, vol. 4 (Rome: Istituto della Enciclopedia Italiana, 1962), p. 547.

22. *Cron. mal.*, pp. 119, 120, 122; the visit with Sforza is also reported by Broglio, p. 142, who dates the visit a day later, 10 August. Apparently the sale of Pesaro had not altered the necessity of maintaining good diplomatic relations with Sforza; indeed, Broglio states that Polissena also brought food with her to Sforza's camp ("et portolli assai rifrescamento a ornare in canpo").

23. *Cron. mal.*, p. 119; Massèra, "Amori e gelosie," p. 68 n. 1. Malatesta's letter to his father Sigismondo, written at age six, is given by Pound, ND70[10] 10.180–199.

24. Luigi Osio (ed.), *Documenti diplomatici tratti dagli archivi milanesi* (Milan: tip. di Giuseppe Bernardoni di Giovanni, 1864–72; rpt., Milan: Cisalpino-Goliardica, 1970), vol. 3, p. 283 n. 2; Massèra (ed.), *Cron. mal.*, p. 84 n. 6.

25. See Massèra, "Amori e gelosie," p. 67 n. 2; I find no record of the date of Galeotto's death.

26. *Cron. mal.*, pp. 128–29:

Morì la magnifica madonna Polisena, donna del nostro magnifico signore. Ala sua sepoltura glie fonno dopieri centoventi. Fo seppelita a Sam Francesco in Arimino cum tutto el populo. Fo vestita tutta la sua fameglia de novo. El vescovo de Cesena cum tutta la chierisia d'Arimino fo ala sua sepultura. *Cuius anima requiescat in pace.*

27. MAS, Convenzioni con le potenze estere, Registro P, ff. 44[r]–48; the clause is reported by Giovanni Soranzo, "Un'invettiva della Curia Romana contro Sigismondo Malatesta" [part 1], *La Romagna* 8 (1911), pp. 174–75.

28. MAS, Carteggio generale, Francesco Sforza to Ottone del Carretto, 10 January 1461; passages are given by Soranzo, "Un'invettiva" [part 2], p. 170.

29. Soranzo, "Un'invettiva" [part 2], p. 171.

30. [Pius II], "Delatio criminum ipsius [Sigismundi Malatestae] facta in consistorio publico per advocatum fisci," in Giovanni-Benedetto Mittarelli (ed.), *Bibliotheca codicum manuscriptorum monasterii S. Michaelis venetiarum prope Murianum una cum appendice librorum impressorum seculi XV.* (Venice: ex typographia Fentiana, 1779), cols. 704–15. The passage quoted here appears in col. 709:

Successere tertiae nuptiae, et novas pecunias nova uxor adduxit, filia Francisci Sfortiae tunc comitis Cotignolae, nunc Mediolanensium clarissimi et excellentissimi ducis. Cui, quamvis esset modestissima, et honestate singulari praedita, non tamen fortuna melior, aut vir mansuetior quam priori fuit. Non tulit casti consortium lecti Sigismundus, sed atrox et sanguinarius parricida, hanc quoque sanctissimam conjugem absque ulla culpa strangulavit, quamvis mortis causam post mortem quaerens nullam invenerit.

31. MAS, *Archivio Sforzesco*, Carteggio estero, Romagna; Niccolò de Palude (governor of Pesaro for Alessandro Sforza) to Francesco Sforza, 13 August 1462. The entire letter is reported by Luigi Fumi, "L'atteggiamento di Francesco Sforza verso Sigismondo Malatesta in una sua istruzione del 1462, con particolari sulla morte violenta della figlia Polissena," *Archivio storico lombardo* 40 (1913), pp. 170–80. The transcription appears on pp. 174–75 n. 1. Niccolò states specifically that he had written earlier, which must mean 12 August, to Sforza about the defeat at Senigallia: "Perchè essendo già perduta Senegaglia, *como è stato denotato* a la vostra excellentia . . ." (italics mine). Nothing before this in the letter refers to the loss of Senigallia, and therefore the reference must be to a prior dispatch. The letter by the other Sforzescan agent appears in MAS, *Potenze estere*, Roma; Agostino Rossi to Francesco Sforza, 14 August 1462, Monte Baroccio. It is cited by Soranzo, *Pio II*, p. 299 n. 2.

32. MaAG, *Dispacci degli ambasciatori del Gonzaga inviati a Roma o ad altre corti;* copy of Federigo da Montefeltro to Piero his *cancelliere*, 13 August 1462, from camp near Senigallia, preserved in Cardinal Francesco Gonzaga to his mother, 19 August 1462, Pienza; cited by Soranzo, *Pio II*, p. 301 n. 1.

33. See above, note 31.

·34. MAS, *Archivio diplomatico*, Bolle e brevi, Pio II; Pius II to Francesco Sforza, 16 August 1462, Pienza. The letter is discussed by Soranzo, *Pio II*, pp. 303–4, cited by him p. 304 n. 1, and transcribed in full pp. 487–88, doc. 25. That Pius II's letter of 16 August reached Sforza by 23 August is evident from the following: the letter by Federigo from Senigallia dated 13 August (cited note 32) reached his *cancelliere* in Rome, then was sent on to Pienza, where it was transcribed by Cardinal Gonzaga on 19 August, which is to say six days later; therefore it is clear that Pius II's letter from Pienza, dated 16 August, would have reached Sforza in Milan by 23 August, or seven days later.

The six-day period required for Federigo's letter to travel to Pienza is also useful for correcting an error made by Soranzo when discussing the significance of Pius II's letter of 16 August, in *Pio II*, p. 303. Soranzo assumes that Pius is writing immediately after learning about Sigismondo's defeat outside Senigallia on 13 August, "poche ore dopo l'arrivo della felice novella." But this is an error. First, it is unlikely that Pius would receive this news only three days after the battle, given that it took Federigo's letter six days to reach Francesco Gonzaga located, like Pius, in Pienza. Second, intrinsic evidence from the letter indicates that Pius II knew only a report that Sigismondo had taken the city and its fortress, not the later report that he had lost it shortly thereafter. For Pius never mentions a victory for the ecclesiastical forces near Senigallia, only their defeat, their loss of Senigallia, and his grave displeasure at learning about this: "Licet ammissio civitatis Senogalliensis nobis displicuerit multum et ad diminutionem honoris nostri non dubie cesserit." These words make clear that Pius is referring not to Sigismondo's loss of Senigallia on 13 August, as Soranzo supposes, but to the events of 12 August alone, when Sigismondo had first seized and occupied it. Third, intrinsic evidence from Sforza's letter of 23 August makes clear that he, too, understood Pius II's reference to the "ammissio civitatis Senogalliensis" in this way. When Sforza recounts the news of the ecclesiastical victory at Senigallia, he calls it "una buona et relavata novella" in obvious contrast to the bad and old news reported by Pius's own letter.

The altered understanding of the chronological relations between the two letters also has implications. Pius II's intention, of 16 August, to press on with the campaign seems less the vindictive gesture suggested by Soranzo and more a sign of his determination to proceed despite recent setbacks; and his request for counsel from Sforza becomes less a calculated ploy designed to win support for his own aims and more a genuine request for advice on a difficult point in a field where Sforza had obvious expertise.

Soranzo's determination to portray Pius II as a man blinded by vindictiveness also affects his discussion of a papal brief written by Pius to Federigo da Montefeltro on 13 August 1462. Soranzo claims that Pius ordered Federigo to continue the struggle with Sigismondo "avuta la notizia . . . della vittoria sul Cesano" (*Pio II*, p. 304). Yet if the battle on the Cesano was just ending "prima della levata del sole del 13 agosto," as Soranzo himself convincingly demonstrates on pp. 301 and 301 n. 1, then it is manifestly impossible that news of the battle could in any way have affected Pius's brief written the same day.

These points are important because Soranzo's authority, which is considerable and in general rightly so, has been invoked as proof that modern historians have come to conclusions similar to Pound's (see pp. 141–43). Although this claim is absurd when formulated in this way (the fact is that Pound read Soranzo, not that they actually arrived at similar conclusions), scholars should not assume that Soranzo's work is flawless. The errors outlined here show that he sometimes colored his interpretations of documentary evidence to make them agreeable to his theses; and similar errors in his use of the material from Amiani regarding Polissena's death (see p. 115) make clear that his evidence must be examined carefully and independently.

35. MAS, *Archivio Sforzesco*, Carteggio estero, Roma; Francesco Sforza to Ottone del Carretto, 23 August 1462; the entire letter is reported by Luigi Fumi, "L'atteggiamento di Francesco Sforza," pp. 170–80; all the passages quoted appear on pp. 172–74.

36. Enea Silvio Piccolomini, Papa Pio II, *I commentarii*, ed. Luigi Totaro (Milan: Adelphi, 1984), pp. 366, 368: "Duas uxores, quas duxerat ante Isottae contubernium, alteram post alteram seu ferro seu veneno extinxit." The passage's parallelism suggests that Sigismondo had poisoned ("seu veneno") his second wife. However, the earlier oration/bull had explicitly accused him of poisoning his first wife, Ginevra; if one wished to assert continuity between the two documents, one could reason that the same charge was intended here, and therefore that the charge of stabbing ("seu ferro") was made with reference to Polissena. But humanist rhetorical theory placed little value on specific details

or factual precision in a modern sense, and one would be ill advised to make too much of this minor discrepancy.

37. Giovanni Simonetta, *Rerum gestarum Francisci Sfortiae mediolanensium ducis commentarii*, ed. Giovanni Soranzo, in *Rerum italicarum scriptores*, 2nd edn., ed. Giosué Carducci, Vittorio Fiorini, Pietro Fedele, vol. 21, part 2 (Bologna: Zanichelli, 1932–43), p. 335:

> Nam Sigismundus Francisci congressum plurimum formidabat, cum ob Polysenam uxorem suam, Francisci filiam, suo iussu immerito necatam, quo patrem acerbiore dolore premeret et ne, propter inexplebile et exacerbatam in ipsum patrem odium, virilem ex ea prolem susciperet et Ysottam pellicem, quam perdite adamabat, deinde in uxorem duceret, et ita mulierem ingenuam atque pudicissimam, acerbissima morte affectam, pestifero morbo correptam simulans, vita functam vulgari iussit.

38. My account here somewhat simplifies the matter. First, the 1461 oration-invective was subject to its own history of transmission. There are two surviving manuscripts that report the oration independently: (1) Ravenna, *Biblioteca Classense 284;* (2) Venice, *S. Michele di Murano, 1130.* Other copies are mentioned as having been received by contemporaries, but have not survived; apparently they were sent to various courts or political centers of northern Italy in 1461. Second, it was early in 1462, most likely, that the oration was incorporated into the *Discipula veritatis,* and this version is conserved in five more manuscripts. Two are miscellaneous collections of writings by Pius II: (3) Vatican, *Chigiano I.V.175;* and (4) Vatican, *Chigiano I.VI.212.* The other three have an entirely different morphology; they contain a collection of some fifty political letters by Pius II, and all are held in the Vatican: (5) *Chigiano I.VII.249;* (6) *Chigiano I.VIII.285;* and (7) *Urbinate lat. 404.* One of them (6) is a vellum deluxe manuscript and bears the papal arms, suggesting that this was a personal if not official collection of Pius II. Two of them (5 and 6) were owned by his nephew, Francesco Tedeschini Piccolomini, later Pius III. Further, it is this collection of Pius's letters that was printed as a book in the three editions from Milan mentioned above. The editions are described in *Indice generale degli incunaboli delle biblioteche d'Italia,* vol. 4 (Rome: Libreria dello stato, 1964), nos. 7787–89. For a full discussion of the manuscripts and their diffusion, see Augusto Campana, "Poema antimalatestiano di un umanista spagnolo per Pio II," in *Atti e memorie della deputazione di storia patria per le Marche,* series 3, vol. 4, fasc. 2 (1964–65), pp. 189–212. And finally, in 1779 the text of the invective alone, before its incorporation in the bull, was printed independently for the only time as part of a documentary collection; the edition was based on the manuscript given above as (2). On this, see above note 30. According to Gregorio Giovanardi, "Un frate minore martire del sigillo sacramentale a Rimini," *Studi francescani* 1 (1914), p. 350 n. 1, there is also an 1884 edition of the *Epistolae* (Rome: Zarotti, 1884), but I have been unable to find it and so have

not discussed it here; perhaps the reference is only a mistake for the 1487 edition. On the problematic place of *Discipula veritatis* in the official registers of papal bulls, and its relation to *Licet natura*, see Franco Gaeta, "La 'leggenda' di Sigismondo Malatesta," in P. J. Jones et al., *Studi malatestiani* (Rome: Istituto storico italiano per il medio evo, 1978), pp. 159–96, and in particular pp. 164–71.

39. Fra Jacopo Filippo Foresti, *Supplementum chronicarum* (Brescia: Boninus de Boninis, 1485), fol. 343ʳ:

> Hic tres successive suscepit uxores primam Crimignole Comitis filiam a qua dote maxima accepta mortuo predicto: illam repudiavit. Secundam Nicolai estensis marchionis filiam nomine Genevram: optimam mulierem: quam et paulopost veneno sustulit. Tertiam autem Francisci Sfortiae filiam modestissimam, quam etiam sine ulla culpa tandem ipsemet strangulavit: nulla ab eisdem suscepta prole. Hunc itaque virum et si infinitissimis sceleribus inquinatissimum fuisse scribat Pius Pontifex: in rebus tamen bellicis strenuum: et in disciplinis doctum et doctorum virorum amantissimum fuisse deprehendimus: ac in omnibus gerendis liberalissimum et splendidissimum.

In the subsequent Latin editions the passage appears on fol. 284ʳ (1486); fol. 250ʳ (1490); fol. 246ʳ (1492); fol. 406ʳ (1503); fol. 406ʳ (1506); fol. 381ᵛ (1535). (It was not possible to ascertain the folio number for the 1513 edition.) Ten stylistic alterations are introduced into this passage in the 1503 edition, none of them significantly altering its sense. Italian editions reported the same passage as follows (1553, fol. 308ʳ):

> In questo caso nientedimeno e summamente infamato che successivamente ebbe tre donne. La prima fu figliola del conte Carmignola dalquale per lei hebbe una gran dote, ma essendo poi morto non la volse menare & repudiolla. La seconda c'hebbe fu madonna Gineura dignissima donna & figliola del Marchese Nicolo da Este, & questa si dice che in breve tempo fece morire di veleno. La terza poi & ultima fu figliola del Duca Francesco modestissima e bona, & questa senza alcuna cagione proprio l'annego, o voglio dire strangolo, & de nesciuna non hebbe mai figliuoli.

I have compared this text only with that of the 1520 edition, in which there are no substantive variants.

40. P. Haroldi, *Epitome annalium ordinis minorum* (Rome: tip. Tinassii, 1612), vol. 1, p. 1257. This is cited by Giovanardi, "Un frate minore," p. 352 n. 9. Fra Paolo Clerici Veronese, unedited ms. in the *Archivi di stato* of Ferrara and Modena; the work is cited by Cesare Clementini in 1627, *Raccolto istorico*, vol. 2, p. 363, but with no reference to its location. It is also cited by Giovanardi, "Un frate minore," p. 363 n. 2, who mentions "gli Archivi Estensi di Ferrara e Modena," but does not indicate a collection, file, or other call number. Luke Wadding, *Annales Minorum, in quibus res omnes trium ordinum a S. Fran-*

cisco institutorum ex fide ponderosius asseruntur, calumnia refelluntur, praeclara quaeque monumenta ab oblivione vendicantur, vol. 5 (Lyons: sumptibus Claudii Landry, 1642), p. 247. Catholic Church [A. R. P. Arturo], *Martyrologium Franciscanum, in quo sancti, beati, aliique servi Dei . . . trium ordinarum . . . S. Francisci . . . recensentur . . . cura et labore A. R. P. Arturi* (Paris: tip. Conterot, 1653; 1st edn., Paris: Apud Dionysium Moreau, 1638), p. 385; cited by Giovanardi, "Un frate minore," p. 352 n. 8. D. Silvio Grandi, *La vita del cristiano paragonata a quella di alcuni santi e beati riminesi* (Rimini: tip. Ferraris, 1702), narrazione XII, divisione 4; cited by Giovanardi, "Un frate minore," p. 352 n. 1. P. Flaminio Bottardi da Parma, *Memorie istoriche delle chiese e dei conventi dei Frati Minori dell'Osservante e riformata provincia di Bologna,* vol. 2 (Bologna, 1760), p. 465. P. Francesco Antonio Righini, [*Zibaldoni*], unpublished mss. in RBCG, vol. 12, ch. 6, art. 3, and vol. 14, pp. 5, 287. Giambattista Braschi, *Diatribe,* cited by Giovanardi, "Un frate minore," p. 352 n. 3, who reports that the manuscript is conserved in the Biblioteca Malatestiana at Cesena, and that it narrates the murder on p. 398. Giacomo Villani, *De vetusta Arimini urbe et eius episcopis,* cited by Giovanardi, "Un frate minore," p. 352 n. 6, who reports it conserved in RBCG, scaf. V, 51 (Fondo Gambetti), p. 427. Giacinto Picconi da Cantalupo, *Centone di memorie storiche circa la Minor. della Provincia di Bologna* (Parma: tip. SS. Annunziata, 1911), vol. 2, p. 357.

41. Those assigning the martyred confessor to Ginevra are Grandi, Bottardi, Braschi, and Picconi; partisans of the anonymous "moglie" are Haroldi, Wadding, Arturo, and Villani (see note 40).

42. P. Gregorio Giovanardi, O. F. M. (ed.), "Cronaca del P. Alessandro Righetti, Minore Conv[entuale]," *Studi Francescani* 2 (1915–16), pp. 29–40, 177–208. The manuscript is conserved in RBCG, Miscellanee I, n. 10 A, B. It is written in an eighteenth-century hand and conserved in vol. 8 of the works of Francesco Antonio Righini (a Franciscan brother who left his papers to the library, although the hand is not that of Righini himself). The document purports to be a copy from an autograph original (the title reads: "Copia di una pergamena autentica ritrovata nell'Archivio dei M. RR. pp. Minori Conventuali di San Francesco di Rimini"). The original was still preserved in the eighteenth century and was cited or described by several writers of the period. From the archive of the convent it passed into the hands of the notary Michelangelo Zanotti (died 1830), who placed it in volume XI of his collection of *Monumenti riminesi autografi* (as appears from the indices of these), where it was also seen by another Riminese scholar of the nineteenth century, Gaetano Urbani. Information on the manuscript is given by Giovanni Soranzo, "Due delitti attribuiti a Sigismondo Malatesta e una falsa cronachetta riminese," *Atti del R. Istituto Veneto di scienze, lettere ed arti* 74 (1914–15), part 2, pp. 1894–96. Among scholars of Pound it has been cited for thirty years as an authentic quattrocento testimony. On this problem see chapter 3.

43. Of course the decision to abandon the daughter of Carmagnola was made not by Sigismondo himself, then only fifteen years old, but by the regency council governing on behalf of him and his brothers.

44. Francesco Sansovino, *Della origine, et de' fatti delle famiglie illustri d'Italia* (Venice: presso Altobello Salicato, 1582), fol. 235ᵛ: "Conciosia che oltre alla prima, avelenò la Gineura figliuola di Nicolò Marchese di Ferrara che fu la seconda, & strangolò la Drusiana [*sic*; an error for Polissena] figliuola del Conte Francesco Sforza, che fu la terza." New editions of Sansovino appeared in 1609 (Venice: presso Altobelli Salicato) and 1670 (Venice: Come e La Nou). See Giovanni Battista Pigna, *Historia de principi d'Este* (Ferrara: apresso Francesco Rossi, 1570), pp. 600–601; (Venice: apresso V. Valgrisi, 1572), p. 754; and in a Latin translation by Giovanni Barone, *De principibus Atestinis historiarum libri VIII* (Ferrara: excudebat Victorius Baldinus, 1645), p. 624.

45. See John Addington Symonds, *Sketches and Studies in Italy and Greece,* 2nd series (London: Smith, Elder, 1898; New York: Charles Scribner's Sons, 1898; 1st edn., 1874), p. 19. All other citations are to this edition, cited as Symonds, *Sketches.* In discussing the church of San Francesco in Rimini and the tomb of Giorgios Gemisthos there, Symonds writes: "Upon the tomb we may still read this legend: 'Jemisthii Beizantii philosopher sua temp principis reliquum Sig. Pan. Mal. Pan. F. belli Pelop adversus Turcor regem Imp ob ingentem eruditorum quo flagrat amorem huc afferendum introque mittendum curavit MCCCCLXVI.' Of the Latinity of the inscription much cannot be said." Such remarks leave no doubt that Symonds was wholly ignorant of Renaissance epigraphy, and one may assume the like for paleography, where the conventions for abbreviations are similar. Consequently Symonds was incapable of reading an original letter from the period, and so incapable of studying anything but printed sources.

46. Symonds, *Sketches,* p. 17, p. 17 n. 1. And John Addington Symonds, *The Renaissance in Italy,* vol. 1: *The Age of the Despots* (New York: Henry Holt, 1888; 1st edn., 1876), p. 172.

47. On Simonetta see Giovanni Soranzo, "Prefazione" to Giovanni Simonetta, *Rerum gestarum Francisci Sfortiae mediolanensium ducis commentarii,* ed. Giovanni Soranzo, in *Rerum italicarum scriptores,* 2nd edn., ed. Giosué Carducci, Vittorio Fiorini, Pietro Fedele, vol. 21, part 2 (Bologna: Zanichelli, 1932–43). The belief that the work was written at the behest of Sforza himself was expressed by Paolo Giovio (see Soranzo, "Prefazione," p. xxx). Giovanni was a brother of Cicco Simonetta, the head of the Sforzescan chancery who controlled the duchy's domestic affairs after Sforza came to power in 1450. Giovanni benefited from his brother's power and prestige, and appears to have been susceptible to bribery. On 11 September 1479 both he and Cicco were arrested in the course of courtly intrigues involving Bona di Savoia and Lodovico il Moro. Cicco was beheaded on 30 October 1480, while Giovanni was released two days later. By 1482 he had returned to court, having regained favor through his his-

tory of Sforza, which pleased Lodovico. It was at Lodovico's request that Lorenzo il Magnifico "suggested" to Landino the idea of translating Simonetta's work.

48. On the manuscript tradition see Luigi Totaro, *Pio II nei suoi Commentarii* (Bologna: Pàtron, 1978), 211–28. There are eleven manuscripts from the sixteenth century, and one from the seventeenth. There are also two from the period of Pius II himself, and they have been the basis for all modern editions. One is *Vaticano Reginense Latino 1995*, an earlier recension with autograph corrections by Pius; the other includes later revisions dating from as late as June 1464, *Corsiniano 147* of the Biblioteca della Accademia dei Lincei. The unpublished portions of the work were edited by Giuseppe Cugnoni, "Aeneae Silvii Piccolomini Senensis qui postea fuit Pius II P.M., Opera inedita," in *Atti della R. Accademia dei Lincei* 280 (1883–84), *Memorie della classe di Scienze morali, storiche e filologiche* series 3, vol. 8, pp. 495–549; the passage regarding Polissena appears on p. 509. Two translations have been published based on *Vat. Reg. Lat. 1995:* one in English by F. A. Gragg, *The Commentaries of Pius II*, in *Smith College Studies in History* 22 (1936–37), 25 (1939–40), 30 (1947), 35 (1951), 43 (1957); another by Italian by Giuseppe Bernetti, *I commentarii* (Siena: Cantagalli, 1972–76). A bilingual edition based on *Corsiniano 147* has been published by Luigi Totaro, *I commentarii* (Milan: Adelphi, 1984), who is also preparing a critical edition based on the same manuscript. There is also a more comprehensive critical edition, Pii II, *Commentarii rerum memorabilium que temporibus suis contigerunt*, ed. Adrian van Heck (Città del Vaticano: Biblioteca Apostolica Vaticana, 1984).

49. Clementini, *Raccolto istorico*, vol. 2, p. 363. His reference to Fra Paolo Clerici Veronese is clearly based on Pigna's account in the *Historia de principi d'Este*, as seen in both his diction and syntax. The following transcription reproduces Clementini's lineation in order to indicate the ambiguities created by the typographical treatment of his "quotation" from Fra Paolo Clerici Veronese:

> Alli due di Giugno mille quattrocento quarantanove il
> secondo giorno della Pentecoste morì Polissena, mo
> glie di Sigismondo Pandolfo, e figlia del Conte Fran
> cesco Sforza d'improviso, non senza sospetto d'un
> asciugatoio involto al collo, e però da Pio Secondo,
> fù scritto, che di tre mogli, c'hebbe Sigismondo d'u-
> na si liberò col repudio, dell'altra col veleno, e della
> terza col laccio, senza occasione alcuna, e concorda
> "Paolo Clerici Veronese, frate Carmelitano in una di-
> "ligente Cronica, dicendo, che portavano tutte tre le
> "dette Signore immaculata fama di pudiche. Fù sepel
> li[t]a con molto onore, essendovi cento venti doppieri,
> nella Chiesa di San Francesco, e vestita tutta la fa-
> meglia à bruno, alla cui sepoltura intervenne il Ve-
> scovo di Cesena, col Clero di Rimino. Scrive il Si-
> monetta, che morta la sudetta Polissena, Sigismondo

pigliò un'altra Polissena, ma forse lo dice per ischer-
zo; poiche egli s'accasò con Isotta de gli Atti Rimi-
nese già sua Dama.

50. In some cases it was true that Clementini availed himself of unpublished
or archival sources, although not in the passage regarding Polissena. For ex-
ample, he repeatedly cites the notarial *rogiti* of Francesco Paponi, which con-
tain many documents pertaining to the day-to-day economics of the Malatestan
court and still need to be published in a systematic form. He also examined
other documents that were available only in Rimini (the papers of Claudio Paci,
also cited by Clementini repeatedly) or have subsequently disappeared since
his examination of them. See for example *Raccolto istorico*, vol. 2, p. 356, where
Clementini cites the defense of Sigismondo's conduct vis-à-vis Alfonso of Na-
ples which was prepared by Giacomo Anastasio, a document that has not been
relocated since then.

For an example of Clementini's reputation by the next century see Anony-
mous (ed.), *Lettere d'uomini illustri, che fiorirono nel principio del secolo deci-
mosettimo, non più stampate* (Venice: nella stamperia Baglioni, 1744), who re-
marks on Clementini's history, on p. xii, "Quest'opera è rara, e stimata
grandemente." Equally revealing is how Clementini's claims form the center of
the 1718–19 debate between Giuseppe Malatesta Garuffi and the pseudony-
mous "N. N." See Giuseppe Malatesta Garuffi, "Lettera apologetica scritta all'
Illustrissimo Signor Carlo-Francesco Marcheselli, Nobile Riminese, dal Signor
Arciprete D. Giuseppe Malatesta Garuffi, in difesa del Tempio famosissimo di
san Francesco, eretto in Rimini da Sigismondo-Pandolfo Malatesta in tempo,
che teneva il dominio di detta città," *Giornale de' letterati d'Italia* 30 (Venice,
1718), pp. 155–86, with his discussion of the alleged murder on pp. 162–63,
indicating his sense that Clementini's version of the charge was the most dam-
aging. In reply to Garuffi, see the pseudonymous N. N., "Lettera scritta al Molto
Reverendo Padre F. Giulio di Venezia, Predicatore chiarissimo, Commessario di
Santa Terra, Exministro provinciale dell'ordine de' Minori Osservanti, da N. N.
del medesimo ordine, sopra le opposizioni fatte al celebre storico Francescano
F. Luca Wadingo, dal Sig. Arciprete D. Giuseppe-Malatesta Garuffi, in una Let-
tera Apologetica, in difesa del famosissimo tempio di san Francesco, eretto in
Rimino, da Sigismondo-Pandolfo Malatesta, registrata nel tomo XXX. articolo
VI. del nostro Giornale a pag. 155," *Giornale de' Letterati di Italia* 31 (Venice,
1719), pp. 82–158. On p. 106 "N. N." also rehearses the testimony of Clemen-
tini, emphasizing the authority he had come to enjoy by this time (pp. 94–95):
"i suoi libri avidamente cercati, anche dagli Oltramontani, sono giunti ad un
prezzo di gran lunga superiore a quello, che converrebbe alla loro mole."

51. Gianmaria Mazzuchelli, *Notizie intorno ad Isotta da Rimino* (2nd edn.,
Brescia: dalle stampe di Giambatista Bossini, 1759). The first edition was pub-
lished in *Raccolta milanese dell'anno 1756*. The second edition claims, on the

title page, to be "accresciuta dall'autore." All subsequent references to this work are from the second edition. On p. 7 Mazzuchelli reports the murder.

Questa [Polissena] gli morì nel 1448. o, com' altri vuole, sul principio di Giugno del 1449; e al riferire d'Enea Silvio, di Fra Filippo da Bergamo, e del Clementini, non ebbe migliore sorte della prima [moglie]; perciocchè si dice che morisse soffocata da lui con un aciugatoio avvoltole strettamente al collo: e perciò dal citato Enea Silvio fu scritto, che di tre mogli, ch'ebbe Sigismondo (perciocchè forse gli fu ignota la quarta, cioè la nostra Isotta) di una si liberò col ripudio, dell'altra col veleno, e della terza col laccio.

On pp. 7–8 n. 12, he thanks "[il] chiarissimo Sig. Dottor Giovanni Bianchi di Rimino, che con su lettera mi ha dato in ciò saggio egualmente della sua gentilezza, che della sua singolare erudizione."

52. On Bianchi see A. Fabi, "Bianchi, Giovanni," in *Dizionario biografico degli italiani*, vol. 10 (Rome: Istituto della Enciclopedia Italiana, 1969), pp. 104–12. On Mazzuchelli's role in diffusing knowledge of the chronicle by pseudo-Alessandro, and on specific passages quoted by Yriarte, Beltramelli, Pound, see chapter 3, pp. 174–77.

53. Mazzuchelli, p. 10: "e forse i suoi amori con essa [Isotta] furono la cagione della morte della mentovata Polissena sua seconda moglie, certo essendo ch'egli amava appassionatamente Isotta, allorchè Polissena viveva."

54. Amiani, *Memorie istoriche dela città di Fano*, vol. 1, p. 410:

Continuava la Peste a desolar la Città . . . quest'anno, in cui dilatandosi per tutta l'Italia il mal contaggioso . . . il quale finalmente per intercessione del glorioso nostro Protettore S. Paterniano in Fano cessato, Donna Violante moglie di Malatesta Novello da Cesena venne ad abitare nel Palazzo di Sigismondo, dal Consiglio al suo arrivo regalata di Cere, e Confetture (o). Fu seguito il dilui esempio da Margherita ancora, Vedova di Galeotto Roberto Malatesta, che Rimini abbandonò, dopo che nel secondo giorno di Pentecoste, che fu ai 2. di Giugno morir vide Polissena moglie, come si è detto, di Sigismondo Malatesta, e figliuola del Conte Francesco Sforza fatta, come parecchi scrissero dal Marito strangolare, che però da Pio II. ebbe a dire, che di tre sue Mogli Sigismondo, d'una si liberò col Ripudio, dell'altra col Veleno, e della terza col Laccio, ancorchè tutte pudiche, e savie. Il nostro Pubblico spedì a Rimini immantinente Angelo di Gabriele de' Gabrielli, Malatesta d'Andrea Torelli, Taddiolo di Niccola di Andrea Galassi, e Niccola di Pier-Antonio di Gio: Francesco Bertozzi vestiti a lutto, perchè assistessero al Funerale di Polissena, dal quale agli 8. dello stesso Mese ritornati portarono lettere di Sigismondo al nostro Comune con la morte del Vescovo Bartolommeo Malatesta, e con l'avviso, che il Papa avevagli rinnovato l'Investitura di Cervia per Lui, Fratelli, Figliuoli, e Nipoti legittimi, e naturali, nel modo, e forma, che a' suoi Progenitori era stata conceduta da Bonifazio VIII.

55. On Amiani's testimony see Soranzo, "Un'invettiva" [Part 2], pp. 169–75; see also Massèra (ed.), *Cron. mal.*, pp. 128–29 n. 16. On the death of Bartolomeo de' Malatesti, see *Cron. mal.*, p. 127.

56. Francesco Gaetano Battaglini, *Della vita e de' fatti di Sigismondo Pandolfo Malatesta Signor di Rimino, Commentario*, in Basinii Parmensis poetae, *Opera praestantiora nunc primum edita et opportunis commentariis illustrata* (Rimini: ex typographia Albertiniana, 1794), vol. 2. pp. 420–21. Battaglini does not mention Simonetta by name but his referent is unmistakable:

> Altri all'opposto scrissero, lui avere schivato a tutto potere di venire alle mani col suocero; non per intelligenza che avessero insieme, ma perchè temeva, che se l'avversità della sorte lo avesse fatto perditore e prigioniere del Conte [Francesco Sforza], non avesse dovuto pagare il fio della morte data a Polissena. Imperocchè questa Signora sendo morta in Rimino il primo dì di giugno, chi metteva studio a denigrare in qual si fosse modo la reputazione di Sigismondo, disse ciò essere stato procurato da lui col veleno. Ma io presterò più fede a chi scrisse, lei aver dovuto soccombere alla pestilenza; la quale in que' giorni oltremodo inferocendo nelle parti nostre, tolse pure dal mondo il nostro Vescovo Bartolomeo de' Malatesti; laonde la moglie del Signor di Cesena [Violante] e la vedova del Beato Galeotto [Margherita] presero conforto di ridursi in Fano.

It is possible that Battaglini's mention of "that author" is a reference to Nolfi. Yet it seems unlikely, since textual evidence indicates that he is following Amiani at this point, and since elsewhere he cites Amiani ten times in the course of his notes, but never mentions the manuscript history of Nolfi. Finally, Battaglini's mistaken report that the charge was poison may be a *lapsus mentis* or may reflect the influence of the ambiguous syntax of Pius II's *Commentarii*.

57. Gaetano Moroni, "Rimini o Rimino," in Gaetano Moroni (ed.), *Dizionario di erudizione storico-ecclesiastica da S. Pietro ai nostri giorni*, vol. 57. (Venice: tip. Emiliana, 1852), pp. 246–304. The section on Sigismondo Malatesta covers pp. 280–83; the charge appears on p. 281: "Sigismondo I [*sic*] appassionato per Isotta, volle rimuovere l'ostacolo per sposarla, e fin dal giugno 1449 fece strangolare la bella e già da lui tanto bramata Polissena, come affermano con Amiani diversi storici." The only author whose work was in print at this time and who claimed that the passion for Isotta had led to Polissena's murder was Simonetta (see the quotation on p. 90). But Moroni's references and knowledge show that he had never read Simonetta. Instead he repeatedly reveals the influence of Mazzuchelli, especially when touching on Isotta, and it is clear that he is giving a "hard" interpretation to the passage from Mazzuchelli quoted earlier (see note 53).

58. Moroni, "Rimini," pp. 290–91:

> L'orda era guidata da Pietro Renzi, che si spacciava per capo del governo provvisorio. . . . Per ben 3 giorni gemè Rimini sotto le cupide e crudeli voglie della masnada, solo intenta a rapine, dissennati nella impotenza degli esecrandi mezzi cui si appigliarono. Vedendosi il Renzi deluso nelle speranze . . . fuggì co' suoi, liberando dall'anarchia la città, che per altro non tardò a ricuperare l'ordine, il quale si consolidò dopo giunte le milizie papali di varie armi, accolte, dai saggi abitanti con festevoli dimostrazioni. . . .

59. See Massimo d'Azeglio, *Degli ultimi casi di Romagna* (Italia, 1846). The book was published clandestinely in Tuscany, but fiercely asserted its national interest by declaring its place of publication as "Italia"—a country that did not yet exist. D'Azeglio wrote it after touring Romagna incognito in September 1845, and the revolution broke out while he was still there on 23 September.

60. Moroni declares on his title page that he served first as "primo aiutante di camera di Sua Santità Gregorio XVI," then as "secondo aiutante di camera di Sua Santità Pio IX." He also makes his cautionary point quite explicitly, "Rimini," p. 282: "Yet his apparent felicity [with Isotta], by which it seemed he could repose quietly in the arms of a love now become legitimate and virtuous, became the very source of his undoing, since it left him without the protection of powerful princes, which was necessary to sustain his regime." Finally, he unveils a redemptive conclusion, claiming that Sigismondo had been converted to the faith through the love of Isotta before he died (p. 283).

61. On Litta see Luigi Passerini, "Necrologia di Pompeo Litta," Appendix to *Archivio storico italiano* 9 (1853); Bernardino Bianchi, *Pompeo Litta* (Milan: Redaelli, 1856); Giovanni Scardovelli, *Il conte Pompeo Litta-Biumi* (Bologna: Stabilimento tipografico Zamorani e Albertazzi, 1891); and Vittorio Cian, "Un genealogista patriotta," *Miscellanea d'erudizione*, vol. 1 (1905), Supplement to Fascicle 2, pp. 7–18.

62. New firms included Treves in 1861, Bietti in 1868, Hoepli in 1871, Baldini and Castoldi in 1872.

63. Luigi Passerini, "I Malatesta di Rimini," *tavola XIII* in *Dispensa 161* (Milan: Tipografia delle famiglie italiane, 1869) of Pompeo Litta, *Famiglie celebri italiane* or *Storia delle famiglie celebri d'Italia* (Milan: Tipografia delle famiglie italiane, 1819–74, *Dispense* 1–176; and Turin: F. Bassadonna, 1875–83, *Dispense* 177–84):

> [Polissena] morì il dì I giugno 1449, assai probabilmente di pestilenza: abbenchè sia stato scritto che l'infedele consorte la facesse strangolare per punirla delle sue infedeltà. Anche a queso proposito vuol notarsi che i rapporti tra Sigismondo e lo Sforza restarono per alcun tempo benevoli, e che giammai fu parlato di questa tragedia nei gravami che il suocero in seguito messe più volte in campo per dolersi del genero; il quale certamente non l'avrebbe scordata se pur fosse avvenuta, nè avrebbe gettato all'infelice Malatesta la tavola di salvezza quando stava per perdere quel poco che gli restava del proprio stato.

Passerini pointedly concludes:

> I sudditi non per tanto l'amarono perchè li sgravò di alcune imposte; perchè il suo governo, per quanto aspro e disastroso, era assai più umano di quello che pesava sulle limitrofe terre soggette alla Chiesa; perchè infine splendido e magnifico in tutto, fece fiorire in Rimini le lettere, le scienze, le arti.

64. Werner Kaegi, *Jacob Burckhardt*, vol. 2: *Das Erlebnis der geschichtlichen*

Welt, and vol. 3: *Die Zeit der klassischen Werke* (Basel-Stuttgart: Benno Schwabe, 1950 and 1956). Note that Burckhardt did not visit Rimini during his 1845 journey to Italy or during subsequent journeys until August 1878 (Kaegi, vol. 3, p. 485; vol. 4, pp. 448, 452–56). Burckhardt knew of the town and the church only through published works, particularly the *Commentarii* of Pius II, whose influence is apparent in his quotation of the inscription on Isotta's tomb— a quotation not of the inscription itself, but of Pius II's abbreviated citation. On this see chapter 1, pp. 34–35.

65. Jacob Burckhardt, *The Civilization of the Renaissance in Italy,* tr. S. G. C. Middlemore (New York: Harper & Row, 1958), pp. 50 (unscrupulousness), 235 (monster), 442 (verdict of history).

66. On the libraries see Nikolaus Pevsner, *A History of Building Types* (Princeton: Princeton University Press, 1976), pp. 106–9. The Bibliothèque Nationale owed much to the reading room of the British Library, with its great dome of glass and iron (1854–56), which in turn was perhaps influenced by the dome of the Coal Exchange (1847–49, by J. B. Brunning). An example of how dramatically the new library removed spatio-temporal constraints is offered by the case of the German professor Heinrich Leo who, writing around 1830, complained that he was unable to locate a copy of Clementini's history of Rimini (1617, 1627), which by then had become extremely rare. Now, however, such a work was readily available to anyone living in the metropolitan capitals of London, Paris, or Berlin.

67. Ministère de l'Éducation Nationale, *Catalogue général des livres imprimés de la Bibliothèque Nationale* (Paris: Imprimerie Nationale, 1897–1981). This work was published over such an extended period of time that it seems best to summarize its information in the form of a convenient table (see table 2, p. 104).

68. On the Milanese *Archivio di stato* in this period see Nicola Raponi, "Per la storia dell'Archivio di stato di Milano: erudizione e cultura nell'*Annuario* del Fumi (1909–19)," *Rassegna degli archivi di stato* 31 (1971), pp. 313–33, which cites the antecedent literature on the archive on p. 314 n. 1, and on Fumi on p. 317 n. 4. Also see Alfo R. Natale, "Milano," in Piero d'Angiolini, Claudio Pavone (eds.), *Guida generale degli archivi di stato italiani,* vol. 2 (Rome: Ministero per i beni culturali e ambientali, 1983), pp. 897–907, with bibliography on p. 901. The first director was Luigi Osio (director 1852–73), the second Cesare Cantù (director 1873–95).

69. The data on railroads is drawn from Sergio Romano, *Storia d'Italia dal risorgimento ai nostri giorni* (Milan: Mondadori, 1978), pp. 40–41, who reports it from the standard source, ISTAT (ed.), *Sommario di statistiche storiche dell' Italia 1861–1955* (Rome: Istituto di statische, 1976). Information on Rimini and tourism is given by Niveo Matteini, *Rimini, i suoi dintorni, la riviera di Romagna* (Rocca San Casciano-Bologna: Capelli, 1963); Luigi Silvestrini, *Un secolo di vita balneare al lido di Rimini* (Rimini: Tip. Garattoni, 1965); Touring

Club Italiano, *Emilia-Romagna*, 5th edn. (Milan: Touring Club Italiano, 1971), p. 691; Angelo Turchini, "Bagni e sviluppo della città (1875–1915)," *Storie e storia: quaderni dell'istituto storico della resistenza e della guerra di liberazione del circondario di Rimini*, no. 7 (September 1979), pp. 135–56; and Giulio Cesare Mengozzi, *Cronache balneari riminesi* (Rimini: Bruno Ghigi Editore, 1976).

70. On Baedeker and Tauchnitz see Paul Fussell, *Abroad: British Literary Traveling Between the Wars* (Oxford: Oxford University Press, 1980), pp. 61–62. There is no study of the larger deluxe travel books, due to the general lack of interest in publishing history, though anyone who works in the period will recognize the description.

71. Symonds *Sketches and Studies*, pp. 22, 31. (See note 45.)

72. "The more picturesque pieces" and "the use of travelers" are from Symonds's "Prefatory Note" to the Tauchnitz edition; both quotations and the information on the Berenson copy are given by Paul Fussell (see n. 70), pp. 61–62.

73. Charles Yriarte, *Les Bords de l'Adriatique* (Paris: Hachette, 1878), pp. 525–36 on Rimini, quotation on p. 533. (His journey by train from Ravenna to Rimini is recounted on p. 526.) Yriarte registers precisely the process of producing "cultural images" on p. 533: "C'est l'église de San Francesco [de Rimini], assez peu connue en somme, très-peu reproduite, si peu, que nous avons dû renoncer à en trouver les photographies dans toute l'Italie, et faire faire à Rimini même dix clichés différents par M. Trevisani, afin de pouvoir un jour l'illustrer, après avoir cherché les documents d'archives." The rapid production of images permits the stabilization of the intellectual itinerary that corresponds with both a geographic route and a cultural history. A series of images becomes a pilgrimage through both specific locales and a terrain of history. Indeed, the relationship between the travel and historical itineraries is very clear, as the same family of images appears in both genres. Thus in *Les Bords* we find engravings of the bridge of Tiberius and the arch of Augustus on pp. 529, 531; the same objects are then reproduced in the biography of Sigismondo on pp. 57, 60. The photographs produced by Trevisani serve for the biography as well, for example on p. 196. Thus a stable family of images is created, which varies little from work to work. For example, Yriarte's *Les Bords* is accompanied by seven engravings, while Jackson's *The Shores* (see note 74) is furnished with eight; but at the core of both sets is the same nucleus of four images: the piazza of Julius Caesar, now *Piazza dei Tre Martiri* (Yriarte, p. 527; Jackson, p. 520); the bridge of Tiberius (Yriarte, p. 531; Jackson, facing p. 243); the so-called Rocca (Yriarte, p. 533, Jackson, facing p. 245); and of course the church of San Francesco (Yriarte p. 534; Hamilton, facing p. 248). The variant scenes are those with "local" color: Yriarte chooses the port and its boats (p. 535), while Jackson shows horses drinking at the fountain in Piazza Cavour (p. 252). Moreover, such works suggest how an image created *by* the metropolitan centers is then inter-

nalized by the inhabitants of the peripheral country (as Italy then was), for Yriarte's *Les Bords* is translated into Italian and undergoes at least two editions (Milan: Treves, 1883 and 1897).

74. F[rederick]. Hamilton Jackson, *The Shores of the Adriatic, the Italian Side: An Architectural and Archaeological Pilgrimage* (London: John Murray, 1906), p. [v].

75. Edward Hutton, *Sigismondo Pandolfo Malatesta, Lord of Rimini: A Study of a XV Century Despot*. (London: Dent, 1906; New York: Dutton, 1906). (This work was revised and reissued in 1926 under a new title, *The Mastiff of Rimini: Chronicles of the House of Malatesta* [London: Methuen].) See also Edward Hutton, *The Cities of Romagna and the Marches* (London: Methuen, 1913); this was given a second edition in 1925, and both the first and second editions were printed in simultaneous American editions by Macmillan, New York. On Beltramelli's activity for the *Corriere della sera*, see R. Bertacchini, "Beltramelli, Antonio," *Dizionario biografico degli italiani*, vol. 8 (Rome: Istituto della Enciclopedia Italiana, 1966), pp. 56–60. His travel books include *Ravenna, la taciturna* (Florence: Alinari, 1908), *Attraverso la Svezia* (Rocca San Casciano: Capelli, 1908), *L'Arno* (Florence: Alinari, 1909), *Il diario di un viandante: dal deserto al Mar Glaciale* (Milan: Treves, 1911), and *Paesi di conquista* (Ferrara: A. Taddei, 1915).

76. Yriarte wrote nine books of art history, including biographies or studies of Goya, Gavarni, Millet, Civitale, Tissot, Fortuny, Paolo Veronese, and Masaccio, as well as a study on the Parthenon. Edward Hutton wrote five art historical books on Hogarth, Perugino, the Sienese school of painting, the Cosmati workers of Rome, and representations of Christ in Italian painting; he also edited the history of Italian art by Crowe and Cavalcaselle and translated another history of Italian art by Adolfo Venturi. Moreover, his numerous guidebooks were keenly oriented toward art history; his *Cities of Umbria*, for example, was subtitled *An Account of the Artistic Features of Umbrian Cities*. As for Frederick Hamilton Jackson, he wrote studies titled *Intarsia and Marquetry* (London: Sands & Co., 1903) and *Mural Painting* (London: Sands & Co., 1904) and served as vice president of the Society of Designers. Finally, one notes that both Beltramelli and Hutton wrote books on Ravenna, and that both Jackson and Yriarte gave the city extensive treatment in their books on the shores of the Adriatic.

The titles of Hutton's art historical books are: *Perugino* (London: Duckworth, 1907), *William Hogarth* (London: International Art Publishing, [1908]), *The Sienese School in the National Gallery* (London: Medici Society, 1923), *The Life of Christ in the Old Italian Masters* (London: Chatto & Windus, 1935), and *The Cosmati: The Roman Marble Workers of the XIIth and XIIIth Centuries* (London: Routledge and Kegan Paul, 1950). His editions and translations are Joseph Crowe and Cavalcaselle, *A New History of Painting in Italy* (London: J. M. Dent, 1908–9), and a translation of Adolfo Venturi, *A Short History of Italian Art* (London: Macmillan, 1926).

77. Symonds, *Sketches*, p. 17.

78. On Yriarte in Italy and his liberal activities see Angelo de Gubernatis, *Dizionario biografico degli scrittori contemporanei* (Florence: Le Monnier, 1879), p. 1075. For further sources regarding his life, see chapter 3, note 20. For his use of Burckhardt see Charles Yriarte, *Un Condottiere au XVᵉ siècle. Rimini: Études sur les lettres et les artes à la cour des Malatesta* (Paris: Jules Rothschild, 1882). On p. 74 he cites Burckhardt's judgment: "Burckhardt le compte parmi les initiateurs de l'humanisme." On p. 77 he gives a French translation of another passage by "Jacques" Burckhardt.

79. Yriarte, *Un Condottiere*, pp. 373–451, offers a massive appendix of notes and documentary transcriptions, the latter executed quite poorly with gross errors in attributions and dating as well; on some of these errors see chapter 3, pp. 179–86. On p. 153 n. 1 he explicitly cites the Bibliothèque Nationale's copy of Mazzuchelli, and one can safely assume that he read the others there as well. On p. 196 he states that the engraving presented on this page is based on a photograph made by Trevisani; in *Les Bords*, p. 533, he recounts how he paid Trevisani to take photographs for him in preparation for a possible book. See the quotation in note 73.

80. Yriarte's discussion of the murder accusation appears in two places, pp. 162–63 and 288–89. He attests to his faith in Clementini on p. 138, calling him an "historien austère." On p. 163 he explains the distinctive feature in the murder charge: "on va jusqu'à désigne l'instrument du crime; et Clementini dit qu'il l'étrangla avec une serviette qu'il serra étroitement autour de son cou." And on p. 288 he concludes: "La meurtre de la Sforza est plus probable, à cause des détails pratiques donnés par Clementini."

81. Yriarte, *Un Condottiere*, p. 163:

> Il est très singulier, et cette circonstance est toute à l'honneur d'Isotta, que pas un des historiens ou chroniqueurs, en vertu de l'axiome célèbre *is fecit cui prodest*, n'ait accusé la maîtresse de Sigismond de complicité. Il semblait que, libre de toute chaîne, le seigneur de Rimini eût voulu secouer le lien conjugal pour épouser Isotta; mais nous voyons que six années après, il n'avait pas encore accompli le voeu de sa maîtresse; il faudrait donc, si on persistait à accuser de ce nouveau crime, lui en laisser la responsabilité tout entière.

It needs to be said that Yriarte was not actually drawing on all the sources that he claims. His reference to a *Genealogie* by Litta is a makeshift recollection, and his allusion to a *Vie de Sigismonde* by Pius II is pure bluff. The real source behind Yriarte's passage on p. 163 emerges from his footnote at the bottom of the page, which ostensibly cites Clementini:

> I.—"Si disse che morisse con un asciugatoio alvoltole [*sic*] strettemente [*sic*] al collo."—Clementini.

Textual collation, however, shows that he is not quoting from Clementini (vol. 2, p. 363), whose text reads "asciugatoio *involto* al collo," but from Mazzuchelli

(p. 7), whose text reads "asciugatoio *avvoltole strettamente* al collo." Thus the reference is a bluff: the sentence ascribed to Clementini is from Mazzuchelli, the only author whose name is *not* mentioned on this page. From Mazzuchelli, too, derives Yriarte's reference to the chronicle of "Alessandro de Rimini" (Mazzuchelli, p. 7 n. 12), along with his reference to Pius. Yriarte did, no doubt, consult Clementini at various points in his work, but he was not doing so here, as he claimed, and it is unlikely that he ever consulted either the chronicle of pseudo-Alessandro or Pius II except through Mazzuchelli's citations. More important, however, is the influence of the sources here. Essentially his portrait of Isotta stems from the pre-Romantic view of Mazzuchelli as sharpened by the more overt Romanticism of Moroni (whom he does cite on p. 155). On his use of Moroni for his portrait of Isotta see chapter 3, pp. 169–71; for now suffice it to note how Moroni's religious view of Isotta is assimilated to Yriarte's aestheticism and conservatism, and how sharply this differs from Passerini's rejection of the charges. Yriarte had been horrified by the experience of the Commune, which he witnessed at first hand, and afterward turned increasingly conservative with Orleanist leanings. See his *Les Prussiens à Paris et le 18 Mars* (Paris: H. Plon, 1871) and *Les Princes d'Orléans* (Paris: H. Plon, 1872).

82. Pasquale Villari, "Rimini," *Encyclopaedia Britannica*, 9th edn. (Edinburgh: A. & C. Black, 1886), vol. 20, pp. 558–60, on p. 557; and 11th edn. (1911), vol. 23, pp. 344–47, on p. 345.

83. F[rederick]. Hamilton Jackson, *True Stories of the Condottieri* (London: Sands, 1903), p. 253.

84. Hutton, *Sigismondo*, p. 196 n. 1. Hutton, *Romagna*, p. 110. In *Sigismondo*, pp. 195–96, within the fictional portion of the work Hutton underscores his view with a Nietzschean twist on the Burckhardtian motifs; his fictional narrator comments on the claim that Sigismondo has declined to engage in battle with Sforza in 1449 because fearful of possible vengeance: "Such is the world which, envying a great man his force and genius ascribes to him every abomination that mediocrity may imagine."

85. André Maurel, *Petites villes d'Italie, IIᵉ série: Émilie–Marches–Ombrie*, 10th edn. (Paris: Hachette, 1920), pp. 152–53. Ermolao Rubieri, *Francesco I Sforza*, vol. 1 (Florence: Le Monnier, 1876), p. 201.

86. Luigi Tonini, *Della storia civile e sacra riminese*, vol. 5, p. 205. (See note 20.)

87. Antonio Beltramelli, *Un tempio d'amore* (Palermo: Remo Sandron, 1912), p. 38, "due misere creature che trascorrono breve tempo alla corte di Rimini e muoiono senza aver conosciuto la gioia"; and p. 50, "Ella visse lunghissimo tempo al fianco di Sigismondo eppure non una volta fu incolpata di avere avuto parte nei delitti ch'egli commise." The reference to "Ginevra Sforza" appears on the same page. What Beltramelli finds especially praiseworthy in Isotta is interesting. For him: "it is in this complete surrender of her spirit and her life, in this unlimited loss of the self, in this blind faith that she had placed in a

man accused, if not guilty, of having killed at age 22 his first wife, Ginevra Sforza [*sic*]—in this fierce and passionate love is all her greatness." Or in the original: "e in questa compiuta dedizione dell'anima e della vita sua, in questo dimenticarsi illimitato, in questa cieca fidanza ch'ella aveva posto in un uomo incolpato, anche se non colpevole, di avere ucciso a 22 anni la sua prima moglie, Ginevra Sforza [*sic*], in questo passionato e fiero amore è tutta la grandezza di lei."

88. Giovanni Soranzo, "Un'invettiva della Curia Romana contro Sigismondo Malatesta" [part 1], *La Romagna* 7 (1910), pp. 462–89; [part 2], *La Romagna* 8 (1911), pp. 150–175; [part 3], *La Romagna* 8 (1911), pp. 241–288.

89. On Soranzo (1881–1963) see Anton Maria Bettanini, "Giovanni Soranzo," *Atti della Accademia Patavina di Scienze, Lettere ed Arti*, 75 (1963–64), pp. 49–54; and Piero Zerbi, "Giovanni Soranzo," in Università cattolica del Sacro Cuore, *Annuario per l'anno accademico 1963–1964* (Milan: Società editrice vita e pensiero, 1964), pp. 431–36, including a bibliography of his works. Soranzo taught in the *liceo* of Thiene and Padua before taking up his position in Rimini from 1906 to 1911. From 1911 on he taught at the *Istituto magistrale* in Padua as professor of medieval and modern history. In 1921 he accepted a position in the faculty of social sciences at the newly founded *Università cattolica* in Milan, though he retained his position and home in Padua. See Giovanni Soranzo, "Di una cronaca sconosciuta del secolo XV e del suo anonimo autore," *Nuovo archivio veneto*, new series, vol. 13, part 1 (1907), pp. 68–101. Soranzo discusses a chronicle that he had discovered and appeals to others for help on p. 69: "giacchè temo che a me, lontano per dovere professionale da un centro cospicuo di studi, possano sfuggire notizie magari preziosissime, e quindi mi sia reso impossibile di preparare con sollecitudine e con diligenza l'edizione di questa cronaca." He signs and dates the article from Rimini, 9 January 1907.

90. Soranzo, "Un'invettiva" [part 1], p. 463, "non sufficientemente provate o addirittura ingiustificate"; and p. 464, "rendere meno severo e meno ingiusto il giudizio degli storici moderni intorno alla figura di Sigismondo Pandolfo Malatesta."

91. Soranzo, "Un'invettiva" [part 2], pp. 169–75 for his discussion of the allegation.

92. Vincenzo Nolfi, *Historia di Fano*, RBCG, ms. 114, fol. 103, "in quell'influenza che si fé sentir anche in Rimini," as cited by Massèra (ed.), *Cron. mal.*, pp. 128–29 n. 16. Soranzo cites simply "più copie nella Federiciana e nell-'Arch[ivio]. Comunale [di Fano]," in Soranzo, "Un'invettiva" [part 2], p. 172 n. 1. More precisely, the *Biblioteca Federiciana* in Fano contains four complete manuscripts (Nolfi's autograph and three copies), as well as one fragmentary transcription. On these see Albano Sorbelli, *Inventari dei manoscritti delle biblioteche d'Italia*, vol. 38 (Florence: Leo S. Olschki, 1928), p. 61 (no. 80; Nolfi's autograph), and vol. 51 (Florence: Leo S. Olschki, 1932), pp. 27–30 (nos. 16, 18, 20, the three complete copies; no. 17, the fragmentary transcription).

93. Soranzo, "Un'invettiva" [part 2], pp. 172 and 172 n. 2, on Nolfi's claim and council records; p. 174 on Broglio. Broglio, p. 147 (see note 18); Polissena's death is reported on p. 160, but no cause is given. At the time when Soranzo wrote, the chronicle was unpublished except for a few quotations given by earlier writers.

94. Massèra (ed.), Cron. mal., pp. 128–29, n. 16.

95. Soranzo, "Un'invettiva" [part 2], pp. 174–75.

96. Luigi Fumi, "L'atteggiamento di Francesco Sforza verso Sigismondo Malatesta in una sua istruzione del 1462, con paticolari sulla morte violenta della figlia Polissena," Archivio storico lombardo 40 (1913), pp. 170–80.

97. Gregorio Giovanardi, O. F. M., "Un frate minore martire del sigillo sacramentale a Rimini nel secolo XV," Studi Francescani 1 (1914), pp. 349–67.

98. Giovanni Soranzo, "Due delitti attribuiti a Sigismondo Malatesta e una falsa cronachetta riminese," Atti del R. Istituto Veneto di scienze, lettere ed arti 74 (1914–15), part 2, pp. 1881–1902, with discussion of Sforza's motives on p. 1885, "un abile pretesto." Apparently Soranzo failed to see the chronological relations between Sforza's letter and the various battle communications discussed earlier in this chapter.

99. Gregorio Giovanardi, "Cronaca del P. Alessandro Righetti, Minore Conv[entuale]., scritta su pergamena nel 1532," Studi francescani 2 (1915–16), pp. 29–40, 177–208. See the remarkable footnote by Giovanardi beginning on p. 191 n. 2 and extending to p. 200, and the footnote on the death of Polissena beginning on p. 201 n. 1. See also his further arguments in Gregorio Giovanardi, "Ancora sul martire del sigillo sacramentale a Rimini," Studi francescani 3–6 (1916–20), pp. 3–31; and "Replica del P. Giovanardi," Studi francescani 7 (1921), pp. 278–88.

100. Giovanni Soranzo, "Ancora sulla Cronaca del presunto P. Alessandro Righetti," Atti del R. Istituto Veneto di scienze, lettere ed arti 76 (1916–17), part 2, pp. 323–34; and "Ultima mia parola sul martire del sigillo sacramentale a Rimini," Studi francescani 7 (1921), pp. 268–78.

101. Piero Parodi, "Nicodemo Tranchedini da Pontremoli genealogista degli Sforza," cited in note 8. Tranchedini was in Sforza's service for quite some time before 1435, when he is listed as his cancelliere. For sources on his life, again see Parodi, p. 335 n. 2.

102. Massèra (ed.), Cron. mal., pp. 128–29, n. 16.

103. Phillip J. Jones, The Malatesta of Rimini and the Papal State: A Political History (Cambridge: Cambridge University Press, 1974), pp. 201–2. Jones states in his preface, dated July 1973: "This work was originally written, some twenty years ago, as a doctoral thesis in the University of Oxford" (p. vii). It should be noted that Soranzo's views did not carry the field immediately. In fact they were opposed by a major authority, Corrado Ricci, whose magisterial volume on the Tempio Malatestiano appeared in 1924. Eager to retain key elements in the late Romantic interpretation of Sigismondo and the Tempio, Ricci sought

to preserve the traditional reading of the cipher *S* entwined with *I* (see chapter 3), as well as the charge about the murder of Polissena. In a footnote he addressed Soranzo's claims: "The variety or the inconsistency of certain details [in the allegations] and the fact that Francesco Sforza availed himself of the story in a moment useful for his political ends are not, it seems to us, sufficient to weaken the substantial truth of the fact affirmed by so many contemporaries." See Corrado *Ricci, Il tempio malatestiano* (Milan-Rome: Bestetti & Tumminelli, n.d. [but 1924]; rpt., Rimini: Bruno Ghigi Editore, 1974), p. 30 n. 12. The passage where Ricci reports her death in the text proper is also important for subsequent debate (p. 24): "And Polissena? Alas, Polissena was destined to a quite different form of humiliation [from what Isotta's father suffered]; she was destined to die a little later (1 June 1449), suffocated at the orders of Sigismondo, in the monastery of Scolca, in the sweet solitude of the suburban hills where she had retired in order to flee the plague and be distant from Isotta."

Scholarly consensus notwithstanding, popular tradition continues to report the timeworn accusations. See for example, Alberto Ricci, *Sigismondo e Isotta (gli ultimi Malatesta)* (Milan: Edizioni Athena, 1929), pp. 62–63, who ignores the entire debate from 1910 to 1924, and who borrows heavily from Yriarte. Of course the *Encyclopaedia Britannica* in its 1929 edition reprinted the article from its 1886 edition, rehearsing the same charges. And tourists toting Michelin green guidebooks to Italy can still read, when they reach Rimini, how Sigismondo "repudiated his first wife, poisoned his second, and strangled his third, and then made an irregular marriage with his favorite mistress Isotta" (1981 edition, p. 198).

104. See Ezra Pound, "Paris Letter: January, 1922," *Dial* 72. 2 (February 1922), p. 192. See Ezra Pound to John Quinn, 10 August 1922; NYPL, *MD*, JQP, Box 34, f. 4; and to Dorothy Shakespear, 29 July 1922; BLUI, *PM.3*, 1922. For Pound's long-standing interest in the Renaissance, see his first publication in prose, "Raphaelite Latin," *Book News Monthly* 25.1 (September, 1906), pp. [31]–34. From the London period see Ezra Pound, "Patria Mia," published in eleven installments in *The New Age* from 12 September to 14 November 1912, reprinted in *SP*, pp. 99–141; and Ezra Pound, "The Renaissance," published in three installments in *Poetry* 5.5 (February 1915), 5.6 (March 1915), and 6.2 (May 1915), reprinted in *LE*, pp. 214–26. For Pound, ideas of the Renaissance were never far removed from assessments of cultural life in the United States, as is clear from the titles of these two essays. "Patria Mia" turns out to contain some of Pound's most extended remarks on the Italian Renaissance, while "The Renaissance" contains Pound's evaluation of the contemporary scene. And the same nexus also recurs in January 1922: when he considers a canto on the Renaissance, he also plans another canto on the United States. Sometime in the second half of 1921, for example, Pound writes autograph notes on the back of a letter from William Carlos Williams, dated 4 January 1921: one jotting records a plan for "Canto X" to treat "Civ[ilization].

Am[erican]." (See William Carlos Williams to Ezra Pound, 4 January 1921; BLSUNY, *PC*.) A few months later, on 13 January 1922, when he sends a draft of Canto VIII to Ford Maddox Ford for criticism, he adds a letter mentioning his "hope to confine" future cantos "to American language from now on." (But this may be only an ironic comment on the lush diction so characteristic of this canto.) See Ezra Pound to Ford Maddox Ford, 13 January [1922]; published in Brita Lindberg-Seyersted (ed.), *Pound/Ford: The Story of a Literary Friendship* (New York: New Directions, 1982), p. 63.

105. "We are planning to get to Italy in April, if nothing prevents[;] trying a new slice, Perugia, and Siena, the middle bit": Ezra Pound to "Grandmother" [Mary Weston], 3 February 1922; NHBY, *PA*, Series 2, Box 52, f. 1967. "[I] HAVE bought the Baedeker, so don't worry about that": Ezra Pound to Agnes Bedford, 16 March 1922; BLUI, *PM.2*, Bedford, 1922.

106. On Pound's use of Beltramelli see chapter 1, pp. 30–32, 37–47. The relative rarity of the book makes it likely it was purchased in Rimini, where perhaps it was sold at a tourist stand near the Tempio itself. In a letter dated 15 September 1922, Pound states that he does not recall having seen a bookstore when he visited Rimini, making it likely that he bought the book at the church itself. See Ezra Pound to [Aldo Francesco Massèra], 15 September 1922; RBCG, *Fondo amministrativo*, 1921–24: Pound reports his visit to the city in May, then adds, "Ma non ritegno il nome ni indirizzo di libreria alcuna" [*sic*].

107. On Pound's travels and drafts, see appendix 2. The passages quoted from Draft *A* are respectively lines 18, 54, 69, and 75. His doubts about the charges regarding Ginevra are registered in lines 72 and 95. Beltramelli's view of Isotta's patience appears in the passages cited in note 87.

108. *N1*, notes 1, 2.1, 3, 4, listing topics of interest. The one on Polissena is note 4. It should be added that neither Symonds nor Beltramelli mentions Polissena's illegitimate birth, the subject of Pound's note; some of the factual information in Draft *A* clearly comes from the lost reading notes designated *Nα*, as we have seen, and these apparently contained notes from Symonds and another source that has not been identified.

109. Heinrich Leo, *Storia degli stati italiani* (Florence: Società Editrice Fiorentina, vol. 1, 1840; vol. 2, 1842), tr. Eugenio Albèri and Adolfo A. Loewe from the original German work published in five volumes, *Geschichte der italienischen Staaten* (Hamburg: Friedrich Pethes, 1829–37). On Heinrich Leo see Christoph Freiherr von Maltzahn, *Heinrich Leo (1799–1878): Ein politisches Gelehrtenleben zwischen Romantischem Konservatismus und Realpolitik* (Göttingen: Vandenhoeck & Ruprecht, 1979). On Albèri see F. Fronzi, "Eugenio Albèri," *Dizionario biografico degli italiani*, vol. 1 (Rome: Istituto dell' Enciclopedia Italiana, 1963), pp. 634–36; see also the massive apologetic by Giorgio Cucentroli, *Eugenio Albèri* (Florence: Associazione artistico-letteraria internazionale, 1970). Nothing whatever is known about the other translator, Adolfo A.

Loewe, who clearly worked under Albèri's direction. His only published work is a *Regolamento per la Società filarmonica di Firenze* (Florence, 1833), which I have not examined. A critical edition of Pound's notes taken from Leo appears in Lawrence S. Rainey, "The Earliest Manuscripts of the Malatesta Cantos by Ezra Pound" (diss., University of Chicago, 1986), pp. 422–63, with a discussion of them on pp. 129–47.

110. The *Cronaca* (*Chronica* is Leo's spelling, copied by Pound) is cited by Leo nineteen times, all in the course of Book 8 on the history of the papal state (all references appear in vol. 2, pp. 25–79), and one of his citations appears just below a passage registered by Pound in his reading notes (*N1*, 18; the citation is in vol. 2, p. 37, col. b, n. 2), making it clear that Leo is his source here.

111. The first fascicle of the Massèra edition (fascicle 184, published in 1922) covered only events up through August of 1440; all the events regarding Polissena (from her betrothal in 1441 to her death in 1449) are treated in the second fascicle (fascicle 201, published in 1924). For a full citation of the edition see note 8.

112. The peculiarity of Pound's citation of Clementini indicates that he is drawing on Leo's only mention of Clementini (vol. 2, pp. 63–64 n. 3), in which Leo notes that Le Bret (his source at this moment) "scrive principalmente dietro l'autorità del Clementini, *Istoria de' Malatesti*, opera che io non possego." But Leo's comment (and Pound's note) present a version of the book's title that differs greatly from the original, *Raccolto istorico della fondatione di Rimino, e dell'origine e vite de' Malatesti*. This is because Leo's reference to Clementini derives from Johann Friedrich Le Bret (1732–1807), *Geschichte von Italien und allen allda gegründeten alten und neuren Staaten* (Halle, 1778–87), ten books published in seven installments as volumes 40–46 of the *Algemeine Welthistorie von Abbeginn der Welt bis auf gegenwartige Zeit* (Halle, 1744–91), where reference to Clementini is made in vol. 45, p. 311 n. *c: Clementini Storia di Rimini*. Alas, the work of Le Bret was also not quite original: it was a translation/adaptation of a British behemoth entitled *An Universal History from the Earliest Account of Time to the Present, Compiled from the Original Authors*, which went through at least eight different editions ranging from seven to sixty-seven volumes between 1736 and 1768. In short, the title that reached Pound was the consequence of a long process of transmission: from the original work by Clementini (1617, 1627) to the British *Universal History* (ca. 1750), to its translation/adaptation by Le Bret in German (1759–67), to Leo (1829–37) and thence to the Italian translation of Leo by Albèri (1840, 1842)—which Pound was consulting in June of 1922! Little wonder that Pound would have difficulty finding the book when he returned to Paris.

Yet even when he had managed to locate it, his understanding of it was also conditioned by other sources that he was reading concurrently. A sign of this appears in an entry made sometime between 30 October and 15 November

1922, when Pound drew up a list of "BOOKS WANTED," which he sent to various booksellers in London and Florence (NHBY, *PA*, Series 5, Box 63, f. 2430.7; formerly 40.7). Item eight on his list reads:

> Clementini. C. Raccolto istorico, della origine e vita dei Malatesti, Rimini. 1617.

Here too the title differs from the original, again because it has been mediated through yet another work, in this case the bibliography given by Soranzo, *Pio II*, p. 516. (This version of the title eliminates all reference to the city of Rimini, and instead mentions only the "lives" of the Malatesta family members—harmonizing with Pound's belief that Renaissance history was best understood as a setting for "the most living individuals," as he expressed it in January 1922.)

113. Clementini himself had assumed the cost of publishing and binding the book, and the total number of copies must have been five hundred or less. By 1719, less than a century after publication, one writer said that Clementini's volumes were "eagerly sought after, even by foreigners" ("avidamente cercate, anche dagli Oltramontani") and added that they had reached "a price much higher than their size would warrant" ("un prezzo di gran lunga superiore a quello, che converrebbe alla lore mole"); see "N. N." (cited note 50), p. 95. In 1744 another writer described his work as "rara"; see Anonymous (cited note 50) in the "Tavola degli autori delle lettere . . . ," pp. xii–xx. By around 1830 Leo confessed that he could not locate a copy (see note 112); and by 1884 Carlo Tonini described the two volumes as "rarissimi," obtainable only at a "carissimo prezzo." See Carlo Tonini, *La Coltura letteraria e scientifica in Rimini dal secolo XIV ai primordi del XIX* (Rimini: tip. Albertini, 1884), vol. 2, p. 138.

114. The hand of the note is not Pound's, and remains unidentified, though the writer is clearly English. A statement of account dated 31 December 1922 also shows that Pound ordered other books from Hoepli when he was in Paris throughout the period July–November 1922; see NHBY, *PA*, Series 5, Box 63, f. 2430.10 (formerly 40.10). Also, in a letter dated 15 September 1922, Pound complains that "Hoepli of Milan does not seem to be able to find the books very quickly." For its location, see note 106.

115. Bride Scratton to Ezra Pound, 7 July 1922, apparently quoting a missing letter from Pound; NHBY, *BP*, Series 1, f. 3. His activities in this period were extremely heterogeneous: on 6 July he received a visit from Paul Morand, coming to check the final revisions on Pound's translation of his *Ouvert la nuit*; on 11 July he hosted an exhibition of paintings by Tami Koumé; on 13 July he saw off his wife Dorothy on her trip to England, was visited by Francis Bacon, and dined with Louis Berman; and on 16 July he wrote a raft of letters to catch up on his correspondence.

116. Pound's reading of the chronicle is inferred from a passage in Fragment *a*, lines 21–22, where he briefly recounts an incident that is otherwise reported only by Lazzaro Bernabei, *Cronache anconitane*, in C. Ciavarini, ed., *Collezione di documenti storici antichi inediti ed editi rari delle città e terre marchigiane*

(Ancona: Tipografia del Commercio, 1870), vol. 1, p. 167. Bernabei's work, a 1492 redaction of earlier chronicles, reports a story from 1445, when Sigismondo is trapped within the city gate of Ancona and exchanges comments with an enemy soldier. (The incident is apocryphal, since Sigismondo himself did not attack Ancona in that year under the circumstances described by Bernabei; it is nevertheless retained in the final version of the Malatesta Cantos, in ND70[10] 8.126 –34.) Pound's use of Bernabei was first pointed out by Ben K. Kimpel and T. C. Duncan Eaves, "Pound's Research for the Malatesta Cantos," *Paideuma* 11 (1982), p. 412 and p. 412 n. 27). Pound's notes taken while reading Bernabei have not survived.

117. Ezra Pound to Dorothy Shakespear Pound, 20 July [1922]; BLUI, *PM.3*, 1922. The passage discussed by Pound here is found in Amiani, *Memorie istoriche*, vol. 1, p. 372. Pound's notes taken while reading Amiani are not preserved. There are, however, two later transcriptions of material derived from Amiani, which he evidently copied from his original notes, and which appear in manuscripts containing heterogeneous materials: NHBY, *PA*, Series 5, Box 63, f. 2430.6 (formerly 40.6), from October–November 1922; and f. 2436.3 (formerly 46.3), dated by Pound, "Dec. 24" [1922]. Both the transcriptions refer to materials incorporated in the final version of the Malatesta Cantos.

118. Ezra Pound to Dorothy Shakespear Pound, 21 July [1922]; BLUI, *PM.3*, 1922.

119. This early set of notes on Yriarte has not survived; their character is inferred from several incidents recounted in Draft *C1*, all clearly derived from Yriarte, even though the draft itself was written before Pound received his copy of Yriarte on 3 August. The incidents appear in lines 6, 20–21, 53–58, and 65. (The date when Pound received his copy of Yriarte is discussed later.)

120. The transmission of this tradition is distinctive. Sources contemporary with Ginevra do not mention her location at the time of her death. However, the anonymous *Cronaca Malatestiana* mentions that her first child, Roberto Novello, died on 18 December 1438 "a Scolca, in caxa del Vescovato" (*Cron. mal.* p. 74). Apparently it was this passage that caught the attention of Charles Yriarte, who proceeded to make the villa into the setting for the death of Polissena as well. Yriarte stated this explicitly in a footnote, and also suggested it by reporting the infant's death at Scolca in a passage contiguous with another reporting Ginevra's death (Yriarte, *Un Condottiere*, p. 137–38, p. 220 n. 1). From Yriarte the mistake was transmitted to Edward Hutton, author of the historical novel on Sigismondo published in 1906 (see note 75). When Hutton treated the death of Ginevra he set a scene that was fraught with foreboding. His fictional narrator is depicted "returning towards Rimini by night, for it was very hot," when he decides to visit "Madonna Ginevra, who kept herself in close retreat at Scolca." The villa is situated in a valley ("the Villa lies in a pleasant valley among the woods," though in reality it is located on a hilltop). As the narrator enters "the wood [where] it was still very dark and close," he hears "a sound of

stirring leaves," draws off the path to "where the trees were thicker"—and in the dark, glimpses a figure who resembles Sigismondo, but is not clearly visible. The rest of the narration is predictable. He reaches the villa, is given breakfast, and then hears a scream as a maid rushes into the room and cries "Madonna is murdered" (Hutton, pp. 102–6). Needless to say, Hutton's place in the historiographical tradition is unique: no one else sets the scene so vividly or fully, or in terms that unmistakably suggest Pound's own phrase, "in the swamp."

Yet the setting is only one element in Pound's peculiar account of the deaths of Ginevra and Polissena; the other is his quotation of a phrase in Italian—"con voce di veleno." Ultimately the phrase derives from Clementini, who reports that Ginevra died "non senza sospetto di veleno." But Pound's reading notes on Clementini date from a period much later than this draft, and therefore the passage must have reached him through some intermediary source. Which one? Clementini's passage was not reported by Symonds, Beltramelli, Amiani, or Yriarte, sources that Pound possessed or had consulted by now. It is, however, reported by Hutton in his novel when he turns to discuss the charge that Sigismondo had murdered, not Ginevra this time, but his second wife Polissena—and it is exactly here that he quotes the entire passage from Clementini given earlier (see pp. 94 and 277 n. 49; Hutton, p. 196 n. 1). From the parallelism of Clementini, as reported by Hutton, Pound draws the phrase *col repudio* and anglicizes it to "repudiated"; then he takes the phrase *col veleno* and integrates it into his own creation "con voce di," a streamlined version of Clementini's "non senza sospetto di." And the suspicion that Pound knew the passage of Clementini through Hutton is corroborated by another source: Pound's own reading notes on Clementini, made only a few weeks after this draft. They show that although Pound recorded the fact of Polissena's death when he read about it in Clementini, he did not take notice of the phrase under discussion—for the obvious reason that he was already familiar with it through Hutton.

To summarize, Pound's passage in *C1* about Polissena's death emerged from an intricate history of transmission: the phrase in Italian ("con voce di veleno") had come from Pius II to Clementini to Hutton to Pound; and the report of "the swamp" descended from the 1449 chronicle to its 1729 edition to Yriarte to Hutton to Pound. In both cases, then, the immediate source was Edward Hutton's novel. Further, it is equally clear that in late July Pound was reading a copy of it that was not his own, for his quotations are vague and inexact. This is confirmed by another document, a letter of 29 August 1922, in which Pound inquires about purchasing a copy of the Hutton novel—making clear that as yet he did not own it. Ezra Pound to Dorothy Shakespear Pound, 29 August 1922; BLUI, *PM.3*, 1922: "*IF* you are in Charing X rd. stir up ole [Friedrich] Neumayer [the bookseller] to hunt for Rimini stuff. I shd. like the Hutton vol. if he can find it." Neither Pound's nor Dorothy's surviving letters mention Hutton's work before this, but it is apparent that some letters have been lost.

121. Ezra Pound to Agnes Bedford, 1 August 1922; BLUI, *PM.2*, Bedford, 1922; and Ezra Pound to Dorothy Shakespear Pound, [autograph note on envelope postmarked] 3 August 1922; BLUI, *PM.3*, 1922.

122. Ezra Pound, NHBY, *Ymn* 25 opposite Yriarte pp. 137–38. The horizontal line indicates a page break. For a preliminary discussion of the marginalia see Daniel Bornstein, "The Poet as Historian," *Paideuma* 10 (1981), pp. 283–91. He remarks, p. 281: "The most striking feature of these markings is that almost all of them call attention to Yriarte's sources." However, it should be noted that Pound's markings total 150, in contrast to the "75 or so" reported by Bornstein (p. 290). Bornstein cites only 26 of the markings and offers no critical transcription or systematic edition.

123. Regarding Clementini, see *Ymn* 14 opposite Yriarte p. 82 n. 1. Regarding Battaglini, see *Ymn* 26 opposite Yriarte p. 138 n. 26; and *Ymn* 128 on Yriarte p. 460 (part of an index made by Pound that refers back to earlier entries). Regarding Pius II, *Commentarii*, see *Ymn* 69 opposite Yriarte p. 287; and *Ymn* 147 on Yriarte p. [461] (another entry in Pound's own index). Regarding Mazzuchelli, see *Ymn* 9 opposite Yriarte p. 67 n. 1, and *Ymn* 40 opposite Yriarte p. 153 n. 1.

124. *Ymn* 44 and 45, opposite Yriarte pp. 155, 155 n. 1; and *Ymn* 144, on Yriarte p. [461] (an entry in Pound's index to his marginalia).

125. NHBY, *PA*, Series 5, Box 63, f. 2430.4 (formerly 40.4).

126. The town councils of Macerata (1441) and Recanati (1442), the anonymous chronicle of Rimini (1442), the *condotta* between Sigismondo and Francesco (1451), Broglio (ca. 1470), Simonetta (ca. 1475), the anonymous chronicle of the Biblioteca Concina, and the "Genealogy" of Nicodema Tranchedini (ca. 1480). (The last two are cited in note 8.)

127. NHBY, *PA*, Series 5, Box 63, f. 2432.5 (formerly 42.5; Clem. 4). The notes cited here were taken as Pound read Clementini, vol. 2, pp. 363–65. The reference is to the account by Girolamo Muzio, *Storia de' fatti di Federico di Montefeltro, duca d'Urbino* (Venice: Giovanni Battista Ciotti, 1605), a celebratory work commissioned by Guidobaldo II della Rovere.

128. Ezra Pound to Dorothy Shakespear Pound, 21 July 1922; BLUI, *PM.3*, 1922.

129. Ezra Pound to Dorothy Shakespear Pound, 29 July 1922; BLUI, *PM.3*, 1922.

130. Ezra Pound to Dorothy Shakespear Pound, [28 July 1922]; BLUI, *PM.3*, 1922. Pound's letter to Dorothy of 20 July shows that he had read as far as vol. 1, p. 386, which contains the last incident mentioned in his letter; the rest of the material on Sigismondo runs through p. 442, where the first volume ends, and some twenty pages of the second volume.

131. Ezra Pound to John Quinn, 10 August 1922; NYPL, *MD*, JQP, Box 34, f. 4.

132. NHBY, *PA*, Series 5, Box 63, f. 2432.18 (formerly 42.18), referring to Soranzo, *Pio II*, p. 227, where the discussion begins, and also quoting from Soranzo, p. 228.

133. NHBY, *PA*, Series 5, Box 63, f. 2432.7 (formerly 42.7; Clem. 5). The note is found opposite his reading notes on Clementini, vol. 2, pp. 268–370.

134. Ezra Pound to Dorothy Shakespear Pound, 29 August 1922; BLUI, *PM.3*, 1922.

135. Soranzo, *Pio II*, p. 230: "tutte le accuse e tutte le relative testimonianze contro Sigismondo facevan capo non ad argomenti e a prove di fato irrefragabili, ma alle dicerie che correvan tra il volgo, alla pubblica fama, fondamento di accusa molto instabile."

136. Draft *D1*, NHBY, *PA*, Series 5, Box 63, f. 2436.7 (formerly 46.7).

137. Draft *D2*, NHBY, *PA*, Series 5, Box 63, f. 2436.12 (formerly 46.12).

138. Draft *E*, NHBY, *PA*, Series 5, Box 63, f. 2443.5 (formerly 53.5).

139. Draft *G2*, NHBY, *PA*, Series 5, Box 63, f. 2439.3 (formerly 49.3).

140. Draft *H*, NHBY, *PA*, Series 5, Box 64, f. 2448.1 (formerly 58.1).

141. On the trip to Pisa, see Rainey, "The Earliest Manuscripts of the Malatesta Cantos," pp. 587–92; for some of the documentary sources, see note 152. Pound went there to see a statue of Isotta degli Atti formerly attributed to Agostino di Duccio, which is recalled many years later in ND70[10] 76.227–29:

> οἵ βαρβαροί have not destroyed them [the clouds]
> as they have Sigismundo's Temple
> Divae Ixottae (and as to her effigy that was in Pisa?)

On the trip to Orbetello with Ernest and Hadley Hemingway, see Carlos Baker, *Ernest Hemingway: A Life Story* (New York: Bantam, 1970; 1st edn., 1969) pp. 140–41. (However, Baker's report that all four went to the Lago di Garda is mistaken.) For his presence in Rome on 16 February, see the document in chapter 3, note 110. For his request for admission, see Vatican, Archivio di Stato, *Fondo amministrativo*, "Registro degli studiosi ammessi all'Archivio Segreto vaticano," vol. 21 (anni 1913–27). Pound's signature appears under the year 1922–23, *numero d'ordine* 107; he reports that he is staying at the Pensione Rossi, via Babuino 186, and lists his research topic as "famiglia dei Malatesta."

142. NHBY, *PA*, Series 5, Box 63, f. 2433.2 (formerly 43.2), p. "9." The note transcribed here was taken during his reading of [Pius II], "Delatio criminum ipsius [Sigismundi Malatestae] facta in consistorio publico per advocatum fisci," in Mittarelli, *Bibliotheca codicum manuscriptorum*, (see note 3) cols. 704–15, in particular col. 709:

> hanc quoque sanctissimam conjugem absque ulla culpa strangulavit, quamis mortis causam post mortem quaerens, nullam invenerit. Audiebant eius confessionem ex more Christiani viri religiosi regulam divi Francisci observantes, hos Sigimundus ad se vocat, quaeruntur non solum coniugis, sed aliarum quoque matronarum

secreta, nihil dicentes, nihil mali pandentes, diversis cruciatos tormentis neci tradidit.

143. For Pound's travels after Rome, see his letters and postcards to Dorothy Shakespear Pound, 17 February–4 April 1923; BLUI, *PM.3*, 1923.

144. RBCG, shelf mark 4.R.IV.15, formerly DP.I-B.199 and EP. 1053; described in *Indice generale degli incunaboli delle biblioteche d'Italia*, vol. 4 (Rome: Libreria della stato, 1964), nos. 7787–89. Pound reports on his reading of this volume in Ezra Pound to Dorothy Shakespear Pound [24 March 1923]; BLUI, *PM.3*, 1922: "The bull 'Discipula Veritatis' (vs. Sig.) is labeled EP 1053. It *was* labele[d] (earlier cataloging [*sic*]) some time ago D.P.I.B.199." Obviously he was pleased to note that the former shelf marks corresponded with the initials of himself and his wife.

145. "[I] have discovered that Soranzo still exists": Ezra Pound to Isabel Pound, 24 February 1923 (from Rome): NBHY, *PA*, Series 2, Box 52, f. 1967. For Pound's source of this news and its place in his research for the Malatesta Cantos, see chapter 3, pp. 191–97. See also Ezra Pound to Dorothy Shakespear Pound, 31 March 1923 (from Venice); BLUI, *PM.3*, 1923: "Have cards to both Soranzo & Grigioni[,] both of whom I want to see." Though I assume that Pound received a "card" or letter of introduction to Soranzo from Ricci, it is also possible that he received it from Santi Muratori, whom he met in Rimini and in Ravenna just before going to Venice. Despite Pound's interest in meeting Soranzo, the encounter appears not to have taken place. Soranzo held simultaneous appointments at two universities: the *Istituto magistrale* in Padua (1911 on), and the *Università cattolica* in Milan (1921 on). His principal address was in Padua, however, and he commuted to Milan only when he was teaching. This would have made it difficult for Pound to meet him, and no documents survive that record an encounter. For information on Soranzo's life and career, see note 89.

146. NHBY, *PA*, Series 3, Box 63, f. 2432.37.

147. Draft *X1*, NHBY, *PA*, Series 5, Box 64, f. 2452.1 (formerly 62.1); the revisions are made on the carbon copy, Draft *X2*, NHBY, *PA*, Series 5, Box 64, f. 2453.1 (formerly 63.1). In effect the draft records three versions of this line; its changes are more easily perceived in a transcription that omits the cancellations in each version and registers only the additions.

[1.] And then Polixena died, Polixena Sforza,
[2.] And Polixena ⟨*Sforza*⇒⟩ died,
[3.] And Polixena ⟨*his second wife*⟩ died,

148. The first version is found in NHBY, *PA*, Series 5, f. 2456.1 (formerly 66.1); the second in NHBY, *BP*, Series 2, f. 37. The latter served as the setting copy for the serial publication of the Malatesta Cantos in *The Criterion* 1.3 (July 1923).

149. "Beautiful inutility" is from "Paris Letter: December 1922," *The Dial*

74.1 (January 1923), p. 90. In an essay written in autumn 1922, Pound concedes the role of biological and empirical determinants in human life, but argues that these "leave a residuum" still unexplained, "the quality that Yeats calls 'intensity'." (See "On Criticism in General," *The Criterion* 1.2 [Jan. 1923], p. 144.) The term recurs throughout Pound's writings of this period. For example: "It is only by incalculable intensity of life, an intensity amounting to genius, that one can escape, even momentarily, from the pressure of this circumjacence, free oneself, or one's audience of six, from the bonds of blatant actuality." ("Paris Letter: February 1923," *The Dial* 74 [March, 1923], p. 279).

For an excellent account of the anthropological premises of modernism, on which I draw here, see Hartwig Isernhagen, "'A Constitutional Inability to Say Yes': Thorstein Veblen, the Reconstruction Program of *The Dial*, and the Development of American Modernism after World War I," *Yearbook of Research in English and American Literature* 1(1982), pp. 153–90.

150. On circulation for *The Criterion* see T. S. Eliot to Richard Cobden-Sanderson, 31 August 1922 and 1 October 1922; both in *The Letters of T. S. Eliot*, ed. Valerie Eliot, vol. 1: *1898–1922* (New York: Harcourt Brace, 1988) pp. 568, 579.

151. See Donald Gallup, *Ezra Pound: A Bibliography* (Charlotesville: University of Virginia Press, 1983), pp. 37–39 (A26), 45–47 (A31), and 77–79 (A61) for the 1948 edition discussed below.

152. Nancy Cunard to Ezra Pond, [11, 16, 20, 22, 26, 27 October] 1922; BLUI, *PM.1*, Cunard. Cunard reports that she has visited Venice and Padua, and plans to travel to Rimini and Ravenna (apparently at Pound's suggestion); she requests him to "send . . . list of *all* to see, to do, where to sit, and where to lie, and what toast to drink to you in which café." She also recounts her errands to bookstores on Pound's behalf, and requests more explanation on his plans for the Malatesta Cantos. In particular, she has recently purchased an encyclopedia in Venice, and she makes extensive transcriptions of it, preserved in NHBY, *PA*, Series 5, Box 63, f. 2431.3 (formerly 41.3). The articles are all from Louis Moréri, *Le Grand Dictionnaire Historique* (Paris: 1743–49, sold by F. Pitteri, Venice).

153. On the 1923 journey to Pisa see Ernest Hemingway to Gertrude Stein, [11 February] 1923, in Carlos Baker (ed.), *Ernest Hemingway: Selected Letters 1917–1961* (New York: Scribner's, 1981), p. 79, which is erroneously dated [18 February] by Baker; and Nancy Cunard to Ezra Pound, [16 February 1923]; BLUI, *PM.1*, Cunard, 1923. I wish to thank Professor Baker for sharing with me his own doubts about the 18 February date of the Hemingway letter.

154. Robert Mayo, "A Guide to Ezra Pound's Canto (IX)," *The Analyst* 7 (April, 1955), p. 9.

155. John Hamilton Edwards and William W. Vasse, *Annotated Index to the CANTOS of Ezra Pound: Cantos I–LXXXIV* (Berkeley: University of California Press, 1957), p. 197, s.v. "[Sforza, Polissena]."

156. Carroll F. Terrell, *A Companion to the Cantos of Ezra Pound*, vol. 1 (Berkeley: University of California Press, 1980), p. 44.

157. Terrell, *Companion to the Cantos*, p. x.

158. The misinformation on the convent of Scolca probably comes from Ricci, *Il tempio malatestiano* (see note 103), who in turn derives it from either Hutton or Yriarte (see note 120).

159. Terrell, *Companion to the Cantos*, p. 62; Christine Froula, *A Guide to Ezra Pound's Selected Poems* (New York: New Directions, 1983), p. 143. A more accurate view would be that Pius II's style generally marked a high in the humanist neo-Latin of his time; in the oration specifically under discussion, it simply conformed to the generic norms of invective—a genre often offensive to modern tastes, but much enjoyed in the Renaissance.

160. Edwards and Vasse, *Annotated Index*, p. [ix].

161. Terrell, *Companion to the Cantos*, p. ix.

162. See Jerome J. McGann, "The Monks and the Giants: Textual and Bibliographical Studies and the Interpretation of Literary Works," in Jerome J. McGann (ed.), *Textual Criticism and Literary Interpretation* (Chicago: University of Chicago Press, 1983), pp. 180–99, reprinted in his *Beauty of Inflections: Literary Investigations in Historical Method* (Oxford: Oxford University Press, 1985), pp. 69–89. For an assessment of McGann's larger enterprise, see John Sutherland, "Publishing History: A Hole at the Centre of Literary Sociology," *Critical Inquiry* 14 (1988), pp. 574–89.

163. Still the best accounts are those of Giorgio Pasquali, *Storia della tradizione e critica del testo* (Florence: Le Monnier, 1934; 2nd edn., 1952), and Sebastiano Timpanaro *La genesi del metodo del Lachmann* (Florence: Le Monnier, 1963; Padua: Liviana, 1981). See also the older survey of J. E. Sandys, *History of Classical Scholarship*, 3 vols. (Cambridge: Cambridge University Press, 1908), and Rudolph Pfeiffer, *The History of Classical Scholarship* (Oxford: Oxford University Press, 1968, 1976). See also Anthony Grafton, "The Origins of Scholarship," *American Scholar* 48 (1979), pp. 236–61; and "From Politian to Pasquali," *Journal of Roman Studies* 67 (1977), pp. 171–76. Representative of the classical position of Lachmann is Paul Maas, *Textual Criticism*, tr. Barbara Flowers (Oxford: Oxford University Press, 1958).

164. Maas, *Textual Criticism*, p. 3.

165. Ibid.

166. An exception to this theoretical position has been the work of Giorgio Pasquali, *Storia della tradizione e critica del testo*, and those who have been his heirs, such as Giuseppe Billanovich, *La tradizione di Livio e le origini dell'umanesimo* (Padua: Antenore, 1981). Much of their work concerns problems in the reception history of classical authors in the later Middle Ages and the Renaissance, when the texts of the authors differed greatly from the reconstructions made by modern classicists.

167. An economical survey of the hermeneutical traditions is given in Robert

Palmer, *Hermeneutics: Interpretation Theory in Schleiermacher, Dilthey, Heidegger, and Gadamer* (Evanston, Ill.: Northwestern University Press, 1969).

168. For accounts of canon formation, see Robert von Hallberg (ed.), *Canons* (Chicago: University of Chicago Press, 1984).

169. Geoffrey Hartmann, *Criticism in the Wilderness* (New Haven: Yale University Press, 1980), pp. 41, 274.

170. Geoffrey Hartmann, *Saving the Text* (Baltimore: Johns Hopkins University Press, 1981), p. xv.

171. See Jacques Derrida, "White Mythology," in *The Margins of Phiosophy,* tr. Alan Bass (Chicago: University of Chicago Press, 1982).

172. Allen Tate, "New England Culture and Emily Dickinson," in *Symposium* 3 (1932), pp. 206–26. The essay has been reprinted countless times. See Jerome J. McGann, *The Beauty of Inflections* (Oxford: Oxford University Press, 1988), pp. 222–32. Tate's "reading" would not be "better" if it were based on a "correct" text, but it would articulate more coherently and more clearly its own engagements with it at a specific intersection of transmissional and cultural history.

173. D. F. McKenzie, *Bibliography and the Sociology of Texts* (London: The British Library, 1986), pp. 10–18.

174. Michael Harper, "Truth and Calliope: Ezra Pound's Malatesta," *Publications of the Modern Language Association* 96 (1981), pp. 86–101, all quotations from p. 92.

175. Ibid., pp. 87 (accuracy), 89 (ignores), 92 (correcting), 100 (conclusions similar).

176. Jones, *The Malatesta of Rimini*, pp. vii, 176, 177 n. 1. (See note 103.) Further, Jones has clearly understood the implication of Fumi's discovery of the 1462 letter. He notes that the charge of murdering Polissena was "upheld, though from suspect motives, *by Sforza* in 1461 and 1462" (p. 202 n. 1; my italics, while the allegations against Sigismondo were "transmitted to posterity" *by pope Pius II*. He perceives, in short, the discrepancy between the charge's production and transmission histories, which is exactly how debate on the murder came to assume its particular character, with its opposition between secular or "pagan" culture and ecclesiastical orthodoxy or conventional piety. It is no accident that Soranzo's 1910–11 article, written before the 1462 letter from Sforza had been discovered, bears the revealing title: "An invective *by the Roman Curia* against Sigismondo Malatesta." For Soranzo assumed, based on the evidence then available, that the charges had stemmed from the church; Jones, however, knows that the matter was more complicated.

177. Froula, *To Write Paradise*, pp. 159, 160, 160 n. 1. (See note 3.) Her uneasy assimilation of diverse critical modes appears in the contradiction between her belief that some claims are "founded in fact," even though all should be equally a "captive of the linguistic mode"—another instance of the contradictory treatment of fact that prevails in modern literary studies.

178. Froula, *Guide to Ezra Pound's Selected Poems*, p. 143.

179. On transferential relations see Dominick LaCapra, *History & Criticism* (Ithaca, N.Y.: Cornell University Press, 1985), p. 123.

180. The following discussion draws on Jürgen Habermas, "What Is Universal Pragmatics?" in *Communication and the Evolution of Society*, tr. Thomas McCarthy (Boston: Beacon Press, 1979), pp. 1–68. At the risk of oversimplification, Habermas argues that human speech acts imply a regulative ideal of perfect communicability, a counterfactual standard that can also serve to measure imaginatively the inadequacies of our actual efforts. One effect of this argument is to shift issues of meaning away from problems of reference and representation to questions of procedure, or communicative conditions.

181. Louis Mink, quoted in Dominick LaCapra, *History & Criticism*, p. 33. See LaCapra's entire essay on the subject of narrative and history. Also, for a critical survey of theories of narrative and their relations to historiography, see Hayden White, "The Question of Narrative in Contemporary Theory," in *History and Theory* 23 (1984), pp. 1–33.

182. René Wellek, *The Attack on Literature and Other Essays* (Chapel Hill: University of North Carolina Press), p. 98. Roland Barthes, *Image, Music, Text*, tr. Stephen Heath (New York: Hill & Wang), p. 147.

183. It should be noted that *Studi francescani*, which contained Giovanardi's articles on the chronicle of pseudo-Alessandro, was available in the libraries of the Vatican and Florence, so that this material could, conceivably, have been located by Pound.

184. Francis Steegmuller, *Cocteau: A Biography* (Boston: Little Brown, 1970; 2nd edn., Boston: Godine, 1986), pp. 277–78.

185. Ezra Pound, *Introduzione alla natura economica degli S.U.A.* (Venice: Casa Editrice delle Edizioni Popolari, 1944), tr. Carmine Amore, rev. John Drummond, in *SP*, pp. 167–85, quotation on p. 169.

186. Froula, *To Write Paradise*, p. 160.

187. See the classic study by H. Stuart Hughes, *Consciousness and Society: The Reorientation of European Social Thought, 1890–1930*, rev. edn. (New York: Vintage, 1977; 1st edn., 1957).

188. Sergio Romano, *Giovanni Gentile: la filosofia al potere* (Milan: Bompiani, 1984), p. 31.

189. Giovanni Gentile, "Il concetto della storia nelle sue relazioni col concetto dell'arte," in *Studi storici* 6 (1897), pp. 137–52, reprinted in Giovanni Gentile, *Frammenti di estetica e letteratura* (Lanciano: Carabba, 1921), quotations on pp. 390–91, 389. For Gentile's positions on history see Mario Signore, "Storia e storicismo: alcuni scritti gentiliani sulla storia," in Ugo Spirito (ed.), *Enciclopedia '76–'77: Il pensiero di Giovanni Gentile (Atti del convegno tenutosi a Roma dal 25 al 31 maggio 1975)*, 2 vols. (Rome: Istituto della Enciclopedia Italiana, 1977), vol. 2, pp. 797–806. See also Vito A. Bellezza, *La problematica gentiliana della storia* (Rome: Bulzoni, 1983).

190. For Yeats's interest see his addresses, "The Child and the State," delivered to the Irish Literary Society on 30 November 1925, and "The Condition of Schools," delivered to the Irish Senate of 24 March 1926, in Donald R. Pearce (ed.), *The Senate Speeches of W. B. Yeats* (Bloomington: Indiana University Press, 1960), pp. 168–74, 106–12, and particularly pp. 170–73 and 110–11. Yeats is especially referring to Gentile's most sustained attempt to create a popular exposition of his work, *La riforma dell'educazione: discorsi ai maestri di Trieste* (Bari: Laterza, 1920), tr. Dino Bigongiari, with an introduction by Benedetto Croce, as *The Reform of Education* (New York: Harcourt, Brace, 1922; London: Ernest Benn, 1923). For the influence of this work on Yeats's famous poem, "Among School Children," see A. Norman Jeffares, *A New Commentary on The Poems of W. B. Yeats* (Stanford: Stanford University Press, 1984), pp. 250–55. On his reading of Gentile's other principal work in English, particularly *The Theory of Mind as Pure Act*, ed. H. Wildon Carr (London: Macmillan, 1922), see W. B. Yeats, *A Vision* (New York: Collier Books, 1966), p. 81 n. 1 and elsewhere, and Connie K. Hood, "The Remaking of *A Vision*" in *Yeats: An Annual of Critical and Textual Studies* 1 (1983), pp. 33–67, with extensive reference to Yeats's letters and notebooks recording his reading of Gentile. For Eliot, see especially his notes on J. A. Smith's lectures on logic and Giovanni Gentile: CHH, bMS Am 1691.14 (15). On Smith's relation to Gentile, see H. S. Harris, "Introduction" to Giovanni Gentile, *Genesis and Structure of Society* (Urbana: University of Illinois Press, 1966), pp. 14–24.

191. On Gentile's life see Sergio Romano, *Giovanni Gentile*, on which I rely here. (Gentile's exact title was minister of public instruction.)

192. ND70^{10} 89.209.

193. Froula, *To Write Paradise*, p. 158.

3. Reception

1. See James Boswell, *The Life of Samuel Johnson* (London: Dent, 1973), vol. 1, p. 414; and Daniel Coit Gilman, "The Utility of Universities: An Anniversary Discourse," in *University Problems in the United States* (New York: Century, 1898), p. 46; cited by Burton J. Bledstein, *The Culture of Professionalism* (New York: Norton, 1978; 1st edn., 1976), p. 292.

2. See *Civilisation: Its Cause and Cure and Other Essays*, 2nd edn. (London: Swan Sonnenschein, 1891), pp. 46–47. Carpenter was quite explicit in his primitivism; his next sentence states, "The same sense of vital perfection and exaltation which can be traced in the early and pre-civilisation peoples—only a thousand times intensified, defined, illustrated and purified—will return to irradiate the redeemed and delivered Man." Carpenter's book was in its thirteenth edition by 1921, an average of one edition every two and a half years between 1890 and 1921. For one view of his place in Edwardian cultural discussion, see Edith Ellis, *Three Modern Seers* (New York: Mitchell Kennerley, 1910).

3. Friedrich Nietzsche, *Menschliches, Allzumenschliches I*, no. 237, in Gior-

gio Colli and Mazzino Montinari (eds.), *Sämtliche Werke. Kritische Studienaus-gabe* (Munich-Berlin: DTV and de Gruyter, 1980), vol. 2, p. 199. The English translation is my own; it differs from the 1909 edition in rendering *Kultur* as "civilization" rather than "culture," in order to make it synchronize with the standard translation of Jacob Burckhardt's *Die Kultur der Renaissance in Italien.* Compare Friedrich Nietzsche, *Complete Works*, ed. Oskar Ludwig Levy (New York: Russell & Russell; rpt. of 1909–11 edn.), vol. 6, pp. 220–21. For a fine survey of Nietzsche's place in discussion contemporary with Pound, see David Thatcher, *Nietzsche in England 1890–1914* (Toronto: University of Toronto Press, 1970), particularly chaps. 6 and 8.

4. On Burckhardt, his treatment of Sigismondo, and its place in the historio-graphical culture, see chapter 2, pp. 101–2.

5. Ezra Pound, *GK*, p. 159, in a chapter titled "Examples of Civilization."

6. Jacob Burckhardt, *The Civilization of the Renaissance in Italy*, tr. S. G. C. Middlemore (New York: Harper & Row, 1958; 1st edn., 1886), vol. 1, p. 235. The italics for "her" are mine.

7. ND70[10] 9.238–250.

8. For example, in the *Oratio pro Caecina* Cicero describes a "senator populi Romani, splendor ordinis, decus atque ornamentum judiciorum" (*Caecina*, 10). Other instances can be found in any concordance.

9. Vergil, *Eclogues* 4, 11, "decus hoc aevi" (Vergil to Pollio) and 5, 34, "tu omne decus tuis" (regarding Daphnis); *Aeneid* 6, 546, "decus nostrum" (to Aeneas); 9, 18, "decus coeli" (Turnus to Iris); 10, 507, "decus magnum" (nar-rator to Pallas); 11, 508, "decus Italiae" (Turnus to Camilla); 12, 142, "decus fluvium" (Juno to Juturna). Vergil is the earliest author specifically to use the phrase that appears here, "Italiae decus."

10. On Basinio's life and work, see Augusto Campana, "Basinio da Parma," in *Dizionario biografico degli Italiani*, vol. 7 (Rome: Istituto della Enciclopedia Italiana, 1965), pp. 89–98, with complete references to primary and secondary literature.

11. The entire poem is modeled on the *Aeneid.* For particular borrowings see V. Zabughin, *Vergilio nel Rinascimento italiano*, vol. 1 (Bologna: Nicola Zani-chelli, 1921), pp. 289–93, 312–25 (notes).

12. For the letter to Sigismondo, which is in manuscript, see Campana, "Basinio da Parma," p. 95a; the other verse epistle begins "O Decus Ascu-leum," and is printed in Christophor Preudhomme, ed., *Trium poetarum elegan-tissimorum, Porcelii, Basinii, et Trevani opuscula nunc primum diligentia . . . edita* (Paris: apud Simonem Colinaeum, 1539), fols. 86–87. Basinio's work on epigraphic inscriptions appears in the epitaph for Giusto de' Conti, carved in the sepulchre that adorns the right flank of the church of San Francesco, and in a distich carved for a portrait of Sigismondo; see Campana, "Basinio da Parma," pp. 90b, 93a, 96b. Campana alters his earlier attribution to Basinio of the Greek epigraphs at the sides of the church in his "Ciriaco d'Ancona e Lorenzo

Valla sull'iscrizione greca del tempio dei Dioscuri a Napoli," *Archeologia classica* 25–26 (1973–74), pp. 84–102.

13. The standard work on the Italian Renaissance medals is G. F. Hill, *A Corpus of Italian Medals of the Renaissance Before Cellini*, 2 vols. (London: British Museum, 1930). Hill's enumeration of the medals is the basis for all subsequent discussion and is followed here. However, Hill also wrote an important article specifically dealing with the medals of Matteo de' Pasti, "The Medals of Matteo de' Pasti," *The Numismatic Chronicle*, series 4, vol. 17 (1917), pp. 298–312, in which he gave a separate enumeration solely of de' Pasti's medals. In subsequent notes, reference to a specific medal is given first by the number from the 1930 *Corpus*, then by the number from the 1917 essay.

14. First medal, Hill 167/9a; second medal, Hill 170/10a.

15. Medals having the longer inscription but unsigned by de' Pasti are: Hill 168/9b, Hill 169/9c, and Hill 171/10b.

16. Medals having the briefer inscription and unsigned by de' Pasti are: Hill 187/24, which depicts an elephant on the reverse; Hill 188/25 and Hill 189/26, which depict a book on the reverse.

17. The medal with the 1447 date is Hill 169/9c. De' Pasti's presence in Rimini appears in a document of 19 June 1449, furnished by Corrado Ricci, *Il Tempio Malatestiano* (Milan-Rome: Tumminelli e Bestetti, n.d. [but 1924]; rpt., Rimini: Bruno Ghighi, 1974), p. 104. The medal of Sigismondo found at Verucchio is Hill 180a/19. The archaeological evidence is assembled by Pier Giorgio Pasini, "Note su Matteo de' Pasti e la medaglistica malatestiana," in *La medaglia d'arte: Atti del primo convegno internazionale di studio, Udine, 10–12 ottobre 1970* (Udine: ciac libri, 1973), pp. 41–75; he reports the finds at Verucchio on p. 54, and the finds with medals of Isotta on pp. 55, 61– 62. Also on de' Pasti see Giovanna de Lorenzi (ed.), *Medaglie di Pisanello e della sua cerchia* (Florence: Museo Nazionale del Bargello, 1983), pp. 49–54, reporting on the medals of Isotta on pp. 50–51.

18. Julius Friedländer, *Die italienischen Schaumünzen des fünfzehnten Jahrhunderts*, 3 vols. (Berlin: Weidmann, 1882–87); Aloiss Heiss, *Les Médailleurs de la Renaissance* (Paris: J. Rothschild, 1881–85); Alfred Armand, *Les Médailleurs italiens des quinzième et seizième siècles* (Paris: E. Plon, 1883).

19. Charles Ephrussi, "Les Médailleurs de la Renaissance," *L'Art: Revue illustrée* 9.3 (1883), pp. 243–52, p. 243. Compare the remarks of Alfred Armand, *Les Médailleurs italiens*, who commented that "le goût du public pour les médailles italiennes . . .s'est développé d'une manière sensible pendant ces dernières années," a fact witnessed "par l'empressement avec lequel ces médailles sont recherchées et par l'élévation croissante de leur prix" (p. i).

20. In 1881 Yriarte was also named an *inspecteur des beaux arts* for the homonymous ministry in France, and in 1889 he became a member of the ministry's *conseil supérieur*, where it appears that he played an active role in purchasing works for the Louvre. On Yriarte's life see Albert Kaempfen, "Charles

Yriarte," *Gazette des Beaux-Arts* series 3, vol. 19 (1898), pp. 431–33. His appointments are reported by Maurice Tourneux, "Yriarte, Charles-Emile," in *La Grande Encyclopédie*, vol. 31 (Paris: Société Anonyme de la Grande Encyclopédie, 1902), p. 1290. On his role as consultant to Sir Richard Wallace, see his own memoirs published posthumously: Charles Yriarte, "Mémoires de Bagatelle: VI," *La Revue de Paris* 10 (1903), pp. 380–414; and Charles Yriarte, "The Hertford House Collection Bequeathed to the British Nation," *Pall Mall Magazine* (1900), pp. 4–18. Note that the Wallace Collection contains two medals by de' Pasti: one depicts Sigismondo Malatesta, the other Isotta (Wallace Collection S 329, Hill 174/14; and Wallace Collection S 330, Hill 189/26). It is likely that one or both were purchased by Wallace under the influence of Yriarte; the editor of the *Pall Mall Magazine* remarks that "Yriarte was the expert by whose opinion Sir Richard Wallace was guided in many of his purchases" (p. 18). In addition, one notes that the medal of Sigismondo was apparently purchased in 1866 from Tito Gagliardi, a Florentine dealer, and that Yriarte himself discusses his collaboration with Gagliardi in *Un Condottiere au XVe siècle. Rimini: Études sur les Lettres et les Arts à la cour des Malatesta* (Paris: J. Rothschild, 1882), on p. 153 n. 2. The second medal was purchased in 1869 through another dealer. On both medals see *Wallace Collection Catalogues: Sculpture*, ed. J. G. Mann (London: Trustees of the Wallace Collection, 1981), pp. 121–22.

21. The medal shown on p. 142 of Yriarte, *Un Condottiere*, is Hill 167/9a. Taken together, three engravings of de' Pasti medals were included by Yriarte. The other two appear facing one another on pp. 148 and 149. On p. 148 (fig. 74) we see the shorter form of the dedicatory inscription, reading:

· D · ISOTTAE · · ARIMINENSI ·

This clearly depicts the obverse of Hill 187/24 (*not* the similar Hill 188/25; note the differences in inscriptional pointing). The other engraving given on the facing page (p. 149, fig. 75) does not show the reverse of the same medal, though that is what is plainly suggested by its collocation and caption: instead it represents the reverse of Hill 167/9a—which is to say, the same medal shown seven pages earlier, on p. 142. (Note de' Pasti's signature in fig. 75; whereas the reverse of the medal shown in fig. 74 should show no signature at all.) In short, Yriarte combines the obverse of Hill 187/24 with the reverse of Hill 167/9a to suggest a third that never actually existed. The error is typical of the dilettantism that characterizes his work.

22. Robert Mayo, "A Guide to Ezra Pound's Cantos (IX)," *The Analyst* 7 (April 1955), p. 19. (Hereafter this is cited as Mayo, "IX.") Following Mayo, though with some confusion, are John Hamilton Edwards and William W. Vasse, *Annotated Index to the CANTOS of Ezra Pound* (Berkeley: University of California Press, 1957), p. 63. More confused is Peter Brooker, *A Student's Guide to the Selected Poems of Ezra Pound* (London: Faber & Faber, 1979), p. 256. He

apparently assumes that there is only one medal by de' Pasti, and like Edwards and Vasse, he fails to perceive that the phrase "decus Italiae" is nowhere to be found in Yriarte, *Un Condottiere*, p. 155. He also cites "a concealed inscription on Isotta's tomb," but this is irrelevant since it was not published until 1924, a year *after* the Malatesta Cantos had been published. (On this inscription and its discovery, see pp. 195–96.) Brooker ignores the study by Pasini, *La medaglia d'arte*, and continues to repeat the 1446 dating of the Isotta medals, apparently borrowing from Mayo and from Edwards and Vasse.

23. Yriarte, *Un Condottiere*, p. 150:

> On connaît huit médailles d'Isotta; sept sont de Matteo da Pasti, la huitième est de Pisanello. Sur les sept de Matteo une seule est datée 1447 et les cinq autres sont de 1446. A part celle au livre ouvert, qui consacre le souvenir des Élégies, il n'y a pas, dans les signes ni dans les légendes, d'allusion à des faits spéciaux. Ici elle est de profil avec l'inscription: *Isottaei. Ariminensi.forma.—et.virtute.Italiae. decori.* Et au revers, l'éléphant des Malatesta, avec la signature *opus Matthaei de Pastis. V. (Veronensis)* M.CCCC.XLVI. Là on a substitué à l'éléphant au revers, dans une plus petite forme, un génie qui vole et porte une couronne. La seule qu'on connaisse du Pisanello la représente aussi de profil avec la même coiffure que dans les médailles de Matteo; au revers figure le Sigismond, en armure.

Yriarte violates conventions for the rendering of points and maintenance of the medal's capitalization. More important, he substitutes *Isottaeus* for *Isote*, and so dedicates the medal to a book written in her honor rather than to her. In another case he 'corrects' the Latin to make it conform with classical Latin or with modern Italian: he replaces the *E* of *ISOTE* with *ae*, and he substitutes a double *t* for the single *T*, producing *Isottaei*.

24. Yriarte, *Un Condottiere*, p. 150 n. 1.

25. On Pound's purchase of the Yriarte copy and the date he received it, see chapter 1, note 28, and chapter 2, pp. 120–21. Ezra Pound, *Ymn* 37[a] and 37[b], in Yriarte, p. 150.

26. *Ymn* 143; the index is on p. [461] of his copy of Yriarte.

27. Ezra Pound to Dorothy Pound, [10 March 1923]; BLUI, *PM.3*, 1923.

28. *GK*, p. 159.

29. Armand, *Les Médailleurs italiens*, vol. 1, p. 13, note A; G[eorge]. F[rancis]. Hill, *Pisanello* (London: Duckworth, 1905), p. 164; G. F. Hill, "The Medals of Matteo de' Pasti," p. 312. See also G. F. Hill, *A Corpus*, vol. 1, p. 10 n. 33, who dismisses it yet again. The medal was also discussed by Francesco Gaetano Battaglini, *Memorie istoriche di Rimino e de' suoi Signori artatamente scritte ad illustrare la zecca e la moneta riminese*, ed. Guid'Antonio Zanetti (Bologna: nella stamperia di Lelio dalla Volpe, 1789; rpt., Rimini: Bruno Ghigi, 1976), pp. 38–39 n. 60. Pound owned a copy of this work, but when he acquired it is unclear.

30. Its extrinsic features match those of Pound's letters in this period, and it is typed in the distinctive bright blue ribbon also characteristic of his work at

this time. It shows signs of only light correction and revision: two cancellations and one revision in typescript (lines 12, 40), one cancellation (24.1–24.3), one correction in pencil (9), and one autograph note in blue ink (45).

31. Yriarte, *Un Condottiere*, p. 157 n. 2; because of an intervening illustration covering two pages (pp. 158–59), the note is continued on p. 160. The argument by Yriarte is silly: having discovered that a letter by Isotta to Sigismondo was written in the hand of a secretary, he reasons that this could occur only if Isotta herself were unable to write. But of course nearly all figures of a higher social status at this time employed secretaries to write their correspondence, and on this basis Yriarte's charge was already dismissed in 1886 by Pasquale Villari in his article "Rimini," *Encyclopaedia Britannica*, 9th edn. (Edinburgh: A. & C. Black, 1886), vol. 20, pp. 555–60. (Hereafter this is cited as Villari, 1886.)

32. Jacopo Ammanati-Piccolomini, *Commentarii*, in Pius II, *Commentarii* (Frankfurt: in officina Aubriana, 1614), Book I, p. 359. See also his *Epistolae*, in the same volume, ep. 41, p. 488.

33. For this interpretation see Gioacchino Paparelli, *Enea Silvio Piccolomoni: l'umanesimo sul soglio di Pietro*, 2nd edn. (Ravenna: Longo, 1978), p. 175.

34. On the life of Ammanati the indispensable study is Giuseppe Calamari, *Il confidente di Pio II: Card. Iacopo Ammanati-Piccolomini (1422–1479)*, 2 vols. (Rome-Milan: Augustea, 1932). I have relied on it throughout. Also useful is Sebastiano Paoli, *Disquisizione istorica della patria, e compendio della vita di Giacomo Ammanati Piccolomini, Cardinale di S. Chiesa, detto il papiense, vescovo di Lucca, e di Pavia* (Lucca: apresso Pellegrino Frediani, 1712).

35. Jacopo Ammanati-Piccolomini, *Commentarii*, Book 5, p. 403:

> Sed accidit per eos dies Sigismundum, qui a Peloponesiaco Venetorum bello in Italiam redierat, valetudine assidua fatigatum Arimini vita excedere relicta arcis civitatisque custodia Isottae uxori, quam Pellicem prius, inde matrimonio adiunctam perdite amaverat.

36. In 1459 Ammanati probably accompanied Pius II to the Diet of Mantua, and there he might have met the Riminese signore. Yet the nature of his position, the press of his official duties at so crucial an event would hardly have permitted him to engage Sigismondo in conversation about personal sentiments. Yet perhaps a second occasion presented itself a few years later. After the election of Paul II to the papacy in 1464, Ammanati kept his distance from the papal court and spent his time at his house behind Sant'Angelo, where he conducted a sort of academy. Among his frequent visitors was Bartolomeo Scacchi, known as Platina, who had been an abbreviator under Pius II but had lost his post when Paul II purged the papal court of figures too closely linked with his predecessor (including Ammanati). Platina was implicated in the alleged conspiracy to overthrow Paul II, as were two members of Ammanati's own household. Platina

writes that during his interrogation for the conspiracy he was asked about his recent conversations with Sigismondo Malatesta (frequently in Rome between June 1466 and early 1468). This might suggest that Sigismondo, via Platina, met Ammanati during this period. The speculation is plausible, though unsupported by any documentation. Yet would they have discussed Sigismondo's feelings about Isotta? It seems unlikely: Platina reports that he and Sigismondo talked "about arms, about literature, and about distinguished men of the past and the present"—in short, the topics typical of humanist bureaucrats, topics far removed from intimate questions of the heart. Nothing indicates it would have fared otherwise between Sigismondo and Ammanati. One notes in passing that Ammanati's devotion to the church is beyond question; that two members of his household were implicated in the conspiracy only shows how little the "conspiracy" had to do with a neopagan revival, as was imagined in the nineteenth century and is implied by Pound in the Malatesta Cantos. See Bartolomeo Scacchi (Platina), *Platynae historici liber de vita Christi ac omnium ponteficium*, ed. Giacinto Gaida, in *Rerum italicarum scriptores*, 2nd edn., ed. Giosué Carducci and Vittorio Fiorini, vol. 3 (Città di Castello, 1934), p. 384.

37. Terrence, *Heautontimorumenos* 97, "eius filiam ille amare coepit perdite," and *Phormio* 82, "hanc ardere coepit perdite." See Plautus, *Cistellaria* 238, "amare coepit perdite." See Catullus 45, "ni te perdite amo," and 104, "non potui, tam perdite amarem." *Perdite* is also used with *se gerere* in a letter from Cicero to Atticus (9.2a.2); with *conor* in Quintilian (2.12.5); with *facere* in the pseudo-Quintilian *Declamationes* (1.16); and with *dedolo* in Apuleius, *Metamorphoses*, as well as by Augustine in the *Confessions* (10.37). Taken together, these names and works epitomize the achievements of humanist philology in the century before Ammanati: Apuleius's *Metamorphoses* was virtually unknown before its possession by Boccaccio; Cicero's *Ad Atticum* was one of Petrarch's most precious possessions (lost again upon his death), and its recovery a second time in 1392 by Coluccio Salutati aroused great joy. Plautus was likewise recovered in 1429 by Nicholas of Cusa, and Catullus was yet another author who elicited intense new interest during the quattrocento. On all these see L. D. Reynolds and N. G. Wilson, *Scribes and Scholars*, 2nd edn. (Oxford: Oxford University Press, 1974), pp. 118, 120, 123. As for the *fortuna* of Quintilian in the quattrocento, its main steps are well known—Poggio's recovery of the complete *Institutio* in 1416, Valla's effort in mid-century to make it the central text for humanist rhetorical and philological theory. Of all these authors, only Terence and Augustine were widely known or read in the Middle Ages.

38. Although we can identify some sociolinguistic aspects of the locution *perdite amare*, it is harder to specify its exact semantic perimeters because we lack a systematic lexicon of humanist or quattrocento Latin, or for that matter a lexicon of contemporary notarial, juridical, or theological Latin.

39. Giovanni Simonetta, *Rerum gestarum Francisci Sfortiae mediolanensium ducis commentarii*, ed. Giovanni Soranzo, in *Rerum italicarum scriptores*, 2nd

edn., ed. Giosué Carducci, Vittorio Fiorini, and Pietro Fedele, vol. 21, part 2 (Bologna: Nicola Zanichelli, 1932–43), p. 335. The passage is quoted in full in chapter 2, note 37.

40. Giuseppe Garuffi, "Lettera apologetica, scritta all'Illustrissimo Signor Carlo-Francesco Marcheselli, Nobile Riminese, dal Signor Arciprete D. Giuseppe Malatesta Garuffi, in difesa del Tempio famosissimo di san Francesco, eretto in Rimini da Sigismondo-Pandolfo Malatesta in tempo, che teneva il dominio di detta città," *Giornale de' letterati d'Italia* 30 (1718), p. 181. Although Garuffi quotes here exactly the passage by Ammanati that I have given, he cites only "*lib. V. Comment.*" (p. 181, note a); but in another discussion of Ammanati on p. 168 he cites the exact number of the page in the 1614 edition of Ammanati, leaving no doubt that it served as his source.

41. Gianmaria Mazzuchelli, *Notizie intorno ad Isotta da Rimino*, 2nd edn. (Brescia: dalle stampe di Giambatista Bossini, 1759), p. 32 and 38–39. Note that Mazzuchelli, on p. 32 n. 44, refers to Ammanati as "Piccolomini," a usage also found in the text proper, where he is called "il celebre Cardinal Jacopo Piccolomini detto il Cardinal di Pavia" (p. 32). The use of Ammanati's adopted name alone (Piccolomini), coupled with the fact that his major work (the *Commentarii*) had the same title as Pius II's, may have contributed to the confusion of the two figures on the part of Yriarte, discussed later in this chapter. In the second quotation and discussion, pp. 37–38, Mazzuchelli refers to Ammanati in the text proper as "il mentovato Cardinal di Pavia" (and again on p. 39 as "il Cardinal di Pavia." On Mazzuchelli and the context of his work, see chapter 2, pp. 94–97.

42. Mazzuchelli, pp. 36–37 for the first quotation of pseudo-Alessandro (on this chronicle see chapter 2, pp. 92, 95); p. 37 for the quotation from Clementini, stating that Sigismondo loved Isotta "per le doti dell'animo, e per essere letterata, e di gran governo." See also p. 37 for Mazzuchelli's claim that "Sigismondo non aveva in alcuno . . . maggior confidenza che in lei" and for "il poter di questa sopra l'animo di lui." See p. 38 for "ch'ella fu capace di ridurlo verso il fine della sua vita al pentimento delle sue irregolarità, e de' suoi peccati."

43. Gaetano Moroni, "Rimini o Rimino," in Gaetano Moroni, *Dizionario di erudizione storico-ecclesiastica da S. Pietro ai nostri giorni*, vol. 57 (Venice: tip. Emiliana, 1852), p. 282 col. a:

> Vuolsi che Sigismondo I non solo fosse tratto ad *amare perdutamente* Isotta per la singolarissima sua beltà, ma ancora per l'eccellenti doti del suo ingegno da lei coltivato in ogni maniera di studi, sublimandosi nelle contemplazioni della filosofia, nutrendosi del continuo pascolo dell'istoria, e felicemente dalla poesia traendo diletto.

(Italics mine.) Note how Moroni's phrase, "l'eccellenti doti del suo ingegno," echoes Clementini's locution ("per le doti dell'animo") as paraphrased by Mazzuchelli. This constitutes one more testimony that Moroni is drawing from Mazzuchelli here. Moroni, p. 383: "Si narra che Isotta lo rimettese nel sentiero della virtù. . . ."

44. His use of Moroni appears in *Un Condottiere*, p. 155 and 155 n. 3, where he translates the long passage by Moroni given above, then cites Moroni explicitly (and as usual, incorrectly). However, note that the quotation given by Yriarte is partly his own invention; he splices together one passage from Moroni p. 282 col. a, with another from Moroni p. 283 col. b, and inserts some phrases of his own. Also, elsewhere on p. 155 Yriarte shows that he is borrowing material from Mazzuchelli, though again without acknowledgment. For example, he cites in reverse order exactly the same quotations that Mazzuchelli had used: the chronicle of pseudo-Alessandro, Cesare Clementini, and Jacopo Ammanati. Further, when he quotes a passage originally written by Clementini (Yriarte, *Un Condottiere*, p. 155 n. 2), his version coincides with Mazzuchelli's report of it (p. 37) in six variants against the original, so that he is clearly quoting not the original, but Mazzuchelli's report. (In addition he introduces five new variants of his own!)

45. On Burckhardt and Yriarte, see chapter 2, pp. 107–10.

46. Yriarte, *Un Condottiere*, p. 155: "elle était la vertue même" (although Yriarte attributes this phrase to Moroni, it is his own invention and therefore I have quoted it as such; nothing resembling it is found anywhere in Moroni). Yriarte, *Un Condottiere*, p. 156: "Quant à ses emportements de luxure, non moins habile aux choses du coeur et des sens qu'aux choses de la politique, Isotta savait que le caprice léger et les fureurs bestiales ne dureraient qu'une heure. . . ." Yriarte, *Un Condottiere*, p. 155: "Il n'y a pas une note discordante dans tous les témoignages de l'histoire, depuis les chroniqueurs contemporains jusqu'aux plus modernes." And Yriarte, *Un Condottiere*, p. 155: "On peut récuser les poètes pensionnaires qui vont la diviniser dans leurs éloges, mais on est forcé de s'incliner devant le jugement du plus sévère des justiciers et du plus cruel ennemi de Sigismond. Le pape Pie II a écrit: 'Il a aimé éperdument Isotta et elle en était digne.'"

47. Palermo: Remo Sandron, 1912. On Beltramelli, see chapter 1, pp. 31–33, 36–37, 46–47, and chapter 2, p. 113.

48. For incisive comments on the ideological and stylistic features of Beltramelli in this period, see Benito Mussolini, "'I Canti di Faunus' di Antonio Beltramelli," in *Opera omnia di Benito Mussolini*, ed. Edoardo and Duilio Susmel, vol. 1 (Florence: La fenice, 1951), pp. 193–97.

49. Beltramelli, *Un tempio d'amore*, pp. 50–51:

Ella visse lunghissimo tempo al fianco di Sigismondo eppure non una volta fu incolpata di avere avuto parte nei delitti ch'egli commise. Pio II, lo storico che nulla risparmia al Malatesta, anzi soverchia la misura, dice: "Sigismondo amò perdutamente Isotta ed ella ne era degna."

La parola del nemico non potrebbe esere più chiara nella sua concisione. Isotta esce pura dalla vita del suo tempo attraverso la quale passò amando e dolorando, nobile e grande più che creatura.

50. Ezra Pound to Homer Pound, 3 October [1922]: "I am plugging along on my Malatesta cantos; will take years an' years at the present rate" (NHBY, *PA*, Series 2, Box 52, f. 1967. The brief remarks communicate vividly Pound's sense of being overwhelmed by the masses of material that he has gathered, and his problems in finding means to assimilate it all.

51. Ezra Pound to James Sibley Watson, Jr., 4–5 January 1923; NYPL, *BC*, JSWP. "I shd. very much like to know, from you, who presumably have not mugged up the history of Romagna, whether I have made the *main* points of the story CRYSTAL CLEAR." These remarks accompany his submission of a preliminary typescript, and indicate his concern that readers might have difficulties. Apparently Pound was also convinced that he had found reasonable or at least serviceable solutions to this problem; in 1938 he wrote, "No one has claimed that the Malatesta Cantos are obscure" (*GK*, p. 194).

52. NHBY, *PA*, Series 5, Box 63, f. 2437.3 (formerly 47.3). The citation from "Leo (Enrico)" is from Heinrich Leo; on Pound's reading of this work, see chapter 2, p. 119.

53. On Pound's alterations in this first draft, it should be noted that both *e* and *ed* mean "and" in Italian, but that *ed* is used if the following word begins with a vowel. From his first draft employing this material, Pound had problems with the quotation marks; here he adds quotation marks *after* he has already written out the passage. Further, he elects to replace an earlier (illegible) variant of the word *e* with *ed*. A week later Pound rewrote this passage again: this time he added it to a draft of the so-called "post-bag" sequence (letters to Sigismondo by quattrocento contemporaries), scrawling it on the verso of the last page. In the new version he pared away the two lines that separated the first half of the quotation from the second. In addition, he gave no quotation marks at all, and wrote the Latinate *et* in place of either *e* or *ed*.

54. Mazzuchelli, *Notizie intorno ad Isotta da Rimino*, p. 7 n. 12, states that the chronicle "se crede composta da F. Alessandro da Rimino Procuratore di quel suo Convento, sebbene altri la creda scritta da Autore più recente." The circumstances surrounding Mazzuchelli's knowledge of the chronicle indicate it was Bianchi who suspected the work was more recent. The original Italian by Mazzuchelli (pp. 36–37) reads:

Ma Sigismondo troppo alieno aveva l'animo dal recar disgusto alla sua Isotta, la quale in Rimino era pur divenuta il suo più forte appoggio: *Erat haec*, così nella Cronica di Rimino viene descritta (49) *pulchra aspectu, plurimis dotibus locupletata, foemina belligera, fortis, & constans in proposito, grata populo, & placita oculis Principis, ex qua nonnullos habuit filios, & filias, inter quos Pandulphum, & Lucretiam.*

At the bottom of p. 37, n. 49 explains: "Which is to say, in the manuscript chronicle composed by Fra Alessandro of Rimini, cited above in note 12"— which is to say p. 7 n. 12, where he thanks Bianchi for having furnished him with a transcription of the chronicle.

55. Giovanni Soranzo, "Un'invettiva della curia romana contro Sigismondo Malatesta," [Part 1] *La Romagna* 7 (1910), pp. 462–89; [Part 2] *La Romagna* 8 (1911), pp. 150–75; [Part 3] *La Romagna* 8 (1911), pp. 241–84.

56. Gregorio Giovanardi, O.F.M., "Un frate minore martire del sigillo sacramentale a Rimini nel secolo XV per opera di Sigismondo Pandolfo Malatesta," *Studi francescani*, new series, 1 (1914), pp. 349–67. For Giovanardi's later studies and the development of his debate with Soranzo, see chapter 2, pp. 115–16.

57. Giovanni Soranzo, "Due delitti attribuiti a Sigismondo Malatesta e una falsa cronachetta riminese," *Atti del Reale Istituto Veneto di scienze, lettere ed arti* 74 (1914–15) [Part 2], pp. 1881–1902. On the debate with Giovanardi, see chapter 2, pp. 115–16.

58. One may speculate whether Pound might have persisted in using this passage even if he had known about Soranzo's 1915 article. Consider the case of Corrado Ricci, an art historian and cultural administrator whose major study of the Tempio appeared in 1924 (see note 17). Ricci was clearly acquainted with Soranzo's 1915 study dismissing the chronicle as spurious, for he cited it at one point in his own book (Ricci, *Il Tempio Malatestiano*, p. 30 n. 12). Nevertheless, he quoted the passage about Isotta from the pseudo-chronicle as valid evidence that Isotta was "la consigliera devota, prudente, forte, sicura, che all'ingegno penetrativo accoppiava il corragio dell'azione" (pp. 25–26; quotation on p. 26).

Ricci's practice is particularly suggestive insofar as it converges with his overall effort to conserve the key claims in the legend of Sigismondo. He rejects, for example, Soranzo's 1910–11 argument showing that Sigismondo had not murdered Polissena Sforza, even though he is aware that the charge renders Sigismondo an unsympathetic figure (on this see p. 288 n.103). Likewise, he rejects the results of an earlier study by Soranzo, published in 1909 (see Giovanni Soranzo, "La Sigla ✠ di Sigismondo Pandolfo Malatesta," *La Romagna* 6 [1909], pp. 306–24.) In that study Soranzo examined the entwined letters *S* and *I* that are carved throughout the church of San Francesco, demonstrating that the cipher denoted only the name of Sigismondo, and that the belief that it referred to both Sigismondo and Isotta was a romantic misunderstanding.

Equally important is the state of Soranzo's own knowledge in 1909, as demonstrated in this article. Though Soranzo demonstrates the romantic misunderstanding of the cipher, he innocently quotes the passage on Isotta from the chronicle of pseudo-Alessandro as valid evidence about the rapport between Isotta and Sigismondo, terming it "the most balanced" assessment of Isotta (see

Soranzo, "Sigla," p. 324: "Son convinto che di tutti più equanime sia l'elogio del cronista contemporaneo Alessandro da Rimino intorno a questa donna famosa [Isotta]." Six years later, in 1915, Soranzo himself first demonstrates that the entire chronicle was a forgery. Note also that even Soranzo, in 1909, is not free of the effects of Yriarte; his quotation of the passage on Isotta from the chronicle of pseudo-Alessandro derives not from the manuscript itself, but from Yriarte, since his quotation corresponds with Yriarte's (see Yriarte, *Un Condottiere*, p. 155) in every point against Mazzuchelli (see Mazzuchelli, *Notizie intorno ad Isotta da Rimino*, p. 37).

This background underscores the irony directed against Soranzo in Ricci's quotation. For Ricci, after all, firmly rejects Soranzo's 1909 claim that the letters *S* and *I* refer only to Sigismondo. Yet when he quotes the passage regarding Isotta from the pseudo-chronicle, he cites as his source precisely the 1909 article by Soranzo—the one written six years *before* Soranzo had dismissed it as a forgery, the one whose central argument Ricci himself rejected.

59. First marking *Ymn* 44, on Yriarte, *Un Condottiere*, p. 155; second *Ymn* 45, opposite Yriarte, *Un Condottiere*, p. 155, n. 1; third *Ymn* 144, on p. 461.

60. Since the fragment appears in close proximity to a bibliographical note regarding the copy of Mazzuchelli in the Bibliothèque Nationale of Paris, one may wonder if Pound was drawing from Mazzuchelli's report of the passage, rather than from Yriarte's. Not so: Pound's draft fragment contains the words "et fortis," so duplicating the only substantive variant (*et*) that Yriarte had introduced into the Mazzuchelli version; further, he also copies Yriarte's treatment of accidentals when he uses a minuscule *p* in the word *principis*, rather than the majuscule *P* given by Mazzuchelli.

61. There is one small difference. In the Watson version the string of Italian and Latin citations does not lead to the canto's conclusion, as it does now, but constitutes a pause in the midst of a narrative. It was only several months later that Pound decided to place the citations at the end of the second canto and the center of the sequence.

62. Robert Mayo, "IX," p. 19. Edwards and Vasse, *Annotated Index*, urge the reader to "see Yriarte," while Brooker, *Student's Guide*, more cautiously states that the passage is "derived from Yriarte." George Kearns, *Guide to Ezra Pound's Selected Cantos* (New Brunswick, N.J.: Rutgers University Press, 1980), attributes the lines to "assorted documents and inscriptions." Carroll F. Terrell, *A Companion to the Cantos of Ezra Pound*, vol. 1 (Berkeley: University of California Press, 1980), p. 48, attributes these lines to "a 15th-century chronicle of Rimini." He is followed by Marjorie Perloff, *The Poetics of Indeterminacy: Rimbaud to Cage* (Evanston, Ill.: Northwestern University Press, 1983; 1st edn., Princeton: Princeton University Press, 1981), p. 187: "The four Latin lines . . . come from a fifteenth-century chronicle attributed to Alessandro da Rimini." Christine Froula, *A Guide to Ezra Pound's Selected Poems* (New York:

New Directions, 1982), p. 148, claims that these lines are "from Broglio's 'Chronicle'," referring to the *Cronaca universale* of Gaspare Broglio (RBCG, ms. SC-MS 1161).

63. Terrell, *A Companion*, p. 48; Froula, *A Guide*, p. 148.

64. On Draft *C3* see Lawrence Rainey, "The Earliest Manuscripts of the Malatesta Cantos by Ezra Pound" (diss., University of Chicago, 1986), pp. 163–74 (dating), 259–61 (description), 566–600 (text and apparatus). On Pound's copy of Yriarte and the date he received it, see chapter 2, pp. 120–21.

65. Yriarte, *Un Condottiere*, pp. 389–92. His discussions of the poem appear on pp. 139–42, 288–320, 388–89. Further page references are given in the text.

66. The poem is found on fols. 275^r and following.

67. "Chacune des ses stances nous explique le sujet d'un des bas-reliefs sculptés par Agostino di Duccio, dans l'une des chapelles de San Francisco."

68. "Matteo les a traduits en cire ou en terre dans ses compositions . . . et Agostino di Duccio a traduit en marbre les compositions du maître. Cela ne fait point de doute pour nous.

"Le sculpteur, qui flatte son maître et seigneur, et se plaît à ces représentations étranges, tire du marbre un à un des symboles et chacune des constellations que Sigismondo a invoquées" (pp. 219–20).

69. The Florentine manuscript is Florence, Riccardiana 1154, the same manuscript used by Pietro Bilancioni for his edition of sonnets attributed to Sigismondo. See the discussion that follows. Bilancioni was born in Rimini. A lawyer and bibliophile, he assembled a large collection of transcriptions of poems written in Italian from the thirteenth through the fifteenth centuries, gathered from both manuscript and printed works, called the *Apografi Bilancioni*. His papers were acquired in 1878 by the city library of Bologna at the suggestion of Carducci. An index of them was published by Carlo and Luigi Frati, *Indice delle carte di Pietro Bilancioni: contributo alla bibliografia delle rime volgari de' primi tre secoli. Parte prima: rime con nome d'autore*, (Bologna, tip. Fava e Garagnani, 1893); they are still an important source for knowledge of early poetry in Italian. When Charles Yriarte examined them around 1880, they were scarcely known.

70. BNF Palatino Capponiano 152, on fols. 130^r and following.

71. It is unclear whether Yriarte actually saw Bilancioni's papers or knew only a transcription of it sent him by Professor Gino Rocchi, whose letter to Yriarte is cited as the basis for a rough summary of the poem (see pp. 393–94). In either event, the report given by Yriarte is not very trustworthy. The Palatino Capponiano 152 reads, "Quale Elena e equale a te"; Bologna, University of Bologna, ms. 1739 reads, "Qual Helena quale a te." A critical text would read: "Qual'Helena equal t'é o qual'Isotta?"

72. Villari, 1886, p. 558.

73. Karl Baedeker, *Italy: Handbook for Travellers*, vol. 2: *Central Italy and Rome* (Leipzig: Baedeker, 1900), p. 104. Same author, title, and publisher, but 1908 edition, vol. 2, p. 99. This is useful because we know that Pound used a Baedeker when he took his 1922 trip to Italy and saw the Tempio Malatestiano for the first time. To one correspondent who helped him acquire books from London he wrote on 16 March 1922: "HAVE bought the Baedeker, so don't worry about that." See Ezra Pound to Agnes Bedford, 16 March 1922; BLUI, *PM.2*, Bedford, 1922.

74. Edward Hutton, *Sigismondo Pandolfo Malatesta, Lord of Rimini. A Study of a XV Century Italian Despot* (London: J. M. Dent; New York: E. P. Dutton, 1906), nine pages, pp. 207–15; "wonders," p. 215; singing soldiers, p. 192; see also pp. 88–92, where Hutton presents his translations of some of the other poems attributed to Sigismondo by Yriarte. Hutton seems never to have doubted the truth of Yriarte's claims.

75. Edward Hutton, *The Cities of Romagna and the Marches* (London: Methuen, 1913), p. 116.

76. Ezra Pound, *Ymn* 28 in Yriarte, *Un Condottiere*, p. 139.

77. Ezra Pound, NHBY, *PA*, Series 5, Box 63, f. 2436.4 (formerly 46.4), note [4] based on Yriarte, *Un Condottiere*, p. 141: the poem addresses itself "au vieux roi Salomon, qui, 'vaincu par l'amour d'une païenne, adora à genoux les idoles'" (p. 141).

78. Edward Carpenter (see note 2).

79. Ezra Pound, *Ymn* 29–30 in Yriarte, *Un Condottiere*, p. 140, regarding lines 9 and 11; and NHBY, *PA*, Series 5, Box 63, f. 2436.4 (formerly 46.4), draft fragment between notes [30] and [31]. Note that I give a comma for Pound's period at the end of line 2, and also *will* for *wil, mantel* for *mentel*, and *d'indi* for *dindi* and *d indi*.

80. *SR*, p. 89. This chapter of *SR*, was first published in 1912 as an independent essay, then incorporated into the second or 1932 edition of *SR* as chapter 5, where it is reprinted in all subsequent editions. In the discussion that follows all quotations are from pp. 88–89. Pound also translates the entire poem by Daniel in *SR*, pp. 33–34. An edition of Arnaut Daniel in use when Pound wrote gives the Provençal text of these lines as follows:

> Em fetz escut de son bel mantel endi
> Que lausengier fals, lenga de colobra,
> Non o visson, don tan mals motz escampa.

See U. A. Canello, *La vita e le opere del trovatore Arnaldo Daniello* (Halle: Max Niemeyer, 1883), pp. 111–12.

81. In an essay published in the spring of 1920, Pound stated that his 1912 view of the mantle had changed in the intervening years: "I had once thought of the mantle of indigo as of a thing seen in a vision, but I have now only fancy to

support this." See Ezra Pound, "Arnaut Daniel," in *LE*, p. 111. By this he seems to mean *vision* in a strictly psychological or hallucinogenic sense. Obviously I am employing the word here more loosely.

82. Ezra Pound to William Bird, 25 January 1925: BLUI, *BP*, Pound.

83. *GK*, p. 159. The comparison depends on an anachronism whereby the values of Romantic or avant-gardist originality are imposed over the conformist culture of the Renaissance courts. Indeed, study of the artists employed by Sigismondo Malatesta shows him consistently imitating the patterns of taste and patronage established at other, more important courts, never acting as an initiator of new tastes or styles. The gothic elements in the sculptural decorations in the Tempio's interior are decidedly behind contemporary taste in Florence, for example—assuming for a moment that this notion of "ahead" or "behind" has any meaning at all.

84. See chapter 1.

85. Luigi Orsini, *Il Tempio Malatestiano* (Florence: Fratelli Alinari, 1915; rpt. 1927), pp. v, vi. This publication was a trilingual work (Italian, French, English); in discussion below I quote from the Italian portion and make my own translation. The format of the work suggests that it was sold at the Tempio itself as a guidebook. Orsini argued that the Tempio was the product of a triad "ideally united by the thread of beauty, of will, and of art." Incidentally, Orsini collaborated with Beltramelli on a 1907 opera and also became a party militant. One notes that the same point of view regarding the church as an epic poem was expressed by Giuseppe Albini in 1907: "The true poem, the solid and flourishing epic in which were written the loves of Sigismondo and Isotta, is only and always the miraculous Tempio Malatestiano." See "Il *Liber Isottaeus* e il suo autore," in *Memorie della R. Accademica delle scienze dell'Istituto di Bologna, Classe di Scienze Morali: Sezione storio-filologica*, series 1, vol. 1 (1906 – 7), pp. 139 – 60, on p. 151.

86. NHBY, *PA*, Series 5, Box 65, f. 2443.4 (formerly 53.4).

87. Yriarte cites Riccardiana 1154 because it served as the basis for the only edition (prior to 1983) of poems attributed to Sigismondo: Pietro Bilancioni (ed.), *Sonetti riferiti al nome di Sigismondo de' Malatesta da un codice della Riccardiana* (Ravenna: tipografia di Gaetano Angeletti, 1860). The work was published as a wedding present, and the number of copies must have been exiguous. None is reported in the Bibliothèque Nationale of Paris, which explains why Pound did not consult it there. Yriarte mentions Bilancioni and/or Riccardiana 1154 on pp. 140 n. 1, 388, 393. Pound records one or both from Yriarte in *Ymn* 31 and 141, and NHBY, *PA*, Series 5, Box 63, f. 2430.6 (formerly 40.6), f. 2432.60 (formerly 42.60), and f. 2441.6 (formerly 51.6). His transcriptions are found in NHBY, *PA*, Series 5, Box 63, f. 2432.10 (formerly 42.10). That Pound is consulting Bilancioni is also apparent by his copying the lineation given by Bilancioni, which of course does not appear in the manuscript. The poems in the Riccardiana are found on fols. 75 – 82ᵛ. A recent edi-

tion of the same poems—none of which is quoted by Pound in the final version of the Malatesta Cantos, is given by Angelo Turchini, (ed.), *Isotta bella sola ai nostri giorni: sonetti di Sigismondo Pandolfo Malatesta* (Rimini: Edizioni Luisè, 1983).

88. One can be certain that Pound consulted both the manuscript and the published transcription because his notes duplicate certain graphemes found only in the manuscript (abbreviations typical of quattrocento Italian), while his orthography in every case copies the spelling of the published transcription, along with its accidentals. Yriarte, *Un Condottiere*, cites BNF Palatino Capponiano 152 under its former catalogue number, Palatino 419, on p. 394. Pound copies the information from Yriarte in NHBY, *PA*, Series 5, Box 63, f. 2441.6 (formerly 51.6) and f. 2430.6 (formerly 40.6), the latter made in late November 1922. His transcriptions from the manuscript are found in NHBY, *PA*, Series 5, Box 63, f. 2432.10 (formerly 42.10), along with specific page references to Francesco Palermo, *I manoscritti Palatini di Firenze*, vol. 1 (Florence: R. Biblioteca Palatina, 1860), a work that served as the main catalogue of the BNF at that time and was probably brought to Pound's attention by library employees. The catalogue includes heterogeneous information also copied by Pound. Pound reached Florence on 3 March 1923, and stayed until 7 March.

89. Aldo Francesco Massèra, "I poeti isottei," *Giornale storico della letteratura italiana* 57 (1911), pp. 1–32. His discussion of the *serventese* appears on pp. 5–6, of its author on pp. 15–21, of the *capitolo ternario* on pp. 6–7. The manuscripts attributing the poem to Serdini are found in Guglielmo Volpi, "La vita e le rime di Simone Serdini detto il Saviozzo," *Giornale storico della letteratura italiana* 15 (1890), pp. 1–78. The poem is discussed on pp. 26–28, and a bibliography of manuscript testimonies appears on p. 68, item no. 37, with another manuscript mentioned on p. 78 n. 1. For a more recent discussion of them, see Emilio Pasquini (ed.), Simone Serdini da Siena detto il Saviozzo, *Rime* (Bologna: Commissione per i Testi di Lingua, 1965), pp. cccxxxix–cccl, with critical edition on pp. 225–27.

As for Massèra's projected biography of Isotta, it was left unfinished when Massèra died in 1928; the manuscript is in RBCG, where Massèra was the director for so many years. In 1923, when Pound visited Rimini during his research tour, Massèra was not inclined to open the library for him, and Pound was pleased when his fascist hotel-keeper forced Massèra to open it. Pound recounts the incident in *Jefferson and/or Mussolini* (New York: Liveright, 1970; 1st edn., 1935), pp. 26–27.

90. Pasquale Villari, "Rimini," *Encyclopaedia Britannica*, 11th edn. (Cambridge: Cambridge University Press, 1911), vol. 23, p. 346.

91. Orsini, *Il Tempio Malatestiano*. See note 85.

92. Robert Mayo, "A Guide to Ezra Pound's *Cantos* (VIII)," *The Analyst* 5 (October 1954), p. 8, declares that the passage in Canto 8 is "based upon a . . . love poem of Sigismundo." Fred Moramarco, "The Malatesta Cantos," *Mosaic* 12

(1978), p. 111, reports: "this quotation [is] from one of Sigismondo's own poems." Kearns, *Guide to Ezra Pound's Selected Cantos*, p. 43, describes the passage as "a sample" of "Sigismundo's own poetry." Terrell, *A Companion*, vol. 1, p. 38, calls it "a poem by Sigismundo in praise of his mistress . . . Isotta degli Atti." Michael Harper, "Truth and Calliope: Ezra Pound's Malatesta," *PMLA* 96 (1981), p. 94, describes it as "Pound's adaptation of Sigismundo's love poetry." William Cookson, *A Guide to The Cantos of Ezra Pound* (New York: Persea Books, 1985), p. 38, labels the passage "a snatch of his [Sigismondo's] love poetry."

93. See Giovanni Soranzo, "La sigla," pp. 306–24, especially 319–22 for examples. See p. 316, citing the testimony of Broglio on f. 167, who states: "Tucti li essi tagliati verifica el nome del Signore miser Sighismondo di Malatesti: questo voi ligitori lo intendete."

94. On Garuffi see Carlo Tonini, *La coltura letteraria e scientifica a Rimini dal sec. XIV ai primordi del XIX* (Rimini, 1884), vol. 2, pp. 98–113, 124–27, 154–58, 173–75.

95. Giuseppe Garuffi, "Lettera apologetica," p. 163: "E per questa cagione volle cifrare insieme col proprio il nome di lei in questo modo, come in varj marmi si vede, ⚭ cioè *Sigismundus Isotta*." And pp. 174–75: "costumanza antica di scrivere i nomi colle due prime lettere majuscule." (See note 40.)

96. Mazzuchelli, *Notizie intorno ad Isotta da Rimino*, p. 28: "Ed è assai ciò verisimile."

97. Giovambattista Costa, "Il Tempio di S. Francesco di Rimino, o sia descrizione delle cose più notabili in esso contenute," in Giuseppe Rocchi (ed.), *Miscellanei di varia lettura*, vol. 5 (Lucca, 1765), p. 88: "per indicare il suo nome." On Costa see Carlo Tonini, *La coltura letteraria* vol. 2, pp. 541–44; and Carla Ravaioli, "Gian Battista Costa pittore riminese del secolo XVIII," in Società di studi romagnoli: Comitato di onoranze a Carlo Luchesi (ed.), *Studi riminesi e bibliografici in onore di Carlo Lucchesi* (Faenza: Fratelli Lega, 1952), pp. 173–81.

98. Francesco Gaetano Battaglini, *Memorie istoriche di Rimino* (see note 29), pp. 178–79: "approfittando del somigliante cominciamento del nome suo e di quello della giovane amante delle lettere S, ed I ne formò quella sigla, della quale fu sì pomposo ad ogni occasione" and "che in tutte le azioni sue ad altro e' più non mirasse, che ad honorar questa femmina." See pp. 259–61, 264, 269–73. See also Francesco Gaetano Battaglini, *Della vita e de' fatti di Sigismondo Pandolfo Malatesta*, in Basini Parmensis poetae, *Opera praestantiora nunc primum edita* (Rimini: ex typographia albertiniana, 1794), vol. 2, p. 401–2.

99. Luigi Nardi, *Descrizione antiquario-architettonica con rami dell'arco di Augusto, ponte di Tiberio e Tempio Malatestiano di Rimino* (Rimini: Marsoner e Grandi, 1813; rpt., Rimini: Luisè Editore, 1980), p. 51. The new edition by Luisè includes a "Nota Bio-bibliografica" on Nardi by Piero Meldini, director of

the Biblioteca Civica Gambalunga of Rimini, with full references to earlier studies on Nardi. See John Addington Symonds, *Sketches and Studies in Italy and Greece*, Second Series (London: Smith, Elder & Co.; New York: Charles Scribner's Sons, 1898; 1st edn., 1874), p. 30.

100. Yriarte, *Un Condottiere*, pp. 103, 146, 191, 198 (quotation).

101. For the 1886 *Encyclopaedia Britannica*, see note 72. See Palmiro Premoli, *L'Italia geografica* (Milan, 1896), vol. 1, p. 328; and Edward Hutton, *Sigismondo Pandolfo Malatesta*, pp. 93, 192, 204, 206. See Luigi Arduini, *Gli scultori nel tempio malatestiano di Rimini* (Rome: Stabilimento danese, 1907), p. 12; and Giuseppe Albini, "Sigismondo e Isotta: poema drammatico in un-'atto," *Romagna* 5 (1908), pp. 321–25. For the 1911 *Encyclopaedia Britannica*, see note 89. See Beltramelli, *Un tempio d'amore*, p. 35; André Maurel, *Petites villes d'Italie*, vol. 2: *Émilie–Marches–Ombrie*, 10th edn. (Paris: Hachette, 1920), p. 151.

102. Lodovico Pogliaghi, "Sigismondo Malatesta dedica ad Isotta il Tempio di San Francesco," p. [401] in Francesco Bertolini, *Il Rinascimento e le signorie italiane* (Milan: Treves, 1897). See figure 11. This image was also reproduced by Luigi Portigliotti, *Donne del Rinascimento* (Milan: Treves, 1927), p. 113. Portigliotti's work was part of a new interest in Sigismondo that flourished during the fascist era, which included a revival of interest in Yriarte's book, of which a virtual translation is given by Alberto Ricci, *Sigismondo e Isotta (gli ultimi Malatesta)* (Milan: Edizioni Athena, 1929), a work that also reproduces engravings directly borrowed from the 1882 Yriarte. See also Luigi Portigliotti, *Condottieri* (Milan: Treves, 1935), dedicated to Mussolini, pp. 133–55.

103. For Soranzo see notes 58 and 93.

104. Ricci, *Il Tempio Malatestiano* (see note 17), pp. 315–19. Ricci's theory was first announced three years earlier by Giorgio Sangiorgi, "Reliquie tessili rinvenute nella tomba di Sigismondo Pandolfo Malatesta in Rimini," *Rassegna d'arte antica e moderna* 7 (1921), pp. 73–84. On p. 73 he writes that the Tempio was "dedicato in segreto all'amore di Sigismondo per Isotta." Sangiorgi was a student of Ricci, and the journal *Rassegna d'arte antica e moderna* was edited by Ricci. The idea plainly derived from him.

105. Beltramelli, *Un tempio d'amore*, p. 35: "Da quel tempo egli fece sua la divisa di Isotta, divisa che non doveva abbandonare mai più, e l'atto cavalleresco sorpassò intenzionalmente la costumanza cortese." On Pound's purchase of this book see chapter 2, p. 117. Of course, Beltramelli's mention of courtly custom was pure bluff; he knew nothing about the practices of Renaissance courts, cited no documents or testimonies, and had no interest in locating or studying them.

106. The first entry is *Ymn* 32, on Yriarte, *Un Condottiere*, p. 146:

Prov.   Sigismondo lui donnait des témoignages publics de
son attachement, et, du vivant même sa femme, ne portait jamais
customs.   dans les fêtes, dans les tournois et dans les cérémonies publiques,

d'autre devise que celle de sa maîtresse. Il avait enlacé son chiffre au
Y. ignorant sien, et sur son cachet, dans ses armes, sur les armures de ses sol-
dats, aux murs des monuments, au frises des églises, au fronton
of middle des autels, il déclarait publiquement que sa destinée était liée à celle
de son amante.

ages

Pound's second entry is *Ymn* 17 on Yriarte, *Un Condottiere*, p. 103, opposite
his discussion of the uniforms worn by condottieri and their soldiers, in which
he claimed that Sigismondo obliged his men to wear the cipher representing his
love for Isotta: across from the discussion Pound carefully entered in pencil a
vertical line that would earmark this passage for further attention:

> Sigismond
> Malatesta avait imposé à tous ses cavaliers les *Imprese* qu'il avait ajou-
> tées à son écusson depuis qu'il était l'amant d'Isotta, et chacun des ca-
> valiers de sa suite portait sur l'armure de son cheval sa devise unie à
> celle de l'amante de Sigismondo.

His third entry is made later in an index at the back of his Yriarte copy (p.
[461]) in order to help him recall his most important marginalia, and is *Ymn*
135: *103*. The reference is clearly to *Ymn* 17 on page 103.

In addition to *Ymn* 17, 32, and 135, Pound also made a separate set of
typescript reading notes, NHBY, *PA*, Series 5, Box 63, f. 2436.4 (formerly
46.4) (ca. 15 September 1922), which also contains a note again based on
Yriarte, p. 103:

> (later. S and I on the shields.)

This note, along with *Ymn* 17 and 135, is the third time that Pound records his
interest in the display of the sign on military uniforms and paraphernalia, and I
draw attention to it here in anticipation of later discussion. Also, in referring to
"two marginalia and one reading note" in the text, I do not include *Ymn* 135
because it was probably written in November or December 1922 and so falls
outside the limits specified by "between 1 August and ca. 15 September."

107. For example, NHBY, *PA*, Series 5, Box 63, f. 2432.7 (formerly 42.7),
explicitly cites Soranzo, "Un'invettiva" in the offprint form with the shelf mark
of Paris, Bibliothèque Nationale, K.4609. Because the other manuscript evi-
dence is especially complicated, it suffices to cite abundant testimony con-
served in the final version of the Malatesta Cantos: note how Pound's treatment
of Sigismondo's 1450 effort to recuperate Pesaro depends on Giovanni Soranzo,
"Un fallito tentativo di Sigismondo Pandolfo Malatesta," *Le Marche* 10 (1911),
pp. 221–34, conserved as an offprint in BNP K.1342; again, how his treatment
of the cession of Cervia derives from Giovanni Soranzo, "La cessione di Cervia
e delle sue saline a Venezia nel 1463," *La Romagna* 6 (1909), pp. 201–19,

conserved as an offprint in BNP K.1340; and finally how his treatment of Sigismondo's letter to Mohamet stems from Giovanni Soranzo, "Una missione di Sigismondo Pandolfo Malatesta a Maometto II nel 1461," *La Romagna* 6 (1909), pp. 43–96, conserved as offprint in BNP K.1346. These, together with the article "Un'invettiva," constitute four of the five articles by Soranzo that are conserved as independent offprints by the BNP. Surely it is unlikely that Pound would have taken the time to look up these four and not the last, whose title announced quite plainly its relevance for the history of Sigismondo Malatesta: "The Sign SI of Sigismondo Pandolfo Malatesta."

108. Yriarte, *Un Condottiere*, reproduces two letters in facsimile on pp. 157–58, one by Isotta to Sigismondo, written in the hand of her secretary; one by the secretary herself to Sigismondo, reporting on Isotta's activities. In the first, the secretary renders Isotta's signature as *Yxotta Ariminesse*. In the second, the secretary gives Isotta's name. It appears in the first line of the facsimile as an abbreviation: *m.*ª *Y.*ᵗᵃ. And it appears in the fourth line, this time with an accidental omission of the second letter in her name: *Iotta*. In addition, Yriarte gives a translation into French of the letter from Isotta (pp. 157, 160, 162), and at the conclusion of it he gives her signature as (p. 162): "YXOTTA DE RIMINI." In short, the facsimile presents Isotta's name three times, and the translation includes a fourth. In two instances it begins with *Yx*; in one instance with *Y* alone (the abbreviation); and in one with *Io*. Not once do we see the name in the form given by Pound, *Ixotta*, even though this is clearly the passage that he is responding to and writing about in Fragment *b*, his earliest use of the spelling (a quotation of this draft fragment appears in the discussion of "Italiaeque decus" on p. 165).

Pound's procedure can be better understood if we glance at the transcription of the letter dictated by Isotta and written by her secretary that is offered by Yriarte, *Un Condottiere*, p. 395. Yriarte, although he includes a small error in his transcription (*Ariminessie* for *Ariminesse*), correctly gives Isotta's name as it appears in the signature: *Yxotta Ariminessie*. In addition to this, Yriarte also includes a transcription of a letter sent him by Luciano Banchi (then director of the *Archivio di Stato* of Siena) (p. 396). Banchi's missive discusses the letter to Sigismondo by Isotta's secretary, in particular the first line reading:

Ogi m.ª Y.ᵗᵃ me à fatto scrivere dela filiuola del S.ᵉ Galiazioi

(My transcription is almost diplomatic for obvious reasons.) But in his discussion Banchi offered two different readings of this line: in one case he resolved *m.*ª as *madonna Ixotta*, and in another as *mad. Ysotta*. Were these divergent readings really due to Banchi, or to Yriarte's transcription of his letter? We cannot be certain, but a clue may be the printed subtitle that appears above Yriarte's presentation of the Banchi letters:

LETTRES ÉCRITES AU NOM D'ISOTTA PAR UN SECRÉTAIRE QUI SIGNE
D. DE M. ET PARFOIS SIGNE POUR ELLE: *Ixotta Ariminensis*

Here, as one can see, Yriarte claims that the secretary signed Isotta's name as *Ixotta*—even though he himself has correctly transcribed the signature as *Yxotta* on the page immediately preceding.

Yriarte, in short, presented Pound with the following choices, aside from the modern spelling of *Isotta:*

secretary: *Yxotta Ariminesse* (facsimile, p. 158)
secretary: *m.ᵃ Y.ᵗᵃ* (facsimile, p. 159)
secretary: *Iotta* (facsimile, p. 159)
Yriarte: YXOTTA DE RIMINI (translation, p. 162)
Yriarte: Yxotta Ariminessie (transcription, p. 395)
Yriarte: *Ixotta Ariminensis* (subtitle, p. 396)
Banchi: *madonna Ixotta* (letter, p. 396)
Banchi: *mad. Ysotta* (letter, p. 396)

Since Pound's initial use of the spelling *Ixotta* takes place in a discussion dependent on the section from pp. 157 to 162, it would seem logical for him to copy one of the first four spellings. And in any event, the spelling he does write is attested only in an obscure footnote regarding Banchi.

Pound's own manuscripts also show that, on at least one occasion, he was aware of the documented testimony regarding Isotta's name, for in late August or early September 1922 he wrote the documented spelling twice in a first draft for what eventually became modern Canto 9, an experiment in translating the letters the Malatestan court had written to Sigismondo when he was away in late 1454, campaigning on behalf of Siena. Among them was the letter from Isotta degli Atti, a translation of which obliged him to confront the question of her signature. In his first typescript of this draft Pound gave a version based on a cursory consultation of Yriarte's transcription and his own sense of how the letter "should" end. The result was simple: "Yxotta da Rimini." Later, however, Pound revised the typescript by comparing his version against Yriarte's and making appropriate corrections. First he canceled the phrase "da Rimini" and replaced it with the reading given by Yriarte, p. 395: *Ariminessie*. Then, without altering this first correction, he copied his earlier reading once more in the margin: *Yxotta da Rimini*. Finally, as a heading above his translation of the letter, he wrote her name a third time: *Ixotta*. For whatever reason, Pound had reverted to his preferred reading. And since he later decided to eliminate Isotta's letter from the canto altogether, he was no longer obliged to confront his only record of the discordant testimony. Thereafter in all drafts Pound always wrote *Isotta* or *Ixotta*, never *Yxotta* or *Ysotta*.

109. On Boni, see his obituary in *The New York Times*, Saturday, 11 July 1924, p. 11, col. 6. Boni gained passing notoriety in 1919 when he greeted President Woodrow Wilson as he entered the Coliseum. Quote from Ezra Pound to Isabel Pound, 24 February 1923, Rome; NHBY, *PA*, Series 2, Box 52, f. 1968.

110. The letter was formerly in the possession of Mary de Rachewiltz, and I

wish to thank her for permitting me to consult it before donating it to the Be-
inecke Rare Book and Manuscript Library of Yale University in 1989. The doc-
ument was among several preserved in Pound's copy of Charles Yriarte, *Un Con-
dottiere au XVᵉ siècle* (1882); at present these have the provisional call number:
Uncat. Za file.204. The letter is written on a small calling card, measuring 212
× 134 mm, folded in half to make two leaves 134 × 106 mm. Printed in the
top left is the simple address: PALATINO E FORO. Below and right is the date
in Boni's hand: *16.2/23*. This, of course, permits us to date his meeting with
Pound quite exactly. It should be noted that Boni's hand is small and affected by
age, making it difficult to read at several points. In the following transcription
an illegible word is registered by square brackets enclosing an elipse, while a
doubtful reading is registered by square brackets enclosing a question mark
immediately before the word. The letter reads:

Caro Ricci
   Ezra Pound, l'arci-arci-critica americano desidera di consoscerti per arrivare a
conoscere col tuo aiuto quel Sigismondo di cui devi averti copiato qualche segreto
misterioso.
   Sarai ad ogni modo in [?] grado [. . .] di poterlo conoscere di persona molto
dotto e produttivo.

> *Affezionatissimo vostro,*
> *Boni*

111. See Renzo de Felice, *Mussolini*, vol. 2: *Il fascista: I. La conquista del
potere, 1921–1925* (Turin: Einaudi, 1966), chap. 5, "Prime esperienze di gov-
erno," pp. 388–517.

112. On Gentile at this time see Renzo de Felice, pp. 386–87, and Sergio
Romano, *Giovanni Gentile: la filosofia al potere* (Milan: Bompiani, 1984), pp.
165–82.

113. On Ricci's life, see the Reale Istituto d'archeologia e storia dell'arte, *In
memoria del Com. Corrado Ricci* (Rome: R. Istituto d'archeologia e storia del-
l'arte, 1935). It contains a biography, a bibliography of his numerous works
(over nine hundred by the time of his death), and moving reminiscences by
friends and colleagues. Especially important is the article on "Il carteggio"
("The Correspondence") by Santi Muratori, pp. 159–74. Among the correspon-
dents whom I discuss elsewhere in this study are: Lodovico Pogliaghi, Alfredo
Oriani, Luigi Orsini, Antonio Beltramelli, and Giovanni Gentile. On Ricci's
earliest collaboration with Gentile, in a series of lectures sponsored by the Fon-
dazione Leonardo in 1921, see Gabriele Turi, *Il fascismo e il consenso degli
intelletuali* (Bologna: Il Mulino, 1980), pp. 27–28. On his participation at the
convention of 29–30 March 1925, see Emilio R. Papa, *Fascismo e cultura* (Ven-
ice-Padua: Marsilio Editore, 1974), p. 162. On Ricci's lecture of 8 February
1933, see *La Tribuna* (Rome), 9 February 1933, p. 3, headlined: "Le grandi
imprese archeologiche compiute a Roma," with "kicker" reading, "La lezione
di Corrado Ricci per l'inaugurazione dei corsi dell'Istituto Nazionale Fascista di

Cultura." For the quotation from Mussolini see Ricci's extensive obituary in *The New York Times*, Wednesday, 6 June 1934, p. 23, col. 3.

114. The letters from Antonio Beltramelli to Ricci are all in RaBC, *Fondo Ricci*, Carteggio, vol. 12, nn. 2722–2777; I quote from the letters of 24 February, 15 March, and 23 March 1907, all of them previously unpublished:

24 febbraio 1907

Caro Signor Ricci—
    Siccome preparo una conferenza su Rimini e più specialmente sul tempio malatestiano e su Isotta, Le sarei grato s'ella volesse mandarmi provisoriamente il discorso che tenne in Rimini commemorandovi l'Alberti.
    La ringrazio di vivo cuore.

Con affetto, Suo
A. Beltramelli.

16 marzo 1907

Caro signore Ricci—
    La ringrazio molto per il grato dono del suo magnifico discorso su l'Alberti. Come per Ravenna [refers to Ricci's guidebook to Ravenna] anche per Rimini l'opera sua mi è stata guida gradevolissima e calda ispirattrice. Io non mi movo per le mie terre a cantarne le forze e le bellezze senza aver Lei come "duce"—Ora la mia conferenza su la terra di Isotta è quasi compiuta e ne sono sodisfatto. Debbo leggerla a Genova e Bologna e a Napoli, ma a Roma la gaia società femminile del Collegio Romano mi ha bellamente scartato come un piccolo importuno che ha troppo ardimento. Vorrei tentare, tanto per non rimanere proprio come un povero piffero, l'Associazione della Stampa. Le pare cosa fattibile? Pottrebbe aiutarmi? Una sua parola sarebbe sufficiente all'accettazione: può dirla? Perdoni la seccatura e mi creda con ammirazione e con affetto,

Suo
A.B.

23 marzo 1907

Caro signor Ricci—
    Le mando il Carlino [*Il Resto del Carlino*, newspaper from Bologna] con un breve resoconto e un brano della mia conferenza. Come vedrà, ci sono *molte remiscenze* del suo bellissimo discorso . . . però prima di conchiudere ne faccio pubblica ammenda.
    Sarà possibile venire a Roma? Mi ricordi e mi creda con ammirata simpatia,

Suo
Antonio Beltramelli

115. A minute report on the restorations is given by Giuseppe Gerola, "Nella soprintendenza ai monumenti della Romagna," s.v. "Rimini," in *Felix Ravenna* 2 (1912), pp. 293–300. On p. 297 n. 1, he mentions Ricci's recent work in the building, and Ricci himself discusses it in Ricci, *Il Tempio Malatestiano* (see note 17), pp. 436–37, specifically dating it to 1912. He discusses the sepul-

chral inscriptions on pp. 436–37 (report and transcriptions) and pp. 446–48 (figures 534–36).

116. NHBY, *PA*, Series 5, Box 63, f. 2430.5 (formerly 40.5). The claim is also confirmed by a comparison with letters in Ricci's hand from the 1920s preserved in the Archivio of the Istituto Nazionale d'Archeologia e Storia dell'Arte, Rome. (I wish to thank Fausto Zevi and Kenneth Haynes for their kindness in communicating these materials.) Their meeting is also confirmed by other evidence. In the Malatesta Cantos Pound devotes several lines to Sigismondo Malatesta's "theft" of precious stones from the walls of San Apollinare in Classe near Ravenna in 1448, and he takes pains to quote from three documents that are located in the municipal library of Ravenna. Although parts of these documents had been quoted and were known as early as 1572, 1582, and 1762, they were not published in their entirety or with indications of their modern locations until the appearance of Corrado Ricci's work in 1924. Since study of Pound's research practices is sufficient to indicate that he could not have located such documents on his own, we must suppose that Ricci also gave him information about these, as part of his effort to provide Pound with "qualche segreto misterioso," as Boni had termed it.

The three documents are: (1) RaAS, Cancelleria vol. 7, N. 6, ff. 4^r, 5^r, 6^r, which is partly quoted by Ricci, *Il Tempio Malatestiano*, p. 486, doc. IV; (2) RaAS, Corporazioni religiose soppresse, Abbazia di San Apollinare in Classe, Pergamene, XX, no. 8, first published in Giovanni-Benedetto Mittarelli and Anselmo Costadoni, *Annales Camaldulenses*, vol. 7 (Venice, 1762), pp. 228–29, and later in Ricci, *Il Tempio Malatestiano*, p. 586, doc. 5; (3) RaAS, Corporazioni religiose soppresse, Abbazia di San Apollinare in Class, vol. 229; this document was partially published in Mittarelli and Costadoni, and in Ricci, *Il Tempio Malatestiano*, pp. 586–87, doc. 6. Documents 1 and 2 were also known to Girolamo Rossi, *Historiae ravennates* (Venice: 1572; I cite from the second edition, Venice, 1589), pp. 632–33. His discussion was followed by Francesco Sansovino, *Della origine, et de' fatti delle famiglie illustri d'Italia* (Venice: presso Altobelli Salicato, 1582), p. 367. Document 3 was quoted incidentally by Mittarelli and Costadini, *Annales Camaldulenses*, vol. 7, pp. 228–29, 293–94.

117. For the letter see note 109. Pound and Ricci clearly discussed at least two subjects: the inscription on the tomb, and the alleged theft of materials from San Apollinare. On the first and its place in the Romantic interpretation, see chapter 1, pp. 33–37. For representative discussions of the second, see Charles Yriarte, *Un condottiere*, pp. 193–94; Edward Hutton, *Sigismondo Pandolfo Malatesta*, p. 202; and Edward Hutton, *The Cities of Romagna*, pp. 193–94. Finally, it is worth noting that Pound also mentions Ricci in *Jefferson and/or Mussolini* (New York: Liveright, 1970; 1st edn., 1935), pp. 84–85. He discusses signs of "the Italian awakening" in the 1920s, and cites two: a new interest in books, and a new interest in restorations, of which latter Ricci was an

example: "Someone mentions the Senatore Corrado Ricci and no one knows who else or how many other sensibilities have been employed." One letter from Ricci to Pound, from 1932, is conserved in NHBY, *PA*, Series 1, f. 1476. No letter from Pound, however, is conserved among Ricci's correspondence at RaBC.

118. Ricci, *Il Tempio Malatestiano*, p. 319.

119. RAS, *Fondo Notarile*, Francesco Paponi 1451–53, fols. 94^r–95^r, *rogito*, 27 July 1452. Pound's notes are in NHBY, *PA*, Series 5, Box 63, f. 2432.53 (formerly 42.53). Pound mistakenly reads and transcribes the date as "1453." His entry reads:

> *94   Isotta. Time of Pope Nic.*

Because Pound had little training in paleography, he could read only certain scripts, such as humanist, and some versions of *cancelleresca* if strongly influenced by humanist script; notarial scripts and *mercantesca* were entirely beyond him, and he seldom could distinguish more than five words in succession. This means, of course, that he could view history only through the princely letters of the dominant classes, and could never gain access to the social lives of other socioeconomic strata. Moreover, despite a vivid and sincere interest in economics, he could never read the primary sources in which economic matters were routinely transacted, since these always employed notarial and *mercantesca* scripts. The situation is sometimes especially sad or ironic when, as here, Pound has come upon an original, unpublished document that plainly interests him, but he can do no more than make out the names of one or two participants in the transaction, with no sense of what the transaction itself is.

It should be noted that Pound also examines another document, the *rogito* of a wedding dowry on behalf of one Isotta di Giovanni da Rimini, dated 7 June 1453, consigning property to Pietro de' Visconti and his son Enea (the latter destined to be her husband). The document is in the same volume of Francesco Paponi, 1451–53, fols. 122–24. In his initial attempt at a transcription he records "Ysotta fili Johi s Guilaraz" [*sic*] from the minute of the *rogito;* "Ysotta adulta" from line 16 of the document; and "Ysotta sprestbile" [*sic*] from line 22. Yet in his summary note, he records: *122 Isotta.* The initial transcription is NHBY, *PA*, Series 5, Box 63, f. 2432.50 (formerly 42.50), the summary f. 2432.53 (formerly 42.53); the two leaves have separated from each other subsequently. Pound's transcriptions containing the sign are found in NHBY, *PA*, Series 3, 2432.31, on his pp. 2, 3, and 2432.40, his p. 2.

120. Ezra Pound to John Quinn, 29 May 1923; NYPL, *MD*, JQP, Box 34, f. 5: "[I] have been snowed under, or at least working on my Malatesta Cantos steadily and without let up from middle of Feb. until about five weeks ago [i.e., 25 April]; and doing overdue job to pay rent from then up till a day or so ago." Cf. Ezra Pound to Isabel Pound, 11 May 1923; NHBY, *PA*, Series 2, Box 52, f. 1968: "Am playing this machine several hours daily. It leaves one very little

to say." Further signs that Pound was busy with the translation emerge in Ezra Pound to Homer Pound, 19 May 1912, NHBY, *PA*, Series 2, Box 52, f. 1968: "⟨Hope to⟩ see daylight, probably wrongly, ⟨i.e. hope ungrounded⟩ a few days hence." Clearly Pound was approaching the end of the translation, which he must have finished some eight days later as he says in the letter to Quinn cited above.

121. On Strater, see Henry Strater, *Works of Sixty Years by Henry Strater* (Ogunquit, Maine: [Henry Strater], 1979). It should be mentioned that Strater returned briefly to the United States in 1919 where he studied at the Art Students League (New York) and the Pennsylvania Academy of the Fine Arts. When he returned to Europe in June 1920, he worked independently in Madrid and studied intermittently at the Academia Real de San Fernando during the autumn and winter. In *Bridge at Ondarroa* (1920) he experiments with slight dislocations of perspective à la Cezanne and adopts the muted grays and earth tones of Spanish painting. In early 1921 he moved to France, where he summered at Montigny-sur-Loing and wintered at St. Jean, Cap Ferrat. For the sober taste of this period one need only recall contemporary works by Léger and Le Corbusier, or the arrival of the *Neue Sachlichkeit* in Germany in 1925 and thereafter.

122. Henry Strater, interview with author, 29 December 1984, Palm Beach, Florida. All subsequent direct quotations from Strater are from this source, unless specified otherwise.

123. Ezra Pound to Homer Pound, [ca. 15 January 1923]; NHBY, *PA*, Series 2, Box 52, f. 1968.

124. Ezra Pound to William Bird, 16 April [1924]; BLUI, *BP*, 1924. Pound's letters from January 1923 in Rapallo give no indication of these discussions, and mention only playing tennis in connection with Strater. Writing to Hemingway on 22 January, for example, he reports that "Ole Stret and I [are] gettin' about ready to go to Cans [sic] and play the lady champeens." It is likely that the discussions took place only after both Pound and Strater had returned to Paris in April 1923. (See Ezra Pound to Ernest Hemingway, [22 January 1923]; Boston, Kennedy Library, E. Hemingway Collection, Pound.)

125. Some influence by Pound appears already in Strater's actions in Rapallo and thereafter in his tour of Italy between January and April 1923. While in Rapallo he did a gouache called *Rapallo Courtyard,* and three watercolors entitled *View of Rapallo, Mountains at Rapallo,* and *Rapallo* (perhaps influenced by Dorothy Pound's watercolor activity). After Ernest Hemingway arrived in Rapallo on 4 February, Strater completed his oil *Boxer Portrait* of him. When the Pounds and Hemingways left on 12 February, Strater set off on a brief tour of Tuscany, including stops in Florence, Siena, and Perugia. In Florence he painted an oil portrait of an unidentified individual, *Florentine,* and throughout his tour he was especially impressed by the work of Piero della Francesca, probably influenced by Pound's outspoken admiration for the artist. He returned to

Paris in late April 1923; see Ezra Pound to Homer Pound, 24 April 1923; NHBY, *PA*, Paige Transcriptions, No. 634: "Marse Henry (Stretter) back from Italy."

126. Henry Strater, interview with Michael Culver, 15 March 1982, quoted in Michael Culver, "The Art of Henry Strater: An Examination of the Illustrations for Pound's *A Draft of XVI. Cantos*," *Paideuma* 12 (1983), pp. 447–78.

127. Ezra Pound to William Bird, 21 April [1924]; BLUI, *BP*, Pound. Compare also Ezra Pound to William Bird, [6 April 1924]; BLUI, *BP*, Pound: "Hell—I told him to cut off the tail of the P—at least I thought I did." Also compare Ezra Pound to William Bird, 10 April [1924]; BLUI, *BP*, Pound: "I *never* sanctioned any love knots in the lower right hand corner."

128. When Strater abruptly left Paris in August 1923 he took the book with him, provoking nearly two years' letters from Pound demanding that he return it. Strater left by 24 August 1923. "Strater gone to bedside of his grandmother in N. Y., so designs for my edtn., de Luxe, are delayed": Ezra Pound to Homer Pound, 24 August 1923; NHBY, *PA*, Series 2, Box 52, f. 1968. This means that Pound's collaboration with Strater lasted only some four months, from ca. 24 April to ca. 24 August 1923. Strater's first efforts were devoted to Canto 4, then to Cantos 5–7 and the Malatesta Cantos (or Cantos 8–11). The evidence that Strater consulted the Yriarte edition is threefold. (1) The illustrations by Strater show many detailed borrowings from the Yriarte book. (2) Strater admits that he consulted the book in his interview with Michael Culver (see note 125). (3) Strater's letters to Pound show that Pound repeatedly asked him to return the copy of Yriarte. On 13 January 1924 Strater writes to Pound: "As for that Yriarte, you forgot already what you sed, 'Tek it, Hen'y, ah ain got no mo use foit.'" See Henry Strater to Ezra Pound, 13 January 1924; NHBY, *PA*, Series 1, f. 1705. And again, more than two years later in November 1926, Pound has apparently complained that Strater had the Yriarte copy rebound; Strater replies, "Re Yriarte how thell could the book be preserved, without rebinding? If I had known that you valued the cover more than the contents, I would have kept the latter. But I admit it is a loss to the world. The cover was in a class with the Opera." See Henry Strater to Ezra Pound, 15 November 1926; NHBY, *PA*, Series 1, f. 1705.

129. Ezra Pound, *A Draft of XVI. Cantos* (Paris: Three Mountains, [1925]). The illustration appears as the headpiece to Canto 8, on p. 27.

130. Carpenter, *Civilisation: Its Cause and Cure*, pp. 46–47. (See note 2.)

131. *A Draft of XVI. Cantos*, p. 42. *Ymn* 17 in Yriarte, *Un Condottiere*, p. 103, quoted in note 106. The typescript note is NHBY, *PA*, Series 5, Box 63, f. 2436.4 (formerly 46.4), also quoted in note 106.

132. *A Draft of XVI. Cantos*, p. 37.

133. Here also Strater has borrowed from Yriarte, whose engraver depicts several horses with caparisons bearing the entwined cipher (Yriarte, *Un Condottiere*, p. 171, fig. 86); thus Strater borrowed the cipher from these designs

and added it to his own, since the specific horse which he copied did not have the sign.

134. See the account by Giovanni Soranzo, *Pio II e la politica italiana nella lotta contro i Malatesti (1457–1463)* (Padua: Fratelli Drucker, 1911), pp. 288–89.

135. *A Draft of XVI. Cantos*, p. 38.

136. See for example: Mayo, "IX," p. 19; and Hugh Kenner, *The Pound Era* (Berkeley: University of California Press, 1971), p. 254. Kearns, *Guide to . . . Selected Cantos*, p. 53.

137. Events of 16 August 1944 are recounted by Augusto Campana, "Vicende e problemi degli studi malatestiani," in *Studi romagnoli* 2 (1951), pp. 1–15. The official report of damage to the building is given by Emilio Lavagnino, *Cinquanta monumenti italiani dannegiati dalla guerra* (Rome: Istituto poligrafico dello stato, 1946), which is also available in translation as *Fifty War-Damaged Documents of Italy* (Rome: Istituto poligrafico dello stato, 1946), with a report on the Tempio on pp. 96–99. Also important for the damage and restoration procedures, and for photos of the damage, are: Alfredo Lenzi, Corrado Capuzzuoli, Giuseppe Rinaldi, "Il restauro del tempio malatestiano a Rimini," *Giornale del genio civile* 85 (1947), pp. 381–91; Roberto Pane, "Restauri del tempio malatestiano a Rimini," *Atti del V Convegno Nazionale di storia dell'architettura (Perugia—23 settembre 1948)* (Florence: R. Noccioli, 1957), pp. 643–47; Emilio Lavagnino, "Il restauro del tempio malatestiano" in *Bollettino d'arte* 35 (1950), pp. 176–84; and Italy, Ministero della Pubblica Istruzione, *La ricostruzione del patrimonio artistico italiano* (Rome: Ministero della Pubblica Istruzione, 1950), pp. 92–107. The building's current form is the outcome of a vast labor of reconstruction. Every block in the exterior walls was numbered and removed, and the entire edifice reassembled. The delicate labor was funded with 15 million lire by the Italian government and sixty-five thousand dollars from Samuel Kress, the latter solicited by Bernard Berenson and Doro Levi through the American Association for the Restoration of Italian Monuments. Work began in October 1947 and was completed on 30 December 1949.

Some information on the bombing of the city is given by Lavagnino, *Fifty Monuments*, p. 98. See also Touring Club Italiano, *Emilia-Romagna*, 5th edn., (Milan: Touring Club Italiano, 1971), p. 677; Carla Catolfi Ferri, Ferrucio Farina, and Emilio Salvatori (eds.), *Macerie: Rimini bombardata fotografata da Luigi Severi* (Rimini: Bruno Ghigi Editore, 1984), where Severi's life and activities in Rimini are also recounted in the introduction. See also Bruno Ghigi, *La guerra a Rimini e sulla linea gotica dal Foglia al Marecchia* (Rimini: Bruno Ghigi Editore, 1980). The monastery was badly damaged in a massive bombing of 28 December 1943. The Tempio suffered its worst damage in the bombing of 29 January 1944, which also struck the monastery/museum again. Because many paintings of the sixteenth and seventeenth centuries were too large to be easily hidden, they had been left in the museum. Twenty-three were destroyed, along with two bronzes; another twenty were damaged. The numismatic collections became the favorite prey of robbers, who stole some fifty-three medals linked with the Malatesta family. Even after the city's liberation there was further damage to the cultural heritage. In an effort to find firewood in the bitter winter of 1944, some inhabitants began to burn the frames and canvases that had remained exposed. Worse yet was the fate of the only portion of the monastery/museum, that had survived. Its supporting beams were repeatedly vandalized for firewood, weakening the structure's last support. On 14 November 1946 it collapsed of its own accord, the last testimony to six hundred years of history.

138. On the press in the Republic of Salò, see Ugoberto Alfassio Grimaldi, *La stampa di Salò* (Milan: Bompiani, 1979), and Phillip V. Cannistraro, *La fabbrica del consenso: Facismo e massmedia* (Bari: Laterza, 1975). Also useful is Silvio Bertoldi, *Salò: Vita e morte della Repubblica Sociale Italiana* (Milan: Rizzoli, 1976), chap. 14. Bertoldi reports (p. 22) that Rivoire was among the earliest of the journalists to support Mussolini after the news of his "rescue" by the Germans was released on 13 September 1943 . Grimaldi notes (p. 44) the effort to foreground news about Anglo-American destruction of the cultural patrimony, citing a directive of the Ministry of Popular Culture (headed by Fernando Mezzasomma), dated 8 November 1943, which urges newspapers "to stress in their headlines the criminal Anglo-American attack against the Vatican City and to describe minutely the historical and artistic importance of the buildings and works struck by them."

139. A clipping of the article, probably made by Pound, was formerly preserved in his copy of Charles Yriarte's book, *Un Condottiere au XVᵉ siècle*; the clipping is now in NHBY, with the provisional call number: Uncat. Za file.204. A preliminary report of the clipping, without reference to its source, title, or date, is given by Barbara C. Eastman, "The Gap in *The Cantos:* 72 and 73," *Paideuma* 8 (1979), pp. 415–27, on p. 424 n. 19: "Hugh Kenner has discovered a wartime clipping from an Italian newspaper among Pound's papers, reporting extensive damage to Rimini and especially to the Tempio Malatesiana [*sic*]. Almost certainly, this was the foundation for Pound's bitter imaginings in Canto 73." The use of the term "imaginings" may suggest that she does not believe the building was actually damaged. Certainly this is the case with Massimo Bacigalupo, who comments on "Pound's belief, luckily unfounded, that the Tempio Malatestiano had been severely damaged," in his "Poet at War: Ezra Pound's Suppressed Italian Cantos," *South Atlantic Quarterly* 83 (1984), pp. 69–79, on p. 76. But as I have shown, the building was damaged indeed (see note 137).

140. Twenty-six lines from Canto 72 were published on 15 January 1945 in *La Marina Repubblicana* 2, no. 2, p. 2. All of Canto 73 was published on 1 February in the next issue of the same journal, p. 7. See Donald Gallup, *Ezra Pound, A Bibliography* (Charlottesville: University Press of Virginia, 1983), C1697b, C1699a (hereafter cited as Gallup, followed only by the item number).

For further information see Eastman, "The Gap in *The Cantos*." All citations are from ND70[10].

141. See Manlio Torquato Dazzi (tr.), Albertino Mussato, *L'Ecerinide* (Città di Castello: S. Lapi, 1914). Also relevant is his later book, *Il Mussato preumanista* (Verona: Neri Pozza, 1964).

142. An array of clippings from articles that report the battle for Rimini from both the northern ("occupied") and southern ("liberated") zones of Italy is given in Bruno Ghigi, *La Guerra a Rimini* (see note 137), pp. [349]–[368]; the article on "45,000 Dead" appears on p. [366], though without mention of the date or page (25 September 1944, p. 1, cols. 7–9). Not included is the article from the *Corriere della sera* of 24 September, p. 1, cols. 4–6, with headline reading: "Aspra lotta per il possesso dei monti del settore centrale." It reports:

> Nel settore adriatico gli "alleati" si trovano ora presso Rimini, città tuttora in saldo possesso dei Germanici. Il nemico non è dunque riuscito a conseguire lo sfondamento. Esso è arrivato a forzare l'uscita dalla montagna, ma finora soltanto all'estrema ala destra e in un punto così stretto che non gli consente di constituire una base per operazioni di un certo respiro.

The article that is Pound's source appears in *Corriere della sera* 1 October 1944, p. 1, cols. 7–8. For a transcription and translation, see appendix 3.

Finally, one implication of these arguments is a revision of the dating of Canto 72 proposed by Barbara C. Eastman, "The Gap in *The Cantos*" (see note 139), who urges that Canto 72 be dated "between the autumn of 1943 and the spring or early summer of 1944 because of historical details within it" (p. 421). (Bacigalupo, "Poet at War," dates both 72 and 73 rather vaguely to "1944.") Instead it is clear that Canto 72 was composed only after 4 June 1944, when it was prompted by the newspaper article of that date. Moreover, it was probably not completed until much later. In particular, it refers to Gemistos Plethon in a fashion that seems incomprehensible except in the light of the seizure of Rimini by the Greek Brigade on 21 September 1944.

Canto 73 was clearly composed between 1 October 1944 (the date of the article that is its source) and 15 January 1945 (date when it was probably submitted for publication). It may be that composition extended throughout this entire period, or that the concluding lines were added later. Their militant hope for a resurgence of the fascist regime would have been inappropriate in the wake of the losses suffered by German forces in August and September 1944, and indeed would have been implausible until the collapse of the Allied offensive in Italy (along the Gothic line) in late October. Allied forces issued an official order to halt the offensive on 28 October, an order that acknowledged that the drive had already stopped several days earlier. If this event is a precondition for Pound's hopes, then it is clear that his composition extended to at least November 1944. Still, I suspect it extended even later, perhaps as late as December 1944. Its optimistic call for a *riscossa* (reconquest) in the *inverno* (winter) seems to reflect the curious mood that prevailed in the wake of Mussolini's last public address at the Teatro Lirico of Milan on 16 December that year. In particular, Pound's use of the term *riscossa* (lines 17, 104; see the translations in the text) may echo Mussolini's concluding sentence: "Camerati, cari camerati milanesi! È Milano che deve dare e darà gli uomini, le armi, la volontà e il segnale della *riscossa*." ("It is Milan that must give and will give the men, the arms, the will, and the signal for the reconquest.") On the speech, its wide diffusion, and its reception, see Bertoldi, *Salò*, pp. 364–68. On the 1944 military campaign see Douglas Orgill, *The Gothic Line: The Autumn Campaign in Italy in 1944* (London: Heinemann, 1967). On Pound's article in the newspaper, see Gallup, C1681.

143. Dorothy Shakespear Pound to Olivia Shakespear [15 May] 1922; private collection. I am grateful to the owner for his permission to quote from this letter, and for his repeated kindness and support.

144. Giovanni Gentile, "La filosofia dell'azione del Laberthonnière," *La Critica* 4 (1906), p. 433; this important essay is reprinted in *Il modernismo e i rapporti tra religione e filosofia*, 2nd edn. (Bari: Laterza, 1921), pp. 16–29, with quotation on p. 18.

145. Giovanni Gentile, "La Rinascita dell'idealismo," in *Saggi critici. Serie prima* (Naples: Ricciardi, 1921), pp. 1–25, quotation on p. 11. Ezra Pound, NHBY, *PA*, Series 5, Box 63, f. 1.

146. Draft *C1*, NHBY, *BP*, Series 2, f. 22. It should be noted that on the typescript revision of this draft, *C2*, Pound adds an autograph dedication of the canto to T. S. Eliot, which is then deleted in later revision. On the arch in Rimini see Guido Achille Mansuelli, "L'arco di Augusto in Rimini," in *Emilia Romagna* 2 (1944), pp. 109–95, and particularly his discussion of its name and function on pp. 109–11. See also his later essay, "La posizione storica dell'arco di Rimini," in *Atti del V Convegno Nazionale di storia dell'architectura (Perugia—23 settembre 1948)* (Florence: R. Noccioli, 1957), pp. 167–71; and "Il monumento augusteo del 27 a.C., nuove ricerche sull'arco di Rimini," *Arte antica e moderna* 8 (1959), pp. 363–91. For a representative assessment of the arch and the church of San Francesco, see Nikolaus Pevsner, *History of Western Architecture* (Harmondsworth: Penguin, 7th edn., 1963; 1st edn., 1943), pp. 188–91. For assessments more contemporary with Pound see Yriarte, *Un Condottiere*, p. 191; Hutton, *Sigismondo Pandolfo Malatesta*, pp. 170–71, 203; Hutton, *The Cities of Romagna*, p. 114; and Beltramelli, *Un tempio d'amore*, pp. 57–58.

147. The destruction is detailed by Mansuelli, "L'arco di Augusto in Rimini," p. 111. For a description of the gate before the "restoration" see Luigi Tonini, *Rimini dopo il mille*, ed. Pier Giorgio Pasini (Rimini: Bruno Ghighi, 1975; the manuscript dates from ca. 1880), pp. 127, 127 n.172, 129, and 129 n. 174. An engraving shows the earlier environment of the arch on p. 129. Other illustrations of it before the 1937 monumentalization appear in Charles Yriarte,

Les Bords de l'Adriatique (Paris: Hachette, 1878), p. [553]; and Yriarte, *Un Condottiere*, p. 57. On the "restoration" see the official publication commemorating its completion by Salvatore Aurigemma, "La Porta augustea di Rimini," *Ariminum, numero speciale per il bimillenario augusteo* (Rimini: City of Rimini, 1938).

148. Roland Barthes, *Image, Music, Text,* tr. Stephen Heath (Hill & Wang, 1971), p. 147.

149. Paul de Man, "Criticism and Crisis," in *Blindness and Insight,* 2nd edn. (Minneapolis: University of Minnesota Press, 1983), p. 17.

150. Geoffrey Hartmann, "Looking back on Paul de Man," in Lindsay Waters and Wlad Godzich (eds.), *Reading de Man Reading* (Minneapolis: University of Minnesota Press, 1989), p. 19.

151. Paul de Man, "Criticism and Crisis," pp. 15 ("tendency"), 16 ("Europe"), 14 ("hindsight").

152. Arthur C. Danto, *Narration and Knowledge* (New York: Columbia University Press, 1985), p. 18. I am paraphrasing his remarks as closely as possible here.

153. Jürgen Habermas, "A Review of Gadamer's *Truth and Method,* in Fred R. Dallmayr and Thomas A. McCarthy (eds.), *Understanding and Social Inquiry* (Notre Dame, Ind.: University of Notre Dame Press, 1977), p. 339.

154. Antonio Gramsci, "Discussion before the Political Commission" at the Third National Convention of the Italian Communist Party, in Gramsci, ed. Elsa Fubini, *La costruzione del Partito communista (1923–1926),* pp. 481–88, esp. p. 483. Angelo Tasca, in *Bollettino: Documenti del III Congresso Nazionale del Partito Comunista Italiano* (n.p., n.d. [but 1926]), p. 29, cited by Renzo de Felice, *Mussolini,* vol. 1: *Il rivoluzionario,* p. xxii.

155. Hayden White, "New Historicism: A Comment," in H. Aram Veeser, *The New Historicism* (New York: Routledge, 1989), p. 296.

156. Luigi Pasquini, *Gente del mio tempo* (Rimini: Maggiolis, 1979), pp. 215–17, for the text. I present a free adaptation, not a literal translation. However, I include the Italian for most of the statements attributed to Pound. Information on Pasquini's life and works is furnished by Silvano Cardellini in the "Presentazione" to the same volume, pp. 11–17.

Appendix 1

1. The only previous study to examine these manuscripts in detail is that of Peter D'Epiro, "A Touch of Rhetoric: Ezra Pound's Malatesta Cantos" (diss., Yale University, 1981), published with minor revisions under the same title (Ann Arbor: University Microfilms, 1983). Because he has no methodological foundations for dating the manuscripts, D'Epiro relies on intrinsic characteristics alone. The result is often guesswork, and the ordering of the manuscripts that he proposes is mistaken. Still, D'Epiro was correct in calling attention to the disorganized state of the manuscripts.

Currently all the Malatesta manuscripts and many related documents (with the exception of two) are found in the Pound Archive at the Beinecke Rare Book and Manuscript Library of Yale University. Within the archive is a series of folders formerly labeled "The Cantos Folders," containing material related to the composition of *The Cantos*. The Malatesta materials were formerly contained in Folders 40–70; under a recent reorganization, they are now found in Series 5, Folders 2430–60. A single file may contain anywhere from five to two hundred leaves, or one to more than sixty different documents. Moreover, a single manuscript is sometimes scattered in more than one file. Such problems make it difficult to find a simple means of indicating the actual location of any single text. For our purpose, it will suffice to give the locations only of "the Sirmione manuscripts," the earliest drafts and notes for the Malatesta Cantos, composed between about 9 and 20 June 1922. To do so, two devices are adopted. First, each text is assigned an editorial siglum; second, each siglum is correlated with the actual place of the manuscript within "The Cantos Folders" by means of the list of manuscripts given below. In the list, each manuscript or documentary item is assigned a number, of which the first unit indicates the folder containing it, the second its place within the folder. Thus "2432.5" indicates Folder 2432, the fifth item within it. (An item is any group of papers whose intrinsic or extrinsic characteristics are discrete from groups of papers immediately preceding and following.) This indication of the item may be followed by an additional description indicating where the text under discussion is located within the item—that is, in those cases where a manuscript or documentary item contains more than one text. The additional description indicates the leaf and the side of the leaf containing the text in question.

List of "The Sirmione Manuscripts"

Sigla	Cantos Folders
A	2430.7
B	2431.8, 2^{r-v}
N1	2431.5; 2431.6, fragment B^v
N2	2431.6, fragment A^{r-v}, fragment B^v
N3	2431.8, 1^r

2. For Pound's travels in Italy in 1922, see appendix 2.

3. Ezra Pound to T. S. Eliot, 18 May 1923; private collection, Mrs. Valerie Eliot.

4. I wish to acknowledge the courtesy and kindness extended to me repeatedly by Omar Pound in the course of this work, particularly in regard to information from the correspondence of Ezra and Dorothy Pound during the years 1922–23.

5. Ezra Pound to John Quinn, 9 June 1922; NYPL, *MD*, JQP, Box 34, f. 4.

Ezra Pound to Agnes Bedford, 16 June 1922; BLUI, *PM.2*, Bedford, 1922. Ezra Pound to John Quinn, 20 June 1922; NYPL, *MD*, JQP, Box 34, f. 4. Ezra Pound to Agnes Bedford, 29 June 1922; BLUI, *PM.2*, Bedford, 1922. In giving the measurements for these letters I refer only to the original size of the sheet, though in fact two of the letters (16, 29 June to A. Bedford) are only half-sheets, each 211 × 270 mm. Also, these letters by no means constitute all the letters written by Pound from Sirmione (nor is the like assumed for other periods or locations discussed subsequently), for too much of Pound's correspondence is still in private hands to permit a complete census. Nevertheless, the letters I have examined are sufficient to permit an accurate chronology of the extrinsic characteristics of the correspondence. Of course all descriptions such as "the first letter from Sirmione" refer only to the body of material described here, and not to the entire corpus of extant documentation.

6. Ezra Pound to Agnes Bedford, 28 May 1922; BLUI, *PM.2*, Bedford, 1922. Ezra Pound to W. C. Williams, 29 May 1922; BLSUNY, *PC*. (I am grateful to Saundra Taylor for information regarding the letters to Agnes Bedford, and to Robert Bertoff regarding the letters to William Carlos Williams.) Compare also Ezra Pound to Homer Pound, 22 May 1922; NHBY, *PA*, Series 2, Box 52, f. 1967. For permission to examine the originals of Pound's letters to Homer and Isabel Pound, I am grateful to Mary de Rachewiltz.

7. All of Pound's letters from 4–5 July 1922 until 5 January 1923 are written on various kinds of typing paper.

8. There is also a fifth manuscript with matching features, but its intrinsic characteristics leave no doubt that it was written after Pound returned to Paris on 2 July.

9. Ezra Pound to John Quinn, 9 June 1922.

10. Ezra Pound to John Quinn, 20 June 1922; Ezra Pound to Agnes Bedford, 29 June 1922.

Appendix 2

1. Noel Stock, *The Life of Ezra Pound* (Harmondsworth: Penguin, 1974; 1st edn., 1970), pp. 310–12; Peter D'Epiro, "A Touch of Rhetoric: Ezra Pound's Malatesta Cantos" (diss., Yale University, 1981), pp. 24–25; and Humphrey Carpenter, *A Serious Character: The Life of Ezra Pound* (Boston: Houghton Mifflin, 1988), p. 418. The other biographies of Pound are so poor that they scarcely merit mention. Further references to Stock and D'Epiro are given by their names only.

2. On his reading of Berman, see carbon of Ezra Pound to Louis Berman, 1 March 1922, and Ezra Pound to James Sibley Watson, Jr., 1 March 1922; both NYPL, BC, *JSWP.*

3. On the Bel Esprit project, see Ezra Pound to Jeanne Robert Foster, 12 March 1922; CHH, bMs 1635. See Ezra Pound to T. S. Eliot, 14 March, 1922;

BLUI, PM.1, Eliot; printed in T. S. Eliot, *Letters of T. S. Eliot*, ed. Valerie Eliot, vol. 1: *1898–1922*, pp. 511–15 (hereafter this volume is abbreviated as *LOTSE 1*). See Ezra Pound, "Credit and the Fine Arts: A Practical Application," *The New Age* 30.22 (30 March 1922). The article was composed on 13 March 1922. See Ezra Pound to William Carlos Williams, 18 March 1922; BLSUNY, *PC*. See Ezra Pound to Agnes Bedford, 18 March and 19 March 1922; BLUI, *PM.1*, Bedford, 1922.

4. For Pound's role in the publication of *The Waste Land*, see Lawrence S. Rainey, "The Price of Modernism: Reconsidering the Publication of *The Waste Land*," in Ronald Bush, ed., *T. S. Eliot: The Modernist in History* (Cambridge: Cambridge University Press, 1990), pp. 90–133.

5. Pound followed the release of Morand's book closely; he promised to send a copy to John Quinn as soon as it appeared. See Ezra Pound to John Quinn, 21 February 1922; NYPL, *MD*, JQP, Box 34, f. 4.

6. "Visas for Italy in order, and we shd. leave on Monday" (or 27 March), Ezra Pound to Isabel Pound, 22 March 1922; NHBY, *PA*, Series 2, Box 52, f. 1967. See also his postcard to Agnes Bedford, postmarked 27 March 1922, Paris: "Address from now till next time Fermo in Posta[,] Sienna" [*sic*] (BLUI, *PM.2*, Bedford, 1922). And see his postcard to Scofield Thayer, also postmarked 27 March 1922, Paris, which likewise reports his next address as "Fermo in Posta" in Siena; NHBY, *DP*, Series 4, Box 38, f. 1073. See also Ezra Pound to Wyndham Lewis, 5 April [1922]: "I had left Paris before you wrote re/ Schiff.—I left on March 27th." The letter appears in Timothy Materer (ed.), *Pound/Lewis: The Letters of Ezra Pound and Wyndham Lewis* (New York: New Directions, 1985), p. 130.

7. Ezra Pound to Homer Pound, 29 March [1922]; NHBY, *PA*, Series 2, Box 52, f. 1967.

8. "Got here last night": Ezra Pound to Jeanne Foster, 5 April 1922; CHH, bMs Am 1635.

9. Ezra Pound to John Quinn, 4 April 1922; NYPL, *MD*, JQP, Box 34, f. 4.

10. Ezra Pound to Jeanne Foster, 23 April 1922; CHH, bMs Am 1635.

11. Ezra Pound to Scofield Thayer, [6 April 1922]; NHBY, *BP*, Series 4, Box 38, f. 1072. In the September 1921 issue of *The Dial* he had published a translation of "Turkish Night."

12. Ezra Pound to Homer Pound, 11 April 1922; NHBY, *PA*, Series 2, Box 52, f. 1967.

13. Ezra Pound to Homer Pound, 12 April 1922; NHBY, *PA*, Series 2, Box 52, f. 1967. Ezra Pound to John Quinn, 12 April 1922; NYPL, *MD*, JQP, Box 34, f. 4. Ezra Pound to Jeanne Foster, [15 April 1922]; CHH, bMs AM 1635.

14. Peter D'Epiro mistakenly reports: "Between April 13 and May 3 he visited, among other places, Ancona, Rimini, and Ravenna (*Paige*, no's. 612–13; 616)."

His error stems from two sources. The first is a group of letters contained in the so-called Paige Transcriptions. (These are the documents cited in D'Epiro's parenthetical note; they are transcriptions of letters by Pound that were made by D. D. Paige in the late 1940s when he was planning to edit Pound's *Selected Letters.*) Paige Transcription no. 612 reports a letter from Pound to Kate Buss dated 4 May, Venice; and Paige Transcription no. 613 reports a letter to Homer Pound dated 22 May, also from Venice. The second source is Noel Stock, who reports a third letter, dated 6 May, and also from Venice: ". . . Pound went to Venice; from there on 6 May he wrote to Mrs. [Jeanne] Foster" (Stock, p. 311). Because all three letters are said to be from Venice, D'Epiro is led to assume that Pound stayed in Venice throughout the period from 4 to 22 May. This assumption he tries to integrate with two other items of information. First, Noel Stock claims that "*after* touring central Italy Pound went to Venice" (p. 311, italics mine). Second, the letter of 22 May (Paige no. 613) reports that Pound has been traveling in central Italy, specifically Assisi, Ancona, and Rimini. D'Epiro therefore reasons that these travels must be the ones referred to by Stock, therefore anterior to the stay in Venice, and therefore prior to May 4. Whence his conclusion: "Between April 13 and May 3 he visited, among other places, Ancona, Rimini, and Ravenna (*Paige*, no's. 612–13; 616)."

The problem arose through mistakes that were made in reading or understanding the addresses of two letters. Paige apparently failed to perceive that the Venice address for the letter of 4 May (Paige no. 612) did not indicate Pound's location when he was writing the letter, but anticipated where he would be when Buss's reply would reach him. On 4 May Pound was not in Venice, but either in Cortona or en route for Perugia. (See the arguments in the text proper.) Noel Stock simply misread the address on the letter of 6 May: Pound's letter of that date to Jeanne Foster bears the address "Perugia" in his own hand, and the word Venice appears nowhere near it. Once these mistakes have been eliminated, the grounds for D'Epiro's inference disappear. Pound did indeed go to Ancona, Rimini, and Ravenna: but he did so *after* 6 May, not before. Specifically, his journey to these cities took place from ca. 12 May to ca. 21 May. For the arguments, see the text proper.

15. Ezra Pound to Scofield Thayer, 23 April 1922; NHBY, *DP*, Series 4, Box 38, f. 1072.

16. Ezra Pound to John Quinn, 6 May 1922; NYPL, *MD*, JQP, Box 34, f. 4.

17. Ezra Pound to Jeanne Foster, [6 May 1922]; CHH, bMs 1635. Ezra Pound to Scofield Thayer, 6 May 1922; NHBY, *BP*, Series 4, Box 38, f. 1072.

18. Ezra Pound to John Quinn, 6 May 1922.

19. Ezra Pound to Scofield Thayer, 6 May 1922.

20. Dorothy Shakespear Pound to Olivia Shakespear, [15 May 1922]; private collection. I am grateful to the owner for generously allowing me to examine this document.

21. Ezra Pound to Homer Pound, 22 May 1922; NHBY, *PA*, Series 2, Box 52, f. 1967. On the contract with Liveright, see p. 48.

22. Victor Llona to Ezra Pound, 19 May 1922; "Memorandum of Agreement," 22 May 1922; both in BLUI, *PM.1*, 1922.

23. NHBY, *PA*, Paige Transcription no. 612. On the problems connected with this letter see note 14 above.

24. Ezra Pound to Agnes Bedford; BLUI, *PM.1*, Bedford, 1922.

25. On 17 May Eliot informed Richard Aldington: "I am off on Saturday [20 May] to Lugano for a fortnight's rest; I hope to cross over into Italy and see Ezra for a few days." On 20 May he wrote to Gilbert Seldes, "I am writing on the eve of a 4'nights holiday"; and to Richard Cobden-Sanderson, "I am just off for a fortnight's holiday." His plans clearly called for an excursion lasting from 20 May ("Saturday") to 4 June (a Sunday), and for his return to work on Monday, 5 June. To return to London on Sunday, 4 June, he would have had to leave Verona sometime late Friday, 2 June. All the quotations here are from *LOTSE* 1, pp. 525, 526.

26 In addition, two performances were offered on 4 June (Sunday), and a final performance on 6 June (Tuesday). This information is from *L'Arena* (Verona): advertisement of 27 May (p. 2, col. 4); advertisement and preview of 31 May (p. 2, col. 4); advertisement of 1 June (p. 2, col. 3); review of 2 June (p. 2, col. 6); review of 3 June (p. 2, col. 5); and review of 4 June (p. 2, col. 4); announcement of 7 June (p. 2, col. 3).

27. The passages are from Draft *C1*, lines 82–85. Although the draft is frankly autobiographical, biographical inferences must be made with caution.

28. Draft *C1*, NHBY, *BP*, Series 2, f. 22. Draft *C3*, NHBY, *PA*, Series 5, Box 63, f. 2440.1.

29. ND70[10] 29.143–46; 78.137–40 and 141–42.

30. Letters and envelope from Scratton to Pound, [21 February], [1 March], 6 March [1922], 21 June, 14 July 1922; NHBY, *PA*, Series 1, f. 3. Eliot's meeting with Pound in Verona is also confirmed by his letter to Sidney Schiff, dated "early June 1922" by Valerie Eliot (mostly likely 6 June), in which he reports on his recent vacation: "[. . .] and I also went to Verona and saw Pound" (*LOTSE* 1, p. 528).

31. Ezra Pound to John Quinn, 9 June 1922 and 4 April 1922; NYPL, *MD*, JQP, Box 34, f. 4.

32. Ezra Pound to John Quinn, 20 June 1922; NYPL, *MD*, JQP, Box 34, f. 4.

33. Ezra Pound to Agnes Bedford, 29 June 1922; BLUI, *PM.1*, Bedford, 1922.

34. Ezra Pound to Wyndham Lewis, 14 July 1922; in Materer (ed.), *Pound/Lewis*, p. 130.

35. Ezra Pound to Homer Pound, [16 July 1922]; NHBY, *PA*, Series 2, Box 52, f. 1967.

36. The notes are designated *N2*; NHBY, *PA*, Series 5, Box 63, f. 2431.6 (formerly 41.6).

37. "Got back from Italy a fortnight ago": Ezra Pound to Harriet Monroe, 16 July 1922; in *SL*, p. 182.

38. Ezra Pound to John Quinn, 4–5 July 1922; NYPL, *MD*, JQP, Box 34, f. 4.

Index

References to pages with figures are in boldface type; a *t* after a page number refers to a table.

Academies in eighteenth century, 94–95
Ackroyd, Peter, 61
Adorno, Theodor, 6, 7
Aeneid, 160
Agostino di Duccio, **15, 16, 18,** 179, 227, 296n.141
Alberti, Leon Battista, 9–13, **10, 11, 12, 13,** 70
Albini, Giuseppe, 36, 188
Alfonso V, king of Naples, Aragon, and Sicily, 86, 87–88, 116, 125
Amiani, Pietro-Maria, 94, 103, 104*t;* and Battaglini, 98; on murder of Polissena Sforza, 96–97; and Pound, 119–20, 121, 293n.117; and Soranzo, 115, 129, 148
Ammanati, Jacopo, cardinal of Pavia, 166–73, 186, 218; in Beltramelli, 171; *Commentarii,* 167–68; on Isotta, 168; life and career, 166–67; in Moroni, 169–70; and Pius II, 166–68, 309n.41; in Pound, 171–73; and Sigismondo, 168, 307n.36; in Yriarte, 170–71; writings, 167–68
Ancona, 166, 236, 237
Ancona, chronicle of, 119
Annotated index to the CANTOS of Pound (Edwards and Vasse), 135, 136
Antheil, George, 70
Antonio, Count, 89
Appel, Karl Otto, 66
Apuleius, 168
Arch of Augustus (Rimini), 84, 105, 220–21, 224, 283n.73, 332n.147
Archives, Italian, 103–4; Florence, 69, 71, 103, 109; Milan, 103–4, 109, 113, 115, 129, 149; Rimini, 197; Siena, 109; Vatican City, 128, 179; and Pound, 69, 71, 115, 128, 129; and Yriarte, 109, 179
Arduini, Luigi, 36, 188
Armand, Alfred, 162, 164
Arturo, A. R. P., 91
Assisi, 236, 237, 240
Atti, Francesco degli, 197
Atti, Isotta degli, 1–2, 85, 118, 120, 122, 149, 166, 197–98; biographies of, 94, 95, 169, 174, 185, 187; bust of (Pisa), 133; in Cantos 72 and 73, 217; and church of San Francesco, 4, 14, 19, 30 32*t,* 33–36, 110–11, 126, 153, 154, 159, 160, 161, 173, 177–86, 188, 209, 227; depictions of (*see also* medals of), 20, **21,** 188, 204, pl. 2; inscriptions to, 19, 30, 32*t,* 33–34, 161–64, 186, 195–97, **196,** 218; medals of, 160–64, 166, 186, 218; poems to, 19, 35, 42, 121, 177–86, 187, 218, 224; and Polissena Sforza, 85, 89, 90, 95–96, 98, 100, 110–13, 149, 153, 154, 161–62; and Provençal culture, 41–42; and sign *SI,* 20, **21,** 187–91, 202–9, 218, 224; and Sigismondo, 1–2, 14, 20, **21,** 33–36, 41–42, 85, 89, 90, 95–96, 98, 110–12, 135, 161–64, 168–73, 177–86, 187–91, 197, 204–6, 209, 218, 227; spelling of name, 8, 22, 188–89, 191, 197–98, 321n.108; tomb of, 1, 14, **18, 19,** 33–34, 35, 195–97, **196**

Atti, Isotta degli (*continued*)
—in Cantos 8–11 (Malatesta Cantos),
176–77, 187, 219–20; draft *A*, 30,
32, 36; fragment *b*, 153, 159, 164–
66; *Ymn*, 41–42, 172–73, 175–76
—discussed by: Ammanati, 168–69; Al-
bini, 36; Arduini, 36; Battaglini, 98;
Beltramelli, 36, 113, 118, 171–72;
Burckhardt, 19, 34, 159; chronicle of
pseudo-Alessandro, 174, 218; Hutton,
36; Maurel, 35–36; Mazzuchelli, 95–
96, 98, 169, 174; Moroni, 98, 100,
169–70; Pius II, 30, 32*t*, 33–34, 206;
Simonetta, 90; Villari, 35, 111–12;
Yriarte, 35, 41–42, 110–11, 170–71,
174–75
Austria, 94, 99
Azeglio, Massimo d', 99

Bach, Johann Sebastian, 227
Baedeker guidebooks, 35, 105, 117,
180, 254n.15, 315n.73
Barthes, Roland, 58, 221
Bartolo di Iacopo Mercati, 85
Baschet, Armand, 65, 265n.80
Basel, 101
Basinio da Parma, 160–61, **205**
Basler Zeitung (newspaper), 101
Bathsheba, 180
Battaglini, Francesco Gaetano, 94, 97–
98, 103, 104*t*, 110, 112, 121, 188,
252n.8, 280n.56; and Hutton, 112; on
murder of Polissena Sforza, 97–98;
and Pound, 121; on sign *SI*, 188
Beardsley, Monroe, 141
"Because I Could Not Stop For Death"
(Dickinson), 141
Bedford, Agnes, 233, 237–38, 241, 242
Bel Esprit, 70, 234, 237
Beltramelli, Antonio, 31, 32*t*, **73,** 171–
72; career, 72–74, 107, 152, 219,
224; on the church of San Francesco,
31, 33, 36, 41; and Convention of Fas-
cist Culture, 72, 152; on Isotta, 31,
33, 36, 188, 189, 217; and Mussolini,
46–47, 53, 72, 74; and Nietzsche,
46, 53; and Pan/Faunus, 53; on Polis-
sena Sforza, 113, 153; and Pound, 31,
32*t*, 33, 36–37, 41, 46–49, 118,
171–72, 189; and Ricci, 194, 195;
role in romantic interpretation of

church of San Francesco, 171–72,
181, 189, 217; on sign *SI*, 188, 189;
on Sigismondo, 46, 47, 49, 72; and
Stirner, 53; *Un tempio d'amore* pur-
chased by Pound, 117, 171, 189,
290n.106
—works, 107, 284n.75; *I Canti di
Faunus*, 53, 74; "Il Fauno," 53; *Un
tempio d'amore*, 31, 33, 74, 181; *L'u-
omo nuovo*, 46–47; reception of, out-
side Italy, 74
Benson, E. F., 51
Benzi, Andrea del, 87, 89, 90, 114,
124, 128
Berenson, Bernard, 106
Berman, Louis, 201; *The Glands Regu-
lating Personality*, 234
Bernicoli, Silvio (1857–1936), archivist
in Ravenna, 79
Bernstein, Michael André, 57, 252n.2,
263n.68
Bertolini, Francesco, 188
Bianchi, Giovanni, 95, 97, 174
Bianchi, Martha Dickinson, 141
Biblioteca Universitaria (Bologna), 180
Biblioteca Malatestiana (Cesena), 164,
213
Biblioteca Nazionale (Florence), 180,
185
Biblioteca Riccardiana (Florence), 185
Biblioteca Vaticana (Vatican City), 179
Bibliothèque Nationale (Paris), 103,
104*t*, 109–10; Pound's studies in, 103,
119–24, 142, 190, 320n.107; works
by Soranzo in, 148, 175, 190,
320n.107; Yriarte's studies in, 109–10
Bilancioni, Pietro, 180, 185, 314n.69,
316n.87
Bird, William, 183
Blackwood, Algernon, 51
Bologna, 8, 28, 105, 129, 185
Boni, Giacomo, 191–92
Booksellers, 230; Messrs. Ellis, 120;
Georg F. B. Neumaier, 120, 254n.17;
Ulrico Hoepli, 119, 123, 241–42,
292n.114; Libreria del Convegno, 241;
Bernard Alfred Quaritch, 120; Suther-
land, 120; Rimini, 290n.106
Bornstein, Daniel, 251n.2
Borsi, Franco, 252n.8
Bottardi da Parma, Flaminio, 91

Braque, George, 198
Braschi, Giambattista, 91
Braudel, Fernand, 153
British Library (London), 103
Broglio Tartaglia di Lavello, Gaspare, 113, 114, 145, 187, 188, 198
Brooke, Rupert, 51
Browne, Thomas, 174
Browning, Elizabeth Barrett, 260n.55
Browning, Robert, 202, 261n.62
Brugnoli, Pier Giovanni, 84
Bruni, Leonardo, 167
Burckhardt, Jacob, 101, 103, 107, 281n.64; on church of San Francesco, 19, 34, 158, 159; on Isotta, 19, 34, 159; and Pound, 117; role in romantic interpretation of church of San Francesco, 19, 34–35, 107; on Sigismondo, 102, 105, 107, 108–9, 158, 258n.39; view of Renaissance, 101–2, 158; and Yriarte, 108–9
Burr, Amelia J. 51
Bush, Douglas, 260n.55
Bush, Ronald, 251n.2
Buss, Kate, 237

Calendrical motifs. See "Kalenda maya"; May Day
Calixtus III, 167
Campana, Augusto, 209–10, 212
Cantos, The (Pound). See Malatesta Cantos; see also under Pound, Ezra
Cappelli, Mario, **214**
Capranica, Cardinal Domenico, 167
Carmagnola, daughter of, 92, 93, 118, 119, 125, 276n.43
Carpenter, Edward, 157, 204; Civilisation: Its Cause and Cure, 157
Carrara, 234
Carretto, Ottone del, 86–89, 129
Casa di Dante, 194
Cattaneo, Carlo, 99, 100
Catullus, 168
Cavalcanti, Guido, 214–15, 216
Céline, Louis-Ferdinand, 224
Centaur, as substitute figure for Pan, 97
Cervia, 97
Cesena, 28; Biblioteca Malatestiana, 164, 213; and 1449 plague, 96–97, 114, 115
Christian era, end of, 35, 43

Chronicle of pseudo-Alessandro. See Pseudo-Alessandro, chronicle of
Church of San Francesco, Rimini, 1, 2, 4, 8–14, **9, 10, 11, 12, 13, 15, 16, 17, 18, 19,** 19–22; Albini on, 36; Arduini on, 36; Baedeker guidebooks on, 35; bas-reliefs in, 14, **15, 17,** 33, 228; Beltramelli on, 36–37; Burckhardt on, 19, 24, 159; Chapel of the Ancestors, 14, **15;** Chapel of San Sigismondo, 9, 43, 44, 161; construction, 9–14; depictions of, 20, **21,** 188, 202, **203,** 204, pl. 1–2; destruction of, 210, **211, 212, 213,** 329n.137; inscriptions in, 14, 19, 33–35, 195–97; Maurel on, 36; and May Day, 41, 44; and neopaganism, 19–20, 33, 35, 36; Pius II on, 30, 32t, 33–34; and poems attributed to Sigismondo, 20, 179–80, 184, 185; reconstruction of, 329n.137; Romantic interpretation of, 14, 19–20, 22, 33–37, 217, 288n.103; and sign SI, 20, 33; and tomb of Isotta degli Atti, 1, 14, **18, 19,** 33–34, 35, 195–97; Villari on, 35; Yriarte on, 35, 179–80, 184–85; zodiacal references in, 14, 20, 179
Church of San Vitale, Ravenna, 193, 236
Cicero, 14, 160, 168; Dream of Scipio, 14
Civilisation: Its Cause and Cure (Carpenter), 157
Civilization, 67–68, 101–2, 126, 131, 157–58, 166, 221; and church of San Francesco, 110, 126, 158, 217; and Isotta, 111, 153, 159, 172–73; Pound's conception of, 117, 131; and the Renaissance ideal, 101–2; and Sigismondo, 107–8, 158
Clementini, Cesare, 94, 95, 96, 103, 110, 112, 119, 121, 145, 278n.50; Pound's reading of, 122–23, 124, 125, 291n.112, 295n.127, 296n.133, 320n.107; on murder of Polissena Sforza, 94; transmission of, 291nn. 12–13
Clerici Veronese, Fra Paolo, 91, 92, 94
Cocteau, Jean, 148
Compagnia della Risata di Polidor. See Guillaume, Ferdinando

Congreve, William, 141
Convention of Fascist Culture, 72, 152, 194
Cook's Travel Agency, 240
Cookson, William, 186
Corriere della Sera, Il (newspaper), 216, 242
Corte, Ilario, 103
Cortona, 235, 237
Costa, Gian Battista, 187–88
Covignano, monastery of, 115, 173, 174
Criterion, The, 27, 70, 132, 230, 234, 239
Croce, Benedetto, 151
Cronaca malatestiana, 44, 84–85, 94, 97, 103, 119, 136, 145
Cubism, 28
Cunard, Bache, 132
Cunard, Nancy, 132–33, 298n.152

Daniel, Arnaut, 182–83
D'Annunzio, Gabriele, 171
Dante Alighieri, 25, 41, 77, 155, 226
Danto, Arthur, 223
Davie, Donald, 251n.2
Davis, Stuart, 106
Dazzi, Manlio Torquato, 164, 213
"Death of Pan, The" (Dunsany), 51
Debussy, Charles, 261n.58
Deconstruction, 58–59, 222
Decus, 160
Deed, André, 54
de Man, Paul, 61–63, 75, 80–81, 221–23, 224
D'Epiro, Peter, 251n.2, 333n.1, 336n.14
Derrida, Jacques, 6, 25, 58–63, 75
"Desperate love," origins of words, 168–69
Dial, The, 47–48, 229, 235, 259n.47
Diana, bas-relief of, 14
Diez, Friedrich, 66
Dionysius, and Pan, 52
Diplomatics, 64–66, 94–95
Dickinson, Emily, 141
Divus, -a, 19, 34
Drafts of The Cantos. See under Malatesta Cantos
Dream of Scipio (Cicero), 14
Drummond, John, 74–75
Dumas, Alexandre, 109
Dunsay, Lord, 51

Ecclesia, 34
Ecole des Chartes, 65
Edwards, John H., 135, 136
Egoist, The, 53
Eliot, T. S., 27, 48, 58, 61, 132, 227, 230; and Bel Esprit project, 70; and draft C1 of the Malatesta Cantos, 220–21, 262n.62; 1922 meeting with Pound in Verona, 54, 233, 234, 237–39, 241
Elite culture, and modernism, 55–57, 67–69, 219
Enciclopedia italiana, 152
Encyclopaedia Britannica: 1829 edition, 112; 1886 edition, 35, 180, 188; 1911 edition, 36, 112, 186, 188, 254n.20
Ephrussi, Charles, 92
Este, Ginevra d': alleged murder of, 92, 93, 110, 112, 272n.36, 293n.120; in drafts for Malatesta Cantos, 118, 119–20, 121, 124, 125, 293n.120
Este, Margherita d', 96, 97, 98, 115
Excideuil, 262n.62
Ezzelino, 214

Fact, 5, 8, 29–30, 67, 72, 225; construction of, 79–82, 137, 143–47; Gentile on, 151; and narration, 145–46; Pound on, 150–51
Fano, 29, 129; history of, 96–98, 114, 119, 123; Sigismondo's alleged rape of bishop of, 258n.39
Farnese, Pierliugi, 258n.39
Fascist Culture, Convention of, 72, 152, 194
Fascist National Institute of Culture (Rome), 194
Fascist Party, 72–73, 152, 193–94
Faunus, 45–46, 53
Federigo da Montefeltro, 88, 183–84, 257n.39
Federigo d'Urbino. See Federigo da Montefeltro.
Fermo, 83
Ferrieri, Enzo, 241
Florence, 28, 107, 115, 129, 240; Archivio di stato, 69, 103; Biblioteca Nazionale, 180, 185; Biblioteca Riccardiana, 185
Foresti da Bergamo, Fra Jacopo Filippo, 91, 92, 95, 118
Forster, E. M., 51

Foscolo, Ugo, 77
Foster, Jeanne, 234, 235
Friedländer, Julius, 162
Froula, Christine, 80, 141–43, 151, 152, 177
Fumi, Luigi, 103–4, 115–16, 119, 142, 148

Gadamer, Hans-Georg, 6
Galla Placidia, 238, 240; mausoleum of, 236–37
Garden God, The (Reid), 51
Garibaldi, Giuseppe, 109
Garnett, Richard, 51
Garuffi, Giuseppe Malatesta, 187
Geertz, Clifford, 3, 5, 6
Geiger, Ludwig, 102
Gemistos Plethon, Georgios, 214, 216, 276n.45
Genoa, 234
Gentile, Giovanni, 151–52, 194, 219, 224
Gherardi da Volterra, Giacomo, 167–78
Ghirardo di Cristoforo da Rimini, 197
Gilman, D. C., 157
Giotto, 236
Giovanardi, Gregorio, 115–16, 119, 142, 148, 175
Giovanna d'Acquapendente, 82
Giovanni di Angelino, 197
Giovio, Paolo, 276n.47
Giudizio universale, Il (Rimini), 210
Gosse, Edmund, 51
Gourmont, Remy de, 259n.46
Grahame, Kenneth, 51
Gramsci, Antonio, 224
Grandi, Don Silvio, 91
Greece, ancient, 39–42
Greek Anthology, 39–40
Griechische Frühling (Hauptmann), 53
Guasti, school of, 103, 109
Guillaume IX of Poitiers, 49, 183
Guillaume, Ferdinando, 54–55, 56, 68, 75

Habermas, Jürgen, 223
Hamsun, Knut, 52
Haroldi, Padre, 91
Harper, Michael, 141–43, 186, 251n.2
Hartmann, Geoffrey, 140, 222
Hauptmann, Gerhart, 53

Heidegger, Martin, 224
Heiss, Alois, 162, 164
Helen of Troy, 42
Hemingway, Ernest, 201, 227
Hill, George Frances, 164
Hoepli, Ulrico, 119, 123, 241–42, 292n.114
Holocaust, 62, 80–81, 133
Homer, 42
Horace, 177
Hours Press, 132
Human, All Too Human, (Nietzsche), 158
Huneker, James, 51
Husserl, Edmund, 222
Hutton, Edward, 36, 107, 134, 284n.76; *The Cities of Romagna and the Marches*, 107, 186, 284n.75; on church of San Francesco, 36; on convent of Scolca, 293n.1; on poems attributed to Sigismondo, 180–81, 186; on Polissena Sforza, 112, 293n.1; and Pound, 121, 254n.17, 293n.120; on sign *SI*, 188; *Sigismondo Pandolfo Malatesta*, 36, 112, 121, 134, 180–81, 188, 284n.75

Ideal text, 139–40
Inscripture, 7, 20, 140
Intensity as standard for civilization, 47, 131–32, 150
"Intentional Fallacy, The" (Wimsatt and Beardsley), 141
Intertextuality, 7, 29, 58, 79
Isotta. *See* Atti, Isotta degli

Jackson, Frederick Hamilton, 106, 112, 284n.76
Jackson, Thomas, 251n.2
Jay, Martin, 23
John Simon Guggenheim Foundation, 70
Johnson, Samuel, 157
Jones, Philip J., 116, 142–43, 252n.8, 300n.176
Joyce, James, 43, 58, 227
Jugend (magazine), 52–53
Jugendstil, 52

Kaegi, Werner, 101
"Kalenda maya," 37–38, 39, 44, 45, 49
Kearns, George, 186

Kenner, Hugh, 57, 263n.8
Kesselring, Marshal Albert, 216

Lachmann, Karl, 138, 139–40
Lago di Garda, 29, 117, 229, 235, 238, 241
Landino, Cristoforo, 93
Landor, Walter Savage, 177
The Last Judgment, Rimini, 210
Latin (language), 34, 160, 168–69. *See also individual works*
Laurent, Paul, **203, 208**
Leo, Heinrich, 119, 257n.39, 290n.109
Lévy, Emile, 66, 254n.21
Lewis, Wyndham, 70, 224
Libraries, national, 103, 109–10, 112–13
Linati, Carlo, 241
Linskill, Joseph, 254n.21
Litta, Pompeo, 100
Little Review Calendar, 43, 45
Liveright, Horace, 48, 198
Llona, Victor, 235, 237
Longenbach, James, 251n.2, 265n.84
Lowell, Amy, 183–84
Lowell, Robert, 224
Lucchesi, Carlo, 210

Mabillon, Jean, 64
Macerata, 83
Macrobius, 14
Mahler, Gustav, 261n.58
Makin, Peter, 251n.2
Malatesta, Bartolomeo de', 97, 98
Malatesta, Galeazzo, 85
Malatesta, Galeotto (di Sigismondo), 85–86
Malatesta, Giovanna (di Sigismondo), 85
Malatesta, Giovanni (di Sigismondo), 85
Malatesta, Malatesta (di Sigismondo), 85
Malatesta, Novello (Domenico), 83, 125, 130
Malatesta, Sallustio, 164
Malatesta, Sigismondo, 1–2, 8–14, **15**, 20, 27, 148, 160, 177, 206; and Alfonso V, 86, 87–88, 116, 125; and Angevins (counts and dukes of Anjou), 86–89; and Isotta degli Atti, 1–2, 14, 20, **21,** 33–36, 41–42, 85, 89, 90, 95–96, 98, 110–12, 135, 161–64, 168–73, 177–91, 197, 204, 205, 206, 209, 218, 227; biographies of, 65, 97,

106, 120–21; and bishop of Fano, 258n.39; and bourgeois culture, 107–11, 127; in Cantos 72 and 73, 213–14; and Carmagnola's daughter, 92, 93, 118, 119, 125, 276n.43; and church of San Francesco, 1–2, 4, 8–14, 20, 27, 33–36, 37–39, 41–42, 44–46, 48–49, 126, 130–32, 160, 161, 177–86, 188, 189, 191, 206, 209, 219, 220, 227; compared with Eliot, 220–21; compared with Guillaume, 56; compared with Mussolini, 46–47, 72, 74–75; compared with Pan, 56–57; compared with Pound, 183–84; compared with Raimbaut de Vaqueiras, 39; depictions of, 14, **15,** 20, **21,** 188, 204, 206, 227, pl. 2, 5, 7; and Federigo da Montefeltro, 88, 89, 183–84; and Ginevra d'Este, 92, 93, 110, 112, 272n.36, 293n.120; inscriptions to, 14; medals of, 161, 163–64; and Provençal culture, 41–42; poems attributed to, 20, 35–36, 42, 121, 177–86, 187, 218, 224, 312n.69; and the Renaissance, 101–2, 219–20; and Risorgimento, 99–101; and Alessandro Sforza, 83 84; and Francesco Sforza, 83, 84–85, 86–90, 93, 94, 114, 118, 123–24, 126; and Polissena Sforza, 83–132, 144–45, 147, 174, 206; and sign *SI*, 20, **21,** 187–91, 202, 218, 224; and tourism, 105–8; and wives, 92, 118, 119–20
—in Cantos 8–11: draft *A*, 3, 30–37, 68, 69–70, 74–75, 118, 120; draft *B*, 37–39, 42–50, *C1*, 120; *C3*, 177, 178, 181, 184; *D1*, 122, 124–25; *D2*, 125, 183; *E*, 125–26; *H*, 127–28; *N*β, 120; *x*, 129; *y*, 182; *Y*, 130; *Ymn 28*, 181; *Ymn 29–30*, 182
—discussed by contemporaries: Ammanati, 168–69, 307n.36; del Benzi, 87, 89, 90, 114, 124; *Cronaca malatestiana*, 84–86; Pius II, 30, 32*t*, 33–34, 87, 89, 90, 93, 114, 123, 136, 206; Scacchi, 68, 307n.36; Francesco Sforza, 86–87, 87–90, 93; Simonetta, 89–90, 93, 114
—discussed by later writers, 34; Albini, 36, 188; Amiani, 96–97, 123; Arduini, 36, 188; Battaglini, 97–98, 188; Beltramelli, 31, 32*t*, 33, 36–37,

41–42, 46–47, 49, 72, 113, 171–72, 188; Burckhardt, 34–35, 101–2, 105; chronicle of pseudo-Alessandro, 92, 174; Clementini, 94, 122; Costa, 187–88; Edwards and Vasse, 135; Foresti da Bergamo, 91; Froula, 143–44; Fumi, 115, 116; Garuffi, 187; Giovanardi, 116; Harper, 142–43; Hutton, 36, 112, 180–81, 186, 188; Maurel, 35–36, 112, 188; Mayo, 134, 135; Massèra, 185–86; Mazzuchelli, 95–96, 169, 174, 187; Moroni, 98–100, 169–70; Passerini, 100–101; Pigna, 92; Pound, 4, 31, 32t, 74–75, 117, 118, 119–20, 122, 126–27, 149, 181–86, 197–98, 202–9; Ricci, 189, 191, 193, 195–97; Rubieri, 112, 123–24; Sansovino, 92; Soranzo, 113–16, 124, 175, 188–89; Symonds, 93, 108–9, 188; Terrell, 135–36, 209; Tonini, 113; Villari, 35, 111–12; Yriarte, 35, 41–42, 108–11, 170–71, 174–75, 178–82, 188, 205
Malatesta, Violante, 85, 96–97, 98, 114
Malatesta Cantos, 2, 3; commentaries on, 134–37, 173, 177, 186, 209, 217–18; composition of, 4, 27–30, 56, 74–75, 103, 118, 123–24, 198, 229–33, 241, 242, 257n.39; and contemporary events, 42–50; criticism of, 69–72, 141–43, 217–18, 251n.2; passages from the final text, 75, 81–82, 131–32, 159–86; publication history of, 132–34; quotation in, 68–72
—Drafts and manuscripts, 5, 8, 28, 29–30, 229–33; A, 29–31, 31, 32t, 118, 120, 126, 241, 258n.39, 334n.1; B, 29–30, 37–50, 118, 120, 126, 233, 241, 257n.39, 262n.22, 334n.1; C1, 29, 55, 74, 220, 239; C2, 120, C3, 120–21, 178, 181, 184, 239; D1, 124–25; D2, 125, 183; E, 125–26; G2, 126; H, 127–28; W, 128, 130, 229–30, 313n.61; X, 130, 297n.147; Y, 130;
—Draft fragments: a, 292n.116; b, 165; m, 126; x, 129; y, 182, 315n.79
—Marginalia in Pound's copy of Un Condottiere: Ymn 9, 121–22; Ymn 14, 121–22; Ymn 17, 319n.106; Ymn 25, 121; Ymn 26, 121–22; Ymn 28, 181; Ymn 29, 30, 182; Ymn 31, 316n.87;

Ymn 32, 41–42, 189–90, 319n.106; Ymn 35, 42; Ymn 37ᵃ, 163–64; Ymn 37ᵇ, 163–64; Ymn 40, 121–22; Ymn 44, 122, 176; Ymn 45, 122, 176; Ymn 69, 121–22; Ymn 128, 121–22; Ymn 135, 319n.106; Ymn 141, 316n.87; Ymn 143, 154; Ymn 144, 122, 176; Ymn 147, 121–22
—Notes assigned sigla: Nα, 117; Nβ, 120, 293n.119; N1, 118–19, 257n.39, 334n.1; N2, 119, 334n.1; N4, 236
—Notes not assigned sigla: from Amiani, 293n.117; from Archivio di stato, Milan, 129; from Archivio di stato, Rimini, 197, 326n.119; from Biblioteca Nazionale, Florence, 185, 317n.88; from Biblioteca Riccardiana, Florence, 185, 316n.87; from "Books Wanted" list, 291n.112; from Clementini, 122–23, 124, 125, 295n.127, 296n.133, 320n.107; from Mitterelli, 128, 296n.142; from Soranzo, 124, 296n.132; from Yriarte, 181, 182, 293n.119, 315nn. 77, 79; Transcription by Ricci, 195–96, **196**
Malatesta da Verucchio, 46–47
"The Man Who Went Too Far" (Benson), 51
"Manifesto of Fascist Intellectuals," 72, 152, 194
Marinetti, Filippo Tomaso, 213
Marsuppini, Carlo, 167
Martini, Ariminuccio, 85
Marx, Karl, 61
Massèra, Aldo Francesca, 185–86, 317n.89
Massignan, Rafaello, 259n.39
Mathews, Elkin, 48
Matteo de' Pasti, 160–63, 166, 179
Maurel, André, 36, 112
May Day, 39–41; and feast of Venus, 40; and Little Review Calendar, 45; in Provençal culture, 39–41; 1442, 84, 269n.17; 1452, 44–45
Mayo, Robert, 134–35, 186
Mazzuchelli, Gianmaria, 94–96; and Ammanati, 169; biography of Isotta, 94, 95, 169, 174, 187; in Bibliothèque Nationale, 103, 104t, 109–10, 121–22; career, 94–95; and chronicle of pseudo-Alessandro, 95, 169; on Isotta, 95–96, 98, 169; and Moroni,

Mazzuchelli, Gianmaria, (*continued*)
169; on Polissena Sforza, 95–96; on
sign *SI*, 187; on Sigismondo, 95, 169,
187; and Yriarte, 174–75
Medals, 160–64, 166, 207; of Isota,
160–64, 166; by Matteo de' Pasti,
160–63; by Pisanello, 206–7; and
Pound, 163–66; by pseudo-Pisanello,
163–64; of Sigismondo, 206–7; by
Sperandio, 162; and Wallace collec-
tion, 162; and Yriarte, 162–63
Medici, Cosimo de', 116
Medici, Giovanni de', 70
Meridiano di Roma (weekly), 227
Merivale, Patricia, 260n.55
Middlemore, S. G. C., 102
Milan, 28; Archivio di stato, 103–4,
109, 113, 115, 129, 149; booksellers,
119, 123, 241–42, 292 n.14; Mu-
seum, 164; Pound's travels to, 28,
240, 241–42; in Renaissance (*see*
Sforza, Francesco); in Risorgimento,
99, 100; Università cattolica, 129
Mino da Fiesole, 70
Mitchell, Charles 252n.8
Mittarelli, Giovanni Benedetto, 104*t*,
128, 296n.142
Miyake, Akiko, 252n.2
Modena, 28, 129
Modernism, 28, 221; and myth, 56–67;
poetics of, 28; and popular culture,
55–56; and quotation, 57–58
Moe, Henry Allen, 70
Le Monde Illustré, 109
Monumenta Germaniae Historica, 65
Moramarco, Fred, 186
Morand, Paul, 224–35, 235, 237, 241
Moroni, Gaetano, 98–101, 103, 104*t*,
169–70, 281n.60, 310n.44
Moulton, Richard G., 66
Mount Mut, 27
Mozart, Wolfgang Amadeus, 227
Muratori, Lodovico, *Rerum italicarum
scriptores*, 64–65, 93, 94–95, 103,
104*t*
"The Music on the Hill" (Saki), 51
Mussato, Albertino, 214
Mussolini, Benito, 216, 224, 331n.42;
and Beltramelli, 46–47, 53, 72, 74;
and Gentile, 151–52, 194; compared
with Sigismondo, 46–47, 74–75; and
Pound, 74–75, 80; and Ricci, 193–95

Nani, Bernardo, 95
Nardi, Luigi, 188, 318n.99
Neopaganism, 19–20, 36, 43, 149
Neuberg, Victor, 51
Neumaier, Georg F. B., 120, 254n.17
Nevinson, H. W., 51
New Age, The (magazine), 47
New Criticism, 134, 136–37, 141, 143,
146
New Directions Publishing Corporation,
133
"New man" motif, 46, 47, 48, 49
Nicholas V, 86
Nicolò, Luigi, **214**
Nicolò de Palude, 88, 271n.31
Nietzsche, Friedrich, 52, 53, 58–59, 74,
157, 158, 171
Nolfi, Vincenzo, 96, 97, 114, 129, 147,
287n.92
North, Michael, 251n.2

Orbetello, 128
Orsini, Luigi, 184, 186
Ouvert la nuit (Morand), 234–35

Paganism: church of San Francesco as
monument to, 19–20, 33–35, 36,
160, 202, 204, 206; Pound's linking of
Tempio with, 38, 43, 45–46, 149,
181, 182; Renaissance Rimini and,
106. *See also* May Day; Pan
Pagliarini, Adelio, **214**
Palermo, Francesco, 185
Pan, 43, 46, 50–53, 55–56, 262n.65; in
Beltramelli, 53; in England, 51; in Eu-
rope, 52–53; in *Little Review* Calendar,
43; meaning of, 50–51, 53, 55–56;
and Nietzsche, 52; in Pound, 51–52
Pan Society, Cambridge, 52
Pan (Hamsum), 52
"Pan" (Huneker), 51
Pan (Meier-Graffe), 52
Pan's Garden (Blackwood), 51
"Pan's Wand" (Garnett), 51
Paponi, Francesco, 197
Paponi, Rodolfo, 197
Paris, 8, 27, 28, 107, 128, 198, 229,
230, 232, 234, 235, 238, 240, 241,
242; Salon d'Automne, 198. *See also*
Biblithèque Nationale
Paris, Gaston, 40–41
Parodi, Piero, 267n.8

Pasolini, Pier Paolo, 25–26, 155

Pasquini, Luigi, 226

Passerini, Luigi, 100–101, 103, 110, 111

Pasti, Matteo de'. *See* Matteo de' Pasti.

Patronage, 47, 68, 69–70

Paul II, 49, 167

Pavia, 167

Pearlman, Daniel, 56–57

Pennabilli, 129

Perdite amare, 168–69

Perloff, Marjorie, 28, 69–72, 80, 251n.3

Perugia, 235, 236, 237, 240, 241

Pesaro, 28, 85, 86, 129, 135, 136

Philology, 64, 66–69; and capitalism, 66–67; and quotation, 64; and socialism, 67–68

Piccinino, Giacomo, 87–88, 257n.39

Picconi, Padre Giacinto, 92

Pienza, 167, 271n.34

Piero della Francesca, 70, 227

Pigna, Giovanni Battista, 92, 94

Pinturicchio, Bernardo il, 236

Pisa, 128, 234, 240

Pisanello (Vittore Pisano), 70, 163–64, 166, 186, 207, **207, 208.** *See also* Pseudo-Pisanello

Pius II (Aeneas Sylvius Piccolomini), 30–35, 96, 100, 113, 118, 119, 136, 170, 171, 186, 217, 218, 271n.34; and Ammanati, 166–68, 309n.41; and Beltramelli, 31, 32*t*; on church of San Francesco, 30, 32*t*, 33–34; on Isotta, 30, 32*t*, 33–34, 206; in Malatesta Cantos, 124, 126–27; on murder of Polissena Sforza, 86, 87, 89, 90, 91, 93, 94, 103, 114, 149; on Sigismondo, 30, 32*t*, 33–34, 87, 89, 90, 93, 114, 123, 136, 206

—works: *Commentarii*, 30, 89, 90, 93, 103, 104*t*, 121, 128, 207–8, 212, 277n.48; *Discipula veritatis*, 91, 94, 103, 273n.38; *Epistolae*, 273n.38; invective, 87, 90, 91, 94, 114, 124, 128, 273n.38

Pius IX, 99, 100

Platina. *See* Scacchi, Bartolomeo

Plautus, 168

Plea of Pan, The (Nevinson), 51

Plutarch, 51, 260n.55

Pogliaghi, Lodovico, 20, **21,** 188

Pontano, Giovanni Gioviano, 258n.51

Pound, Dorothy Shakespear, 54, 117, 120, 124, 217, 230, 234, 236, 241

Pound, Ezra, 1, 2, 3, 4–6, 8, 22–23, 27–30, 36–56, 64–75, 80–82, 93, 94, 117–32, 133, 142–43, 147–54, 158, 160, 162–66, 171–73, 175–78, 180–86, 187, 189–209, 213–22, 224, 226–28, 229–42

—Attitudes toward: civilization, 67–68, 117, 131; fact, 67, 151–52; history, 149–52; individualism, 67–68, 131–32; "new man," 47, 48; patronage, 47, 70–71; philology, 66–69; Provençal culture, 39–42; quotation, 68–72; the Renaissance, 47, 117–20, 288n.104

—Readings of: Amiani, 119–20, 121, 293n.117; Ammanati, 171–73; Battaglini, 121; Beltramelli, 31, 32*t*, 33, 36–37, 41, 46–49, 117, 118, 171–72, 189, 290n.106; Broglio, 198; Burckhardt, 117; Clementini, 122–25, 291n.112, 295n.127, 296n.133, 320n.107; Hutton, 121, 254n.17, 293n.120; Pius II, 128–29; pseudo-Alessandro, 175–76; Ricci, 189, 191–93, 195–97, 325n.16; Soranzo, 123–26, 128–29, 147–49, 190, 197, 297n.145; Symonds, 117, 118; Yriarte, 120, 120–22, 163–65, 175–77, 178–80, 189–90, 202, 302n.18 (*see also* Malatesta Cantos: Marginalia in Pound's copy of *Un Condottiere*; Malatesta Cantos: Notes not assigned sigla)

—Relations with: Nancy Cunard, 132–33, 298n.152; *The Dial*, 47–48, 259n.47; T. S. Eliot, 27, 47, 48, 132, 220–21, 227, 230; Horace Liveright, 48; Elkin Mathews, 48; *The New Age*, 47; Luigi Pasquini, 226–28; John Quinn, 27, 47–48, 234–35, 237–38, 241, 258n.39; Evelyn St. Bride Scratton, 238–41; Henry Strater, 198–202, 327n.125

—Studies of: medals of Isotta 160–64, 166; poems attributed to Sigismondo, 121, 177–86; Francesco Sforza, 118, 123–24, 126–27; murder of Polissena Sforza, 117–32, 147; sign *SI*, 186–98

—Travels: during 1922, 1, 27, 234–42;

Pound, Ezra (*continued*)
  during 1923, 28, 128–30, 191–98;
  during 1963, 226–28
—Writings (poems): "The Faun," 52;
  "N.Y.," 52; "Pan Is Dead," 52; "Tem-
  pora," 52
—Writings (prose essays): "Affirmations,"
  52; *Little Review* Calendar, 42–43;
  "Paris Letter, January 1922," 47–48;
  "Praefatio" to *Spirit of Romance*, 66–
  67; "Provincialism the Enemy," 67–
  68, 265n.84; "Psychology and the
  Troubadours," 39–42; "Raphaelite
  Latin," 66
—Writings (prose books): *Guide to Kul-
  chur*, 150–51; *Spirit of Romance*, 39–
  42, 66–67
—Writings (*The Cantos*), 4, 28, 57, 58,
  79–80, 81–82, 152, 153, 159, 209,
  213, 219, 226; Canto 1, 49; Canto 2,
  256n.30; Canto 4, 262n.62; Canto 12,
  262n.62; Canto 29, 239; Canto 72,
  28, 213–14, 331n.142; Canto 73, 28,
  213, 214–17, 331n.142; Canto 78,
  239; *A Draft of XVI. Cantos*, 28, 132,
  183, 198–209, pl. 1–8; *A Draft of
  XXX Cantos* (Hours Press), 132; *A
  Draft of XXX Cantos* (Farrar), 133; *The
  Cantos of Ezra Pound* (New Direc-
  tions), 133. *See also* Malatesta Cantos
Pound, Homer, 234, 237
Premoli, Palmiro, 188
Priapus, feast of, 45
Provençal culture, 37–42, 41–42, 182–
  83, 184; and pagan origins, 39–42;
  and philology, 66; and Sigismondo,
  41–42, 120
Pseudo-Alessandro, chronicle of, 92, 95,
  115–16, 122, 148, 173–76, 186, 218;
  and Bianchi, 174; and Giovanardi,
  175; and Mazzuchelli, 174; and
  Pound, 175–76; and Ricci, 312n.58;
  and Soranzo, 175, 312n.58 and
  Yriarte, 174–75
Pseudo-Pisanello, medal of, 173, 213,
  218

Quaritch, Bernard Alfred, 120
Queen Mab (Shelley), 60–61
Quinn, John, 27, 47–48, 234–35, 237–
  38, 241, 258n.39
Quintilian, 168

Quotation, 4, 8, 28–29, 37, 57–64; and
  diplomatics, 64–66; and historiogra-
  phy, 58, 65–68; and modernism, 57–
  58, 60; and philology, 64–66; theory
  of, 59–60

Radetzky, J. J., 99
Raduno, Il (newspaper), 72, 74
Railroad, and tourism, 104–5, 106
Raimbaut de Vaqueiras, 37–39, 42, 44,
  49
Ranke, Leopold von, 23
Rapallo, 229, 234
Ravenna, 28, 79, 107, 129, 236, 238,
  284n.76; church of San Vitale, 193,
  236; mausoleum of Galla Placidia,
  236–37; and tourism, 106–7
Recanati, 83–84
Reguardati, Benedetto, 87
Reid, Forrest, 51
Reinach, Solomon, 261n.57
Renaissance, 47, 106; concept of, 99–
  102, 288n.104; and "new man," 47;
  Pound's view of, 117
Renzi, Pietro, 99
Ricci, Corrado, 148–49, 189, **192,**
  193–97, **196,** 204, 205, 208, 218,
  219, 221, 224, 252n.8; and Beltra-
  melli, 195; and church of San Fran-
  cesco, 195–97; on Isotta, 195–97;
  meets Pound, 189, 191–93, 195–97,
  325n.16; and Mussolini, 195; on Polis-
  sena Sforza, 288n.103; on pseudo-
  Alessandro, 312n.58; on sign *SI*, 189,
  197; on Sigismondo, 189; and Soranzo,
  189, 197, 288n.103, 312n.58; tran-
  scription of original inscription on
  tomb of Isotta, 195–96, **196**
Richards, Ivor A., 136
Righini, Padre, 91–92
Rimini, 1, 3, 28, 41, 83, 107, 114, 236,
  237; Arch of Augustus, 84, 105, 220–
  21, 224, 283n.73, 332n.147; Beltra-
  meli on, 41, 107; Biblioteca civica
  Gambalunga, 129, 175, 297n.144,
  317n.89; Booksellers in, 290n.106;
  Bridge of Tiberius, 105, 283n.73; in
  Cantos 72 and 73, 214–15; church of
  San Francesco, (*see main entry*); Grand
  Hotel, 105; Hutton on, 107; Istituto
  Idroterapico, 105; Jackson on, 106–7;
  Kursaal, 105; Main piazza, 84, 210,

212, **214;** Museum, 210; Symonds on, 106, 107; Tempio malatestiano (*see also* Church of San Francesco, Rimini), visited by Pound, 1, 27, 28, 129, 226–28, 236; 1831 Revolt, 99; and tourism, 104–7, 132–33, 283n.73; in World War II, 209–13, 215–16; Yriarte on, 106, 107

Risorgimento, 99–101

Rivoire, Mario, 212

Rivolta ideale, La (newspaper), 72

Rome, 8, 28, 34, 99, 100, 128–29, 240

Romulus, 191

Rossi, Agostino, 88

Rubieri, Ermolao, 112, 123–24

Rudge, Olga, 227

St. Elizabeths Hospital (Washington, D.C.), 27, 133, 184

Saint Francis, 33–34, 236

Saki, 51

Salò, Republic of, 212, 216

Salomne d'Automne (Paris), 198

Salvemini, Gaetano, 194

San Fabiano, battle of, 257n.39

San Francesco (Rimini), church of. See Church of San Francesco, Rimini

San Marino, Republic of, 129

Sansovino, Francesco, 92–93, 118

Santa Maria del Fiore, 13

Scacchi, Bartolomeo, 68, 307n.36

Scolca, monastery and convent of, 85, 135, 136, 293n.120

Scratton, Evelyn St. Bride, 328–41

Secolo XIX, Il, 212–213

Senigallia, battle of, 67–88, 271n.34

Senigallia, Torrione, 161

Serdini, Simone, 185–86, 187

Severi, Luigi, 211–12, **214**

Sforza, Alessandro, 83, 85

Sforza, Bianca, 84

Sforza, Drusiana, 268n.10

Sforza, Francesco, 101, 104, 112, 114–16, 122, 123, 129, 134–35, 148, 149, 271n.34; and murder of Polissena Sforza, 82–85, 86–89; Pound's view of, 118, 123–24, 126–27

Sforza, Giangaleazzo, 93

Sforza, Lodovico (il Moro), 93, 276n.47

Sforza, Polissena, 8, 81–91, 92, 100, 101, 106, 144, 147, 149, 152–53, 161–62, 166, 174, 210; birth, 82–83; children, 85–86; death, 86, 145; funeral, 94, 96–97, 136; in Malatesta Cantos, 81–82, 126–28, 134–37, 153–54; marriage, 83–85, 268n.10; murder of, 81, 86–116, 142, 175, 272n.36, 288n.103; Pound's studies of, 117–32; and plague, 96–97, 98, 100, 113, 114–16, 135, 145; and Sigismondo, 134–36, 268n.10; spelling of name, 81, 127, 135, 136

Shakespear, Olivia, 236

Shelley, Percy Bysshe, 60–61

Sieburth, Richard, 28, 70, 251n.2

Siena, 187, 234–35, 236, 240

Sign *SI,* 20, 35, 187–89, 197; Battalgini on, 188; Broglio on, 187, 198; Costa on, 187–88; in *A Draft of XVI. Cantos,* 202–9; Garuffi on, 187; meaning of, 218; Mazzuchelli on, 187–88; Pound's study of, 189–98; Ricci on, 189, 197; Soranzo on, 188–89; Yriarte on, 20, 188, 256n.29

Simonetta, Cicco, 90–91, 276n.14

Simonetta, Giovanni, 86, 89–90, 92, 93, 94, 97–98, 103, 114, 123, 134, 145, 276n.14

Sirmione, 29, 117, 229, 232, 233, 237, 238, 241, 242

Slatin, Myles, 28

Smith, Justin H., 39–40, 255nn. 21, 24

Socialism, 67–68

Soir, Le (newspaper), 62–63, 223

Soranzo, Giovanni, 113–16, 119, 142, 188–89, 271n.34, 287n.89, 300n.76; in Bibliothèque Nationale, 104*t,* 148, 190; on chronicle of pseudo-Alessandro, 175, 312n.58; *Pio II e la politica italiana,* 123, 126, 190; influence on Pound, 123–26, 128–29, 147–49, 190, 197, 297n.145; and Ricci, 189, 197, 312n.58; on Polissena Sforza, 114–16; on sign *SI,* 188–89

Spello, 236, 237

Sperandio, 162

Starace, Achille, 194

Stirner, Max, 53, 61, 171

Stock, Noel, 337n.14

"Story of a Panic, The," (Forster), 51

Strater, Henry: life and career, 198–202, 327nn. 121, 125, 328n.128; *A Draft*

Strater, Henry (*continued*)
  of XVI. Cantos, headpiece for Canto 8, 202, 204, pl. 1, 2; *A Draft of XVI. Cantos*, headpiece for Canto 10, 204–5, pl. 5, 6, 7; *A Draft of XVI. Cantos*, inset design for Canto 10, 206–8, pl. 8; *A Draft of XVI. Cantos*, headpiece for Canto 11, 205, pl. 3, 4; *Little Nude by a Table*, 198–201, **200;** *Margaret Strater in Red*, 198–201, **199;** *Nude with Black and White Fox Terrier*, 198–201
Surrette, Leon, 255n.23
Symbolism, 28
Symonds, John Addington, 19, 35, 92–93, 188, 258n.39, 276n.45; on murder of Polissena Sforza, 92–93; reading of, by Pound, 117, 118; and Rimini, tourism in, 106; on sign *SI*, 188; on Sigismondo, 109

Tasca, Angelo, 224
Tate, Allen, 141
Tauchnitz, Bernhard, 105, 106
"Teatro della Risata." *See* Giullaume, Ferdinando
Tempio malatestiano. *See* Church of San Francesco, Rimini
Terrell, Carroll F., 135–37, 172, 186, 209
Terrence, 168,
Thayer, Scofield, 235, 236, 259n.47
"Tomb of Pan, The" (Dunsany), 51
"Thi," "Thiy," "Ti." *See* Scratton, Evelyn St. Bride
Three Mountains Press, 70, 132, pl. 1–8
To the Lighthouse (Woolf), 58
Tonini, Luigi, 113
Tontolini. *See* Giullaume, Ferdinando
Tourism, 105–7, 132–33, 283n.73
Tranchedini, Nicodemo, 116, 145, 148, 267n.8
Transmission: of literary materials, ix, 2, 23, 137, 220–26; of sources relating to Malatesta Cantos, 4, 5, 20, 21, 147–54, 218–19, 293n.120; defined, 7–8
Travel books, 105–6
Triumph of Pan (Neuberg), 51
Troubadours. *See* Provençal culture
The Troubadours at Home, The (Smith), 39–40, 255nn. 21, 24

Ulysses (Joyce), 43, 58, 259n.42
Urbino, 129

Valbusa, D., 102
Valla, Lorenzo, 34
Valturi, Carlo, 187
Valturio, Roberto, 44–45
Varani, Giulio Cesare de', 85
Varchi, Bebedetto, 259n.39
Vasari, Giorgio, 14
Vasse, William W., 135–36
Vatican City, 128–29; Archivio segreto, 179; Biblioteca vaticana, 179
Venice, 28, 86, 99, 129, 232, 235, 237, 239; Hotel Danieli, 237; Hotel Savoia, 237
Venturi, Carlo, 185
Venus Genetrix, feast of, 40, 194
Vergil, 160, 166
Verona, 54, 56, 232, 233, 234, 238–41; arena, 54, 56, 238–39, 262n.62; Cafe Dante, 239; piazza dei signori, 232
Veronese, Guido, 167
Verruchio, 161
Vie parisienne, La, 109
Vienna, 107
Villani, Mgr. Giacomo, 92
Villari, Pasquale, 35, 111–12
Villon, François, 148
Visconti, Filippo Maria, 82, 85
Voloshinov, V. N., 69

Wadding, Father Luke, 91
Wallace, Richard, 162
Wallace Collection (London), 162
Waste Land, The (Eliot), 58, 221, 234, 262n.62
Watson, Dr. James Sibley, Jr., 229
White, Hayden, 142, 226
Wimsatt, W. K., 141
Wind in the Willows, The (Graham), 51
Wittgenstein, Ludwig, 223
Wittkower, Rudolf, 252n.8
Woolf, Virginia, 58
World War I, 49–50, 67–68
World War II, 209–13, 215–16

Yeats, W. B., 224
Yriarte, Charles, 20, 35–36, 41, 65, **108,** 112, 142, 145, 186, 204, 205; and Ammanati, 170–71; and archives,

109, 179; and Beltramelli, 171; and Bibliothèque Nationale (Paris), 109–10; and Burckhardt, 108–9; and chronicle of pseudo-Alessandro, 174–75; on church of San Francesco, 20, 35–36, 179–80, 185–86; and Clementini, 285n.80; on convent of Scolca, 293n.120; errors of, 285n.80, 305n.21, 310nn. 44, 46, 314n.71 (*see also* Ammanati, Jacopo; Malatesta, Sigismondo: poems attributed to; Pseudo-Alessandro, chronicle of; Pseudo-Pisanello, medal of; Sign *SI*); influence on Pound, 120–22, 163–65, 175–77, 178–80, 189–90, 22, 302n.18 (*see also under* Malatesta Cantos); on Isotta, 35, 41–42, 110–11, 162–64, 170–71, 174–75; life and career, 65, 109–10, 162, 304n.20; on Sigismondo, 35, 41–42, 109–11, 170–71, 174–75, 178–82, 188, 205; and Mazzuchelli, 170, 174–75; and Moroni, 170; on Matteo de' Pasti, 162–63; on Pisanello, 163–64; on poems attributed to Sigismondo, 20, 35, 178–86; on Polissena Sforza, 110–11, 136; on sign *SI*, 20, 188, 256n.29; and tourism, 106, 107 —works, 65, 284n.76; *Les Bords de l'Adriatique*, 106–7; *Un Condottiere*, 35, 65, 106, 120, 178, **203, 205, 208**

Zagreus, feast of, 43